Local economic development:
A geographical comparison of rural community restructuring

Local economic development: A geographical comparison of rural community restructuring

Edited by Cecily Neil and Markku Tykkyläinen

United Nations University Press

TOKYO · NEW YORK · PARIS

United Nations University Press
The United Nations University, 53-70, Jingumae 5-chome, Shibuya-ku, Tokyo, 150-8925, Japan
Tel: (03) 3599-2811   Fax: (03) 3406-7345
E-mail: sales@hq.unu.edu
http://www.unu.edu

United Nations University Office in North America
2 United Nations Plaza, Room DC2-1462-70, New York, NY 10017, USA
Tel: (212) 963-6387   Fax: (212) 371-9454
E-mail: unuona@igc.apc.org

United Nations University Press is the publishing division of the United Nations University.

Cover design by Jean-Marie Antenen, Geneva

Printed in the United States of America

UNUP-998
ISBN 92-808-0998-9

Library of Congress Cataloging-in-Publication Data

Local economic development : a geographical comparison of rural community restructuring / edited by Cecily Neil and Markku Tykkylainen.
  p.   cm.
Includes bibliographical references and index.
ISBN 9280809989 (pbk.)
1. Rural development – Case studies. 2. Structural adjustment (Economic policy) – Case studies. 3. Resource-based communities – Case studies. I. Neil, Cecily, 1943–
II. Tykkylainen, Markku.
 HN49.C6 L58   1998
 307.1′412 – ddc21
                                                      98-40088
                                                        CIP

Contents

Contents

Figures and Tables

Figures

Tables

Acronyms

CEFTA	Central European Free Trade Association
CIS	Commonwealth of Independent States
CMEA	Council for Mutual Economic Assistance
EC	European Community
EU	European Union
GATT	General Agreement on Tariffs and Trade
GDP	gross domestic product
NGO	non-governmental organization
NIC	newly industrialized country
OECD	Organization for Economic Cooperation and Development
R&D	research and development
RTD	research and technological development
UNESCO	United Nations Educational, Scientific and Cultural Organization
UNU/WIDER	World Institute of Development Economics Research of the United Nations University
WHO	World Health Organization

Preface

Restructuring is a widely used concept that denotes rapid and often far-reaching socio-economic transformation processes in communities, locales, localities, regions, and nations. This book seeks to explain the processes of restructuring in remote resource communities, focusing on the trends of the 1990s. Case-studies of resource communities subject to restructuring are analysed in 12 papers. The empirical material was derived from investigations into resource communities in Poland, Hungary, Bulgaria, Russia, Sweden, Finland, Ireland, the United States, Australia, and Viet Nam. The case-studies explore capitalist and neo-capitalist restructuring in the East and West in traditional, modern, post-industrial, and translocal communities.

The book explores restructuring processes ranging from various policy practices to sector-specific issues from the global to the local level. The book concludes with the presentation of a multicausal theory of local economic development, which is intended to assist in understanding restructuring processes in rural areas and, hence, to help design appropriate responses to the pressures that restructuring generates.

The case-studies demonstrate that communities and entire regions are adapting continuously to changing economic conditions. Such basic concepts as community and local economic policy are also being reshaped. The authors conclude that local economic policy must be reflexive and dynamic. Only economically and socially sustainable solutions that take account of the long-term socio-economic prospects can be recommended. The development policy followed must possess the ability to adapt to new circumstances and it must be proficient in anticipating economic development and individual needs.

Acknowledgements

The research for this book was associated with the research programme of the World Institute of Development Economics Research of the United Nations University (UNU/WIDER). The editors initiated this comparative research project in 1992 and managed it between 1992 and 1997. Although this volume is the product of the hard work of the authors, it is also the main result of the project "The Potential for Local Economic Development in Rural Resource Communities," conducted by the editors.

Many researchers contributing to this project came together in the Annual Meeting of Finnish Geographers in 1992, in the European Summer Institute in Regional Science in 1993 in Joensuu, in the conference of the European Regional Science Association in Moscow in 1993, and in the meetings of a TEMPUS project coordinated by the University of Oxford. Some of the preliminary results of the project were also discussed at the conferences organized by the International Geographical Union and the meetings of the Union's Study Group on Development Issues in Marginal Regions in the early and mid-1990s. The various opportunities for academic discussions provided by these events were of great assistance in conducting the research project.

Comparative analysis and the editorial process were supported by UNU/WIDER under the Finnish Special Programme Fund (contract

ICA W93/10 with the University of Joensuu) and various grants from the Academy of Finland. The costs of the case-studies in Western Australia and Russia were also borne by these sources. The other case-studies were funded from various sources in each country. Technical assistance was received from the University of Joensuu.

Special thanks are due to Christopher Gribbin and Michael Korhonen for the considerable effort they put into assisting with the editing, and to Erja Koponen, Riitta Honkanen, and Timo Pakarinen for redrawing the illustrations.

Although the editors accept full responsibility for the introductory and concluding remarks and for the editorial work, they would like to express their appreciation for the time, work, and thought that a number of contributors put into thorough case-studies in several countries. Finally, the book benefited directly from the suggestions of two anonymous reviewers. They provided insightful comments in their extensive and profound reviews. None the less, we alone bear the editorial responsibility for this final version.

Cecily Neil and Markku Tykkyläinen
September 1997

Part I
Concepts and framework

1

An introduction to research into socio-economic restructuring in resource communities

Cecily Neil and Markku Tykkyläinen

The studies in this book examine the socio-economic restructuring processes currently taking place in a number of rural places. Authorities, companies, and individual households have all been forced to respond to economic processes requiring transformation of the economic sectors upon which they have depended. In most of the situations explored, the pressure to restructure has been an outcome not only of rationalization and shifts in demand but also of associated transformations of national socio-economic institutions and policies. The papers in this book include case-studies from the advanced market economies of the United States, Ireland, and Australia, from Nordic welfare states, and from developing economies in East-Central Europe, Russia, and Viet Nam.

The papers in parts II–V all explore, within national and regional contexts, local adjustment to broader, structural transformations. They examine not only the forces that have necessitated local adjustments but also the different ways in which local people and authorities in various communities have responded to external pressures, and the divergent directions that development has taken as a result of the nature of the adjustments. The case-studies elaborate upon the roles of both external and local capital and know-how in local

3

development, and analyse the innovativeness and the consequences of advanced technology.

In part VI, the role of general and sector-specific transformations and local-specific factors in determining the directions of readjustment in a region is explored, together with the relative importance of local and external decisions and support in determining whether or not the ultimate outcomes are ones that offer local economic stability, and whether they are likely to provide opportunities for or barriers to future local economic development.[1] In concluding, the editors develop a theory of development for understanding the restructuring that has been occurring in resource communities in transition in the late 1980s and early 1990s.

The book examines the socio-economic restructuring processes that have happened worldwide in the 1990s, and evaluates the results of changing local economic policies. Different forms of society clearly presuppose significant differences in the particular economic measures designed to influence the country's resource communities. In most of the countries with which this book deals, however, such policies have been based on *laissez-faire* principles, and most of the papers analyse the deregulation stage of the planning regimes. The aim of this book is to compare local development in the three types of economies – market, welfare, and post-socialist – in order to find a solid theoretical framework for understanding current socio-economic restructuring in resource communities in both old and nascent capitalist systems. It seeks to pave the way for comprehending the new, emerging countryside of the information age, market-led development, and network society.[2]

Resource communities

In resource communities, the unifying social tie is the economic base, which sustains the community. Mining or forest industry towns, fishing villages, and agricultural villages are traditionally considered to be resource communities, as are towns making a living from the oil or chemical industries, or through iron or steel factories. Since recreational centres and holiday resorts use their landscapes and open spaces as resources, the commercialization of the natural landscape for recreational purposes can also be seen as an economic base for a resource community of a distinct type.

A resource community may be a village, a conglomeration of scattered rural households, a commune, a town, or a subdivision of any

4

one of these. Where a community is delimited by a particular geographical area, its key characteristics are likely, at least in part, to be shaped by a common identity and culture in that area (Buller and Wright 1990, 10–14; Butz and Eyles 1997). None the less, in any community, there may exist varying social groups and, hence, heterogeneous aims and targets relating to the development of the community. This is especially true where communities are demarcated according to administrative boundaries rather than some characteristic integral to the community itself. Thus, as some of the following papers demonstrate, a resource community is often an arena for conflicts and diverse interests, which can have important implications for its ability to restructure in particular ways.

The definition of the concept "resource community" rests on the assumption that the use of natural resources is the distinguishing feature of places in rural areas. The definition implicitly assumes that there exist non-resource communities, such as service towns, commuter dormitories, rural suburban areas, rural towns based on footloose industries, retirement communities, summer residential areas, conservation areas, etc. Hence, resource communities are a specific community type and play a distinctive role in the rural spatial structure. This may be one way to define rurality and rural settlement structure (see Hoggart and Buller 1987, 8–18).

Resource communities, however, are not necessarily delimited by a single geographical area. A resource community can also consist of a network of people working in the same resource sector across different localities. One corollary of this is that people may feel that they belong to many communities. The common ties of people involved in a resource business may depend strongly upon their being part of the international staff of a transnational company. A community, for them, may be a group of people in the same company, or in the same field of business, working in various parts of the world. Thus, these people are simultaneously members of an international social network and members of the local community in which they are living. This duality of community commitment may be reinforced by community feeling stemming from strong commitments to leisure activities and the residential environment.

Social interaction takes place in locales (Giddens 1984, 118–119, 164) such as farms, mining areas, villages, towns, local authority areas, etc., but this spatial term, together with the term "locality" (Duncan 1989; Marsden et al. 1993, 135–139), is limited as a common concept in the framework of this study because the associated

5

research deals primarily with the network character of social inter-action. Therefore, the term "community" as a spatially flexible con-cept seems to cover the domain of the social interaction analysed in the case-studies. Nevertheless, social interaction related to develop-ment and the (trans)formation of economic and social space is central in this study.

Most of the papers in this collection refer to development in com-munities associated with a single geographical area. However, multi-local and translocal settings of social interaction are gaining in importance via improved communications and increased spatial divi-sion of labour. As discussed in this book, the sense that people in resource communities have of belonging to both a local community and international social networks is important in understanding the roles that some of the local actors play in development at the com-munity level.

The measurement of place, space, and spatial organization of soci-ety has long been considered in geographical theories and, nowadays, increasingly in sociology. To enhance theoretical understanding, this book aims at illuminating what forms resource communities take and their relations to geographical space, where spatial structures come from, how communities restructure under economic and social pressures, and the factors on which socio-economic development depends.

The changing concepts of local development and restructuring

"Local development" refers to the mobilization and management of resources in order to create wealth in a community. It is linked to economic policy measures adopted by the authorities in a community or region. Local development, like the concept of economic restruc-turing, is an ambiguous concept. New concepts of local development have emerged in recent literature. According to Conti,

the concept of local development ... implies a process of activation of spe-cific territorial factors of transformation. In this light, it is far from those restrictive interpretations of a normative nature ... according to which a process of local development is understood as endogenous development activated almost exclusively by local actors. Local development, on the contrary, does not refer to the idea of "localism", which, theoretically and practically, regards a problem of territorial rooting in the strict sense, and does not even coincide with the idea of a small peripheral area. (Conti 1993, 118)

This means that local economic development and ensuring the continuity of a resource community (in the sense of retaining its common identity and culture) are not necessarily synonymous. Local economic development refers only to the development of the economic basis of a community or simply to the promotion of the competitiveness of enterprises.

"Restructuring" refers to fundamental changes in the organization of a community; for example, changes in the mode of production, major changes in the economic basis of a community (such as the closure of a mine), or changes in the interplay of market mechanisms and local actors. The restructuring concept thus contains a wider theoretical and more fundamental perspective than the policy-oriented concept of local development.

Restructuring is a process that leads to a new or different structure or arrangement of the system under consideration. In earlier geographical and regional studies, the word was employed to describe the behaviour of a firm in its endeavour to improve its competitive position (Cooke 1986, 4). It is now used in a broader sense to describe structural, economic-led changes in a society (Friedmann 1991; Welch 1993), including countries in transition (Scholtès 1996; Stenning 1997). The closure of an old plant, the growth of a new system of production based on new and unique technology, the development of a new economic base, drastic shifts of employment from one sector to another, continuous depopulation of rural areas, the unmanageable growth of cities, the privatization of industrial capital, and changes in the bases of the electoral systems of local councils are all examples of structural change in societies.

The pressures to restructure

The processes that generate the need for resource communities to restructure are numerous and often interrelated. They may stem from international, sectoral, national, or local factors. Some of these processes, such as the exhaustion of non-renewable resources, are inherent in the very nature of many resource communities. Most of the processes affecting communities in the 1990s are not new. Transition, sectoral transformation, different policy-related factors, and the attributes of a locale and locality are all highlighted in the case-studies, one process often reinforcing another. The key processes associated with fundamental restructuring that have affected the researched communities are:

- changes in national policies and prevailing political economies – the collapse of the socialist regimes, the playing down of the welfare economy concept, deregulation, and the reinforcement of other market economic principles;
- shortcomings in public policy – continuing budget deficits, high unemployment rates, and unstable exchange markets – leading to uncertainty in the examined communities;
- sectoral restructuring resulting from shifts of demand from one sector to another;
- the globalization of economies;
- the collapse of the socialist trade bloc, and the associated reorganization of international trade and tourism;
- economic pressures leading to the search for more efficient production through the introduction of robotization, computer-mediated communications, and telecommunications into industrial processes; and
- the revival of local economic policies in many countries, and an associated restructuring of the socio-economic institutions and philosophies.

Each of these processes is discussed briefly below.

Changes in prevailing political economies at the national level

A diffusion of neo-liberal arguments, reactions against an old regime, subjective evaluations of national development potential, the failure of some existing economic systems to meet lifestyle expectations, and the profit-maximizing logic of globalizing capitalism have all combined to induce major changes in national economies over recent decades. Appelbaum and Henderson (1992) suggest a two-dimensional typology to help understand national-level transformations of political economies in the 1990s. The first dimension distinguishes between planned economies and market economies, the second between economies based on ideology and those based on rationality. These two dimensions thus provide a fourfold classification of the political systems currently undergoing transition, the different classifications being defined as follows:

1. *Market rationality*. Market rationality, according to Dahrendorf (1968, 219), is based on the assumption that a "smoothly functioning market is to the greatest advantage of the greatest number" and requires a "politically passive ... hands-off attitude in matters of legislation and decision making." The term has been

redefined by Appelbaum and Henderson (1992, 19) to include "the regulatory function of the state, which is viewed in such political economies as providing a framework wherein investment, production, and distributional decisions (which remain the preserve of business) can operate in a relatively efficient manner."

2. *Market ideology.* In market ideology, "public policy is oriented above all towards assuring the free market operations ... [M]arket ideological régimes arise from ideological dogma: ... [a belief in] the wisdom and benevolence of an invisible hand in a supposedly unfettered market" (Appelbaum and Henderson 1992, 19).

3. *Plan rationality.* In plan rationality, "state regulation is supplemented by state direction of the economy as a whole. Here, national economic goals are identified, and the state operates with various degrees of influence or pressure to urge companies to act in accordance with these goals. The economy remains largely in private hands, and companies compete with one another under the watchful discipline of the market; yet the state also intervenes to achieve national goals where necessary. Should a sector be lacking, for example, what is deemed essential to economic growth, the state will likely induce it, often through price supports, subsidies, and favourable credit arrangements" (Appelbaum and Henderson 1992, 19–20).

4. *Plan ideology.* Plan ideology also arises from ideological dogma. It is based on a belief in "the wisdom and benevolence of state managers in a command economy ... [T]he state owns and controls most if not all economic units. Resource allocations and investment decisions are a state rather than a corporate or market function, supposedly serving an overriding concern with equity in the distribution of wealth and income. Ideological dogma, rather than pragmatic analysis of consequences, dominates policy choices and applications" (Appelbaum and Henderson 1992, 20).

This is a static but comparative conceptualization. Other models, such as those based on national-level perceptions of the need to restructure, set in motion by periods of particular turbulence (Britton et al. 1992), offer more dynamic explanations of political economic restructuring. It is also only one of a number of ways of looking at the political economic environment, but it helps us to understand what are the ideological, national values that influence the availability of local policy instruments in communities.

Most of the countries from which the case-studies in this collection have been drawn have recently changed position in this typology.

Plan ideology has been abandoned in Europe and Viet Nam. Hungary has moved from plan ideology to market rationality. Some East European countries, such as Poland, have moved from plan ideology to something akin to a market ideology and back again. Australia in 1996 had been showing signs of moving, at least partially, from market rationality to market ideology.

Some Nordic countries have reduced welfare spending. Finland, for example, is moving in the direction of a market ideology; although public opinion is against the demise of the welfare state, increased public debt has forced a reduction both in welfare spending and in employment in the public sector (Wiberg 1997; Willner 1998). Thus, in general, the national movement has moved in the direction of an increasing commitment to a market economy, although this movement has not necessarily taken place in fixed stages. Politico-economic environments are, nevertheless, evolving, and there are neither perpetual structures nor predetermined stages in development. Therefore, the above framework should be developed, too.

The manifestations of change in the socio-economic transformations of the 1990s have been quite varied. However, the ultimate effect for most of the rural resource communities researched has been a reduction in the role played by the states in their local economy, and the need to adapt to changes that were not necessarily compatible with the desired course of economic development of their region. Moreover, restructuring has often been imposed without any local involvement in decision-making in a traditional sense, that is, in the form of strong involvement by the local community. At the same time, "liberalization" has provided a new opportunity in some countries not only for new business enterprises but for informal organizations and self-help groups to become a force in local development. In some cases, the impact of non-governmental organizations, local or external, can be particularly strong when the options open to local communities are associated with negative environmental impacts. The need to adapt to new political and institutional settings has had profound impacts on most of the communities discussed below.

As the case-studies below show, the ways in which people have adapted, at the community level, to these transformations in political systems are not necessarily what might be predicted from the nature of the transformations at the national level and the systems of production aspired to in national policies. A striking feature of restructuring in a number of the case-studies is the development of diverse methods of production at the local level, which may coexist with the traditional system of production.

The "crisis" in the public sector

Apart from any changes presupposed by the transformation of their national politics, it has become increasingly difficult for most central and local governments to sustain the level of external funding on which some communities have become dependent owing to the decline of their economic base. This has affected not only the communities studied in the developing economies of Eastern Europe, but also the Nordic communities. It has affected the support that can be offered in times of natural disaster to the agricultural communities studied in South Australia, thus substantially altering the viability of farming in the peripheral region in which the communities are situated and in other peripheral agricultural regions in Australia.

In most of the countries experiencing a public sector "crisis," the crisis has been associated with changes in national policy. Politicians have opted to encourage private service enterprises, rather than the provision of public services. Privatization has occurred and social benefits have been considered a burden, not a necessary part of social infrastructure. As unemployment has increased in many countries, the contradiction between the goals of the past social model and the actual situation has become more obvious. In the countries in transition toward a market economy, many parts of the public sector have collapsed. Because many resource communities have been, and still are, dependent on government assistance or have been associated with public sector employment, these communities tend to be particularly vulnerable to such restructuring.

Sectoral restructuring

Most of the communities examined in this collection of papers have been affected, to a greater or lesser extent, by the fact that the demand for certain products has declined or failed to expand, forcing sectoral restructuring in the region or country. Agricultural, mining, and forestry communities have all been affected by this process, leading to rationalization in an effort to increase the efficiency of production in many sectors. This has resulted in reductions in the demand for local labour and in plant closures.

11

Communities where the economic base consists of traditional primary production (mining, bulk or staple production in agriculture, etc.) have been the most affected by rationalization and stagnant demand. Specialization in supplying a product that has a positive or more positive elasticity of income is a common remedy in this situation, but it cannot be applied in every locality.

Sectoral restructuring does not, or should not automatically, mean the shrinking of local economies. The disbandment of communities and associated local economies may be the only viable option in some extreme cases, such as the closure of a mine in an isolated area totally dependent on mining. At the broader level, however, sectoral restructuring contains a potential for growth. It leads to new businesses, different business cultures, and a new networking of enterprises, in both resource-based sectors and beyond. Tourism, for instance, has increased the viability of some local economies, although, as the papers below show, whether or not it ensures the viability of the original community as a social entity depends very much on the circumstances surrounding its introduction.

The globalization of economies

Owing to improved telecommunications, the decline in the relative prices of some forms of transportation, and the increased integration and liberalization of international economic relations, a globalization of economies has taken place. Resultant changes in the spatial organization of firms have increased the role of both the material and the non-material network relations that link the various regions with the outer world (Cappellin 1992, 2, 5). These changes have been further stimulated by the diffusion of new technological innovations, such as the new information technologies, which horizontally affect all economic sectors through the rapid birth of high-tech firms. This trend has been defended by the classical arguments of increasing efficiency generated by specialization, on the grounds that "the globalization of economies has meant making use of differences and a trend towards specialization of each firm and of each regional and national economy in those types of production where they have a comparative advantage, in particular with respect to their specific know-how" (Cappellin 1992, 5–7).

For resource-based companies and entrepreneurs in a number of production sectors, globalization, together with changes in government control, has led to a new market situation, which is neither protected nor regulated by state authorities to the same degree that it had been earlier. An unprotected situation is not new for Australian farmers. In Europe, agriculture is carried on in different economic environments. For instance, farmers are operating either within the trade bloc markets, such as the European Union, or outside these blocs, as in the case of Hungarian, Bulgarian, and Polish farms. Likewise, the mining sector is not controlled by military interests to the same extent as before, thus allowing mining companies to operate widely in the international market (Humphreys 1995). Further, transnational companies can relocate particular operations rapidly. In urban areas, the relocation of a company's operation may result in economic hardship for a segment of the population; in a resource community, it may remove a community's *raison d'être*. Whether this globalization is allowed to lead to the closure of certain industries in the national economies, and whether it leads to the marginalization of large numbers of communities in some fringe regions of the new trade blocs, are central issues of the globalization of industrial activities.

The reorganization of international trade

A further international pressure forcing restructuring in the 1980s and 1990s was the integration of economies into trade blocs and the liberalization of world trade by the General Agreement on Tariffs and Trade. The break-up of the Council for Mutual Economic Assistance, on the other hand, left the primary producers in the East-Central European countries without their traditional market, meaning that exports to Russia ceased. This caused severe problems in countries such as Hungary in the early phase of transition. The East-Central European countries are seeking to become members of the European Union in order to lessen the problems of the limited export market.

The liberalization of trade may create opportunities for specialized products, because it greatly expands the market for such products. On the other hand, less competitive companies and enterprises are forced to close as the production of the most efficient producers expands. Thus, communities with many marginal producers, or with producers that were protected by national subsidies before liberalization, are now faced with the need to restructure.

13

The introduction of improved technology

Innovations induce improvements in production technology and products, often leading to a reduction in employment. A new, modernized plant usually employs fewer people than the plant it replaced, and, in spite of this reduction in labour, production increases – the efficiency of resource sectors has increased considerably in recent years. In most countries, employment has decreased in agriculture, forestry, mining, etc. with the continuous introduction of modern technology.

There has been considerable discussion of a new techno-economic paradigm (Freeman 1988, 11). Known as the fifth Kondratiev wave, the new mode of growth started to emerge in Western economies after the oil crisis. It is characterized by the introduction of computers, advanced telecommunications, robotics, biotechnology, and remote control systems into production. According to Freeman and Perez (1988, 53), on the management side this wave consists of networks of large and small firms based increasingly on computer networks and close cooperation in technology, quality control, training, and "just-in-time" production planning. "Keiretsu" and similar conglomerations take care of the financial operations of the companies and networks of companies.

Technological changes have been fundamental in many resource communities. A new techno-economic paradigm emerges in a world still dominated by an old paradigm, and begins by demonstrating its superior competitiveness in a few pilot projects. Thereafter it expands rapidly. As Freeman and Perez (1988, 58) argue,

A new techno-economic paradigm emerges only gradually as a new "ideal type" of productive organization, to take full advantage of the key factor(s) which are becoming more and more visible in the relative cost structure. The new paradigm discloses the potential for a quantum jump in total factor productivity and opens up an unpredictable range of new investment opportunities. It is for these reasons that it brings about a radical shift in "engineering" and managerial "common sense" and that it tends to diffuse as rapidly as conditions allow, replacing the investment pattern of the old paradigm.

The full constellation – once crystallised – goes far beyond the key factor(s) and beyond technical change itself. It brings with it a restructuring of the whole productive system.

This is what is happening in progressive resource communities, as the Western Australian case illustrates.

The revival of local economic policies

A considerable shift in regional policy doctrine has taken place in the past two decades. Investments in infrastructure, various private/ public and local/central partnerships, and the deregulation and opening of local economies for competition have replaced Keynesian-type regional policies, which emphasized regional assistance through financial incentives to growth. In contrast, in accordance with the now widely accepted supply-side approach, one country after another has employed applied research and technology in its less developed regions, improved communications networks, ameliorated market rigidities, and attracted foreign capital to communities. Housing, infrastructure, cheap premises, and favourable business environments are developed by authorities and development corporations at the local level. Development authorities are often ready to support companies to train labour in greenfield projects. Local economic policy concentrates on enabling a community to remain a viable candidate in the international competition between localities seeking to sell themselves as suitable locations for industries.

This kind of policy opens up many countries to foreign competition, and it increases the specialization of production. Former socialist countries have joined in the competition between localities. So far, inexpensive skilled labour has been their advantage, and a poorly developed institutional business environment their disadvantage. Throughout the world, local economies are creating opportunities for integration in the worldwide production chains. If successful, this development leads to increased wealth. In the event of failure, it may lead to social dumping and the emergence of low-wage factories and sweatshops. Successful or otherwise, this process leads to resource communities becoming more and more sensitive to the economic fluctuations originating from international markets. The case-studies of the book reveal how the more open and market-led policies work in practice and what their consequences are.

The need to restructure: A crisis or an intermittent process?

The varying nature of the processes that generate pressures to restructure at the local level means that restructuring can take different temporal forms. For some communities discussed in this book, the need to restructure has arisen from a sudden crisis in a situation that has been economically stable for decades. This is most likely to be true of mining communities, single-industry communities, and communities where the conditions for profitable production suddenly disappear with a single production plant.

In the more diversified communities examined, the need to restructure can be seen as a continuous, if intermittent, evolutionary process, although it can be equally distressing for those affected. It can be the outcome not just of sectoral pressures, but also of centralized planning philosophies that involve constant adjustments to a nation's economic system in the hope of achieving overall optimal economic efficiency. The transition of the 1990s in the former socialist countries was not a totally new experience. In the capitalist economies, a similar intermittent or evolutionary process was caused by market forces. Socio-economic restructuring has thus been a feature of both economic systems.

To understand the particular directions that development takes, it is necessary to examine the current restructuring processes in different time–space settings (see Thrift 1983). Where restructuring has been an ongoing, intermittent, process, each stage of local adjustment is influenced by past transformations, and the constraints and opportunities that they have created for new initiatives. This development process may be intentional, with a clear sense of a desired ultimate outcome; in other words, many socio-economic structures and forms of advanced society may be deliberately chosen, as Lash and Urry (1994) show in comparing the German model of society with the Anglo-American neo-liberal model.

Restructuring: A source of progressive or non-progressive economic change?

Development is commonly expected to involve progress (Gore 1984, 241), often in the sense of increasing economic efficiency as a result of policy measures. In many economic usages, restructuring contains the implicit notion that the changes involved are the effects of market forces, which should lead the society to a more efficient economic system (e.g. World Bank 1996). However, the papers in this collection clearly illustrate that restructuring in a community is not always progressive in local economic terms. In some cases, restructuring arising from local adjustment to external pressures has resulted in a resource community with a stable and reasonably secure position in the national economic system. In other cases, it has led to out-migration and other processes likely, in the long term, substantially to reduce the community's or region's options for future economic progress. In still other cases, local adjustment to external pressures has led to the evolution, at the local level, of an advanced or alternative system of production, resulting in gradual regeneration of a socio-economic system at the local level.

The relativity of progressive change

Communities exist in various socio-economic circumstances: some people live in a subsistence economy, and some are surrounded by advanced technology. These local circumstances influence the perception of what is considered progressive. Economic turmoil has led to the adoption of a subsistence economy in some communities, as the case-studies indicate. As Evers (1988, 39) points out, in industrialized as well as in developing societies, the intertwining of several sources of income and different kinds of labour is by no means unimportant, although it is overlooked by many studies. Thus, household survival may depend upon successfully intertwining economic activities in the formal, or state-regulated, sector of the economy with activities in the subsistence sector, in which all consumption-oriented economic activities are intended for private use. Furthermore, survival may include participation in the informal sector (the sector of the economy that consists of small-scale production) or it may include rendering services for cash or barter. Only the formal sector operates within state regulation or influence.

As some of the neo-capitalist case-studies in this book show, one way in which households disadvantaged by national restructuring can survive is through such intertwining of economic activities. Intertwining is also a basis for innovative restructuring and development. It is important, therefore, that the growth of informal activities, as a part of restructuring, is seen not just as a negative phenomenon but as a part of an adjustment process. If low-income households are to survive they may need to derive their income from various sources, but this represents only one of many adaptations in countries undergoing transformation to a market economy. Intertwining bridges the divide between two economic systems during the stage of transition and becomes a part of training in the ways of economic behaviour in capitalism. Intertwining can also be a feature of restructuring in cities in advanced market economies, such as the United Kingdom and the United States (Evers 1988; Roberts 1994) and Italy (Mingione 1991), where the social structure of cities is moving towards a polarization between high-income and low-income jobs and between employed and unemployed people.

In contrast with the strategies of development occurring in the conditions of crisis in the transitional countries, the idea of progress may be emphasized very differently in welfare states and highly industrialized societies. An example that highlights the complex definition of "progressive development" is to be found in Finland, where the government accepted the programme "Finland's Way to the Information Society" to be carried out as a national project on 18 January 1995. The reasoning behind this strategy reveals one concept of progressive restructuring in the context of an advanced market economy (Ministry of Finance 1996, 6):

Within an open world economy, both firms and national economies must continuously look for ways to improve productivity and competitiveness. In order to secure the well-being of citizens, and the resources required to develop the society, there are no alternatives. Renewal requires readiness for change, as well as know-how and the use of information and technologies of the highest quality.... [Information technology] is an essential competitive factor for products and production. It is also increasingly gaining foothold at a personal level in work, studies, and leisure time activities.... A networked economy, with a developed information network as a basis, provides a real opportunity for Finland as it reduces the problems caused by distance.

The report continues by outlining how the government will provide a favourable framework by promoting information network infrastructures, teleworking, the use of information technology in the provision of public services, digital radio and television broadcasts, training in information technology, multimedia, transport telematics, etc. This programme is utilized in schools and villages, as an introduction to the cyber-society, and many of the most remote communities have been connected to advanced telecommunications and computer networks. These developments are leading to networking and the formation of various cyber-communities. This is a very different vision of progressive development compared with the sorts of visions often held in remote villages in transitional countries. This complicated issue of what is progressive development is discussed in the case-study of Western Australia, which represents a community of the information society.

The case-studies in this book show that great diversity prevails in the outcomes of restructuring. What is progressive or not progressive depends on one's values and norms and the time-scale of evaluation.

In the recent past, however, it appears that restructuring has generally been a response to unsatisfactory socio-economic conditions and is irreversible, although a large number of options exist with respect to how it can be managed locally.

Principles in searching for explanations

An approach using multiple case-studies was considered to be an appropriate research strategy for analysing socio-economic restructuring in the project, because the outcomes of restructuring vary greatly in geographical space and resource communities face diverse future prospects. It has been concluded that the future of resource communities depends on a combination of several economic and local conditions with great spatial and sectoral variety (Tykkyläinen and Neil 1995). Therefore, the investigation of geographical variation in development can fundamentally enrich theory, reinforcing the idea that a broad, globally applicable theory must have a geographical basis.

The case-studies have been deliberately drawn from different parts of the globe, rather than being examples of a broad region such as Eastern, Northern, or Southern Europe. Concern with making comparisons and understanding dynamics was particularly important when selecting cases and analysing the results. Cases were chosen bearing in mind that we were willing to analyse the dilemma of various explanations related to external/internal, exogenous/endogenous, and global/local development dimensions in depth. We were also willing to contribute to the discussion of the coexistence and interaction of global forces and local processes, a sort of "glocalisation" (see Swyngedouw 1992), but discussing it in a rural setting in this project. A broad analysis of various forces was seen as important, and we attempted to avoid the approaches of many past explanations that were derived from analyses on a national, or regional, scale, which pay very little attention to multi-faceted transformation processes in a community.

In a paper presenting a preliminary theoretical analysis, we concluded that geographical differences, the inherited structures of society, and local and sectoral characteristics have all been ignored or underestimated in many explanations of restructuring (Tykkyläinen and Neil 1995). An attempt to contextualize the restructuring in resource communities using existing theories of regional development led to the conclusion that this body of theory is amorphous and

19

that, although there are many theories, any one theory offers only a very partial explanation of development (ibid., 39). The chain of reasoning led to a framework for multicausal analysis incorporating different factors of development. That paper presented the idea that general processes, policy-related factors, local-specific features, and sector-specific processes are independent categories and that the explanation of restructuring in any community involves the inter-action of all four sets of processes. It was also outlined how divergent factors affect development, so that communities emerge, grow, and disband and the economic, social, and spatial structures of communities change continuously.

An earlier version of the paper was sent to all those invited to contribute case-studies for this volume. A leading theme was condensed as follows (Tykkyläinen and Neil 1993, 11):

Inherent for the framework outlined above is the idea that an adequate explanation of restructuring, and the outcomes of local economic development policies, is contingent upon understanding both the general factors and specific factors affecting a community, and that socio-economic restructuring is reforming the spatial shapes and pattern of resource communities. It seeks to offer a framework for comparison and explanation of restructuring, for an assessment of how local development schemes achieve their goals, and for comparative evaluation of the economic, social and environmental effects of schemes. The framework is naturally open to debate and will undoubtedly evolve further as research for this book progresses, and the framework is evaluated in the case studies and in the concluding chapter.

The above ideas of multicausality are revised and developed further in the concluding chapter of this book based on the results of the case-studies.

Comparisons of rural restructuring processes and local economic development in an international context highlight different aspects of transformation, bring out its geographical factors, and provide a broad context to explain restructuring. The selection of the countries and communities incorporated in this volume was based on the principle that it was necessary to incorporate case-studies reflecting a wider range of circumstances if the different kinds of processes and outcomes of rural restructuring were to be realistically investigated. In that way, we aimed to generalize from a set of case-study results to a broader theory. We considered it important to have case-studies from market economies and economies in transition; thus, the case-studies explore capitalist and neo-capitalist[3] restructuring in the East

Table 1.1 **Case-study communities and regions**

	East-Central Europe and Russia	Finland, Sweden, and Ireland	USA and Australia	Viet Nam
Geographically marginal communities facing a reduction in public spending		Härjedalen, Sweden	Cleve, South Australia	
Restructuring of the countryside in countries undergoing transition	Lower Silesia, Supraśl, and Zabłudów, Poland Eastern Hungary Virma and Gridino, Karelia Kuklen, Bulgaria			Rural Viet Nam
The life cycles of resource communities		Vuohijärvi, Finland	Forrestania, Western Australia	
Sectoral shift and diversification – the example of tourism		Kolari, Lapland Irish community network	Kellogg, Idaho	

and West in traditional, modern, post-industrial, and translocal communities (table 1.1).

The case-studies have been divided into four groups, roughly in line with the spatio-economic characteristics of the restructuring processes themselves, and as indicated in the rows of table 1.1. Part II of the book deals with remote communities facing a reduction in public spending, part III deals with transitional economies, part IV elaborates upon the start and restart of industrial activities in remote settings, and part V analyses the challenges of diversification in rural communities, using tourism as an example (table 1.1). Some of the analyses are done at the regional level. The geographical division indicated in the columns of table 1.1 groups the institutional setting of the cases into: transitional economies; subsidized rural West European economies; the more liberal Australian and North American economies; and newly developing economies.

The idea of table 1.1 is to provide an overview of the comparative setting of the research – it does not represent an attempt at any sort of universal classification of the rural situation, nor does it contain any implicit idea of stages of development. The selection of cases also reflects the changing idea of community, from the traditional view to the social networks of an information society. The research project does not focus only on single-resource communities but concerns social networks, such as cooperatives, advisory councils, and multi-local communities.

By incorporating a number of case-studies driven by different circumstances we hope to increase the external validity of this research (see Yin 1990, 40–60). In practice, it is intended to lead to a research situation in which it is possible to explore and compare the dynamics of restructuring across a variety of countries in the hope of finding explanations that are more comprehensive than explanations derived from studies carried out in one country at a particular point in time. The search for a theory of restructuring, a multicausal theory of local development, has been a prime motivating factor in this research endeavour.

Notes

1. In general, this book deals with social networks in various geographical settings and scales focusing on human activities in work and social and political life, and the terms "community," "locality," and "locale" have been found valid and useful. The term "local-specific" includes the ideas of spatial contingency effects, local causal processes, and locality effects in particular places (see Duncan 1989).
2. On the definition of the concepts "network society," "information age," and "information(al) society," see Castells (1996, 21–22, 468–478).
3. Capitalism in Viet Nam is restricted, but the country is clearly on the way to a market economy.

References

Appelbaum, R. P. and Henderson, J. (1992), "Situating the State in the East Asian Development Process," in R. P. Appelbaum and J. Henderson (eds.), *States and Development in the Asian Pacific Rim,* Sage Publications, London, pp. 1–26.

Britton, S., Le Heron, R., and Pawson, E. (eds.) (1992), *Changing Places in New Zealand: A Geography of Restructuring*, New Zealand Geographical Society, Christchurch.

Buller, H. and Wright, S. (1990), "Introduction: Concepts and Policies of Rural Development", in H. Buller and S. Wright (eds.), *Rural Development: Problems and Practices*, Avebury, Aldershot, pp. 1–24.

Butz, D. and Eyles, J. (1997), "Reconceptualizing Sense of Place: Social Relations, Ideology and Ecology," *Geografiska Annaler* 79 B, pp. 1–25.

Cappellin, R. (1992), "Theories of Local Endogenous Development and International Co-operation," in M. Tykkyläinen (ed.), *Development Issues and Strategies in the New Europe,* Avebury, Aldershot. pp. 1–19.

Castells, M. (1996), *The Rise of the Network Society,* Blackwell, Oxford.

Conti, S. (1993), "The Network Perspective in Industrial Geography: Towards a Model," *Geografiska Annaler,* 75 B 3, pp. 115–130.

Cooke, P. (1986), "Global Restructuring, Industrial Change and Local Adjustment," in P. Cooke (ed.), *Global Restructuring, Local Response,* ESRC, London, pp. 1–24.

Dahrendorf, R. (1968), "Market and Plan: Two Types of Rationality," in R. Dahrendorf, *Essays in the Theory of Society*, Routledge, Kegan & Paul, London, pp. 215–231.

Duncan, S. (1989), "What Is Locality?", in R. Peet and N. Thrift (eds.), *New Models in Geography, Volume II,* Unwin Hyman, London, pp. 221–252.

Evers, H. D. (1988), "Shadow Economy, Subsistence Production and Informal Sector: Economic Activity Outside of Market and State," *Prisma* 51, pp. 34–45.

Freeman, C. (1988), "Evolution, Technology and Institutions: A Wider Framework for Economic Analysis," in G. Dosi, C. Freeman, R. Nelson, G. Silverberg, and L. Soete (eds.), *Technical Change and Economic Theory,* Pinter Publishers, London, pp. 9–37.

Freeman, C. and Perez, C. (1988), "Structural Crises of Adjustment, Business Cycles and Investment Behaviours," in G. Dosi, C. Freeman, R. Nelson, G. Silverberg, and L. Soete (eds.), *Technical Change and Economic Theory,* Pinter Publishers, London, pp. 38–66.

Friedmann, J. (1991), "The Industrial Transition: A Comprehensive Approach to Regional Development," in E. Bergman, G. Maier, and F. Tödling (eds.), *Regions Reconsidered: Economic Networks, Innovation, and Local Development in Industrialised Countries*, Mansell, London, pp. 167–178.

Giddens, A. (1984), *The Constitution of Society. Outline of the Theory of Structuration*, Polity Press, Cambridge.

Gore, C. (1984), *Regions in Question,* Methuen, London.

Hoggart, K. and Buller, H. (1987), *Rural Development. A Geographical Perspective,* Croom Helm, London.

Humphreys, D. (1995), "Whatever Happened to Security of Supply? Minerals Policy in the Post-Cold War World," *Resources Policy* 21, pp. 91–97.

Lash, S. and Urry, J. (1994), *Economics of Signs and Space,* Sage, London.

Marsden, T., Murdoch, J., Lowe, P., Munton, R., and Flynn A. (1993), *Constructing the Countryside,* UCL Press, London.

Mingione, E. (1991), *Fragmented Societies. A Sociology of Economic Life beyond the Market Paradigm,* Basil Blackwell, Oxford.

Ministry of Finance (1996), *Finland's Way to the Information Society. The National Strategy and Its Implication*, Edita, Helsinki.

Roberts, B. (1994), "Informal Economy and Family Strategies," *International Journal of Urban and Regional Research* 18(1), pp. 6–23.

Scholtès, P. R. (ed.) (1996), *Industrial Economics for Countries in Transition. Evidence from Eastern Europe and Asia Pacific*, Edward Elgar, Cheltenham.

Stenning, A. C. (1997), "Economic Restructuring and Local Change in the Russian Federation," in M. J. Bradshaw (ed.), *Geography and Transition in the Post-Soviet Republics*, Wiley, Chichester, pp. 147–162.

Swyngedouw, E. (1992), "The Mammon Guest. 'Glocalization', Interspatial Competition and the Monetary Order: The Construction of New Scales," in M. Dunford and G. Kafkalas (eds.), *Cities and Regions in the New Europe*, Belhaven Press, London, pp. 39–67.

Thrift, N. J. (1983), "On the Determination of Social Action in Space and Time," *Environment and Planning D: Society and Space* 1, pp. 23–57.

Tykkyläinen, M. and Neil, C. (1993), "Introduction," a paper submitted to the participants in the project "The Potential for Local Economic Development in Rural Resource Communities," Joensuu, mimeo.

—— (1995), "Socio-Economic Restructuring in Resource Communities: Evolving a Comparative Approach," *Community Development Journal* 30, pp. 31–47.

Welch, R. V. (1993), "Capitalist Restructuring and Local Economic Development: Perspective from an Ultra-Peripheral City-Economy," *Regional Studies* 27, pp. 237–249.

Wiberg, M. (1997), "Staten har blivit för dyr," *Journal of the Economic Society of Finland* 50, pp. 175–185.

Willner, M. (1998), "Några myter om offentlig sektor och privatisering," *Journal of the Economic Society of Finland* 51, pp. 37–46.

World Bank (1996), *World Development Report 1996. From Plan to Market*, World Bank, Washington D.C.

Yin, R. K. (1990), *Case Study Research*, Sage, Newbury Park, Calif.

Part II
Geographically marginal communities facing a reduction in public spending

2

A rural community faces the turmoil of the welfare state: The case of Härjedalen, Sweden

Lars Olof Persson

Long waves of structural adjustment

This paper examines restructuring in the municipality of Härjedalen, in Norrland, a region in the north-western interior of Sweden. The focus of the paper is how macroeconomic and political shifts at the national and international levels have changed the living conditions and the settlement structure of a relatively isolated region. The aim is to describe the processes of change in a remote Swedish community that has been transformed from a dependence on forest resources and small-scale agricultural exploitation to a dependence on public resources, without developing any local manufacturing industry of importance. For macroeconomic reasons, reflected in national policy shifts, this type of resource community is now facing a reduction in its public resource transfer. I hypothesize that this will have important spatial implications and a more all-pervasive impact than is likely to result from the changes in specific sector policies or in the national regional policy that are expected to take place, partly as a consequence of Sweden's approach to the Single European Market.

Remote marginal regions in Sweden are facing a second period of contraction of their local economic base – the first being the restructuring and reduced labour demand of forestry during the period 1950–

1980, the second being the reduction in the public sector in the 1990s. As in other regions in Sweden, it seems that the only realistic substitute for the expected loss of jobs will be an expansion within the private service sector. In the rural upland region of Härjedalen, this will be in the labour-intensive, but low-capacity, tourist industry, rather than in the more qualified information and knowledge sector (as tends to occur in urban regions; see, for example, Drucker 1993; Reich 1991).

In this paper, the background to this development will be presented, and discussed in terms of both its already observed and its anticipated consequences for the labour market and the settlement structure of Härjedalen. As discussed in more detail below, two particular consequences can be anticipated for this region. The first relates to the level of formal education in the local labour force. This improved moderately during the period of public service expansion, although it is still lower than that of many other regions. In the future, however, it is likely that, as a result of impending changes, Härjedalen will come to lag even further behind other regions in the level of educational attainment of its labour force, thus increasing the regional disparities within Sweden. The second consequence of the expected loss of public service jobs, and their substitution by private sector jobs, relates to the settlement pattern. As long as forestry and small-scale agriculture dominated the local labour market and the local economy in Härjedalen, the settlement structure was scattered. As public services expanded, the population became concentrated in small central places relatively far from the mountains. During the coming period of an expected reduction in public services and an expansion of private services, a new locational shift of economic activity towards the mountainous parts of this vast municipality is anticipated. These parts of the region are more attractive from a tourist point of view. The present administrative and service centre of the municipality may lose some of its importance.

A major task confronting the local government in the next decade will be defending the existing public services and the jobs based in the local administrative centre, while simultaneously stimulating (in a period of shrinking public resources) and supporting new private initiatives in the tourist region.

Härjedalen: A rural "landscape" in a post-industrial economy

The sparsely populated regions closest to core urban regions in Europe are found largely in the central parts of the Scandinavian

Gulf of Bothnia

Fig. 2.1   **Härjedalen in Sweden.**

peninsula. The interior of Norrland in Sweden covers a land area that
is seven times as large as, for instance, the Netherlands, and yet this
vast area has fewer than 500,000 inhabitants (fig. 2.1). As international integration proceeds, not only will these regional contrasts
within Europe become more visible, but economic and political integration will also introduce both threats and new opportunities
(Lundqvist and Persson 1993) to local communities in this semi-
peripheral area. Threats will include the risk of unrestricted market
forces, which may erode the protective sheltering effects of the Scandinavian national welfare system and regional policy. Opportunities
will be created through increasing demand from other European
countries for resources available in the area (mainly recreational and
environmental) and through access to common structural policy

29

measures within the framework of the coherence concept of the European Union.

In so far as the European integration process penetrates these communities, the structural changes, which have already transformed the labour markets of these communities from their former strong dependency on forestry as an export industry to a dependency on service production for local demand, will continue to reshape both the settlement structure and the local labour markets. Rationalization, cut-backs, and the privatization of divisions in the large public sector are expected to be significant catalysts for change. The growth of private services and of a few new industries based on natural resources is also expected to be a driving force (see, for example, Jussila et al. 1993).

Härjedalen is a municipality in one of the sparsely populated regions of Norrland. It is unique in a few ways, but in most respects it is representative of many municipalities in the north-western interior of Sweden (see fig. 2.1). With only 12,400 inhabitants and a land area of 11,400 km^2 (just over one inhabitant per km^2), it ranks as the seventh most sparsely populated of the 285 Swedish municipalities. Härjedalen is a combination of small villages, scattered settlements, and the municipal centre, Sveg. This pattern of resource communities is common in the countryside of Sweden and Finland.[1]

Although administratively it was incorporated (along with six other municipalities) into the county of Jämtland in the early nineteenth century, Härjedalen is one of the two Swedish municipalities that constitute what is traditionally known as a *landskap* in Swedish, denoting a province. The Swedish province is the historical definition of a land area covering a large but well-defined territory that is (or at least was considered to be) culturally and geographically homogeneous. In early medieval times, each of the 24 provinces in Sweden was independent and had its own legislation. Today, the province has no administrative significance, although the concept is still alive and widely used in common parlance as a symbol of regional identity. As an image or trademark, the concept is also sometimes used in regional marketing, such as within the tourist industry.

The reason the municipality of Härjedalen qualifies as a province is probably because, although it is one of the large rural regions least remote from the central urban areas of Sweden, Härjedalen has remained comparatively isolated. It takes approximately two hours to drive from central Härjedalen to any appreciably large urban area (such as the county administrative centre of Östersund). Located on the border of Norway, with the mountains as a dividing range, it has not had, and still does not have, any main east–west communication links.

A major attempt was made to improve accessibility and to promote regional development with the construction of the 1,290 km main Inlandsbanan railroad line by the state between 1908 and 1937. This connects all the western regions of central Sweden to the extreme north, and traverses the eastern section of Härjedalen. There were three reasons for this major railroad project: to stimulate the exploitation of natural resources in the interior of Norrland; to stabilize a settlement pattern with a number of interconnected and economically viable administrative urban centres; and, finally, to establish an alternative transport link to supplement the main railroad line along the coast of the Baltic Sea (largely for military purposes). However, owing to increased motoring and improved highways, the inland railroad never became profitable and was soon outdated. For Härjedalen, the new railroad initiated some growth, at least in the village of Svegsmon (later known as Sveg), which had only 724 inhabitants in 1916 but by 1958 had 2,071 inhabitants. However, the main growth of Sveg occurred for other reasons, and after the railway epoch.

Nevertheless, the rail link has not yet been closed, and its symbolic importance has never become obsolete. As late as the early 1950s, communities in western Härjedalen made every effort to convince the authorities that a west-bound railroad should be built to connect Härjedalen with Norway, thus creating a "coast-to-coast" railway straight across central Scandinavia. However, this project was never implemented.

The relative isolation of Härjedalen has other implications as well. In the early twentieth century, the National Encyclopedia described its regional dialect as "almost impossible to understand (without preparation), only a few dialects being more divergent from the national Swedish language" ("language" in *Nordisk Familjebok* 1910). One of the reasons for this linguistic divergence is that, until 1645, Härjedalen belonged to Norway. Furthermore, earlier outside observers loved to emphasize the almost exotic isolation that they apparently found on their excursions through the province; Härjedalen has been described as "Sweden's Siberia," "the land that God has forgotten," and, alternatively, "the land that God has hidden" (Näsström 1931; Peterson-Berger 1931).

The principal features of the region were described in the following way in 1931:

Härjedalen has always been one of this nation's poorest and harshest historical provinces; its people and nature are less known than people and settlements that are even more remote. This is due to the fact that *Härjedalen* has, until recently, been an isolated and desolate region, surrounded by inhospitable mountains; its communication with other provinces has been limited, its population is small, and it offers few sources of income. The only arable land (found in the river valleys) covers no more than one-half of one per cent of the land area of the entire province, the forests covering approximately 70 per cent. The remaining land area is composed of small mountain lakes, rivers, streams, hills, swamps and bare mountain wilderness. (Näsström 1931)

Its homogeneous rural character was underscored at that time by the fact that Härjedalen was the only one of Sweden's 24 provinces that did not possess a town (*"stad"*) and a town's corresponding rights. Sveg, the local administrative centre of Härjedalen, was appointed as a borough (*"köping"*), with fewer rights and fewer responsibilities than a town, because of its limited population and sparsely populated hinterland. Today, these terms have no significance, since each municipality, regardless of size, has the same responsibilities with respect to the provision of local services and welfare, etc. (see, for example, Häggroth 1993).

Some of these images stressing the uniqueness of Härjedalen may still be valid, although its negative features are seldom referred to nowadays. No doubt, the equalizing effect of the Swedish welfare system, and the regional policy in a general sense, have contributed to the elimination (or, at least, the disguising) of most of the negative features. None the less, the relative isolation, the low level of industrialization, the sparse and ageing population, and the high unemployment are highlighted whenever resource transfers from the government are questioned for some reason.

Paradoxically, and as mentioned before, the reason for stressing the rural and isolated character of the municipality is probably that Härjedalen is one of the most rural and mountainous peripheries close to the urban centres of central Sweden. At least in the past, this sharp urban–rural contrast made the differences in settlement structure, economic conditions, and culture more striking to visitors.

The "favourably located isolation" of Härjedalen has been one of the factors stimulating the tourist industry, based on the demand for recreation in the metropolitan and urban regions in central and southern Sweden. Since the 1930s, western Härjedalen has developed into one of the most important tourist regions in the Swedish mountains, mainly for winter sports. The local government has been actively involved in this development by raising capital, through marketing efforts, through infrastructure investments, and by subsidizing tourist services.

At the same time, Sveg has developed into an administrative and service centre for the entire municipality, and had a population of 4,174 in 1992. Urbanization in the rural peripheries and the expansion of municipal services have been the main reasons for its growth. During the past 30 years, Sveg's share of Härjedalen's population has increased from 25 to 34 per cent, while, at the same time, the total population of the province has decreased by 20 per cent.

The movement towards uniformity and increased equality

Inevitably, in many respects, the uniformity of different regions has increased through the processes of urbanization and social welfare that have been occurring in Sweden for some considerable time. Thus, as early as the 1930s, at the very beginning of the development of the Swedish welfare state, one author noted:

The totalistic "urbs" in which we live has started to impose its planning on Härjedalen. Modern communications have carried the message of our times (both for good and for bad) up to these forest-clad valleys. The provincial profile is fading owing to the exterior uniformity of modern culture, and the romance of the saga and other local traditions are giving way to a new spirit of perhaps materialistic but socially beneficial rationalism. (Näsström 1931)

This "materialistic but socially beneficial rationalism" was introduced as early as 1928, when the social democratic metaphor of "the people's home" was launched. During the period of almost 60 years that followed, this vision more or less guided the development not only of social and labour market policies but also of economic and regional policies in Sweden (Persson 1992; Ginsburg 1992). The official national regional policy goals still affirm that the state should create favourable conditions for employment, social services, and the environment in all regions. Table 2.1 clearly illustrates the resource concentration involved in the growth of the welfare programme since social democratic ideas were launched in the 1930s (and were eventually accepted by the majority of the population).

The implementation of the vision of the welfare state has had a tremendous, although not always fully recognized, impact on a relatively poor, isolated, and sparsely populated community such as

Table 2.1 **The Swedish state budget as a percentage of GDP and three major sectors as a percentage of public spending, 1920–1980**

Fiscal year	State budget (% of GDP)	Major sectors' share of state budget (%)		
		Defence	Social services	Education
1920	8	24	–	12
1930/31	10	16	14	19
1940/41	N/A	52	10	7
1950/51	16	20	25	10
1960/61	22	17	28	12
1970/71	26	13	29	16
1979/80	34	8	26	12

Source: Birgersson et al. (1981).

Härjedalen. In the early 1960s, 50 per cent of the population was more or less dependent on forestry for its income, and manufacturing employed less than 5 per cent of the labour force. One reason for the limited development of forest-based manufacturing industry in the inland area was the cheap transportation provided by floating timber on the large rivers to the coastal industries. Another reason was that during the nineteenth century and the first part of the twentieth century a comparatively large proportion of the forests had been sold by poor, small farmers to large companies searching for a secure supply for their saw mills and pulp mills located on the coast. Currently, in the entire county of Jämtland, less than one-fifth of the timber is manufactured within the county, and in Härjedalen the proportion is even lower.

There is a saying that "the forest is the plough and pasture of Härjedalen" – a saying once true of all of the communities in northwestern Sweden. Technological change, however, induced a rapid decrease in forestry and small-scale farming in the interior of Norrland in the 1960s. At the same time, there was a growth in manufacturing industry in southern and central Sweden. As a result of the emigration of young people from northern Sweden and of urbanization within the extensive inland area, the already sparse settlement was depleted even further in favour of expansion in most of the central regions. In Härjedalen, the rural population decreased from 65 per cent of the municipality in 1960 to only 30 per cent in 1990.

In the course of the past three decades, Härjedalen, once a natural resource community, has evolved into a service economy (see table

Table 2.2 **Employment, by industrial sector: Härjedalen and Sweden, 1965, 1985, and 1990 (%)**

Sector	Härjedalen			Sweden		
	1965	1985	1990	1965	1985	1990
Primary	37	15	12	12	5	3
Manufacturing	7	13	11	32	21	20
Public services	12	33	38	15	34	36
Private services	19	21	22	23	23	25
Other	25	18	17	18	17	16
All sectors	100	100	100	100	100	100

Source: Census of population.

2.2). This major structural change is reflected in the decrease in employment in the primary sector (agriculture and forestry). The primary sector and its associated industries (the food and forest industries, which are included in the manufacturing sector in table 2.2) accounted for 40 per cent of Härjedalen's employment in 1965, but only 17 per cent in 1990. This restructuring process was even more extreme in some other regions, and in Sweden as a whole the corresponding figure was less than 10 per cent in 1990. Unlike other regions, the decline of the primary sector in the marginal regions of the north was not replaced spontaneously by the growth of manufacturing. In fact, very few manufacturing industries were established spontaneously (that is, without any financial support from the regional policy). In Härjedalen, employment in manufacturing industry reached a peak in the 1980s and is, as in other parts of the country, currently decreasing from an already low level (see table 2.2).

Owing to the development of the tourist industry, employment in the private services has increased to almost the same level as that in Sweden as a whole. None the less, it is indisputable that the core of the local labour market of Härjedalen is the public service sector, which has introduced and maintained economic stability and a higher quality of life in this community. By the end of the twentieth century, however, it may be that the size of this sector will place the community once again in a vulnerable position.

The dominance of the public sector in the early 1990s

The public sector in Sweden was developed in order to satisfy very ambitious goals (by international standards) concerning the distribution of welfare and services to every household and individual. As a result, the sector has taken a central position in the labour market in almost every region, and in the national economy as a whole. In Sweden, total expenditure within the public sector represents over half the total value of all services and goods produced (GDP). Half of this expenditure is used directly to redistribute resources between households and individuals (such as pensions, grants for families with children, unemployment allowances, and other subsidies). As a result of the demographic and economic differences between regions, the subsidies received per capita vary. For example, municipalities with a high proportion of elderly people and with a weak labour market receive more money than the others on a per capita basis.

The Swedish welfare model redistributes income to a much larger extent than occurs in most comparable countries. More than 50 per cent of the variation in earned incomes is redistributed in the form of disposable incomes. Most other countries in Europe redistribute less than 40 per cent. As a result, in Sweden the difference in buying power between regions is much less than in most other countries. The regional variation (measured as the average deviation from the national mean) is 6 per cent in Sweden, compared with more than double that percentage in countries such as Finland, Norway, the United Kingdom, and Germany (SOU 1992).

The public production of services that, directly or indirectly, are supplied to households employs one-third of the labour force in Sweden. In sparsely populated northern Sweden, this proportion is generally more than 40 per cent. In these labour market areas, the public sector has (owing to the decrease in the primary sector and the undeveloped manufacturing industry), to some extent, taken the position of an economic base. This is due to the fact that local services and investments in service facilities are largely (more than 50 per cent) funded from external sources. This is an important factor in interregional solidarity, which is rooted in the Scandinavian welfare system. On the other hand, the very volume of public activities creates substantial local demand for goods and services in the private sector.

The growth of public services has had at least two significant effects on the labour market. First, it has created jobs for female labour, which would otherwise have been impossible in resource communities such as Härjedalen. Both the primary sector and manufacturing industry in Härjedalen employ less than 25 per cent female labour, whereas the public services employ 71 per cent (see table 2.3). In

Table 2.3   **Female employment, by industrial sector: Härjedalen, 1985**

Sector	Female % of labour force
Primary	23
Manufacturing industry	24
Public services	71
Private business services	54
All sectors	44

Source: Statistics Sweden.

Table 2.4   **Level of education, by industrial sector: Härjedalen and Sweden, 1990** **(% of labour force in each sector)**

Sector	Härjedalen		Sweden	
	Low[a]	High[b]	Low[a]	High[b]
Primary	57	3	55	3
Manufacturing industry	58	2	50	3
Public services	28	8	23	14
Private business services	39	3	28	9
All sectors	37	6	32	10

Source: Statistics Sweden.
a. Fewer than nine years of education.
b. More than two years university education.

most European countries, only 50 per cent of women are economically active, whereas the corresponding figure for Sweden was 81 per cent in 1990. The uniformity of the labour markets in Sweden is evinced by the fact that, in Härjedalen, labour market participation by women between the ages of 20 and 54 exceeds the national average.

Secondly, by setting formal professional standards for most jobs in public administration, as well as in the social and health services and education, the public sector has contributed substantially to upgrading the formal education level of the labour force (table 2.4). In all subsectors of the local public economy (whether it is child care, schooling, health care, recreation services, etc.), formal educational qualifications are required for most positions. This has, in turn, meant the development of a differentiated secondary and post-secondary school system. Almost two-thirds of the labour force with post-secondary education and three-quarters of the labour force with more than two years of university education are employed by the public sector. In the labour market area of Härjedalen, 83 per cent of employees with more than two years of university education are employed by the public service sector alone. In practice, this means that only 27 individuals in the entire province of Härjedalen who have an advanced university education work for the private sector. For Sweden as a whole, manufacturing industry employs only 4 per cent of the latter kind of theoretically trained labour; in Härjedalen, less than half of this percentage is employed, revealing, *inter alia*, the relatively low level of technology in the underdeveloped manufacturing industry of this community.

It is sometimes argued that the Swedish universities mainly function as occupational schools for public service workers. It could also be argued that, in a remote rural community such as Härjedalen, there would hardly be a functioning labour market for people with higher education if the public sector were not there. None the less, and notwithstanding the role of public service work in upgrading the formal level of education in the Härjedalen labour market, there is a substantial and prevailing gap between this and the level of formal education of the labour market in the rest of Sweden (see table 2.4).

The especially low level of education in business services in Härjedalen is a factor limiting the possibilities of a revival in private industry, regardless of whether it involves branches handling goods or information.

The growth of subsidized consumption

In retrospect, it may seem paradoxical that almost unrestricted growth of the public sector in the past three decades was possible in such a small and open market economy as the Swedish one. However, during the past two decades, the household consumption of goods and services that are organized and financed publicly has increased. This was a consequence both of the automation of the general welfare system, primarily pensions, and of the fact that almost all health and social care is subsidized. Use of the latter service is not related to the real buying power of the household, because it tends to increase disproportionately in relation to the actual income of the household. In 1970, 16 per cent of the total consumption of households was subsidized by the public sector, as against 27 per cent in 1989. In regions that benefit from the redistribution of subsidies to households (that is, sparsely populated regions with an elderly population and a relatively large public service sector), probably more than a third of all consumption is not expressed as a demand on the market. Since total consumption increased by two-thirds in real prices during the period 1970–1990, consumption not related to the private market increased threefold.

Within the framework of total expansion, social transfers (payments directly to individuals) represent an increasing proportion of public expenditure: they constituted 35 per cent in 1970, but increased to 52 per cent in 1990. Within the different sectors of the public services, it is social care that has expanded most (from 13 per cent to 21 per cent in 1989). Education has decreased its share from 30 per cent to 21 per cent, while health care and public administration have remained at relatively the same level (SOU 1992).

Compensation and vulnerability

For most municipalities in the interior of Norrland, total government resources per capita are between 10 and 50 per cent higher than the national average. For Härjedalen, they have been calculated to be 18 per cent higher than the national average (SOU 1989). A "syndrome" of labour market problems, a high proportion of low-income industries in the regional economy, regional policy priorities, and distinctive demographic and population changes all seem to be the common criteria associated with high total expenditures per capita for individuals, firms, and municipal services in a community. There are two ways in which the rural inland communities benefit from a higher resource transfer than is experienced in other regions. The first is through action under government policies designed to compensate for generally weak economic conditions, for example labour market policies and industrial policies. Regional policy instruments are only one component in the battery of possible measures stemming from such policies, though certainly not the largest in terms of resources. It is estimated that explicit regional policy accounts for only 6 per cent of the total compensatory programme. The second way is through direct transfers and payments, that is, income redistribution to elderly people, families with children, and sick people.

A guiding principle of compensatory resources is that regions experiencing high costs for service and goods production should receive compensation for their harsh climates, long distances, and other natural problems. Such characteristics are difficult for individuals, firms, and local authorities to overcome. Even if the arguments are not always explicit, this principle guides measures such as the transportation subsidy, the tax equalization policy (government grants for the equalization of local taxes), and special financial support for agriculture in northern Sweden.

Compensation takes a different form in each economic sector, which sometimes unintentionally results in an overlap. Private firms in less favoured areas may receive subsidies for capital (grants, low-interest loans), labour, recruitment, and employment, and may even be taxed at a lower rate on labour. Compensation under the tax equalization scheme is given to the municipalities in a lump sum.

Owing to the varied age structure and the relatively low level of incomes, local income taxes account for less than 40 per cent of the budget of a municipality such as Härjedalen. The system of government grants to equalize local taxes aims at compensating communes for such deficiencies, and contributes to one-fifth of the budget. This is one of the main incentives for equalizing the standard of services in each region (see table 2.5). The increasing importance of this grant in the regional distribution of welfare is shown by the fact that in 1975, for example, this grant was SKr 1,560 per capita in the county of Jämtland, and, by 1992, it had risen to SKr 10,530 per capita (*Årsbok för Sveriges kommuner 1993*).

Sweden became a full member of the European Union at the beginning of 1995 and, in the environment of increasing internationalization, the large, publicly financed service sector is the main focus of political debate. On the one hand, a large and powerful public sector that intervenes in almost all sectors of society is perceived as an obstacle to the liberalization of markets in Europe. Further, the high level of taxes necessitated by the way in which the public sector is financed raises a question about the possible side-

Table 2.5 **Sources of municipal income: Härjedalen compared with the average Swedish municipality, 1992 (%)**

Source	Average municipality	Härjedalen
Local income taxes	49	38
Tax redistribution	4	20
Specially directed governmental resources	22	23
Local fees	17	9
Other	8	10
Total	100	100

Source: *Årsbok för Sveriges kommuner 1993.*

effects of market distortion. On the other hand, political integration in Europe is perceived as a threat to the distributive role of the national welfare state. Partly independently of developments within the European Union, public finances were rapidly exhausted in Sweden during the deep recession that started in 1990. Unemployment rates in 1993 were more than three times higher than they were in 1990, demanding substantial efforts within labour market policy.

In Sweden, as in the other Nordic countries, the possibility of maintaining a large tax-financed public sector is being challenged, leading to a crisis in the public sector. For sparsely populated and economically weak and vulnerable regions, a substantial reduction in public services and transfers is undoubtedly perceived as a threat to both the present standard of living and employment.

General problems of the 1990s

Even though the levels of public service provision are unlikely to be raised, there will still be a tendency towards increased public consumption. The main reason for this is the qualitative changes in consumption that are expected to occur.

Even if productivity stays the same and the age-specific need for old-age care and health care remains unchanged, some important changes that will have consequences at the national level are:
- an adjustment in the compulsory school age (children being allowed to begin school at the age of 6 instead of 7);
- an increasing number of school pupils;
- less institutionalized care of the elderly;
- changes in the age structure of the population, which are calculated to increase the demand for health care by 0.7 per cent per year.

On the basis of these few assumptions alone, total municipal consumption was expected to increase by 10 per cent during the period 1992–1997. The sectoral distribution is shown in table 2.6.

However, according to the Ministry of Finance, a corresponding expansion in government grants was impossible owing to restructured national finances (SOU 1992). The ministry contended that such an increase in governmental grants to the municipalities could be met only by the reorganization of major transfers within the pension system, etc. As an alternative, other solutions were suggested by the Ministry of Finance:
- increased efficiency in public sectors, mainly by introducing more competition;

Table 2.6 **Sectoral distribution of the expected increase in municipal consumption, 1992–1997 (%)**

Sector	Share
Child care	25
Primary and secondary schools	23
Care of the elderly	18
Health care	28
Other	6
Total	100

- the take-over by private enterprises of segments of municipal activities;
- the dissolving of current public monopolies, leaving the way open to increased privately financed and market-oriented production in health care, social care, etc.;
- an increased proportion of user fees in the financing of public services such as health care.

The government appeared to be suggesting a substantial policy shift with regard to the public sector, and if this programme were to be introduced and fully implemented, Sweden would be abandoning its vision of "the people's home."

Compared with qualitative changes in consumption, demographic changes will be relatively insignificant in the near future so far as any tendency towards an increase in public consumption is concerned (table 2.7).

During the course of the 1970s and 1980s, owing to demographic changes, the demand for child care and old-age care increased more in Härjedalen than it did in the average Swedish municipality (see table 2.7). None the less, according to a population forecast for 1990–2010, the "demographic" structure of demand will not diverge substantially between Härjedalen and other parts of Sweden. However, with only one inhabitant per km^2, and 30 per cent of the population living outside urban areas, the spatial structure of demand may still be very different for Härjedalen.

The significance of local taxes

Swedish municipalities have some features that make them relatively stable by international standards. First, they are self-governed and

Table 2.7 **Change in service consumers, by age group, 1970–1990 and 1990–2010 (forecast) (%)**

	Härjedalen		Sweden	
Sector/age group	1970–90	1990–2010 (forecast)	1980–90	1990–2010 (forecast)
Child care (0–6)	+0.2	+0.7	−1.3	−0.3
Schooling (7–15)	−2.0	+1.1	−1.6	+0.9
Care of the elderly (75+)	+3.9	−0.2	+3.0	−0.4
Total non-working population (0–19, 65+)	+3.4	−2.1	+0.9	0

Source: Statistics Sweden.

have the right to raise local income taxes (to a certain level). Secondly, they have considerable rights as regards physical planning. One general issue raised in the early 1990s with respect to the suggested membership of Sweden in the European Union was the possible impact of membership on the economic independence of the municipalities. Together with the county councils (which are responsible for specialized medical care and regional public transportation), the municipalities account for two-thirds of total public expenditure for both consumption and investment. As mentioned above, approximately 50 per cent of this public expenditure is financed by local taxes, this proportion varying between municipalities according to the local taxing capacity.

The central government's subsidies are paid either for special purposes or for less specific purposes. On average, central government resources account for one-quarter of the total budget. The remainder of municipal income comes from fees and rents.

In discussing the possibilities for and consequences of cut-backs in public resource transfers, it is important to remember that different sectors of municipal activities are financed in different ways. Approximately 50 per cent of the costs of primary and secondary schools are financed by the state, whereas up to 80 per cent of the cost of care of the elderly is financed by local taxes and resources. Approximately 50 per cent of child-care costs is paid for by local taxes, and only a very small proportion is paid for by fees.

Fees are mainly associated with technical supplies and infrastructure (heating, electricity, water, sewerage, and waste treatment). Some service activities, such as child care, care of the elderly, recreation, cultural studies, and music schools, are paid for to a very limited extent by fees (less than 10 per cent in most municipalities). The way such activities are financed will be debated more thoroughly as the Swedish system is compared with that of other European countries. Activities that are currently mostly financed by taxes will be the most vulnerable to cut-backs. Cut-backs in the cultural sector have already been widely debated in some municipalities, and this is increasingly the case so far as schooling and child care are concerned (*Kommunala konsekvenser av medlemskap i EG* 1992).

Most probably, the proportion of fees will increase in all of the above areas. If these fees are related to production costs, they will generally be high in regions with a small and sparse population. Usually, the implementation of scale economies in a service production community will favour a more centralized supply.

A governmental strategy with regional implications

All the main political parties largely agreed upon three fundamental elements in the strategy launched in the early 1990s for a stable Swedish economic policy. These can be summed up in the following way:

1. to take part more actively in European integration ("The Prime Minister's Declaration to Parliament" 1991), leading to EU membership in 1995;
2. to reduce production costs (mainly by limiting increases in wages) and to intensify competition (in order to avoid increased unemployment and to safeguard basic parts of the welfare system);
3. to revive growth through governmental and private investment in infrastructure, and through job training and improving the level of competence in the labour force.

The increasing demand for international competition, the challenges posed by EU membership, and the technological renewal of industry have intensified the Swedish debate on regional development. Specific geographical, institutional, and economic conditions are focused upon in this debate. With a regional concentration of only 21 inhabitants per km^2 (compared with a European average of 147 inhabitants per km^2), Sweden is one of the most sparsely populated nations in Europe.

As the combined result of a political shift towards market solutions, adjustments to European Union rules, and budgetary problems, a substantial reduction in the state budget is anticipated

(Tapper 1992). According to one estimate (assuming a SKr 80,000 million cut-back in the SKr 500,000 million state budget), the per capita net effect means that the central regions, especially the big cities, will benefit from tax reductions and experience a limited contraction of public services. The main reason for the negative outcome in the periphery is the present large dependence on public services and transfers, plus the relatively low income level, which means that the positive effect of tax reductions on buying power is relatively minute. For example, the per capita income level in Härjedalen is approximately 20 per cent lower than that in Sweden as a whole.

It was calculated in 1993 that a hypothetical cut-back in the state budget by 16 per cent would lead to severe reductions in the provision of services in the municipalities. The hypothetical cut-back (the potential positive effects of tax reductions are not considered here) for the cluster of sparsely populated labour market areas to which Härjedalen belongs was among the highest of all regions, more than SKr 8,000 per capita. Compared with the actual situation in 1993, this would represent almost 25 per cent of municipal expenditures per capita. For the average municipality, the corresponding reduction is estimated to be 3–4 per cent of municipal expenditures per capita.

These figures are hypothetical and can be looked at only as examples of what might happen if proposed budget reductions were carried through. Nevertheless, the above example indicates that a spatial perspective is needed with respect to the currently changing macro-conditions. The redistributional effects of policy changes will have to be taken into consideration, as well as the needs and possibilities of the different kinds of peripheral and rural areas. Such a policy cannot be restricted to traditional regional policy; it must embrace all sectors and be strategic and progressive. From that perspective, a major task would be to help the peripheral areas to enter the growing sectors of the economy. Another task, stressing the long-term demographic processes in those regions, would be the development of methods and solutions that facilitate economic and social adjustment.

Visions, strategies, and local response in Härjedalen

The failure to realize the importance of the growth of public services in creating new employment in all regions has often led to a misunderstanding of the dynamics of change, and to an overestimation of the impact of regional policy. For instance, in 1977, the vice-governor of Jämtland County observed that the negative population trend in the county had changed during the early 1970s. He reported that the moderate annual decrease of 400 inhabitants in the 1950s had accelerated to as many as 1,700 annually by the 1960s, whereas the early 1970s showed an increase of 400 inhabitants per year. He raised a question regarding this and also tried to supply the answer:

What was it that halted the negative trend and created a situation for the county which can be considered satisfactory? It is not easy to give a simple answer to that, but it would be very interesting to study the issue scientifically. However, the location policy pursued in the mid-1960's has probably exerted the most important influence over the trend. The government realized that it was not very prudent to relocate thousands of people from their accustomed environments to the industrial regions of southern Sweden. Instead, industrial and other activities should be located in the regions where the labour is to be found. (Calleberg 1977)

At the same time, however, the vice-governor had difficulty in interpreting the employment statistics. He continues:

[F]or some reason, it is difficult to contend that the active location policy has actually increased employment. It is calculated that approximately 300 new jobs were created each year during the 1970's. But at the same time, the number of active farmers decreased by 500 each year, and the number of forestry workers by 260. The reason for this big decrease in agriculture and forestry is evident. It is enough to refer to the agricultural policy that was pursued during the 1960's and the intensive rationalization that took place in forestry. (Calleberg 1977)

The vice-governor goes on to discuss the consequent need for an intensified policy to attract manufacturing industry, and the need for changes in forestry and agricultural policies. However, like many others at that time, and also later, the vice-governor completely failed to notice the contemporary growth of the public sector in his report, "Jämtland County – Now and in the Future."

In spite of that, throughout the 1970s and 1980s, the public sector continued to grow in Jämtland County. By 1991, it employed close to every second "Jämtlander," which is seven times more labour than agriculture and forestry combined employed. Soon after the Swedish parliamentary elections in 1991 (which brought the Conservative–Liberal–Centre coalition into power in the central government), the mayor of Härjedalen municipality published a manuscript entitled "Meeting the Future of the Härjedalen Corporation" (Ring 1991). The description of the municipality as a "corporation" was certainly a very conscious adaptation to the new political mood. The mayor was aware of the increasing financial problems, primarily of the nation and, secondarily, of the municipalities, and declared that he intended to start a "process of strategic planning adjusted to reality and to the preconditions of the future in the municipality, replacing the old sectoral programmes and personal preferences, which pervaded local policy during the period of expansion" (ibid.).

In April 1992, this local process was initiated, first involving officers and consultants, then, later, involving politicians within the municipality, in accordance with the mayor's ideas. He had pointed out that the planning process "must liberate itself from prejudice and obsolete perspectives in its approach to the future. It must not use traditional routines and must not ask the local establishment the usual questions of, 'How are you doing?' or 'What do you want?' No, we must study the progress of both the private and the public sector from on high, like an eagle" (ibid.). The only indication of the goal of the "corporation," as suggested by the mayor, was that it should "reduce peripheral, not primary, municipal activities." He cited social care and education as being the principal tasks of the municipality. One way to interpret this goal is that municipal involvement in economic development projects should be reduced.

After less than a year at work (completed in February 1993), the committee produced a report with 24 concrete suggestions on how to go about reducing municipal costs and concentrating on central tasks within the competence of the municipality. A preliminary analysis of the report, however, shows that there is still a long way to go before the strategic plan that the mayor had hoped for is enacted. This is evident from a brief review of some of the suggestions for various divisions of the "corporation" of the Härjedalen municipality:

- the technical sector: increasing fees for building permits and the selling of industrial buildings;
- the recreational sector: a reduction in staff, to be brought about by, *inter alia*, shortening the opening hours of the municipal swimming pool;
- the cultural sector: the closure of a number of libraries in rural areas and a reduction in municipal purchases of art objects; the municipal music school to be reduced and reorganized;
- the social sector: child-care supervision to be limited, in order to reduce labour costs;
- minor public services: the privatization of the chiropody care of elderly people, and of the maintenance of some tourist services.

It was estimated that the 24 suggestions would translate into less than a 3 per cent cost reduction in the municipal budget. This should be compared with the estimated effects of cut-backs in the central government's resource transfer, calculated by Tapper (1992) to be almost 25 per cent of the municipal budget.

The first comment to be made on this local plan is that it appears difficult to prepare a thorough and credible defensive plan for a municipality facing large cut-backs in its public budget. Secondly, it is probably an even more difficult task to prepare an offensive strategic plan for the community. One reason is probably the strong vested interests that have emerged in different public sectors in the community and that tend to defend the present organization and level of each activity.

By 1995, there had been substantial cut-backs in the municipal budget and in employment. No doubt, productivity has increased in several public subsectors. At the same time, unemployment remains high and there are calls for public expenditure and measures in the employment policy.

The dynamics of the settlement structure

I have stressed that the development of a "Swedish welfare model" (directed primarily towards individuals, not regions) has meant that jobs and services have been provided on an equal basis in all regions. Such a well-distributed system of education, health care, social welfare, etc. has generated jobs and services in regions that would otherwise lag behind. These spatial effects of the welfare system have been largely unobserved, mainly because they are not included in any active regional development strategy. Consequently, when the welfare model is questioned, and when state transfers to individuals and municipalities are expected but must be curtailed, the negative effects on many peripheral and rural areas may come as a surprise. Structural changes determining the future of these areas will occur in other systems, such as the economy and other political fields. These changes will have to be met by local action and creative thinking in each community. The example of Härjedalen shows that local governments are ill prepared for this task.

Hence, the central government needs to adjust its policy changes within different sectors to the problems and prospects of different locations. For a community like Härjedalen, it is important to recognize the following characteristics.

First, it is a resource community with both rural and urban charac-teristics and a moderately developed infrastructure (see, for example, Gade et al. 1991; Wiberg 1990; Persson and Wiberg 1995). The com-munity has been reduced by net emigration from the region and by internal migration to towns and municipalities within the region. Population decline, service problems, and a dominance of declining sectors are standard features. The labour markets in marginal com-munities such as Härjedalen are generally small, but still able to offer employment at almost the same level as in larger regions. For a long time, the average employment ratio has been only a few percentage units lower than in other regions. The differences in unemployment rates were correspondingly small, especially by international com-parison.

Parts of the region, however, are taking advantage of its particular attractions as a place to live in, to invest in, to spend holidays in, etc. In that sense, a social, as well as an economic, change is taking place. Traditional resource-based activities are declining. Hence, spatially dispersed within this marginal zone, one finds a conglomeration of rural localities and small towns with specific scenic, sporting, and wilderness characteristics. In spite of the slower rate of population growth during the recession of the early 1990s, there is a long-term trend towards growth in these localities, in some cases based on per-manent residence, in other cases primarily based on seasonal resi-dence (see, for example, Persson 1992). An increasing number of relatively affluent retired people are searching for attractive sites with good infrastructure and service facilities, and it is likely that the marketing in Central Europe of specific Nordic sites with unique environmental assets will result in expanding tourist business. The long-term increasing individual mobility of the major strata of the population in the advanced economies of Europe will add to the dynamics of these rural localities.

At the same time, within the community of Härjedalen, there are also marginal areas lacking much of the allure and potential of other areas. These marginal areas are characterized by a sparse, ageing, and decreasing population, and have little or no attraction for private investors and limited potential for infrastructural investment. These problems are structural, the areas still having a large share of employment in the declining sectors. The rising costs of maintaining public services such as schools, health care, and postal delivery add to their already insecure future. In Härjedalen, even the present active centre of the municipality, Sveg, has some of these characteristics of

49

marginality. In addition to these problems, the future development of a successful new industry in the Sveg area, based on natural resources (peat industry), is being questioned owing to environmental concerns.

In conclusion, a shift of economic activity towards the mountainous parts of this vast municipality is foreseen. The current local centre of the community may lose some of its importance as the core of the local labour market. Looking at the present attempts at strategic planning in the community, it can be predicted that it will be a major task in the coming years for the local government both to defend the existing public services and jobs in the local administrative centre, and to reallocate shrinking resources in order to support new private initiatives in the tourist region.

Conclusions

Härjedalen is an example of how changes in national policy affect communities on the margin. The public sector, which had been the most reliable employer for decades, suddenly became subject to new principles.

The community illustrates the possible consequences of the shift from the ideological doctrine of the welfare state to the doctrine of the market-led provision of services. This ideological restructuring was the result partly of deep economic crises and partly of pressures to modernize the welfare state model in line with the market ideologies developed in the OECD countries. Nevertheless, it happened without a clear vote in favour of the changes to this direction. The final outcome of restructuring was not so dramatic as the calculations indicated. The Swedish welfare state was able to carry out adjustments without incurring considerable migration and local social crises, because many public sector factors balancing development remained and a radical shift to a neo-liberal local policy was not politically acceptable.

Note

1. I use the term "municipality" to denote the Swedish term "*kommun*," that is, the territory administered by local government. I use "community" as a synonym for municipality, but mainly when the economic and social, rather than the legal or political, structure of the region is stressed. A "county" (*län*) usually consists of several municipalities and is administered by the Regional Administrative Board, which is answerable to the central government.

References

Årsbok för Sveriges kommuner 1993, Statistiska Centralbyrån, SCB-Tryck, Örebro.

Birgersson, B. O., Hadenius, S., Molin, B., and Wieslander, H. (1981), *Sverige efter 1900: En modern politisk historia*, BonnierFakta, Stockholm.

Calleberg, L. (1977), "Jämtlands län – nutid och framtid," *Svenska Turistföreningens Årsskrift 1977*, Esselte Hertzogs, Nacka.

Drucker, P. F. (1993), *Post-Capitalist Society*, Harper Business, New York.

Gade, O., Persson, L. O., and Wiberg, U. (1991), "Processes Shaping the Rural–Urban Continuum. The Cases of Sweden and North Carolina, USA," in M. Ó Cinnéide and S. Grimes (eds.), *Planning and Development of Marginal Areas*, Centre for Development Studies, University College, Galway.

Ginsburg, N. (1992), *Divisions of Welfare. A Critical Introduction to Comparative Social Policy*, Sage Publications, Wiltshire.

Häggroth, S. (1993), *From Corporation to Political Enterprise: Trends in Swedish Local Government*, Ministry of Public Administration, Stockholm.

Jussila, H., Persson, L. O., and Wiberg, U. (eds.) (1993), *Shifts in Systems at the Top of Europe*, Alföld, Békéscsaba.

Kommunala konsekvenser av medlemskap i EG (1992), Kommentus Förlag AB, Stockholm.

Lundqvist, L. and Persson, L. O. (eds.) (1993), *Visions and Strategies in European Integration: A Northern European Perspective*, Springer-Verlag, Heidelberg.

Näsström, G. (1931), "Härjedalen. Kulturbygd och vildmark," *Svenska Turistföreningens Årsskrift 1931*, Centraltryckeriet, Stockholm.

Nordisk Familjebok (1910), Stockholm.

Persson, L. O. (1992), "Rural Labour Markets Meeting Urbanisation and the Arena Society: New Challenges for Policy and Planning in Rural Scandinavia," in T. K. Marsden, P. Lowe, and S. Whatmore (eds.), *Labour and Locality. Uneven Development and the Rural Labour Process*, Critical Perspectives on Rural Change vol. IV, David Fulton, London.

Persson, L. O. and Wiberg, U. (1995), "The Microregional Fragmentation – Contrasts Between Welfare State and Market Economy," *Physica-Verlag*, Heidelberg.

Peterson-Berger, W. (1931), "Genom Dalarna, Härjedalen och andra märkliga trakter," *Svenska Turistföreningens Årsskrift 1931*, Centraltryckeriet, Stockholm.

Reich, R. B. (1991), *The Work of Nations: Preparing Ourselves for the 21st Century Capitalism*, Vintage Books, New York.

Ring, A. (1991), "Möt framtiden i koncernen Härjedalens kommun," *Idéskrift*, 9 December, mimeo.

SOU (1989), 65, *Staten i geografin*, Allmänna Förlaget, Stockholm.

——— (1992), 19, *Långtidsutredningen 1992*, Allmänna Förlaget, Stockholm.

Tapper, H. (1992), *EG, statsbudgeten och den regionala balansen*, Ds 1992:80, Arbetsmarknadsdepartementet, Allmänna Förlaget, Stockholm.

"The Prime Minister's Declaration to Parliament" (1991), Prime Minister's Office, Stockholm (unpublished), 14 June.

Wiberg, U. (ed.) (1990), *Characteristics of the Intermediate Socioeconomic Zones in Sweden and USA*, CERUM Working Paper, CWP-1990:8, University of Umeå, Umeå.

3

Double or quits: Restructuring and survival on the margin of the South Australian wheatbelt

Peter J. Smailes

Introduction

This paper from Australia examines restructuring in communities in a marginal agricultural region. The restructuring examined has been partly a response to local-specific factors, and partly a response to macroeconomic pressures, set in the context of national politico-economic restructuring. In the Australian case, such restructuring has primarily affected the economic system. As is also the case in some of the following papers, the restructuring process has involved an age-related depletion of the population and some redistribution of land – although, in this case, land redistribution has come about as a result of economic rather than political pressures on the individual farm. However, components of the process of politico-economic trans-formation in Australia, such as financial deregulation, have had a strong impact on the rural economic system, especially in communities on the margins, and they have thus affected the economic pressures that farmers have experienced.

The local restructuring process described in this study, undertaken with minimal community-based or regional measures to enhance the competitiveness of business in the locale, can be shown to have had long-term detrimental effects on the economic progress of the region.

Farming in the South Australian wheatbelt is always a gamble, against a trinity of uncertainties: the growing season rainfall, world commodity price fluctuations, and political decisions and events, both local and international. At the start of each year, many farmers already carrying substantial debts must borrow even more money (provided they can find a lender) – perhaps as much as A$50,000–60,000 – to finance the planting of a crop, plus essential carry-on expenses. The gamble often amounts to the classic "double or quits," with "quits" the best possible outcome and "double" referring to debt, not winnings.

The Australasian context

Before proceeding to the case-study, a brief review of the considerable Australasian contribution to the literature on globalization and restructuring is needed. The close similarity between the Australian and New Zealand economies in respect of the processes and impact of globalization is strongly reflected in the literature. From the 1950s to the 1970s, both countries coupled relatively efficient export-based primary industries with a strongly protected and relatively inefficient manufacturing sector, serving a small home market but employing a large and heavily urbanized workforce.

Many scholars have traced, and theorized, the impact of globalization and restructuring of the Australian and New Zealand economies since the mid-1980s, when both countries made major policy shifts under newly elected Labor governments. The Australian realization that radical change was required even at the cost of inevitable social upheaval to keep up with, and preferably join, the rapidly growing economies of its Asian Pacific neighbours is well expressed by Linge (1988, 253–259). Focusing specifically on the globalization of agriculture, and drawing heavily on regulation theory, Le Heron (1993) seeks to place New Zealand and Australian agriculture in the context of United States, European Community, and GATT policy frameworks. At the level of national economic restructuring and macro-level spatial readjustment, a concise summary has been provided for Australia by Fagan and Webber (1994), and for New Zealand by Britton et al. (1992). Britton et al., in their introduction to their edited volume, reject a naive spaceless model of restructuring ("simple restructuring") in favour of "geographic restructuring," incorporating interaction between global, national, and local levels. National-level perceptions of the need to restructure are seen as set in motion by periods of particular turbulence – crises of accumulation – in the world capitalist system. According to this model, these changed national perceptions produce new policies that abruptly change many entrenched ground rules for firms and individuals, producing a crisis of legitimation as the new national "logic" promotes hostility, questioning, and resistance at the local level. The differentiated regional geography of both firms and social class fractions that developed during the "long boom" after World War II no longer yields maximal efficiency under the newly emerging ground rules; but labour, households, and fixed capital cannot be switched overnight, and some regions and fractions of society have to pay the price as newly unleashed market forces work to create a new spatial system. Such a model aptly describes the situation of the Eyre Peninsula regional communities discussed in this chapter.

Not all scholars researching the impact of globalization have adopted the economic rationalist view that in the restructuring process the weaker regions and sectors – such as rural communities dependent on land-based resources – should necessarily be left to pay the price of radical social and economic changes. Lawrence (1987, 1990) has taken a consistently critical stance toward the impact of economic rationalism on Australian rural society, stressing both the dangers posed by deregulation to the social system based on family farming (Lawrence 1990, 106–108) and the environmental non-sustainability of current Australian agriculture (Vanclay and Lawrence 1995). None the less, the transformation of the ground rules continues to work to the detriment of outlying agricultural regions such as the case-study presented here. In a study that complements that of Britton et al. (1992), Sorensen and Epps (1993, 7–31) outline the major events shaping rural Australia, modelling the decision-making processes that influenced the Hawke/Keating Labor government, elected in 1983, to open the Australian economy to international market forces in a manner almost identical to New Zealand's. Legitimation of economic rationalism is shown to have been achieved by a concurrent move to corporatism among key actors, replacing fragmented pressure groups by a virtual consensus between trade unions, big business, and government. Continuing the story in the same volume, Walmsley (1993, 41–56) expands on the way the Australian Labor Party ("the best Conservative government since 1949") tackled the abrupt switch from its traditional socially oriented policies toward economic rationalism. Walmsley's list of the main structural reforms (ibid., 48) illuminates the links between national policy and the Eyre Peninsula case-study, and is worth repeating.

Deregulation in the finance sector:
- the floating of the dollar and the abolition of exchange controls
- reduction of interest rate controls
- entry of foreign banks into the domestic market

Liberalization of foreign investment policy

Tax reform

Industry policy:
- tariff reduction
- encouragement of R&D

Deregulation of the crude oil market

Relaxation of export controls on defence-related goods

Deregulation of domestic aviation

Improved efficiency in government programs:
- means-testing welfare
- user-pays principle and increased cost recovery
- administrative reform

The Eyre Peninsula case-study presented below well illustrates Walmsley's contention that the beneficial effects of these measures bypassed most of rural Australia, whereas the adverse effects were fully experienced. In particular, the largely unforeseen problems caused by financial deregulation, which revolutionized the agriculture–finance relationship (Argent 1996), and the drive for efficiency in public sector service provision have borne down heavily on outlying rural regions such as Eyre Peninsula. Compensations have been few. No foreign bank branches entered Eyre Peninsula, and relaxation of foreign investment controls brought no productive investment there. Airline deregulation brought cheaper travel only to the major national routes; tariff reductions on imported capital goods have so far had minimal effect; and so on.

A number of other locality-specific studies have examined the economic and social effects of restructuring in New Zealand (e.g. Cloke 1989; Pawson and Scott 1992; Wilson 1995) and Australia (e.g. Miller 1995, 1996; Smailes 1996). Insights into the impact of deregulation and globalization on specific sectors of Australian and New Zealand agriculture have been provided by a growing list of contributions (e.g. apples: Grosvenor et al. 1995; sugar: Robinson 1995 and Hungerford 1996; tomatoes: Burch and Pritchard 1996). Many of these contributions, together with other case-studies and linking conceptual overviews, are brought together in Burch et al. (1996). In tracing the transmission of global forces for change down through the national and regional scales of resolution to the locale, and thence to the individual farm, small business, or family, it is fair to say that most work has concentrated on macro-level impacts on structures, sectors, regions, and locales. This chapter focuses on impacts at the grass-roots level in a resource community at the receiving end of the causal chain.

Eyre Peninsula

The case-study concerns a rural resource community at the extreme margin (in terms of climate, remoteness, and economic viability) of global commercial agriculture. The concept of "community" is operationalized at two levels, regional and local. At both levels, the term "community" is merited by virtue of a strong local social system, a sense of belonging and common identity, and a territorial base with administrative and statistical boundaries corresponding quite closely to the spontaneously evolved communities of interest. The study region chosen is the Eyre Peninsula, South Australia, and the local community within the region is the Cleve local government area, on the eastern side of the Peninsula (fig. 3.1).

Eyre Peninsula is a triangular area of agricultural settlement about the size of Switzerland, at the western extremity of the wheat/sheep belt of eastern Australia, and separated from the main settled area of the state to its east by Spencer Gulf and some 150 km of semi-arid pastoral country surrounding Whyalla in the north-east. Along the northern boundary, the Peninsula's settled areas are quite sharply delimited from the inland pastoral country. The region has a population of only 30,000, of which almost 12,000 are located in the regional capital, Port Lincoln. The agricultural census (1990) records only 1,700 rural holdings, with a total full-time workforce of 2,950 men and 1,390 women employed in primary production at the most recent population census (1991). An isolated narrow-gauge rail system feeding a major deep-water port at Port Lincoln in the south and a smaller port (Thevenard, near Ceduna) in the north-west (fig. 3.1) allows for direct export of bulk cereal products. As in much of the Australian wheatbelt, the region's problems relate not to low productivity but to low profit margins; indeed, under normal seasonal conditions, the Eyre Peninsula is extremely productive. In 1990/91,

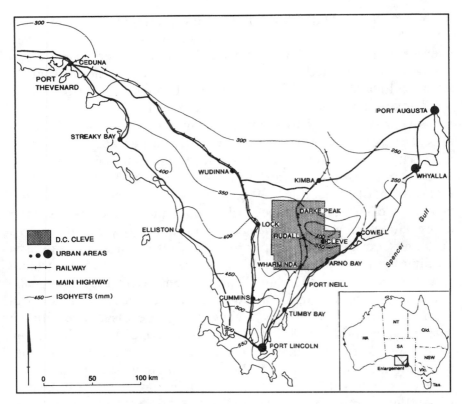

Fig. 3.1 **The Eyre Peninsula and the District Council of Cleve (Source: Smailes 1993, 3).**

for example, it produced some 49 per cent of South Australia's wheat, 23 per cent of its barley, and 14 per cent of its wool.

The region presents a classic case of a resource-dependent community whose economy is dominated by export-dependent primary production (agriculture, grazing, and some fishing, including recent developments in aquaculture) and services to the rural communities. Other sectors are small and poorly developed, so that local alternative employment for those forced or wishing to leave farming is hard to find. In these circumstances, farming families in the area have exhibited a tenacious resistance to displacement from the land. Owing to an ever-tightening cost–price squeeze between rising costs of production and commodity prices fluctuating about a near-horizontal trend line, Eyre Peninsula farmers have been forced to cut costs to the bone, resulting in one of the most extensive agricultural systems

57

in the world in terms of low labour and capital inputs per hectare to offset the meagre returns. To illustrate, in the 1992/93 crop year average costs of production per hectare of wheat in upper Eyre Peninsula were estimated at A$63.10, total machinery hours spent in wheat cultivation, spraying, and harvesting operations at 0.73 hours per hectare, and average yield at 1.0 tonnes/ha. Based on the previous year's wheat prices, a farmer planning to plant in 1992 could expect to receive a gross margin of A$46.90 per hectare of wheat after paying for costs of production plus freight and handling charges to deliver the wheat at Port Lincoln for export (South Australia, Department of Agriculture 1992). Although the gross margin is net of all variable costs, the farmer still has to pay fixed costs such as depreciation on machinery, wages for full-time workers, and interest on loans from this A$46.90 per hectare. This is extremely extensive farming by any standard, made more hazardous by the uncertainty resulting from price and rainfall fluctuations. With such low profits per hectare, the size of farm required to make a reasonable living from traditional agriculture is obviously large, necessarily resulting in a very sparse rural population. Densities are typically well below one person per km^2, resulting in long travel distances and small total populations within, say, an hour's travel from any given point.

Approximately 12 local rural communities may be distinguished within the Eyre Peninsula (fig. 3.2). These are typically focused on a service town of some 450 to 950 people. Only Ceduna in the far west (including its port of Thevenard) is larger. Total community size is about 1,200 to 2,000 people, and in most cases each community is reasonably well defined as a local government area – though Elliston and to a lesser extent Le Hunte district councils each contain two distinct communities. Similarly, in the south, the community focusing on Cummins is included in the Lower Eyre Peninsula council district, centred on Port Lincoln. The small service towns offer very few opportunities for non-farm or off-farm jobs in transport, private and public sector services, and a very few small secondary industries. No larger urban centres are within commuting range, and the largest (the steel-making centre of Whyalla) is itself suffering from heavy unemployment.

General, macro-level factors affecting the restructuring process

As in the cases of New Zealand and Canada, a rural society built upon maximizing production of a limited range of products for export

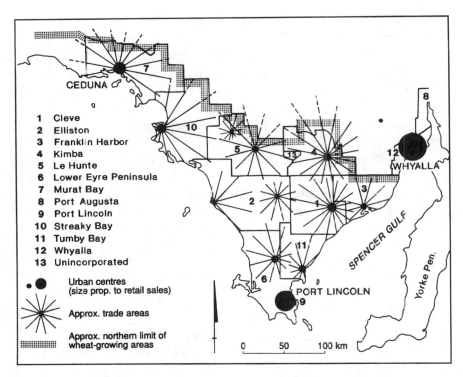

CEDUNA

1 Cleve
2 Elliston
3 Franklin Harbor
4 Kimba
5 Le Hunte
6 Lower Eyre Peninsula
7 Murat Bay
8 Port Augusta
9 Port Lincoln
10 Streaky Bay
11 Tumby Bay
12 Whyalla
13 Unincorporated

Urban centres
(size prop. to retail sales)

Approx. trade areas

Approx. northern limit of
wheat-growing areas

WHYALLA

SPENCER GULF

Yorke Pen.

PORT LINCOLN

0   50   100 km

Fig. 3.2 **Eyre Peninsula local government areas and approximate communities as identified by urban trade areas (Source: Griffin and McCaskill 1986, 103).**

on the world market has been radically affected by the transformation of the United Kingdom and the European Community from importers to net exporters of temperate zone food and fibre products. The emergence of large subsidized surpluses in Europe and the development of a trade war between the European Community and the United States in the early 1990s, in which these two major producers competed for the retention of markets by in effect dumping large volumes of grain and other farm products on the world market, have severely depressed commodity prices. Of particular importance to the Eyre Peninsula and similar regions has been the invasion of traditional Australian markets for wheat. At the same time, the constant rise in prices for farm inputs has consistently worsened the terms of trade for farmers, except in occasional favourable seasons.

In respect of the declining terms of trade for farmers, cost–price squeeze, low world commodity prices, and deregulation of capital flows, Australian farming has much in common with the restructuring

59

forced on other temperate zone exporters. The story for New Zealand is summarized by Britton et al. (1992) and Johnson (1993). Reviews of Australian and EC rural policy are given by Gerritsen (1992) and Manegold (1992). Le Heron (1993) outlines the development and difficulties of the Uruguay Round of the GATT, started in 1986. Despite Australia's prominent role in the Cairns group of nations striving in the Uruguay Round for reduced agricultural subsidization and reduced agricultural protection, benefits to Australian producers from the eventual agreement are limited, with increases in commodity prices estimated at the order of about 8 per cent, phased in over six years commencing 1995 (Durham and Kidman 1994, App. 2), and about 6.5 per cent in the annual value of Australian agricultural exports (MacLaren 1995, 56). Although this gives some hope of greater market stability, it is dependent on actual international compliance with the agreement (Anderson 1995).

Australian financial deregulation

Against this background, a significant event that proved fateful for Eyre Peninsula was the decision by the Hawke government in 1983 to abandon traditional attempts to maintain a fixed exchange rate for the Australian dollar (A$). In that year, Australia "floated" its currency, one of the last OECD countries to do so, thus creating a further element of uncertainty in the farm export trade. This move was rapidly followed by near-complete deregulation of the Australian financial institutions and the granting of licences in 1985 for 16 foreign banks to operate in Australia. The story of these decisions and their impact has been told by many writers and is not repeated here (see, for example, Abbot 1990; Daly 1993; Daly and Logan 1989; Kelly 1992; Stretton 1992).

Removal of restrictions on the flow of international capital has been accompanied by a blow-out of Australia's foreign debt, particularly from 1985 onward (Hefford 1991; Heywood and Tamaschke 1991). Interest rates had fluctuated about a generally upward trend in the first half of the 1980s (fig. 3.3), but fell sharply in 1987, a year that was marked by a severe crash in the Australian stock market. From early 1988, hoping to control inflation and stem the flow of imports, the Australian government embarked on a credit squeeze, deliberately raising interest rates (Hefford 1991). These decisions bore heavily upon both families and small businesses, while not achieving their intended objective (Hefford 1991, 25).

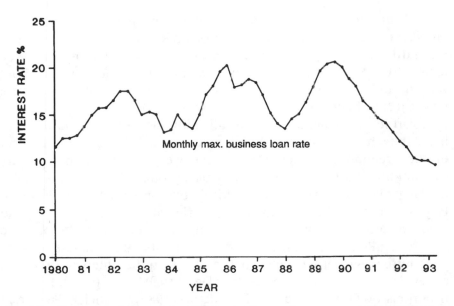

Fig. 3.3 **Changes in interest rates on loans: Quarterly averages, 1981–1993 (Note: Margins are added on many individual loans. Source: Westpac Banking Corporation, August 1993).**

The impact of high interest rates was particularly adverse upon the farms of Eyre Peninsula, for, although its farming is extremely labour and capital extensive in per hectare terms, large areas of land and expensive machinery are needed, requiring very large inputs of capital per holding, with a very low rate of return on investment.

Climatic marginality

The restructuring problems are magnified in much of the Eyre Peninsula by a relatively high risk of drought, coupled with recent revision of the Australian national policy on drought relief. This has transformed droughts (when proclaimed as such by a state government) from the category of a natural disaster warranting near-automatic emergency assistance from the federal government, to a normal risk requiring self-reliance and risk-management strategies on the part of farmers (Commonwealth of Australia, Drought Policy Review Task Force 1990; Simmons 1993). Most Eyre Peninsula farmers would concede that in the long term this is a sensible policy. It has long been known that the chances of seasonal failure of grain crops range from 30 per cent in the wetter south to over 60 per cent

61

on the dry margin in the north and north-west (Trumble 1948). However, the timing of the change of policy was particularly bitter for hard-pressed Eyre Peninsula farmers, because during the 1988 drought the South Australian government failed to access Commonwealth funds, from which other states had drawn heavily, while there was still the chance to do so.

A further environmental factor affecting the future shape of farming is the perceived possibility of long-term climatic change as a result of the greenhouse effect. Despite the well-recognized uncertainty surrounding global warming, it is a background threat hanging particularly over the northern tier of local government areas from Murat Bay to Franklin Harbor, whose territories abut directly on the arid fringe of settlement (fig. 3.2). Such concern is recognized in the state government's Greenhouse Strategy (South Australia, Climate Change Committee 1991, 66), which is based partly on the outcome of a 1988 government-sponsored conference (Dendy 1989). In particular, contributions by Greenwood and Boardman (1989), French (1989), and Reimers (1989) stress the likelihood that, under the most accepted greenhouse scenario, with rainfall about 20 per cent lower in winter and 10 per cent higher in summer, the boundary between the arable and pastoral zones would have to move southward quite substantially. The increase in summer rain would be of little benefit owing to increased evaporation and higher temperatures. The greenhouse scenario also envisages an increase in rainfall intensity and in the frequency of extreme storm events. One of the dangers of the farming system under the present economic pressure is that of overworking or overexposing the land because of the imperative need to produce income (Durham and Kidman 1994).

Although the actual effects of global warming are of course speculative, and impossible to predict accurately, they add an extra element of uncertainty, which may inhibit long-term investments in much-needed public infrastructure, such as extending the Eyre Peninsula water pipeline system westward beyond Ceduna (fig. 3.1) (McColl Carey Associates Pty Ltd 1990) or upgrading Ceduna's port of Thevenard (Mules 1990).

Summary

The above discussion has demonstrated that the entire socio-economic, land-use, and settlement system of the study region is operating in an external environment tending to promote structural change. The main contributing factors can be listed as follows:

- a dependence on the production, with very little subsidization, of a small range of export commodities;
- fluctuating, but generally low, world commodity prices, influenced by the dumping, or the threat of the dumping, of subsidized surpluses;
- a severe cost–price squeeze caused by steady rises in the costs of inputs for production;
- the instability in the financial environment caused by the floating of the Australian dollar in 1983 and the subsequent deregulation of the banking and finance industry;
- very high interest rates on loans, including deliberate policy measures from 1988 that took base interest rates to above 20 per cent per annum;
- a number of years with low or unseasonable rainfall; and,
- the perception by government decision makers of possible long-term climatic deterioration as a result of the greenhouse effect.

The Eyre Peninsula at the start of the 1980s

The Eyre Peninsula communities have been accustomed to droughts and boom/bust cycles since the beginning of European settlement (Heathcote 1992). Earlier periods of crisis had already thinned out the farms. During the 1950s and 1960s, a programme was put in place to amalgamate marginal farms, as a response to the severe droughts and associated wind erosion problems of the 1940s (Williams 1976).

However, by 1969, there were still 2,358 rural holdings on the Peninsula. During the 1970s, the number of holdings was subject to slow attrition, as farms coming up for sale were bought out by neighbours, and, by 1981, there were 2,061 holdings, with an average size of 2,640 hectares. However, over the same period, the total population of the Eyre Peninsula continued to grow, from 30,600 to 33,146 (table 3.1), and, despite fluctuations, farming prospects appeared reasonably favourable.

By the early 1980s, then, one round of adjustment had been completed, and the Eyre Peninsula was a relatively prosperous, if thinly settled, part of the state. Several of its local government areas in 1981 were among those with the highest percentages of high-income families in all of rural South Australia. Cleve, the particular district

63

Table 3.1 **Population change on Eyre Peninsula, 1971–1991**

	1971	1976	1981	1986	1991	% change 1986–91
Cleve D.C.	2,702	2,809	2,710	2,422	1,983	−18.1[a]
Ceduna/Theven.	2,070	2,327	2,794	2,877	2,753	−4.3
Port Lincoln	9,158	10,272	10,675	11,552	11,345	−1.8
Total rural[b]	19,389	19,867	19,677	19,215	17,900	−6.8
Total Eyre	30,617	32,466	33,146	33,644	31,998	−4.9

Sources: Australian Bureau of Statistics, Censuses of 1971, 1976, 1981, 1986, and 1991, Canberra.

a. Affected by boundary change, 1990. Without this, change would be approximately −13.0 per cent.

b. Eyre Statistical Division less Port Lincoln and Ceduna/Thevenard. Includes Cleve D.C.

council studied here, had the fourth-highest median income of the state's 88 rural local government areas (Smailes 1989). Similarly, the age structure was favourable, with relatively high proportions of young people and low proportions in the retirement age groups (Griffin and McCaskill 1986, 92–94).

The development of crisis conditions

As outlined above, the scene for the present round of restructuring in rural South Australia was set during the mid- to late 1980s, and the turn of events may be illustrated using tables 3.2 and 3.3. In interpreting these tables, which are based on financial years ending 30 June, it should be borne in mind that South Australia has a "Mediterranean" climate dominated by winter rain.

The cropping year normally begins in the southern hemisphere autumn months of April or May, following the onset of opening rains; harvesting occurs from about November to January; and the bulk of income from grain is received by about February. Thus, the 1982–83 crop, for example, depends on the 1982 growing season (April–November) rainfall. By about February or March, farmers have to make arrangements to finance the planting of the new year's crop, in time to catch the opening rains.

Table 3.2, which is a very useful barometer of rural economic activity on the Eyre Peninsula, shows summary data for a group of small firms, both farm and non-farm, which form part of one rural accountant's practice. The clients are spread over a large area of

Table 3.2 **Key financial data for a group of small firms (both farm and non-farm) from an Eyre Peninsula rural accountant's practice, 1983–1992 (averages per firm)**

Year	Sales (A$)	Net profit (A$)	Total liabilities (A$)	Interest paid (A$)	Interest as % of sales	Rainfall Apr.– Nov. (mm)	Total farms, Cleve D.C.
1982/83	54,653	556	54,526	5,619	10.3	160	293
1983/84	100,962	22,290	51,558	6,736	6.7	354	291
1984/85	92,575	7,433	60,682	7,010	7.6	312	292
1985/86	88,485	3,261	73,790	10,365	11.7	278	280
1986/87	80,488	3,045	74,413	10,952	13.6	312	269
1987/88	103,141	9,078	77,143	10,338	10.0	203	263
1988/89	103,833	8,704	76,132	11,252	10.8	187	253
1989/90	140,879	32,378	66,175	10,410	7.4	448	247
1990/91	121,056	12,488	84,455	9,361	7.7	252	236
1991/92	154,079	24,142	86,484	8,577	5.6	256	229

Sources: rainfall data for Cleve – Bureau of Meteorology, South Australian Regional Office, microfiche records; number of farms – Australian Bureau of Statistics, Agriculture South Australia, annual agricultural census data, Catalogue No. 7113.4, South Australian Office, Adelaide; financial data – records of private accountant's practice, personal communication, Cleve.

Table 3.3 **Some background trends affecting South Australian farming, 1982–1993**

Year	Average South Australian prices (A$ per tonne)			ABARE indices (1980/81 = 100)		
	Wheat	Barley	Wool	Prices received by farmers (a)	Prices paid by farmers (b)	Farmers' terms of trade (a)/(b)
1982/83	178	155	2,652	104	123	84
1983/84	165	154	2,811	109	134	82
1984/85	185	136	2,818	112	141	79
1985/86	176	123	3,049	112	153	73
1986/87	150	116	3,434	122	165	74
1987/88	169	123	4,903	142	172	83
1988/89	216	169	5,406	157	186	84
1989/90	199	168	4,696	153	199	77
1990/91	138	133	3,474	134	207	65
1991/92	204	145	3,086	134	214	63
1992/93	182	137	2,906			

Sources: prices – Australian Bureau of Statistics, *South Australian Yearbook*; indices – Australian Bureau of Agriculture and Resource Economics, *Quarterly Review of the Rural Economy*, 1983–1988, and *Agriculture and Resources Quarterly*, 1989–1993.

north-eastern Eyre Peninsula. Because the number of cases varied from a minimum of 100 to a maximum of 136, the data are expressed as averages per firm in each year. Well over half of these businesses are farms, and the remainder have their sales affected by farm spending in the same financial year, so the data clearly depict the annual variations in rural economic fortunes.

The story begins in 1982, a year of widespread and severe drought that affected a large area of Australia. Thus, on table 3.2, the small firms had a disastrous year in 1982/83, with profits averaging only A\$556 per firm; a great many obviously made a loss. However, the following year, 1983/84, was a peak farming year, with double the amount of rainfall and commodity prices remaining reasonably high (see table 3.3). The resulting sharp increase in both sales and profits (see table 3.3) tempted many farmers to make purchases of capital goods, such as tractors, headers (harvesting machines), etc., and also land. The competition for land further encouraged the trend for rural land values to climb to unrealistically high levels.

At this point, the 1984 deregulation of the Australian banking industry saw a sharp change in the approach of rural banks to the granting of loans to farmers. Before deregulation, interest rates paid by primary producers were controlled at a level slightly below market rates. Banks could get higher returns elsewhere, and, consequently, adopted a conservative approach to farm applications for loans. After deregulation, however, market rates could be charged and banks became willing lenders, but they began to differentiate their margins between customers according to risk (Parliament of South Australia, Social Development Committee 1994, 13–14). To quote this Committee, "Eager to shore up market share in a deregulated financial market, banks relaxed lending criteria, often with insufficient regard to commercial reality" (ibid., 13).

Thus, used to a regime of intense scrutiny of their ability to repay, farmers were suddenly faced with a plentiful supply of credit. Some farmers claimed that the banks acted irresponsibly at this time, and, although these claims may be exaggerated, they have entered into folk memory as bitter recriminations against the banks. Cronin (1991, 7) provides an example:

At the time of deregulation in 1984 Australian banks went on a lending spree to keep foreign banks out of rural retailing. They also went into direct competition with each other to lock up this area of business. In some cases it was not friendly persuasion, but blatant coercion to borrow money. Banks were allowing their managers great freedom in throwing out half million dollar loans by clients simply telling the bank how much they wanted or saying to a farmer, "Buy the property, then come in and tell us how much you need." ... Even if one bank refused a loan to a farmer an opposition bank in some cases heard about it, chased him down and accommodated him. With example after example over those couple of years, banks threw money at all and sundry, pushing up land values to speculative levels in doing so. In one extreme example, a very large loan was approved when two banks were merging, and no cash flow analysis was done on the farmer's capacity to service the loan or repay it. Now, in case after case, the banks want to place all blame for the present situation on the borrowers.

Disregarding extreme cases, it is certainly true that many of the hardships facing Eyre Peninsula farming households and rural communities today have their roots in the period between 1983 and 1985. In these years, many young farmers trying to enter the industry and many established farmers trying to follow the constantly repeated maxim of "get big or get out" incurred debt from which they have been unable to extricate themselves over 10 years later. Farmers who embarked on land purchases, new plant, and other investments made their calculations on the basis of the then-prevailing commodity prices, interest rates of the order of 12–13 per cent, and high equity in terms of the paper value of their land. These included experienced and skilful farmers and, in many cases, their problems can be traced back to a single, major, and, in hindsight, injudicious purchase.

The events that then transpired saw the annual rainfall total decline for five successive years (using the Cleve recording station as an example), with additional problems of unfavourable distribution of the rainfall over the year; interest rates rising to upwards of 20 per cent on loans first negotiated at much lower rates; a steady deterioration in the farmers' terms of trade caused by rising costs and declining commodity prices; and a collapse in rural land values, which peaked in 1984 but by 1987/88 had dropped by over 50 per cent, to their lowest post-war level in real terms.

The rapid expansion of the interest payment burden on the small firms appears clearly in table 3.2. Net profits reached their lowest ebb in 1986/87. By the end of 1987, the author's random sample of farms in the Cleve district revealed an average net farm income of only A\$3,100 per farm, while a sample of better farms averaged only A\$12,700 net from an average gross return of almost A\$147,000 per farm. A great deal of social stress had become apparent, including family friction, divorce, and even some suicides of farmers.

From table 3.3, it may be seen that commodity prices picked up in 1987/88 and 1988/89, and this is reflected in table 3.2 in the form of improved sales. However, Eyre Peninsula farmers were unable to take full advantage of the situation, owing to continued regional drought conditions. The district of Cleve, being centred in the rather safer rainfall area of the Cleve Hills, suffered less than the surrounding council areas of Franklin Harbor, Kimba, and Tumby Bay (fig. 3.1).

During 1987 and early 1988, hampered by the State Minister of Agriculture's consistent refusal to declare the drought a natural disaster, the farmers made repeated efforts through their state organization to organize rescue packages in order to allow them to carry on. Many mustered their last reserves to plant the 1988 crop, but others were unable to obtain carry-on finance. Finally, on 16 April 1988, as the break of the season was imminent, the state government announced that a A$5 million fund would be made available to farmers at a subsidized interest rate of 10 per cent.

In the end, although 1988 was a good rainfall season in much of Australia, on the Eyre Peninsula the problems redoubled. After a late and slow opening to the season, the crops were eventually planted, but a series of natural disasters struck the growing crops. Three unseasonable spells of very hot, dry weather culminated in a devastating northerly wind storm, which on 7 November 1988 caused an estimated A$15 million worth of damage to the remaining barley crops. This storm swept millions of tonnes of soil from the parched wheat paddocks into the Southern Ocean.

The publicity surrounding the crisis conditions produced a polarization of views between conservationists and farming interests, which was well captured in contemporary letters to the press (for example, *Adelaide Advertiser* 29 August, 23 September, and 19 November 1988). For many farmers, the harvest was minimal and barely worth reaping; negative net incomes were recorded yet again. For those areas slightly more fortunate with respect to the rainfall, the commodity prices, particularly wool prices, were good; and, averaged over all farms, the returns from that year were better than might have been expected.

By early 1989, the struggle for carry-on finance and a rescue package for up to an estimated 400 Eyre Peninsula farmers was even more bitter and intense than in the previous year, and, by now, the first Farmers' Action Groups had arisen to add a more radical dimension to the picture. Banks were picketed and potential purchasers were intimidated at mortgage foreclosure auctions. An organized campaign ("Bankwatch") was mounted to encourage farmers to unite in standing up to the banks (Cronin 1991). The state government continued to refuse to declare the drought a natural disaster, but, following the breakdown of negotiations between the banks, farmer organizations, pastoral companies, and the state government, the government produced its own proposed rescue package (*Eyre Peninsula Tribune*, 12 January 1989). The concept of "viability" became all-important: "viable" farmers were to be helped with loans at interest rates of 8 per cent to buy out their neighbours, while "non-viable" farmers faced surcharges, bringing interest rates up to the order of 22 per cent for any further advances. Farmers negotiated on an individual basis with banks and lending institutions, and many were uncertain, right up to the break of the season, whether they would be granted carry-on finance.

Somehow, the majority of the farmers ended up with enough finance to plant the 1989 crop; some even sowed with little or no superphosphate, for it was clearly a make-or-break situation. Fortunately for the district, a reprieve came in the shape of an excellent season, with commodity prices dropping a little, but still high. Those who had gambled on wall-to-wall wheat were rewarded with a high-profit financial year in 1989/90 (table 3.2), and many farmers were able to breathe again. For those struggling with debts accumulated over the several years of drought, however, a single good year was far from sufficient to bring them back to solvency, though it did allow most farmers enough leeway to finance the planting of the 1990/91 season's crop, in the hope that another good year would bring debts under control – "double or quits" once more.

The seasonal conditions during 1990 again proved favourable, but during that year the Eyre Peninsula's regional woes were overtaken by the definite onset of what the then federal Treasurer (later Prime Minister) Paul Keating called "The recession we had to have" – an expression that became a national byword. In a rising tide of metropolitan bankruptcies, mortgage foreclosures, and unemployment, the Eyre Peninsula lost its uniqueness and newsworthiness as a distinctive rural problem. Worse was to follow later in 1990 with the collapse of wool and wheat prices more or less simultaneously, while the embargo on trade with Iraq further restricted the market, so that, by October 1990, the newspapers were again full of headlines on the rural crisis – but this time nationwide. The Australian Wool Corporation was by then buying up most of the wool submitted for sale at auction, the wool stockpile was seen to be growing at an unsustainable rate, and in February 1991 the Wool Reserve Price Scheme was abandoned.

Nevertheless, the good seasonal conditions made up to some degree for the drop in prices, and the 1990/91 season was a reasonable one for farmers, though nowhere near the levels of the year before. During 1991, the increasing farm subsidy war between the United States and the European Community, intruding on traditional Australian grain markets, caused increasing concern about the future level of grain prices available to Australian exporters. Carry-on finance for the many farmers carrying accumulated debt was available only under the most stringent conditions. For example, a survey carried out in the Smoky Bay district (north-west Eyre Peninsula) in May 1991 showed that 10 out of 21 farmers had been refused carry-on finance, and 5 of those who received it were subjected to punitive conditions such as additional mortgage on land, Bill of Sale on machinery, crop liens, or an agreement to sell their property at the conclusion of the harvest (Smoky Bay Farm Support Group, personal communication). However, once again in 1991, the rainfall was adequate, and low prices were offset, to a degree, by an average to good harvest for the 1991/92 season.

The following season, 1992/93, was bitterly frustrating for farmers. Excellent rainfall during the growing season promised a very heavy yield, but persistent unseasonable rain continued throughout the harvest period, which turned out to be one of the wettest on record. Owing to lodging, sprouting, discolouration, and excess moisture content, the bulk of the Eyre Peninsula wheat was downgraded to fodder grain standard only, resulting in price reductions of some A\$40 per tonne. Low prices were, to some degree, compensated by the large volume harvested, but, once again, hopes of making inroads into debt burdens were shattered.

Towards the end of the 1993/94 season, Eyre Peninsula farmers were once again frustrated, despite having adequate rainfall, by a widespread, severe mouse plague, followed by frost damage to grain and legume crops and disastrous product prices, particularly for barley. Respondents to a 1994 rural poverty survey pointed out that a tonne of barley would not pay for a pair of school shoes (Country Women's Association of South Australia, personal communication).

These continued difficulties and disappointments have meant that, despite a run of seasons with average to high annual rainfall, and the sharp drop in interest rates since their peak in 1990, many farmers have been unable to reduce debt significantly. The situation reported by the Eastern Eyre Rural Counselling Service in June 1991 (personal communication) gives some idea of the extent of the problem in the Eyre Peninsula region generally: at that date, 139 clients of the counselling service drawn from all over the eastern half of the Peninsula had, between them, a debt of A$43.7 million, or an average debt of over A$314,000 per farm. By 1993, some of the most indebted farms had been sold, but the average debt of the 208 clients then on the books was still A$179,350 (Eastern Eyre Rural Counselling Service 1994, personal communication).

Impact of the crisis on the region

Population loss

By 1991, the Eyre Peninsula had already lost (at least temporarily) a very substantial number of rural people. Figure 3.4 illustrates the changes between the 1986 and 1991 censuses, using the smallest available statistical areas (census collectors' districts).

The map demonstrates the heavy rate of loss across the entire region, particularly in the most farming-dependent areas and in a broad belt across the northern part of the settled areas. Across the whole Peninsula, only a handful of districts showed any percentage increase in population at all. The proportion of townspeople to rural dwellers in each local government area is increasing, because the small towns have held their numbers a little better than the dispersed population (mainly farms).

When one examines the change (not mapped) in the number of households – that is, the number of occupied houses – the percentage declines are not so radical. The number of persons per household has shrunk, because young people in particular have left, but the region has continued to attract or retain retirees and semi-retired people, keeping up the number of occupied houses. To demonstrate the way the rural crisis has affected the age structure, table 3.4 concentrates on the changes in three crucial age groups between the 1986 and 1991 censuses: school leavers, young adults, and the retirement age groups. The figures speak for themselves. In some cases the percentage figures appear dramatic because of the small actual numbers involved, but the overall impact cannot be mistaken.

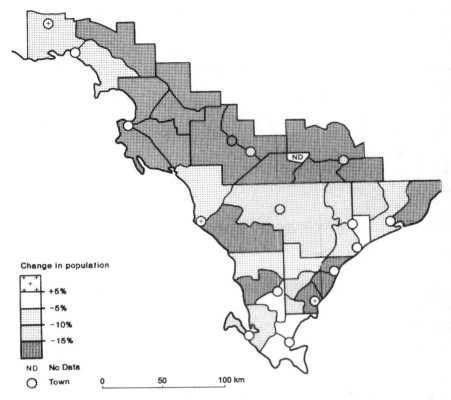

Fig. 3.4 **Population changes in the Eyre Peninsula, 1986–1991 (Source: Australian Bureau of Statistics, Censuses of 1986 and 1991, Canberra).**

Unemployment

The crisis on the Eyre Peninsula, as in other similar Australian rural areas of low population density, has not resulted in exceptionally high local unemployment. Only the larger towns (Whyalla, Port Augusta, and Port Lincoln) exceeded both the national average of 10.73 per cent and the 12.06 per cent of Adelaide, the state capital. The smaller places (including Cleve, with 8.14 per cent) had relatively lower unemployment levels. Kimba, Cleve's neighbour to the north, had one of the lowest unemployment rates in the country (3.90 per cent) in 1992 (Australia, Department of Employment, Education and Training (DEET), Economic and Policy Analysis Division 1993). The reasons are not far to seek. The lower level of unemployment in the

Table 3.4   **Population changes in selected age groups, Eyre Peninsula, 1986–1991**

Local government area	% change by age group, 1986–92			Total population, 1991
	15–24	25–34	65–74	
Cleve[a]	−32.2	−22.0	−13.1	1,983
Elliston[a]	−41.7	−3.4	+40.4	1,323
Franklin Harbor	−27.6	−21.7	+8.5	1,234
Kimba	−34.5	−23.9	−19.1	1,276
Le Hunte	−26.5	−18.2	+67.1	1,697
Lower Eyre Peninsula	−19.1	−12.9	+5.4	3,705
Murat Bay	−15.9	−10.9	+14.4	3,642
Port Lincoln[b]	−15.0	−2.5	+8.6	11,824
Streaky Bay	−34.1	−24.3	+11.5	1,898
Tumby Bay	−20.6	−31.6	−4.8	2,582
Unincorporated	−4.6	−26.5	+140.0	850
Total Eyre Peninsula	−20.7	−10.2	−8.0	32,014

Sources: Australian Bureau of Statistics, Censuses of 1986 and 1991, Canberra.
a. Affected by a minor boundary change.
b. Local government area includes a small proportion of rural people.

smaller rural districts reflects the fact that most job seekers have already left the district. Those remaining included a substantial number of farm wives and other rural women, forced by circumstance to register as seeking non-existent jobs in order to eke out household income with unemployment benefits. The fact that many rural families, formerly proudly independent of social security "handouts," had been forced to swallow their pride and seek whatever income supplement they could obtain is a measure of the severity of the deprivation endured.

The withdrawal of government services

In a community where the great majority of non-primary economic activity is concerned with supplying services to an agriculture-dependent population, the "drought-proof" incomes of public sector employees such as teachers, police officers, and road and rail maintenance workers take on great importance. During the late 1960s and 1970s, a considerable extension of public sector employment occurred in South Australia. Previous studies (Smailes 1991; 1993, 73) have shown that public sector employees comprised almost exactly one-third of the employed workforce in the small towns (but not the surrounding farm areas) of the Eyre Peninsula.

Between 1981 and 1986, this had already begun to contract and, by the 1991 census, public sector employment had fallen only slightly to 29 per cent of the workforce in the small towns mentioned above. Substantial further losses are to be expected as a result of the slashing of state government spending in the early 1990s, precipitated by a A\$3.5 billion bale-out required to prevent the collapse of the government-guaranteed State Bank of South Australia. Furthermore, the Eyre Peninsula was one of the regions selected as a trial area by the Government Agencies Review, a body set up in 1989 and, by 1992, charged with the radical reduction of state government expenditure (cf. the crisis in the public sector depicted in the case-study of Härjedalen in chap. 2).

The impact on the individual community

We turn now from general discussion of the Eyre Peninsula as a region to the specific case-study of the Cleve D.C., summarizing some results of surveys I carried out there in 1987, 1988, and 1992. Space permits only a brief and selective summary.

Direct impact on family farming

The direct impact of the rural recession in the community naturally begins with the farm sector. Some key figures are provided for a core group of 23 farms (out of a random sample of 37 farms) for which comparable and accurate data are available for each of the surveyed years (table 3.5).

It must be remembered that the averages shown are based on a wide spread of values. At the lowest ebb of their fortunes, in 1986/87 and in the drought year of 1988/89, net incomes were negative for many farmers, and, for much of the period surveyed, households were able to survive only through (a) off-farm income earned by one or more family member(s); (b) social service benefits never previously drawn on by farm families; (c) a degree of cost-saving and belt-tightening amounting, in many cases, to self-exploitation; and (d) "living on depreciation" – the annual depreciation on plant and equipment appearing as a cost in the farmer's tax return was actually used for basic household expenses instead of being put aside for plant replacement. At the same time, interest repayments on loans were

Table 3.5 **Key financial data for 23 out of 37 randomly sampled farms in the District Council of Cleve, 1983/84 to 1991/92 (averages per farm)**

	1983/84	1985/86	1986/87	1988/89	1990/91	1991/92
Gross farm income (A$'000)	185.0	110.0	108.0	123.0	147.0	153.0
Net farm income (A$'000)	98.0	14.9	3.1	4.3	18.0	25.5
Off-farm income:						
Farms with off-farm income (A$'000)	9.8	8.1	6.4	12.5	10.4	11.3
Averaged over all farms (A$'000)	2.0	2.3	3.1	5.1	5.3	5.5
Indebtedness at 30 June (A$'000)	73.0	113.0	116.0	156.0	147.0	148.0
Estimated land value/ha (A$)	513.0	348.0	280.0	318.0	235.0	272.0

Source: Author's survey data.

absorbing over 15 per cent of *gross* farm income. Thus by 1988/89 the mean debt per farm had risen to A$156,000, with only very slow debt reduction in the following years.

As shown in table 3.5, some recovery had occurred by 1992, with average farm net incomes rising to A$25,500. However, even this should be compared with the income earned by ordinary wage and salary earners in the state of South Australia. In 1992, the state average wage for full-time adults was A$31,470 – for a much shorter working week, and without all the trauma and uncertainty faced by farmers.

During this period, too, the paper value of the farmers' main asset (their land) also greatly declined. In the speculative frenzy immediately following banking deregulation, the ease of obtaining loans contributed to average land prices in the Cleve district being bid up to over A$500 per hectare. Most farmers agreed that land was then overvalued in terms of its earning power from farming. The low point was reached in about 1991, owing to the effects of the simultaneous drop in world prices for both wheat and wool and the fear of numerous forced sales. By 1990/91 the surveyed farmers estimated their land to be worth only A$235 per hectare on average, and the land market had slowed to a virtual stop, with many farms potentially or actually on the market but no buyers forthcoming. The price realizable for a whole farm on Eyre Peninsula was little more than the cost of a house on a residential site in Adelaide.

Get big or get out?

At the heart of the whole concept of the restructuring of an agrarian society is the question of matching the factors of production – land, labour, capital, management – in such a way that the economist's immediate goals of efficiency and equity in the allocation of scarce resources can be reconciled with the social goals of a sustainable rural society able to provide its people with a reasonable range of services and amenities. In Australia, up to the present, attention has been focused almost entirely on the former, to the detriment of the latter. One of the most significant findings of this study is the inadequacy of the simplistic view implied in the "get big or get out" adage so impressed on Australian farmers, even up to the present. Results here suggest that the rural crisis on the Peninsula is not a small-farm problem but is spread throughout the farm size spectrum.

As would be expected, the bigger farms do tend to have a higher gross value of production, although some productive smaller farms with fewer than 1,000 hectares grossed over A$200,000, even in the drought year of 1988/89. Turning to the distribution of net income, however, the relationship disappears: farms with negative net incomes in that year are spread throughout the size spectrum, as are the highest net incomes of A$40,000 or more.

A clear picture of the relationship between net income and gross income is provided graphically in figure 3.5. There is only a very limited relationship between the scale of farm operations (as measured by gross sales) and farm net income. Clearly the burden of debt is affecting many of the farms with low gross incomes, but indebtedness and the low net income problem are spread right through the farm size spectrum. In a better season (fig. 3.5, 1991/92) the whole scatter of points shifts to the right and there are fewer negative net incomes, but again there is only a very slight tendency for bigger farms to have correspondingly larger net incomes.

What is being argued here is not that farm size is unimportant or irrelevant to farm viability or prosperity, but rather that the problem of low farm incomes and high indebtedness is spread through almost all of the farm size spectrum. Simply amalgamating all the smaller farms would not in any way solve the problem. It would also greatly worsen the economic situation of the local service sector.

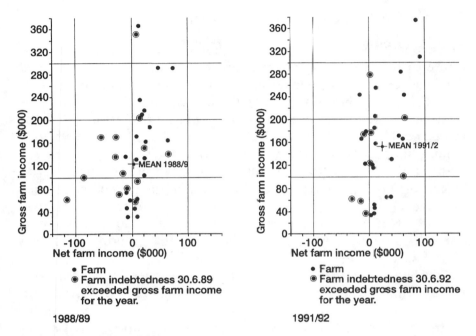

Fig. 3.5 **The relationship between gross and net incomes on a random sample of farms, District Council of Cleve, 1988/89 and 1991/92 (Source: Smailes 1993, 23).**

Changes in the farm household age structure

The 37 farms surveyed in 1992 between them had 60 habitable houses, of which 7 were empty and 16 occupied by families of workers, sons, parents, or other family members, or simply people renting the houses. The most important population data relate to the 37 actual farm households, comprising 131 people in all.

Of the male heads of household on the farms, few are below the age of 40, the average age being 48 years. The average for the female household heads (spouses) was only slightly lower, at 44 years. Secondly, there are very few young men in the 20–29 age group (which would be expected to take over the farms in due course) – only five young men in their twenties and one unmarried young woman in her early thirties were resident in these 37 households (some married sons have established their own household nearby, as noted above). Thirdly, although there are still quite substantial numbers of teenagers and children aged 10–12 of both sexes, there are very few pre-school and primary school aged children on the farms. The situation testifies to the heavy loss of young people from the district.

The next generation on the Cleve farms

The age structure of the farm population is clearly unstable, and the future of family farming depends greatly on whether farmers' sons who have been forced to leave the district for work will return to take over the family farms when conditions improve. People in Cleve often spoke of a "lost generation" of young people forced off the farms, not because of any wish to leave or any lack of need for their labour, but because of the "work for two, pay for one" syndrome.

In all, the 37 surveyed households had 47 former members living away from home, 43 of them being children of the present generation of farmers (the other 4 were hospitalized persons or separated former spouses). Not only has the district lost most of its 20–30 age group, but also, equally importantly, it is losing the children and new households that they would have produced.

To what extent, then, has this loss been worsened by the crisis? Of the "missing" children, 19 had left the farms since 1987, and the parents were asked whether their decision to move had been caused by the rural crisis. Results showed that 8 would have moved in any case, but the other 11, or more than half, moved entirely, or partly, due to the crisis situation on the farms. The excess rate of loss is thus 50–100 per cent higher than it "ought" to be.

Changes in the farm workforce

Between 1987 and 1992, there was a continued slow decline from 66 to 59 (10.6 per cent) full-time male workers on the 37 farms surveyed in both these years. This was partly offset by a slight increase in full-time female employment and a slight rise in part-time employment of both sexes. These changes left the surveyed farms with an average of just over two full-time workers per farm, nearly all family members. When one considers that the 37 farms average 1,742 hectares, or over 3,800 acres, in size, the farms are clearly understaffed and can manage to cover the essential tasks only by what amounts to "self-exploitation" in terms of overwork. As several farmers pointed out, many simply could not manage more land with their current labour resources, or at least not without another round of heavy capital investment in newer and larger plant as well as more land. This is exactly the recipe that got many ambitious farmers into trouble in the mid-1980s.

However, the remarkable thing up to early 1994 was the relatively small number of farms that had actually gone out of business in the Cleve district. This testifies partly to the extreme resistance put up by the farm families to the loss of their farms, but also to the absence of buyers from the market, despite rock-bottom land prices. It can scarcely be doubted that a considerable number of other holdings are hanging on by a slender thread.

The impact on the community business sector

The businesses in the District Council of Cleve, as in many other small country towns, are predominantly locally owned; but some key businesses are Cleve branches of state- or nation-wide organizations, over whose expansion and contraction or relocation decisions local community members have no control. In the case of Cleve, about 80 per cent are locally owned, 14 per cent are branches of state or national organizations, and the remainder include two branches of firms based in other Eyre Peninsula country towns. Thus the local community of Cleve has quite a strong stake in its own business future. Examination of the age of Cleve businesses (the date of origin or of takeover by present operators) showed two peak periods of new business formation: 1955–1969 and 1975 to the present. Since 1985 in particular, a very high rate of business turnover has occurred. The depressed condition of farming has naturally had a major negative multiplier effect. This has been offset, in part, by the concentration of public tertiary sector employment in the town and by those people in the community dependent on pensions, superannuation, welfare payments, etc., which provide low, but stable, incomes. Owing to its favourable central location in the higher and more reliable rainfall zone of the Cleve Hills, the town has also, to some extent, been able to expand its trade area in response to business closures in the surrounding districts (Lock, Kimba, and Cowell). Despite these dampening effects, however, the impact of the farm recession has been severe, particularly upon firms predominantly supplying producer goods and services to farms and other businesses.

In terms of employment, core firms in small Australian country towns try hard to retain key staff, knowing how hard it is to reassemble a skilled workforce in outlying areas once it is lost. Thus, between 1983/84 and 1987/88, there was only a small decline in the workforce. Between 1988/89 and 1991/92, however, several firms were forced to lay off staff, while several others continued in business through extremely difficult times with reduced work hours, largely

Table 3.6 **Summary of employment changes in private business firms in the District Council of Cleve, 1988/89 to 1991/92**

	1988/89 (n = 52)	1991/92 (n = 57)	% change
Full-time, total	224	197	−12
Full-time male	164	145	−12
Full-time female	60	52	−13
Part-time, total	46	53	+15
Casual, total	69	79	+14

Source: Author's survey data.

Table 3.7 **Trends in aggregate turnover for a group of private business firms interviewed in both 1987 and 1992, District Council of Cleve**

	1983/84	1985/86	1986/87	1988/89	1990/91	1991/92
No. of firms	32	32	32	33	33	33
Total turnover	22,779	26,311	25,127	38,545	35,949	35,375
Adjusted for inflation to constant 1990 A$	36,842	38,195	33,614	44,265	35,949	33,353
Consumer price index, South Australia (1990 = 100)	62.2	69.3	75.2	87.6	100.6	106.7

Sources: Author's survey data, 1987 and 1992; Australian Bureau of Statistics, CPI data (March Quarter), South Australian Office, Adelaide.

because of a feeling of responsibility to employees who had been with them for long periods. The overall figures (table 3.6) show a 12 per cent loss in full-time jobs over the three years, only partly compensated by an increase in part-time and casual work. The trends in turnovers for 32 firms interviewed in both 1987 and 1992 appear in table 3.7 (one 1987 firm had split into two branches by 1992). In real-dollar terms, the worst year of the rural crisis was (as with farm incomes) 1986/87, but, by 1992, no real-dollar recovery had occurred.

Figures on gross turnover alone give no indication of the net profitability of businesses. Data on net business profits for the Cleve firms are not available, though they would be highly desirable to match the data on net farm incomes. Such data are simply too sensitive; some businesses declined to reveal even gross turnovers. However, the low level of profits for the Eyre Peninsula in general was shown earlier (table 3.3).

Some further indirect evidence was gained by asking respondents how far their business had recovered in profitability since their worst year in the rural recession. Of the 51 able to respond, over 60 per cent had not yet returned to the same level of profitability as before the crisis, and 12 firms were still well below that level. On the other hand, a significant group of 10 firms were doing better than before the recession, owing in some cases to the elimination of former competition, in other cases to a restructuring of their operations.

Adjustment in the non-farm business sector

In response to questions seeking a ranking of the most important problems experienced as a result of the rural recession, clearly the most serious perceived problem, mentioned by almost half the surveyed firms, was the reduction in profitability of the business. The falling number of customers as the farm population gradually dwindles and business employment drops had the second-highest average score, closely followed by the reduction in turnover (gross sales). The other problems mentioned by more than a quarter of all those interviewed were the rises in wages and salaries and the loss of skilled workers.

All of these problems, particularly customer loss, lower turnover, and lower profits, are obviously interrelated. In terms of restructuring, a very clear finding of the present study is that almost (though not quite) all business firms in Cleve expressed a clear preference for a farm population consisting of many, even if poor, farmers, rather than few, but rich, farmers. This was for a wide variety of reasons, including the greater propensity to trade locally and the dependence of many firms on sales of low-order goods and services with a low income elasticity of demand. Sales of these are more dependent on the number of households than on average household income.

During the rural crisis, Cleve businesses have adopted various strategies to cope with the shrinkage of the local market, some opting for diversification, others for specialization in what they considered that they did best, others seeking to open branches outside the district, and still others switching to alternative lines of business. Generally speaking, up to 1987, Cleve firms had been very successful in coping.

Since then, leading firms have continued to adjust. The biggest and most diversified firm in the Council area moved from a wide diversity of interests to greater specialization, cutting out its transport and fuel distribution operations and closing some of its outlying branches in neighbouring towns – Lock in 1988 and Kimba in 1989. On the other hand, other Cleve-owned ventures in distant areas such as the recently developed mining town of Roxby Downs – where there is a substantial Cleve expatriate community – have been maintained and developed, and new ventures have been established in Whyalla and Clare. For several types of crucial service (medical practice, dental practice, and pharmacy), Cleve firms have established their town as a centre for the surrounding towns, with branch offices/stores in Lock, Cowell, and Kimba. Several other Cleve firms may follow this strategy. The fact that some firms have reduced the spread of their operations has opened up increased opportunities for others, especially in the fields of electrical contracting and rural supplies. One particularly innovative firm has established an export market for local manufactured goods. The above examples of responses to a shrinking local market are, however, not available to all types of business in the town, and serious problems remain for many smaller firms.

Assessment of business operators' view of their prospects for the future showed that, by November 1992, a substantial increase in optimism had occurred, as compared with the two earlier surveys in 1986 and 1987. Assessing their performance in a shrinking local market in comparison with other towns, a greater proportion now felt that Cleve had made gains relative to the situation in the previous survey, gaining particularly from neighbouring towns of about the same size. Since 1987, Whyalla had increased its competitive position in relation to Cleve businesses, while Adelaide was mentioned much less frequently.

From among the other problems experienced by local firms, two in particular deserve mention. The first is the unreasonable difficulty experienced by innovative country firms in raising equity for bank loans to develop their business, partly owing to the fact that buildings and real estate located in a small country town are given a very low value rating as equity by financial institutions. Though expensive to build or convert, such investments may even become liabilities rather than assets, unlike a metropolitan-located factory. This problem not only frustrates and delays risk-taking expansions but puts a subtle pressure on successful firms to move to Adelaide – a pressure antithetical to effective regional development policy. A second problem mentioned by several respondents was the communication difficulty experienced in the country – not only the well-known problem of high telephone costs but, more generally, the transition to electronic communications and making the most of computer technology; and also the problems in obtaining advice and assistance for new developments, particularly with respect to the recruitment of qualified staff in remote locations such as Cleve, the marketing of products and ideas, and how to transform ideas into practice.

Some approaches to solutions

The above discussion has identified some of the global, national, and local causes of the restructuring process affecting Eyre Peninsula, and has demonstrated the severe impact that these processes are having on the demographic structure, social and economic viability, and morale of families, businesses, and communities. Indeed, across the greater part of the South Australian wheat/sheep belt, the continued extent of rural distress is highlighted in an interim report on rural poverty (Parliament of South Australia, Social Development Committee 1994) documenting cases of rural children driven to stealing food, while a rural member of the state parliament reported to the press nearly 30 cases of farmer suicide in his constituency (Austin 1994). Much more evidence could be cited. The question may well be asked: does it matter if this small (on a global scale) piece of the world's ecumene is deserted by its present population and its community structure dissolved? Similar human tragedies are widespread across the globe as farming communities struggle to come to terms with radical change not of their own making. Australia's extreme metropolitan concentration of people, its great need for export income to reduce national indebtedness, its continued high level of metropolitan and urban structural unemployment, and the presence of rapidly growing populations, economies, and potential markets to the near north argue for a national effort to maintain the basic community infrastructures and productive capacity of its agricultural areas so that change can be achieved without collapse. I now turn to examine some of the most pressing needs to achieve this end, and some approaches to solutions.

The scope for self-help

The literature makes it abundantly clear that, at a local level, the forces of globalization can be counteracted to only a limited extent.

In Australia, local self-help is further limited by institutional factors. In the absence of an active regional development policy, the chances of high-tech footloose firms seeking "green-field" sites with low labour costs (Marsden et al. 1990, 9) being attracted to outlying regions such as the Eyre Peninsula are very slim, owing to the small numbers and low density of population. Diversification of the over-specialized local economies is obviously required, but the three tiers of government in Australia (Commonwealth, state, and local) are unsuited to the task. Regional policy is a state responsibility under the Constitution; but the states lack the necessary financial resources for the task, because the great bulk of taxation revenue is raised and distributed by the Commonwealth government. The state is also too large, remote, and metropolitan dominated; for example, South Australia's area of 980,000 km^2 equates roughly to France plus Germany. Local government, while socially very significant in rural areas, is based on populations of typically 1,000 to 3,000, and is far too small, parochial, and bereft of funds to promote significant economic development. To deal with the difficult problems revealed in the case-study, therefore, requires both a substantial source of ongoing funding and suitable political structures to administer it. This in turn requires a much better articulation between the three layers of government, plus the creation of permanent administrative structures at a regional level between state and local government. What are the chances of this, and can these things be achieved through self-help?

Regional development fund

The absence of local investment in off-farm enterprise has been a longstanding problem in Australian regional development and reconstruction, as Eyre Peninsula's recent experience has illustrated. Indeed the financial system to date has acted like a giant vacuum cleaner, sucking every cent of surplus value out of the Peninsula, in a variety of ways. Personal savings in bank accounts, loan repayments and extortionate interest rates, taxation, increased out-of-town bargain chasing for expensive capital goods, all result in the investment of Eyre Peninsula savings elsewhere – dominantly in metropolitan areas or offshore. Although state government recurrent spending on services such as education, hospitals, and police is likely to be providing cross-subsidization to rural areas, the opposite is the case for capital expenditure. Thus for the year 1990, only 1.5 per cent of the State Department of Industry, Trade and Technology budget was spent on regional economic development policy. Likewise in the period 1987–1990, industry investment in metropolitan Adelaide amounted to A$3,340 million compared with only A$581 million for the whole of regional South Australia, of which most went to the single mining project of Roxby Downs (South Australian Regional Development Association 1991). To remedy this situation, intervention by the national government, which controls the bulk of taxation revenue, appeared likely in the early 1990s. It was a key recommendation of a major national report known as the "Kelty Report." As well as proposing major upgrades of regional infrastructure (transport, communications, etc.), the report (Australia, Taskforce on Regional Development 1993, 5–6) recommended legislation allowing regional development organizations to set up Regional Pooled Development Funds under terms that exactly suit the needs of regions such as Eyre Peninsula for local investment capital.

Administrative and local political reform

The above Taskforce's report also addressed the associated need to provide administrative structures at the regional level to allow more regional autonomy in decision-making (Australia, Taskforce on Regional Development 1993, 67–71). Action on this problem has been slowed by a common perception that Australia is already "overgoverned" and by antipathy to the idea of a fourth tier of government, while there would be intense, entrenched opposition to abolition of either the state or the local tier. However, state moves to establish and fund Regional Development Committees in South Australia preceded the Kelty Report. Almost certainly hastened by trenchant criticism of its inadequate regional policy (South Australian Regional Development Association 1991), a network of Regional Development Boards has been established in the 1990s, of which the Eyre Peninsula Board has developed from an initially more limited Port Lincoln based committee, to commence operations in 1993. Already this Board has created its task forces, appointed staff, and produced a major community consultation document (Eyre Peninsula Regional Development Board 1994). Moves have also been initiated by the Australian Local Government Association (1990; 1993) and the Local Government Association of South Australia (1993) to promote much greater cooperation between the three tiers of government and providing support for "Integrated Local Area Planning."

With the Regional Development Board now able, for the first time, to give the region a united voice and a meaningful budget, the necessary ingredients for a successful, cooperative regional development programme are in place. These are necessary, even though not sufficient, conditions to give hope that the communities of Eyre Peninsula can survive the restructuring process. If they are to do so, four major tasks will need to be addressed, with or without the above reforms.

The restructuring of farm debt

The first necessity is to find a means of dealing with entrenched rural debt, if family farming is to survive the restructuring process. At the heart of this problem is the sanctity of financial contracts in the capitalist system. Banks and financial institutions that lent money on the basis of much higher land values and farm returns have (at least overtly) been unwilling simply to cancel debts that farmers are unable to pay back, even though they could obtain tax concessions for the non-performing loans. This is because of the unacceptable precedent such action would set, and the unfairness to clients who had managed to meet their repayments. At the same time, banks have been unwilling to carry out wholesale foreclosures on mortgages of farmers unable to meet commitments, firstly because of the unfavourable publicity and the fierce opposition from Farmers' Action Groups, secondly because it would be likely to leave them with large numbers of basically unsaleable farms on which they would have to pay managers and essential upkeep, and thirdly because they could in any case recoup only a limited amount of their losses by such punitive measures. Paradoxically, crisis conditions thus have an inbuilt thermostat-like mechanism that limits the speed of change, even for farmers not threatened by mortgage foreclosure. Prices are too low for anyone to sell willingly, and existing indebtedness, exhausted private capital reserves, and low farm incomes prevent all but a few from buying. Some solutions contrived between the banks and individual farmers threatened with foreclosure include putting the farm on the market to repay at least part of the debt, in return for agreement (on the terms of which the farmer is bound to secrecy) to cancel the rest of the debt. Such deals, however, are grossly unfair to farmers on surrounding properties. By further depressing land values, these sales artificially reduce the neighbours' equity. Although their land itself is exactly as before, its value as collateral for loans, its role as a superannuation nest egg, and its potential exchange value if the farmer wished to sell out have all been sharply reduced.

To establish the extent of the rural debt problem in South Australia, a major survey was commissioned by the incoming Liberal state government in late 1993. This showed that, of 1,654 broad-acre farms on the Peninsula, 183 (11 per cent) were in "Category C" debt, i.e. regarded by lenders as having no prospect of recovery. Another 262 (16 per cent) in "Category B" were having difficulties in servicing debts owing to the exceptional circumstances outlined above (Durham and Kidman 1994, 39–40). This category included many farmers still attempting to pay off debts mostly incurred in the second half of the 1980s, who would be viable operators if they could eliminate debt. Efforts to find an appropriate method to achieve this have included various forms of deferred payment, set-aside of part of the debt, subsidized interest rates, debt consolidation, and individual sale-and-lease-back arrangements. However, the long run of years with inadequate farm incomes on the Eyre Peninsula has drained the area of its capital reserves.

The particular problems of the region caused it to be used as a pilot project to establish appropriate state-wide regional policy guidelines, and a Task Force set up by the state government to that end treated debt reduction as its most urgent task. Among its 29 recommendations was a re-establishment grant of A\$75,000 per family to assist the 11 per cent of farmers deemed non-viable to leave the industry with some dignity (Parliament of South Australia 1995). A repeat of the state-wide indebtedness survey (Durham and Kidman 1996) showed that, by December 1995, about 100 of these farmers had exited; the region remained the worst affected in the state, but the percentage of "Category C" farm debts had fallen from 11 per cent to 7 per cent.

The diversification of traditional agriculture

The removal of entrenched debt is only a first step toward successful restructuring of the Eyre Peninsula communities and their economic base. At the root of the problem is the excessive dependence of the economy on a limited range of commodities for export. There remains considerable scope for improving farm performance within the confines of traditional farming by relatively simple techniques, already known but not yet widely adopted – for example, the wider adoption of legumes such as lupins and field peas in the rotation, and greater precision in the timing of seeding. Wider experimentation is also occurring in new ideas such as the farming of Australian native wild flowers and fruits – particularly the quondong or native peach – as well as emu and ostrich farming, goat meat, sheep milk products, and oyster, abalone and tuna fish farming. There are undoubtedly many niche markets available for "clean and green" Australian products in Asian markets, and the opportunities for innovation are extensive, though few such products seem likely to achieve mass markets. As in many other parts of Australia, the extreme circumstances of the recession have acted as a catalyst forcing conservative farmers to seek novel solutions.

Alternatives to farming

As shown above, two of the most pressing – and interrelated – problems caused by the rural recession are inadequate farm incomes and the loss of a generation of young people. The need for alternative employment, both part-time, off-farm work as a supplement, and full-time, non-farm work as an alternative, is an imperative. The Cleve study showed, for example, that almost half the surveyed families had off-farm income; however, owing to the low population density, excessive travel distances, and absence of suitable skills, only a minority of the most needy families were able to earn off-farm income. The district does however have innovative firms able to provide non-farm jobs. A particularly instructive example is a business run by a Cleve dentist, combining a dental surgery, a sports store, and a manufacturing business producing spotlights for night shooting, for which a substantial export market has been developed; its latest venture is jewellery production using an anodizing process based on native Australian eucalypt leaves, gumnuts, etc., with great potential for employment. Encouragement of such innovations requires a suitable infrastructure, including networking of potential innovators with local services and suppliers, market identification, assistance with marketing and business skill development, and the provision of risk capital for seeding. Other examples of potential industries awaiting development on the Peninsula include the production of ethanol and high-protein stock feed from poor-quality wheat, and gypsum processing from deposits at Sceale Bay on the western coast.

The human factor

In a remote, thinly peopled region such as the Eyre Peninsula, the loss of every farm family weakens the already fragile community structure. However, there is very little evidence so far in my fieldwork to suggest that the family farm system itself has been radically changed. The loss of farms in the Peninsula has not resulted in "real" or "direct" subsumption, in the sense that the relinquished land has passed into the hands of other local farmers rather than those of major agribusinesses, absentee owners, land speculators, and the like. Even "larger-than-family" farm businesses are unusual, except in cases where relatives have joined to operate several farms. This apparent resistance is due at least as much to the absence of buyers in the land market during the crisis years as to a dogged wish to retain the farm for lifestyle reasons. Yet economically irrational motivation is also important.

Moran et al. (1993) suggest that, to make subsumption theory more empirically useful, better linkage is required between currently theorized macro processes and processes directly driving farm-level decision-making on the ground. Particularly needed are: first, a full, empirically testable understanding of the extent to which family farming is resisting subsumption by pluri-activity; secondly, incorporation of both family and business lifecycle change into subsumption theory; and, thirdly, better understanding of the organizational structures that link the farm with the capitalist economy. To these I would add the need for a much better understanding of all those human factors that come between stimulus and response, causing farm families to "hang on" against all logic. I hope that evidence from the case-studies in this volume will at least assist inductive progress toward these ends. To conclude, I quote an Eyre Peninsula farmer, whose sheep flock was saved by a fodder lift organized by the South Australian Farmers' Federation, writing of his response to the ravages of the 1988 drought (Pfitzner 1992, 13):

So our figures do not add up and will not add up. But we have learnt something about caring. The miracle of the 1988–89 people helping people has given us a courage which had deserted us some months earlier. Are we mad? Do we not understand what is going on? We have been told this at times, but I am going to hang on and hand the family farm to the son who wishes to stay on. And I am going to tell him that the best advice I can give him is this: Keep out of debt, buy only what you can pay for, and be prepared to live simply. Then, when you have a chance to help someone by word, work or in any other way, count it a privilege.

References

Abbot, K. (1990), "Financial Deregulation in Retrospect," *Journal of Australian Political Economy* 27, pp. 88–98.

Anderson, K. (1995), "Agricultural Competitiveness after the Uruguay Round," *Review of Marketing and Agricultural Economics* 63(3), pp. 351–362.

Argent, N. M. (1996), "The Globalized Agriculture–Finance Relation: South Australian Farm Families and Communities in a New Regulatory Environment," in D. Burch, R. E. Rickson, and G. Lawrence (eds.), *Globalization and Agri-Food Restructuring. Perspectives from the Australasia Region,* Avebury, Aldershot, pp. 283–300.

Austin, N. (1994), "Caring Rural MP Is Paying a Heavy Price," *The Advertiser,* 7 May, p. 2.

Australia, Department of Employment, Education and Training (DEET), Economic and Policy Analysis Division (1993), *Natural Labour Markets in Australia,* Australian Government Publishing Service, Canberra.

Australia, Taskforce on Regional Development (1993), *Developing Australia: A Regional Perspective,* vols. 1 and 2, Canberra.

Australian Bureau of Agricultural and Resource Economics (1983–1988), *Quarterly Review of the Rural Economy,* various issues, Canberra.

———— (1989–1993), *Agriculture and Resources Quarterly,* various issues, Canberra.

Australian Bureau of Statistics (annually), *South Australian Yearbook,* South Australian Office, Adelaide.

Australian Local Government Association (1990), *Better Services for Local Communities,* Welshpool, W.A.

———— (1993), *A Guide to Integrated Local Area Planning,* Deakin, A.C.T., Australia.

Britton, S., Le Heron, R., and Pawson, E. (eds.) (1992), *Changing Places in New Zealand: A Geography of Restructuring,* New Zealand Geographical Society, Christchurch.

Burch, D. and Pritchard, B. (1996), "The Uneasy Transition to Globalization: Restructuring of the Australian Tomato Processing Industry," in D. Burch, R. E. Rickson, and G. Lawrence (eds.), *Globalization and Agri-Food Restructuring. Perspectives from the Australasia Region,* Avebury, Aldershot, pp. 107–126.

Burch, D., Rickson, R. E., and Lawrence, G. (eds.) (1996), *Globalization and Agri-Food Restructuring. Perspectives from the Australasia Region,* Avebury, Aldershot.

Cloke, P. (1989), "State Deregulation and New Zealand's Agricultural Sector," *Sociologia Ruralis* 29, pp. 34–48.

Commonwealth of Australia, Drought Policy Review Task Force (1990), *Final Report,* vols. 1–3, Australian Government Publishing Service, Canberra.

Cronin, J. (1991), *Operation Bankwatch,* Eyre Peninsula Action Group, Streaky Bay, S.A.

Daly, M. (1993), "No Economy Is an Island," in S. Rees, G. Rodley, and F. Stilwell (eds.), *Beyond the Market: Alternatives to Economic Rationalism,* Pluto Press, Leichhardt, pp. 72–90.

Daly, M. and Logan, M. (1989), *The Brittle Rim: Finance, Business and the Pacific Region,* Penguin Books, Ringwood.

Dendy, T. (ed.) (1989), *Greenhouse '88: Planning for Climate Change*, South Australia Department of Environment and Planning.

Durham, L. J. and Kidman, R. C. (1994), *Rural Debt in South Australia,* Report to the Minister for Primary Industries, Government of South Australia, Adelaide.

———— (1996), *Rural Debt in South Australia: Report No. 2*, Report to the Minister for Primary Industries, Government of South Australia, Adelaide.

Eyre Peninsula Regional Development Board (1994), *Eyre 2000: A Strategic Advantage.*

Fagan, R. H. and Webber, M. (1994), *Global Restructuring: The Australian Experience*, Oxford University Press, Melbourne.

French, R. (1989), "The Greenhouse Effect and Its Implications for Primary Production in South Australia," in T. Dendy (ed.), *Greenhouse '88: Planning for Climate Change*, South Australia Department of Environment and Planning.

Gerritsen, R. (1992), "Labour's Final Rural 'Crisis'? Australian Rural Policy in 1990 and 1991," *Review of Marketing and Agricultural Economics* 60(2), pp. 95–112.

Greenwood, G. and Boardman, R. (1989), "Climatic Change and Some Possible Effects on the Terrestrial Ecology of South Australia," in T. Dendy (ed.), *Greenhouse '88: Planning for Climate Change*, South Australia Department of Environment and Planning.

Griffin, T. L. C. and McCaskill, M. (1986), *Atlas of South Australia*, South Australian Government Printing Division, Adelaide.

Grosvenor, S., Le Heron, R., and Roche, M. (1995), "Sustainability, Corporate Growers, Regionalisation and Pacific-Asia Links in the Tasmanian and Hawkes Bay Apple Industries," *The Australian Geographer* 26(2), pp. 163–172.

Heathcote, R. L. (1992), "Settlement Advance and Retreat: A Century of Experience on the Eyre Peninsula of South Australia," paper to the International Conference on the Impacts of Climate Variations and Sustainable Development in Semi-arid Regions, Fortaleza, Brazil.

Hefford, R. K. (1991), "Lucky Country or Fool's Paradise?" University of Adelaide, Department of Economics, Working Paper 91-4.

Heywood, K. and Tamaschke, R. (1991), "Australian Deregulation and the Growth of Foreign Debt," *Journal of Australian Political Economy* 28, pp. 54–79.

Hungerford, L. (1996), "Australian Sugar in the Global Economy: Recent Trends, Emerging Problems," in D. Burch, R. E. Rickson, and G. Lawrence (eds.), *Globalization and Agri-Food Restructuring. Perspectives from the Australasia Region,* Avebury, Aldershot, pp. 127–138.

Johnson, R. W. M. (1993), "New Zealand Agricultural Policy Review, 1991–93," *Review of Marketing and Agricultural Economics* 61, pp. 375–400.

Kelly, P. (1992), *The End of Certainty: The Story of the 1990s*, Allen & Unwin, St. Leonards.

Lawrence, G. (1987), *Capitalism and the Countryside,* Pluto Press, Sydney and London.

———— (1990), "Agricultural Restructuring and Social Change in Australia," in T. Marsden, P. Lowe, and S. Whatmore (eds.), *Rural Restructuring: Global Processes and Their Responses*, David Fulton, London, pp. 101–128.

Le Heron, R. (1993), *Globalized Agriculture: Political Choice*, Pergamon, Oxford.

Linge, G. J. R. (1988), "Australian Space and Global Space," in R. L. Heathcote and J. A. Mabbutt (eds.), *Land, Water and People*, Allen & Unwin, Sydney, pp. 239–260.

Local Government Association of South Australia (1993), *Strengthening Local Economic Capacity: Strategic Plan for South Australia.*

McColl Carey Associates Pty Ltd. (1990), *Review of Water Supply to the Area West of Ceduna*, Adelaide, for Engineering and Water Supply Department.

MacLaren, D. (1995), "The Uruguay Round," *Review of Marketing and Agricultural Economics* 63(1), pp. 51–63.

Manegold, D. (1992), "EC Agricultural Policy in 1991–92: CAP Reform Constrained by GATT Negotiations," *Review of Marketing and Agricultural Economics* 60(2), pp. 113–154.

Marsden, T., Lowe, P., and Whatmore, S. (1990), *Rural Restructuring: Global Processes and Their Responses*, David Fulton, London.

Miller, L. (1995), "Agribusiness, Contract Farmers and Land-Use Sustainability in North-West Tasmania," *Australian Geographer* 26(2), pp. 104–111.

—— (1996), "Contract Farming under Globally-Oriented and Locally-Emergent Agribusiness in Tasmania," in D. Burch, R. E. Rickson, and G. Lawrence (eds.), *Globalization and Agri-Food Restructuring. Perspectives from the Australasia Region*, Avebury, Aldershot, pp. 203–218.

Moran, W., Blunden, G., and Greenwood, J. (1993), "The Role of Family Farming in Agrarian Change," *Progress in Human Geography* 17(1), pp. 22–42.

Mules, T. (1990), *The Impact of the Port of Thevenard on Regional Income in the West Coast Regional Economy*, Centre for South Australian Economic Studies, Adelaide.

Parliament of South Australia (1995), *Report of the Eyre Peninsula Strategic Task Force*, Adelaide.

Parliament of South Australia, Social Development Committee (1994), *Rural Poverty in South Australia: Interim Report*, Adelaide.

Pawson, E. and Scott, G. (1992), "The Regional Consequences of Economic Restructuring: The West Coast, New Zealand, 1984–1991," *Journal of Rural Studies* 8, pp. 373–386.

Pfitzner, J. (ed.) (1992), *We Are Hanging on: Voices of Hope in the Rural Crisis*, Lutheran Publishing House, Adelaide.

Reimers, H. (1989), "Climate Change Impact on the Cropping and Grazing Systems of the Cereal Belt and Higher Rainfall Areas of South Australia," in T. Dendy (ed.), *Greenhouse '88: Planning for Climate Change*, South Australia Department of Environment and Planning.

Robinson, G. M. (1995), "Deregulation and Restructuring of the Australian Cane Sugar Industry," *Australian Geographical Studies* 33(2), pp. 212–227.

Simmons, P. (1993), "Recent Developments in Commonwealth Drought Policy," *Review of Marketing and Agricultural Economics* 61(3), pp. 443–454.

Smailes, P. J. (1989), *Impact of the Rural Crisis of 1985–89 on the D.C. of Cleve*, Geography Department, University of Adelaide.

—— (1991), "The Impact of the Rural Crisis of 1985–89 on a Rural Local Government Area and Its Wider Implications: Cleve, Eyre Peninsula, SA," *South Australian Geographical Journal* 91, pp. 24–45.

——— (1993), *Impact of the Rural Crisis on the District Council of Cleve: An Update to 1992*, Geography Department, University of Adelaide.

——— (1996), "Entrenched Farm Indebtedness and the Process of Agrarian Change," in D. Burch, R. E. Rickson, and G. Lawrence (eds.), *Globalization and Agri-Food Restructuring. Perspectives from the Australasia Region,* Avebury, Aldershot, pp. 301–322.

Sorensen, T. and Epps, R. (1993), *Prospects and Policies for Rural Australia,* Longman Cheshire, Melbourne.

South Australia, Climate Change Committee (1991), *The Greenhouse Strategy for South Australia,* South Australia, Department of Environment and Planning.

South Australia, Department of Agriculture (1992), *Gross Margin Budget Guide Book for Upper Eyre Peninsula,* Port Lincoln.

South Australian Regional Development Association (1991), *Regional Economic Development in South Australia,* Adelaide.

Stretton, H. (1992), "Reconstructing the Financial System," in J. Carrol and R. Manne (eds.), *Shutdown: The Failure of Economic Rationalism and How to Rescue Australia,* Text Publishing Company, Melbourne, pp. 154–171.

Trumble, H. C. (1948), "Rainfall, Evaporation and Drought Frequency in South Australia," *Journal of Agriculture (South Australia)* 52, pp. 55–64 and Suppl., pp. 1–15.

Vanclay, F. and Lawrence, G. (1995), *The Environmental Imperative: Eco-Social Concerns for Australian Agriculture,* CQU Press, Rockhampton.

Walmsley, D. J. (1993), "The Policy Environment," in T. Sorensen and R. Epps (eds.), *Prospects and Policies for Rural Australia,* Longman Cheshire, Melbourne, pp. 32–56.

Westpac Banking Corporation (1993), unpublished data, personal communication, August.

Williams, M. (1976), "Planned and Unplanned Changes in the Marginal Lands of South Australia," *Australian Geographer* 13, pp. 271–281.

Wilson, O. J. (1995), "Rural Restructuring and Agriculture–Rural Economy Linkages: A New Zealand Study," *Journal of Rural Studies* 11(4), pp. 417–431.

Part III
Restructuring of the countryside in countries undergoing transition

4

Market forces and community development in rural Poland

Jan Łoboda, Zbigniew Rog, and Markku Tykkyläinen

Introduction

This paper examines the restructuring of rural areas in Poland during the transition towards a market economy. It focuses on rural policy and on its effects on agrarian Poland in general, examining in detail both the effects of restructuring in rural communities in Lower Silesia and local responses to the transition in the local districts of Supraśl and Zabłudów in the Białystok voivodship (fig. 4.1). Resource communities – more precisely agricultural communities – in both regions were subject to pressure to adjust to socio-economic reforms at the national level under socialism. Now, in the 1990s, these regions are being pushed to adjust to the transition from a planned economy and social ownership of the means of production to a market economy. The range of outcomes that have resulted from the latest adjustments in these two regions give some insight into the variety of socio-economic processes that are emerging in the transition to a market economy in rural Poland.

The post-war restructuring of agriculture in Poland was strongly associated with traditional private small farming. Such farms continued to operate under socialist regimes; collective farms played only a minor role in agriculture during these periods. In the 1990s,

Fig. 4.1 **Lower Silesia and the local districts of Supraśl and Zabłudów.**

therefore, restructuring has focused on issues such as the privatization of former state farms, pressures to rationalize private farming,
and the search for ways to diversify the rural economy.

This paper deals with two kinds of areas. Lower Silesia is an
industrialized area, with fertile land and a favourable climate for
agriculture. North-east Poland is a sparsely settled agricultural and
forest region, where local authorities aim to create a development
model suitable for local conditions, based on farming, tourism, and
service provision. In this paper, the different approaches of residents
in these two regions in coping with the problems of transition are
discussed.

Methodologically, this paper consists of macro, regional, and community study approaches. The first part of this paper describes briefly

the post-war structural changes in agriculture in Poland and the contemporaneous transformation of the agrarian structure. This section gives an understanding of the legacy of the earlier attempts to develop agriculture and rural communities in Poland, and the influence of past measures on the present structural problems of rural areas at a macro level.

The second section highlights the impact of the nationwide socio-economic restructuring on the development of agriculture in Lower Silesia. This section also examines the diffusion of innovation in private agriculture and the significance of this diffusion process for socio-economic development. The approach in this part is chiefly regional, and the analysis is based on a survey of farmers' innovative behaviour in Lower Silesia.

The third section of the paper examines the community planning that is emerging and applied in the Białystok voivodship. A case-study approach is undertaken in this section and the investigation deals with two local districts in the vicinity of the regional capital, Białystok. It outlines an idea for a new model of community planning, based on attempts to develop local social capital.

The paper concludes with a brief general discussion of community development and socio-economic restructuring during the transition to a market economy in Poland.[1]

The post-war agrarian agricultural policy

The post-war changes in Polish agriculture have been associated with a series of shifts in emphasis in state-led agricultural policy. Collective and private modes of production were, in turn, called for to enhance agricultural performance.

One outcome of these post-war policy shifts has been fluctuations in the number of family farms over time (Morgan 1992). Land reform in 1944 distributed land to landless peasants and subsequently to Polish settlers in the western part of Poland (Dziewanowski 1984, 77). Both north-east Poland and Lower Silesia have a turbulent agrarian history as massive resettlement programmes were carried out there after World War II (Turnock 1989, 86–89). Family farms were the dominant mode of farming in post-war Poland, despite the recurrent pressures to reduce private farming under socialist governments. Towards the end of the 1980s, the private sector owned 75 per cent of the arable land in Poland. This was clearly less than the corresponding percentage in 1948 (when collectivization began), but this none the less indicates the extent to which, in contrast to what happened in other East European countries, private farming remained viable in Poland under socialism. Further, collectivization was never uniform throughout the country. The private ownership of land remained high in central and south-eastern regions of the country. For instance, in regions such as Łomża, Radom, and Nowy Sącz, the proportion of arable land in private ownership is 95 per cent or more, whereas in Lower Silesia, former German territory, it has remained at 59 per cent (fig. 4.1). None the less, the number of family farms in the country rose and fell in association with policy shifts (Głębocki 1992).

During the intense collectivization of Polish agriculture between 1948 and 1956, the number of individual family farms decreased significantly, large and medium-sized farms frequently being incorporated administratively into collective cooperatives. In the middle of this collectivization period (in 1950), the average size of a private farm was 5.6 hectares (Łoboda 1994, 4).

The political changes in Poland in 1956 initiated a reverse process, which dissolved the majority of cooperative farms and restored family farming. New private farms were established. The policy between 1956 and 1970 also aimed at establishing farms referred to as part-time or "peasant-worker" farms. The size of these farms was 2–3 hectares (Dzień 1973). According to Farkowski (1973), over 26 per cent of all private farms drew incomes from non-agricultural sources and 20 per cent of all private farms were managed by women in 1966. The beginning of the 1970s was characterized by improvements in the economic conditions of family farming, and that period resulted in increased production.

The reform in agricultural policy introduced in 1974, however, made it difficult to increase the domain of private farms. When possible, arable land was transferred to the State Land Fund, and local authorities made it obligatory for collective farms to cultivate these new land areas. Where there were no collective farms, new cooperatives and state farms were established. These actions, intended to improve the condition and structure of Polish agriculture, led to crop specialization and caused a growth of almost 25 per cent in the total area of agricultural land of state farms (Whitaker 1984, 177). The agricultural policy of the 1970s resulted in higher production costs in collective agriculture (ibid., 178), and an increase in the farmers' distrust of government policy. Over 300,000 small farms disappeared between 1970 and 1980, and the average size of a private farm increased from 5.1 hectares to 5.4 hectares during the 1970s (Łoboda 1994, 4).

A worsening situation in agriculture led to the revision of agricultural policy in 1981. Smallholding and agriculture became appealing because of the rapid increase in farmers' incomes in the early 1980s. The food shortage was turned into overproduction in the late 1980s. Nevertheless, agriculture provided only low incomes and the development of both technical and social infrastructures was neglected in many villages. The shrinking of employment in farming continued in the 1980s. Between 1980 and 1987, the number of farms decreased by 215,400. This rationalization took place in private farming, affecting small (0.5–5.0 hectares) and medium-sized (5–10 hectares) farms; the number of large farms (over 10 hectares) increased by 54,000. The average size of a farm increased from 5.4 hectares in 1980 to 7.1 in 1990 (Łoboda 1994, 4).

Liberalization of market forces led to a deep recession in agriculture in 1989–1991 (Wecławowicz 1996, 49). The neo-liberal agricultural policy of the early 1990s, and in particular the introduction of a market economy, induced a crisis in the collective sector of agriculture. In 1991, the corn and potato crops of the state farms fell by about 37 per cent and 80 per cent respectively.

Reforms in agricultural policy led to interest in further increasing the acreage of family farms in the early 1990s. This was accompanied by the sale of redundant land on state farms and cooperative farms in many regions of Poland. The Agricultural Property Agency of the State Treasury was established in Poland in 1992. The Agency took over the assets of the 1,600 state farms, a total of 3.7 million hectares, for sale or lease. This represented one-fifth of the total arable land in Poland.

By the end of September 1995, less than 5 per cent of the land taken over by the Agency had been sold, about 24 per cent was managed by administrators or stewards, some 60 per cent was being leased, and 11 per cent was in the process of transfer to buyers or lessors (OECD 1996, 48). The efficient reorganization of the land of former state farms is a process that will take many years (Anusziewski 1996). The polarization of the land ownership pattern continued in the 1990s, and an increasing number of farmers rely on social security payments. The average size of a private farm rose from 7.1 to 7.8 hectares between 1990 and 1994 (OECD 1996).

Implications of changes for agriculture

The average size of farms is still small in Poland compared with farms in Western Europe. Since the early 1980s, land has been con-solidated, rather than divided into parcels, but this process has been slow. Since World War II, the average size of a Polish private farm has increased slowly, although more rapidly in the 1980s and the early 1990s. In general, the constant decrease in the number of small and medium-sized farms, and, in particular, the rapid increase in the largest farms (over 15 hectares), are recognized to have been the defining characteristic features of Polish agriculture in the 1980s. Employment in agriculture declined by 17 per cent during the 1980s, though agriculture still provided work for 4.3 million people in 1990 (WIIW 1995, 111).

Yields per hectare are low in Poland, a fact that, at least partly, prevented the withdrawal of arable land from production until the period of transition. Arable land has decreased slowly during recent decades – between 1969 and 1991, for example, the total loss was 4 per cent (*Statistical Yearbook of Finland* 1972, 1994). The extent of this withdrawal of arable land from production has varied from region to region. Western parts of Poland have kept a higher than average amount of land in production. There were no significant shifts from one crop to another.

To summarize, the differences in the ownership of arable land by region are significant and are the result of a long historical process. At the very beginning of the privatization phase of the 1990s, family farms were dominant in the central and south-eastern regions of the country, whereas the proportion of arable land owned by family farms was much smaller in the western and south-western regions (in Lower Silesia, a mere 58.7 per cent of farms were family farms) and in the northern regions (for example, in the Stettin voivodship, only 35 per cent of farms were family farms in 1991). State farms, collec-tive farms, and farmers' cooperative groups owned the remaining arable land.

The conditions under which Polish agriculture operated during the socialist period were both unstable and uncertain. Policy changes alternately favoured collective and individual farms. The reason for the shifts in emphasis in state agricultural policy was to improve the efficiency of farming. In fact, the changes did little to improve effi-ciency. In the early 1990s, Poland had 0.38 hectares of field area per inhabitant, which was slightly more than in France (*Statistical Year-book of Finland* 1994), but Polish agriculture was less productive. Moreover, the labour input per hectare in Poland was five times the labour input per hectare in France (ibid.). The number of employees engaged in agriculture in 1990 was greater in Poland than in all EU countries together, excluding the Mediterranean countries. Poland has long lagged behind in the modernization of agriculture, and the disparities between Poland and the Western countries with respect to agricultural productivity and technology have increased over time.

The new liberal policy of the early 1990s, following the principles of a market ideology, triggered wide-ranging restructuring in agriculture: employment in agriculture dropped to 3.7 million in 1993 (13 per cent less than in 1990) and agricultural production declined in 1990–1992 and 1994 (WIIW 1995, 68, 111). Policy changed in 1993, and agricultural production grew again in 1995, and employment in agriculture increased in 1994 and 1995 (WIIW 1996, 80, 135).

Lower Silesia

Before transition, 1975–1990

Lower Silesia is not generally reflective of Polish agriculture because, until 1945, it was part of Germany and, following the peace treaty, was settled by Poles displaced by the westward expansion of the USSR. Thus, from 1945 onward, many of the resource communities had no longstanding ties with the land. Furthermore, before transition agriculture involved the coexistence of collective and declining private farming. Nevertheless, the study of Lower Silesia gives an idea of what has happened in both private and collective farming in the area, where transition has shaped the lives of many individuals in resource communities.

Lower Silesia covers 18,871 km², approximately 6 per cent of the total area of Poland. It is inhabited by nearly 3 million people, which is about 8 per cent of the Polish population. Lower Silesia is located in the south-western part of the country and consists of four voivodships: Wrocław, Legnica, Wałbrzych, and Jelenia Góra (see fig. 4.1). The soil quality in this region is better than the average in Poland (Rosołowska 1992). The best soil for wheat and sugarbeet cultivation occurs in the southern part of the region. The quality of the arable land in Lower Silesia, except for the Jelenia Góra voivodship, is above the average for the country as a whole. Mountainous areas in the Sudeten influence natural conditions near the border in the south. Lower Silesia has also been subjected to heavy air pollution from the nearby industrialized areas in Poland, Germany, and the Czech Republic.

As has happened in rural Poland as a whole, the rural population in Lower Silesia has fallen – from 815,700 in 1989 to 806,500 in 1992 – even though this region is part of the already heavily urbanized area of the country. Since 1980, only the Legnica voivodship has had a positive balance of migration. The other voivodships of the region have all experienced outward migration. The migration of population from the Lower Silesian villages has skewed the population structure, leading to the ageing of the rural population. The number of people employed in agriculture, particularly the number of young women, has also diminished.

The development of agriculture in Lower Silesia has been influenced not only by the pull of job opportunities in cities but also by the slow growth in labour productivity and by agricultural policy. In addition to these supply-side factors, the market for traditional agricultural products has not expanded. The area of arable land decreased by 3 per cent between 1975 and 1990, representing 35,800 hectares in Lower Silesia.

The proportion of arable land owned by family farms decreased in the 1970s, but started to grow again in the 1980s, when restrictions on purchasing land for family farming were withdrawn. In 1990, state farms owned one-third of the land and collective groups and cooperatives only a small fraction. Labour intensity in agriculture in Lower Silesia was three-quarters of the national average.

Agriculture in Lower Silesia could be said to have stagnated during recent decades. The main developments in agriculture between 1975 and 1990 were:
- a tendency for the area of cultivation to be reduced, although slowly;
- the maintenance of labour-intensive production;
- a shift in the emphasis in developing agriculture (from state farms to private farms) towards the end of the period;
- a stemming of overly rapid migration, despite out-migration;
- the inflow of pollution from industrial and urban sources;
- low efficiency, especially in mountainous areas (which are often also border areas).

The privatization of state farms in Lower Silesia after 1990

The proportion of arable land used by family farms is lower in Lower Silesia than the average for Poland. For instance, in 1990, it was, by voivodship, 52.7 per cent in Legnica, 58.0 per cent in Jelenia Góra, 60.0 per cent in Wałbrzych, and 57.8 per cent in Wrocław. Thus, the recent privatization process has had more effect on rural communities here than in many other regions.

State farms are concentrated in 21 (out of a total of 49) voivodships, the majority being in the north-western part of the country, with many located in the former German areas. The four voivodships of Lower Silesia belong to this group of 21 voivodships. The process of privatizing state farms in Lower Silesia involved a large area, and its course was complicated and slow. It was also a controversial process, because state agriculture in Poland was a political instrument, and state farms were expected to be an example and instrument of progressive change within agriculture.

The description of the prevailing conditions at the start of privatization in Lower Silesia in the early 1990s reveals the complexity of the entire process (Łoboda 1994):

- At the end of 1992, there were 144 state farms designated for take-over by the Agricultural Property Agency of the State Treasury. Seven farms were privatized during the first eight months of 1993, and 137 state farms still were in operation.
- The number of applications for the liquidation of state farms increased from 9 in 1992 to 54 by August 1993; the largest numbers of farms planned for liquidation were in the Wałbrzych and Legnica voivodships.
- The number of farms taken over by the Agency increased from 12 at the end of 1992 to 90 by the end of August 1993. The most intense process occurred within the Wrocław voivodship, where 110,000 hectares were taken over.
- The Agency had taken over 29 enterprises by the end of 1992; by the end of August 1993 this figure had increased to 296 enterprises, of which 157 were agricultural enterprises, including 21 alcohol distilleries, 12 food-processing enterprises, 15 butcher's shops, 48 drying houses, 29 fodder mixers, and 3 potato flaking plants.
- Together with these enterprises, the Agency took over the apartments inhabited by the employees and families of former state farms. By the end of August 1993, it had acquired up to 23,165 flats and sold 987.

- The percentage of debts out of the value of fixed assets of enterprises taken over by the Agency was only 21 per cent, being about the same value as the financial assets.
- 10,906 people were employed in either the Lower Silesian farms of the State Treasury (after their take-over by the Agency in August 1993) or other enterprises subsequently taken over. Of these people, 8,780 were employed by the Agency farms and 479 by the new owners. Of the remainder, 1,258 people were dismissed or resigned, and 389 retired or received a disability pension.
- Besides taking over the land and buildings of former state farms, the Agency also took over land from the State Land Fund, the former broker of land.
- In total, in the region, 22,186 hectares were taken over by the Agency at the end of August 1993 – the total area of land taken over was 222,054 hectares; 56,519 hectares were offered for sale, and 804 hectares were sold, including 788 hectares from the State Land Fund. At the same time, 8,246 hectares were leased out, including 107 hectares from the State Land Fund.
- The Agency also offered the communes the free usage of nine flats, one nursery school, and one sports centre. Of these, five flats, the nursery school, and the sports centre had been transferred to the communes in the Wrocław voivodship by August 1993.

The industries associated with agriculture in Lower Silesia were being widely restructured as part of the transition to a market economy. For example, in the early 1990s, the state grain enterprises had a monopoly in purchasing and processing grain in the region. Reforms, a decline in production, and the introduction of free competition resulted in a fall in revenues and poor prospects. Almost half of the state grain enterprises had their bank credit withdrawn because they were considered unable to repay their debts. The credits had been granted for the modernization of these enterprises; however, they worsened instead of improved the plight of enterprises, which had become unprofitable. The immediate reason state enterprises were so unprofitable was the fall in demand, the import of food products, and the decline in relative prices of food products in the early years of the transition.

This detailed account of the process of privatization of agriculture in Lower Silesia demonstrates that the mechanics of the transition to a market economy are complex, and may take a number of years to put in place. The role of the Agricultural Property Agency has been central in Lower Silesia, but it looks as if the introduction of a broker would have been useful, because the central role of the Agency has led to a time-lag in privatization.

Innovativeness in private agriculture in Lower Silesia

State-led privatization is a crucial step in the restructuring of Polish agriculture to meet the demands of a market economy. However, unless further innovations are adopted by farmers at the household level, successful economic development is unlikely. Small-scale farming is an endogenous economic activity, because development is largely based on face-to-face contacts between farmers, trips to nearby centres to buy fertilizers, machinery, etc., and consultations with local advisers. Theories of endogenous development place considerable importance on local initiatives in successful economic development in small-scale agricultural activities. Accordingly, this section looks at the role of innovative practices adopted by private farm owners in the current economic development of agrarian communities in Lower Silesia.

The figures presented in this section are derived from a series of surveys of innovative processes in local communities in this region. These have been systematically carried out since the mid-1970s (Łoboda 1976–1978 and 1987; Krzywiecka 1993). The aims of the research have been, *inter alia*, to explore the way in which information about innovations is introduced to farmers, and to explore the impact of innovation on agricultural performance. Attention has also been paid to the differentiation of communities with regard to their socio-demographic and occupational characteristics and their need for planning services.

The most recent survey, among farmers in 33 randomly selected localities in Lower Silesia, was carried out in 1993, and the following results are based on the analysis of this survey (Łoboda 1994).

Innovative trends

The majority of farms are run by married couples and are peasant farms with a low level of mechanization. Most farmers, according to the survey, had extensive practical experience in individual farming (8–25 years). Hence, they were established farmers. Commitment to continuing in farming, however, was by no means universal. In 1993, 10 per cent of the farmers – predominantly those with small, poorly mechanized farms – worked mainly in non-farm occupations. In addition, 20 per cent of the farmers were earning additional income from casual work in agriculture during the peak seasons or by providing services in the villages, such as locksmithing, bricklaying, or house painting. Further, only just over half the farmers surveyed (56 per cent) intended to continue working in agriculture: 12 per cent wanted to change their profession, but had no clear alternative prospects (this willingness to change occupations has been at the same level since 1976); 7 per cent planned to change their profession and then stay on in the village, while a very small percentage wanted to change their profession and move to a larger town; 25 per cent had other plans, the most frequent aspiration being to sell the farm or to transfer it to a successor. If farmers had implemented the plans they discussed, they would have had a major impact on the restructuring pattern of farming.

Some modernization took place in the early years of the transition. For example, more productive species of plants, new ways of using fertilizers, or the upgrading of farming equipment have been introduced. Several key characteristics of the process of diffusion of innovations in Lower Silesia have emerged from the survey:

- Most farmers mentioned the installation of new machines and the acquisition of new fertilizers as innovations.
- The period between gaining the initial information about a possible innovation and its introduction decreased between 1986 and 1993 – in some cases from 5–7 years to 2.8 years. The period from testing to the full use of an innovation was just over a month.
- At the time of the 1993 survey, the agricultural advisory service was the most important source of information for innovations. The significance of neighbours' opinions and the media had decreased significantly over the preceding seven years.
- Distance influenced the likelihood of adopting innovations: proximity to town favours more frequent visits to town by the farmers, and they are, therefore, more likely to introduce innovations.
- Investment by family farms has decreased during the transition to a market economy in Lower Silesia. However, innovations do not necessarily require a large amount of capital. Improved management and skills are equally important in family farms.

The 1993 survey reveals that the adoption of innovations has not been hampered by the transition and, in fact, now takes place more rapidly than earlier, except in peripheral locations. The role of agricultural advising is considered more important than previously.

Despite these positive aspects, the uptake of innovation is selective. In general, the formal education of farmers is relatively low –

22–52 per cent had not even completed primary school. Those with only primary school education form the largest category in the population so far as educational attainment is concerned, although in the 1993 survey the response "incomplete secondary education" was more frequent. Further, the population employed on individual farms in Lower Silesia is growing older. These population characteristics suggest that the acceptance of innovations necessary for economic development in this region may be hampered.

It is not surprising, therefore, that only one in three farmers plans to buy or lease land from the state farms or cooperative farms that are being privatized. These farmers tend to be the owners of middle-sized farms (5–15 hectares) who aspire to double their acreage. They usually also have the resources and skills to adopt innovations and develop farming.

The study of Lower Silesia confirms the hypothesis that larger farms are more open to innovation. One-third of the farms in the group of smallest farms had not introduced any innovation during the previous seven years. Of the farms with 2–5 hectares, 60 per cent had introduced some form of innovation, as had 67 per cent of farmers with 5–7 hectares. On farms of 7–10 hectares, as many as 86 per cent of farmers had incorporated some form of innovation into their farming practices. Innovation had occurred on 93 per cent of farms of 10–15 hectares, and on all the largest farms (those with over 15 hectares of land).

The technology gap between smaller and larger farms widened between 1986 and 1993. Small farms have lagged behind in the adoption of innovations. In the absence of any policy measures, it may well be that the interaction of national restructuring and the pattern of constraints and opportunities at the local level will result in a fraction of the already well-off farmers increasing their proportion of agricultural production.

Early adaptors are the winners in transition

The survey of Lower Silesia revealed some of the social implications of the transition to a market economy. Transition is socially selective and it will probably lead to a strong rationalization phase in agriculture, in which the smallest and least innovative farms will disappear and employees of state farms will have to search for new jobs. Other likely outcomes are that:

- a new stratum of farmers with medium to large acreage will be able to develop and expand most efficiently;
- some land will be acquired by family farms when the former state and collective farms are privatized by the Agricultural Property Agency of the State Treasury; this transformation will not, most importantly, relieve the problems of low productivity in Polish agriculture;
- growth and development in Polish agriculture will be selective – owing to low demand and high competition, including imports from abroad, investment in agriculture has been low;
- given the rather minimal support of local authorities, the creation of Agencies of Local Development, performing advisory, training, and information-providing functions, will become the factor stimulating the development of Lower Silesian agriculture.

Restructuring will continue in rural communities in Poland. An excess labour force is becoming a significant problem in the rural countryside. The low level of education and the ageing of the rural population, as observed in the surveys in Lower Silesia, may be the first signs of the development of the situation seen in many peripheral areas in the West, where outlying agricultural areas are reservoirs both of a poorly educated workforce and of elderly people. Economic policy should be directed so that economic growth will create new jobs for people from the countryside. Young generations born in the countryside, but not getting a chance to work in farming, should be a special target group of the policy. The coming years will also be very challenging for rural policy, because of the large rural population and the small size of farms.

Local planning experiments in north-east Poland

The borderland

North-east Poland consists of three voivodships, Suwałki, Olsztyn, and Białystok (fig. 4.1). Olsztyn and the western part of Suwałki are a part of Masuria, which was acquired from Germany in 1945. Therefore, there is no unifying cultural heritage in the region. It is an underdeveloped fringe area, mainly agricultural and forest, where agriculture is not very productive. North-east Poland is not industrialized, and it is much more sparsely populated than Lower Silesia. Białystok (275,000 inhabitants) and Olsztyn (160,000 inhabitants) are the biggest cities. The most north-eastern corner consists of a lake and the upland area of Suwałki.

Białystok is the only significant industrial city in the region of north-east Poland, having a textile industry. In spite of the lack of large-scale industrial activity, the region is believed to have some potential for economic development because of its outstanding natural environmental attributes and its advantageous geographical position as a gateway between the East and West.

National parks, nature reserves, landscape parks, areas of protected landscape, and many protected drainage areas are found in north-east Poland. Białowieza National Park in the voivodship of Białystok has a special status, accepted by UNESCO in 1977 as a Biosphere Reserve and, in 1979, as an Object of Human Heritage. Further, north-east Poland is the least polluted area in the country, possessing relatively clean air, water, and soils. These environmental attributes are the unifying factor of communities in north-east Poland.

The north-eastern borderlands are not only unique in Poland with respect to their natural environmental attributes, but also significant in the broader context. They have:
- a unique botanical and climatic zone;
- a watershed dividing the catchment area of the Baltic Sea from that of the Black Sea;
- very important European ecological belts containing forest and boggy ecosystems with varieties of plants and animals unknown in other areas.

Hence, this area is a vital part of the European endowment of flora, fauna, and landscape.

Local planning

The lowest tier of territorial division in Poland is a local district *(gmina)*. The Local Government Act decentralized some tasks to the local districts in 1990. The local district became an investor in the local infrastructure and, as the owner of former communal properties, obtained the power to run, lease, or sell them (Weclawowicz 1996, 173). The government of a district is elected by the locals, and it is responsible for developing its domain. New planning principles have been drawn up by Rog (1993a) to help local districts to cope with the restructuring process in north-east Poland. These ideas reflect the political atmosphere, which favoured local administrative reforms and pilot projects in Poland in 1992–1993 (Grochowski 1997). The aim was to develop an advanced planning method for the local districts themselves and the local, rural communities in Poland within the framework of a new market economy. This market economy represented a market rationality approach, as described in the introduction of this book. This planning approach is intended to promote local economic development and to be implemented by the local authority. The feasibility of implementing local planning in remote rural communities has been investigated in the communities in the vicinity of Białystok. The case-studies – the local district of Supraśl (10,300 inhabitants) and the local district of Zabłudów (11,700 inhabitants) – are both located in the voivodship of Białystok (the average population of a local district in Poland is about 15,600).

The concept of functional local planning

To improve environmental conditions substantially and to stimulate the local economy, it will be necessary to improve the methods of local planning. For north-east Poland, a planning model based on the formation of communities of sustainable development (Rog 1993a, 1993b) is of special interest. In this model, the local district is planned to be a "functional community," which refers to the organizationally integrated, usually powerful, type of local authority that is dominant in northern Western Europe (Horváth 1997). Local districts have many tasks, as listed by Jensen and Plum (1993, 577–578), and in 1990 the domain of local government approached that of the Nordic model. In addition to the traditional tasks of taking care of infrastructure and providing services, it is argued that environmental protection and the interests of different economic activities, of both local and regional significance, should be linked together within these spatial units. The aim of this kind of local planning is simultaneously to increase the well-being of the locals and the sustainability of the local economic-environmental systems.

The principles of increasing the participation of locals and of bottom–up initiatives in local planning have been successfully applied in several countries. It is a planning paradigm that gained popularity in Western Europe in the 1980s as a replacement for the traditional top–down approach. For instance, it has been applied and analysed in local planning for the development of tourism (Aronsson 1989), the development of partnerships between universities and communities (Brown 1989), local development efforts in rural communities (Johansen et al. 1992; Malinen 1991), the establishment of local initiative networks (Stöhr 1992), and the integration of local development work with municipal planning (Wahlström 1989). In Poland, this kind of participative planning is only just starting. So far, privatization and the introduction of a market economy have been more topical than community planning.

The proposed approach is characterized as holistic and integrating. The functional planning process aims to evaluate the local advantages and business opportunities of the communities, the feasibility of industrial development, and the local resources for economic development. In this process, economic activities that are compatible with sustainable development are assessed. A crucial task is then to design a plan that takes into account locational advantages, together with the income, employment, and environmental effects of the planned economic activities. It is equally crucial that the plan is implemented by local authorities in concert with regional planning. The main aim of local economic development policy is that each community should consist of a competitive combination of activities within the framework of a market economy. Local planning is to be directed towards promoting these kinds of networks of competitive small clusters of economic activities.

The four basic types of local development strategies considered suitable for the conditions of north-east Poland are outlined in table 4.1. If industrial activities are appropriate for a community, manufacturing should also be promoted. The most advanced technologies allow for the development of manufacturing without harmful environmental effects. A careful selection of the most feasible elements of different strategies may be the most productive way to implement this scheme within a local district.

Retail trade and allied industries near the border became important industries in the early stage of transition, and now, in the mid-1990s, they are very lucrative. A large number of visitors make shopping trips to Poland from the newly independent countries. Nevertheless, larger centres, such as the city of Białystok, benefit most from this trade. This border trade is not necessarily a permanent phenomenon, and it is therefore not considered central among development strategies. Some communities could also benefit from suburban expansion, and the plans should be integrated with geographically wider regional planning.

In addition to locational advantages in the traditional sense

Table 4.1 **The four basic types of local development strategy outlined for north-east Poland**

Type of community	Economic activity	
	Predominant	Supplementary
Agricultural	Specialized, intensive and traditional farming, local industry, settlement	Forestry, fishing, small and medium-sized industries
Agricultural, ecological	Organic farming, nature and water resources protection	Tourism and recreation, health resort, sustainable forestry, local food processing, fishing
Holiday resort	Spas, golf courses, housing and services for elderly people, organic farming, nature and water resources protection	Tourism and recreation, eco-tourism, local food processing, sustainable forestry, fishing
Recreational	Tourism and amusements, organic and traditional farming, nature and water resources protection	Forestry and sustainable forestry, fishing, local food processing, cross-border trade

(abundant labour, low salaries, natural resources, etc.), the creation of locational advantages through education and social interaction should be considered. This "creative" side of the competitiveness of a region and a community is becoming increasingly important in the development of communities. Malmberg et al. have elaborated on the concept of local milieu as an important factor of development, as follows:

Some basic characteristics of such milieux may be identified. Thus, there are several actors (firms, institutions) that are relatively autonomous in terms of decision making and strategy formulation, and the interaction between these actors contains an element of both cooperation and rivalry. Furthermore, the milieu is characterized by a specific set of material (firms, infrastructure), immaterial (knowledge, know-how) and institutional (authorities, legal framework) elements. These elements make up a complex web of relations that ties firms, customers, research institutions, the school system, and local authorities to each other. The interaction between economic, socio-cultural, political and institutional actors in a given place may trigger learning dynamics and enhance the ability of actors to modify their behaviour and find new solutions as their competitive environments change.... It is an environment within which physical capital and human capital is created and accumulated over time, which translates into sustainable competitiveness among incumbent firms. (Malmberg et al. 1995, 11)

Thus, economic development in a community or in a set of communities takes place through learning and intense interaction. That is seen as an important element of competitiveness.

Functional planning aims at utilizing the benefits of a developing local milieu. The concentration of knowledge in certain localities, the learning process, and the development of economic activities based on interaction between local actors have been considered crucial in this concept of functional communities. The Polish case-studies demonstrate how this process manifests itself in a poor agrarian region.

This idea of functional communities offers an entirely new, local approach to the spatial planning of communities in Poland. If the planning principles are accepted by local authorities and are institutionalized, this method will be the main instrument of local development planning. This framework is likely to be the most efficient instrument of spatial policy, because communal plans are the most powerful blueprints in post-socialist Poland. On the other hand, it creates a new task for local governments, which must create their own planning practices. Close cooperation between the planning team, the authorities of the local district, business, the research and development sector, the provincial administration, local groups, etc., is also necessary to achieve success.

The drive for functional communities in the Białystok voivodship has so far come from expert teams including an environmental manager, an ecologist, a spatial management planner, a medical adviser, and an agricultural adviser (Rog 1993a). The planning process was outlined in close cooperation with local governments and different actors at local, regional, and supra-regional levels at the beginning of the 1990s.

Local districts near Białystok – two case-studies

In the early 1990s, two functional community projects were under discussion: the development of the local district of Supraśl in accordance with ecological principles; and the development of Zabłudów as an area for agriculture and suburban housing. These local districts offer distinct starting points for local economic development and for environmental protection. A large part of the Supraśl local district is situated in the protected areas of Knyszyn Forest, which possesses highly valued natural environmental attributes. The most important task of this project was to assess the sustainable use of natural resources. In the case of Zabłudów, natural environmental attributes are secondary, and economic development is the main issue. Local economic activities find a market in the nearby city of Białystok.

Supraśl: Towards an ecological community
Supraśl is located 14 km to the north-east of Białystok City, along a minor road. It is characterized by weakly developed social and technical infrastructures, a lack of industry, a predominance of people employed in agriculture, infertile soils, and a predominantly forested terrain. In this respect, it is a backward local district that, up to now, has had little opportunity for rapid economic development. On the other hand, it is exceptionally privileged by history and by nature. The town of Supraśl, the centre of the local district, has a 500-year history and plenty of architectural monuments, and is located adjacent to the entrance to the Knyszyn Forest (also known as the Knyszyn Wilderness and Landscape Park).

The first step of the planning process embraced an assessment of the natural environment, socio-economic conditions, and the potential for economic development, including (Rog 1993a):
- the physical geography of the area;
- the main features of the forest areas, forestry, and hunting;
- the attributes of the natural environment, and the protection of these attributes (nature reserves, natural attractions, etc.);
- the micro-climate, the sanitary conditions, the possibilities of establishing recreational activities, and the activities of the health sector;
- land use, including settlement, infrastructure, and architectural monuments;
- social conditions, economic activities, tourism, and the spatial structure;
- water supply, as well as waste and waste water management.

The development of the functional community in Supraśl was prepared with the participation of the local inhabitants and the local government. Because of the outstanding value of the natural environmental attributes, ecological factors were emphasized. Special regard was paid to the protection of nature, the economic use of natural environmental advantages, local skills and traditions in farming, and any opportunities that might attract outside investors and customers. Taking into account the locational advantages of the

116

region, the following economic activities were preferred as the economic base for the local district: tourism and recreation, health services and resort activities, and small-scale farming and high-quality food production.

TOURISM AND RECREATION. Tourism and recreation have gained ground as two of the main economic activities in the locality. There are already many summer cottages within the local district. Tourist services and recreational activities were included in the plan, but taking into account environmental protection needs. It is planned to increase the recreational value of the area by building a large reservoir, which will also supply drinking water for Białystok City. The city has had a problem with its drinking water supply, so it was possible to obtain financial support for the construction of the reservoir.

The natural environmental attributes of the region make it possible to develop tourism, paying special attention to what is known as "agro-tourism" in Poland. Tourism and recreation need to be combined with other businesses in the local district, such as farming. The provision of rural tourism could be targeted at the people of Warsaw, for instance.

RESORT ACTIVITIES AND HEALTH SERVICES. The area under study has a favourable micro-climate, which makes it suitable for holiday resorts, though with strict environmental controls. This represents a business opportunity not only for Supraśl but for north-east Poland as whole because, at present, most Polish health resorts are located in much more polluted areas. The local district of Supraśl could also offer premises for a resort because it contains some rest houses belonging to various institutions that have no funds to maintain them. Białystok City's medical centre is also interested in these premises for convalescent therapy, because they are much more affordable than hospital premises. In either case, this could solve the problem of maintaining the rest houses.

FARMING. Agriculture is the basic source of income for the large majority of inhabitants. However, the entire northern part of the local district is located in the protected Supraśl River drainage area, which is the only source of drinking water for Białystok City. Given the necessity of protecting the water supply, the value of the natural environmental attributes, and the possibility of recreational development in the area, the promotion of organic farming was included in the project. Farming without the use of chemicals would facilitate the protection of the water ecosystems and drinking water. Organic farming is not popular in Poland yet, but it is assumed that it will develop, especially in north-east Poland.

After three years of project implementation, some of the planned objectives have been reached. The community has received financial support to solve the waste water problem and to supply gas to the town of Supraśl. This has resulted in the improvement of the local environment, a necessity for the development of the recreational function. Investors have investigated the profitability of recreational investments. Organic farming has not been successful, being attempted by only a few and usually subsequently abandoned; the higher price of organic produce is the crucial obstacle (Follow-up data 1997). Rural tourism has attracted visitors from Warsaw and is successful on the whole (ibid.).

Zabłudów: Agriculture and suburban housing
Zabłudów is located 18 km south of Białystok City. It has an agricultural character, but the majority of the inhabitants are employed in the city. Zabłudów has no particular natural attributes or need for strong conservation measures. Economic development of the area could take into account the following features: the proximity of Białystok City, with its rapid economic development; the junction of tourist routes; and more efficient use of production facilities belonging to former state and cooperative farms.

The following economic activities and main regional opportunities were considered worth developing: suburban housing, tourism and recreation, organic farming, and ecologically friendly food production.

The most important task of planning in this region is to provide more urban space in the local district to accommodate the expansion of Białystok City. There is a great demand for urban space, because the city is surrounded by protected forests and expansion can take place only in the direction of Zabłudów. The community plan allocates land especially for the following purposes: suburban housing; industrial and commercial activities; and recreational purposes.

The Zabłudów plan also proposes directives for urban and regional authorities in environmental management, including suggestions for an increase in the proportion of forested and water protection areas, as well as measures for economic development in line with the proposed activities. The project was prepared in 1992 and, at the time of writing the final version of the paper, the expansion of Białystok City was the most discernible achievement. The importance of farming in the community is illustrated by the privatization of a large poultry farm, which was one of the key industries in the community in 1997 (Follow-up data 1997).

The future of local planning

Functional planning aims to create sustainable development based on such principles as the locational advantages provided by the region, local skills and traditions, ecologically friendly production, profitability and market demand, the allocation of infrastructure and premises to new activities, and the attraction of external investment. Broad participation by local governments and local groups is necessary to bring people with different interests and ideas together.

The concept of functional planning is comprehensive and integrated, and emphasizes innovativeness and local participation. The basic premises underlying economic development planning for local districts of the Białystok voivodship are that a local authority should be able to develop its domain by:

- activating the local economy by highlighting opportunities for the sustainable use of local resources;
- supplying industrial premises, infrastructure, and land for housing and industry;
- promoting industrial activities by facilitating opportunities for broad networking and cooperation – including cross-border and international cooperation;
- promoting trade, especially in border communities;
- creating a new educational policy for higher and vocational education to meet the regional needs;
- strengthening regional self-government;
- encouraging the active participation of inhabitants in businesses;
- encouraging broad cooperation between local government, administration, universities, businesses, enterprises, and local residents.

It remains to be seen whether these principles will be observed. To be successful, each local authority must have a voice in deciding the planning principles of the community.

Local development – local responses

In the case-studies discussed here, many less competitive economic activities have been inherited from the socialist period. As such, they have been subjected to major restructuring processes. Various developments have occurred in rural communities as responses to these restructuring processes.

In the rural areas of Lower Silesia, decisions on how to adapt to the problems presented by restructuring have been the responsibility of individual households. Some have been able to do this through increasing farm size and adopting innovations; others have survived by intertwining activities from the subsistence, formal, and informal sectors. Advisory services have been provided, but no holistic, integrated planning structures have been instigated.

From the survey of Lower Silesia, it was concluded that the participation of local government in local economic development is rather minimal, and that it is likely that the creation of Agencies of Local Development supplying advisory, training, and information-providing functions will be necessary to stimulate the further development of Lower Silesian agriculture. Even then, the study showed larger farms to be more open to innovation, which, in turn, facilitated further increases in the size of the farms. It seems that the market mechanism is inducing the modernization of rural economies, which did not happen during the socialist era. It is evident that, in the longer run, social and economic pressures and the attempt to join the European Union will necessitate rural initiatives and the regulation of farming according to the agricultural policies adopted elsewhere in Europe. As a consequence, land ownership will gradually become concentrated in the hands of larger family farms, and redundant labour will have to seek a livelihood from other activities or retirement. High unemployment keeps the price of labour low, and, as the opportunities for survival from the increasing intertwining of subsistence, formal, and informal activities decline with the increase in farm size, younger people will most likely be forced to migrate out. If no opportunities exist for displaced farmers or their children, and if no new forms of economic activities (to absorb this displaced labour) emerge locally, increasing social problems are likely to occur in the Lower Silesian rural society.

The restructuring of the local economies in the Białystok voivodship's rural communities reveals the need for planning that seeks to create opportunities for sustainable economic development. One factor underlying this need can be traced to the potential for economic progress in the region. There is no pull of urban agglomeration, nor is there much fertile agricultural land in north-east Poland. Hence, a search for diversification must be based on what the socio-economic characteristics of the community and natural resources offer. Environmental attributes, improvements in technology and education, the availability of premises, and local skills and labour are seen as crucial, rather than the redistribution of the means of production or the expansion of traditional agriculture, for instance.

It is evident that planning is a special precondition of sustainable economic and environmental development, owing to the existence of public goods – that is, goods that involve external consumption effects on more than one individual (Samuelson 1973, 160). The demand for public services, even if they are increasingly privately produced, is strong when societies become more complex. Systematic improvements in the competitiveness of a community and region through education, the construction of infrastructure, and the provision of amenities all require planning and local involvement.

In 1997, community planning was still struggling with the provision of basic infrastructure (roads, streets, electricity, etc.) for the inhabitants of the communities of Supraśl and Zabłudów. The tasks transferred from voivodships to local districts demand financial resources. Community revenues are meagre, however, and the progress of local planning has been piecemeal – communal problems have been solved as they have emerged. Long-range community planning was a goal rather than an everyday practice in the two local districts investigated (Follow-up data 1997). The slow progress of local administration has been attributed to a political factor: the political parties in power and the national government after 1993 have not been eager to introduce efficient local self-governance owing to the costs and political lethargy (Grochowski 1997; Regulska 1997).

The task of local governance is not easy in rural Poland. Many remote villages have an ageing population and resource-based industries face rationalization. Even if new economic activities could be successfully established in rural communities in Poland, this may not resolve the problems of local displaced people, who often fail to find a new job in a city and return to their original domicile. As subsequent case-studies in this book show, new enterprises in a community often do not require the type of labour that has been displaced by the loss or rationalization of previous economic activities.

Poland is still very rural and a country of small agricultural resource communities. In the long run, rationalization of agriculture will cause an increase in the supply of labour in Poland. Millions of people born on the small farms will search for jobs outside the primary sectors. This will lead to severe restructuring of rural areas in coming decades.

In order to create steady growth that benefits as many people as possible, the importance of achieving a balance between local opportunities and market forces, expectations of socio-economic development and local initiatives, planning and involvement must be emphasized above all else. The rural resource communities in Poland face restructuring, whose effects need to be anticipated sufficiently well and balancing measures found. Otherwise, rural Poland will have to cope with even more severe structural unemployment and migration, as has happened in many countries before.

Conclusion

The studies in Lower Silesia and the Białystok voivodship reveal local adjustment problems during the transition to a market economy. Transition led to the rationalization of rural economic activities and the redistribution of the means of production in Poland. This restructuring has been geographically uneven.

The transformation of rural areas in Poland has involved different forces attempting to influence development. For instance, socio-economic philosophies relating to the organization of production have fluctuated, national policy has laid down guidelines for local governance and land-use policy, and local responses in the form of cooperation and planning have varied. Increasingly, the problems of rationalization in agriculture are becoming more severe and each village and region possesses unique conditions of production, which will lead to spatio-economic variations in restructuring.

Note

1. The major part of the paper, including analytical discussions, has been written by Markku Tykkyläinen, who also compiled the paper. The Lower Silesian case is based on the study by Łoboda (1994) and some revisions submitted afterwards, and the case of the two local districts in the Białystok voivodship is based on the study by Rog (1993a) and material from the follow-up study (Follow-up data 1997).

References

Anusziewski, T. (1996), personal communication, University of Joensuu, Joensuu.

Aronsson, L. (1989), "Local Planning for the Development of Tourism," in G. Gustafsson (ed.), *Development in Marginal Areas*, Research Report 89:3, University of Karlstad, pp. 63–75.

Brown, V. (1989), "A University–Community Partnership: Programme and Activities to Enhance Economic Development," in G. Gustafsson (ed.), *Development in Marginal Areas*, Research Report 89:3, University of Karlstad, pp. 97–104.

Dzień, A. (1973), *Part-Time Farmers in Industrial Plants and Agriculture*, PWN, Warsaw (in Polish with English abstract).

Dziewanowski, M. K. (1984), "Historical Setting," in W. Evans-Smith (ed.), *Poland. A Country Study,* United States Government, Headquarters, Department of Army, Washington, pp. 1–93.

Farkowski, Cz. (1973), *Productional Differentiation of Private Farms in Poland*, LSW, Warsaw (in Polish).

Follow-up data (1997), notes and interview material from field trip to Supraśl and Zabłudów, 28 April – 11 May 1997, Janne Antikainen, University of Joensuu.

Głębocki, B. (1992), *The Organization of the Productive Space of Individual Farms*, Research Project No. 5 028 19 101, Warsaw.

Grochowski, M. (1997), "Public Administration Reform: An Incentive for Local Transformation," *Environment and Planning C: Government and Policy* 15(2), pp. 209–218.

Horváth, T. M. (1997), "Decentralization in Public Administration and Provision of Services: An East-Central European View," *Environment and Planning C: Government and Policy* 15(2), pp. 161–175.

Jensen, H. T. and Plum, V. (1993), "From Centralised State to Local Government, the Case of Poland in the Light of Western European Experiences," *Environment and Planning D: Society and Space* 11(5), pp. 565–581.

Johansen, H., Naukkarinen, A., and Väre, T. (1992), "Local Development Efforts in Finland's Rural Communities," in M. Tykkyläinen (ed.), *Development Issues and Strategies in the New Europe*, Avebury, Aldershot, pp. 89–100.

Krzywiecka, J. (1993), "The Diffusion of Agricultural Innovations in Perzów Commune," typescript. Research carried out by the Department of Spatial Organization of the Institute of Geography of Wrocław University, Wrocław.

Łoboda, J. (1976–1978), "The Acceptance of Innovations and the Development of Settlement Systems. Reports of Studies within the Subject: The Regional Settlement Systems," typescript, Institute of Geography of Wrocław University.

——— (1987), "The Flow of Information and the Diffusion of Innovations in Local Societies of the Agricultural Region Using the Example of Lower Silesia," *Acta Universitatis Wroclaviensis*, no. 894, Studies of Institute of Geography, Series B, vol. VI, pp. 15–27.

——— (1994), "Socio-Economic and Spatial Conditions of Agriculture in Lower Silesia in the Context of System Transformation in Poland," typescript submitted to the editors.

Malinen, P. (1991), "Rural Planning Methods in the Rural Development Program of Kainuu," in M. Tykkyläinen (ed.), *Evolving Regional and Local Development*, Occasional Papers 18, University of Joensuu, Department of Human Geography and Planning, pp. 25–39.

Malmberg, A., Sölvell, Ö., and Zander, I. (1995), "Spatial Clustering, Local Accumulation of Knowledge and Firm Competitiveness," paper presented at the Residential Conference of the IGU, Commission on the Organisation of Industrial Space, Seoul, 7–11 August 1995.

Morgan, W. B. (1992), "Economic Reforms, the Free Market and Agriculture in Poland," *Geographical Journal* 158(3), pp. 145–156.

OECD (Organization for Economic Cooperation and Development) (1996), *Agricultural Policies, Markets and Trade in Transition Economies*, OECD, Paris.

Regulska, J. (1997), "Decentralization or (Re)centralization: Struggle for Political Power in Poland," *Environment and Planning C: Government and Policy* 15(2), pp. 187–207.

Rog, Z. (1993a), "Ecological Principles of Community Development in North-east Poland," typescript submitted to the editors.

—— (1993b), "General Assumption of the Baltic Euro-Region," *Economics and Environment, Polish Division* 1(3), pp. 81–89.

Rosołowska, M. (1992), *The Agriculture and Food Economy of the Southwestern Macroregion*, Research Project No. 5 028 19 101, Warsaw.

Samuelson, P. A. (1973), *Economics*, McGraw-Hill, Tokyo.

Statistical Yearbook of Finland 1972 (1972), Central Statistical Office, Helsinki.

Statistical Yearbook of Finland 1994 (1994), Statistics Finland, Helsinki.

Stöhr, W. B. (1992), "Local Initiative Networks as an Instrument for the Development of Peripheral Areas," in M. Tykkyläinen (ed.), *Development Issues and Strategies in the New Europe*, Avebury, Aldershot, pp. 203–209.

Turnock, D. (1989), *Eastern Europe. An Economic and Political Geography*, Routledge, London and New York.

Wahlström, L. (1989), "Integrating Local Development Work with Municipal Planning," in G. Gustafsson (ed.), *Development in Marginal Areas*, Research Report 89:3, University of Karlstad, pp. 77–88.

Wecławowicz, G. (1996), *Contemporary Poland. Space and Society*, UCL Press, London.

Whitaker, D. P. (1984), "The Economy," in W. Evans-Smith (ed.), *Poland. A Country Study*, United States Government, Headquarters, Department of Army, Washington, pp. 163–222.

WIIW (Wiener Institut für Internationale Wirtschaftsvergleiche) (1995), *Countries in Transition 1995*, WIIW Handbook of Statistics, Vienna.

—— (1996), *Countries in Transition 1996*, WIIW Handbook of Statistics, Vienna.

5

Coping with socialist restructuring and the transition to a market economy in rural Hungary

István Süli-Zakar, Attila Sántha, Markku Tykkyläinen, and Cecily Neil

Introduction

Hungary has experienced many phases in the degree of state control over its economic development since World War II. A number of not always compatible factors – such as ideology, a commitment to socialist planning principles, attempts to decentralize economic power, the importance of agriculture in foreign earnings, and the importance of providing food to citizens through agricultural production – have led to significant variations in national economic policies. Constant adaptation by households and collective enterprises at the local level resulted in relatively wealthy rural communities compared with other East European countries, but also in migration from rural areas. In some regions, this socialist restructuring was, at times, successful in terms of economic progress. The adaptation that occurred was challenged in the early 1990s, when rural resource communities were faced with the new post-socialist era, with its privatization and its restructuring of the entire rural economic system in Hungary.

As this paper shows, however, the inhabitants of the peripheral region of eastern Hungary have been adversely affected by structural shifts and unstable policies, both during the socialist era in the 1950s and 1960s and later on, when the transition to a market economy started. In the absence of any opportunity in the socio-economic situation to adopt what Hirschman (1970) refers to as a "voice" strategy, the only option left for many locals has been "exit" (i.e. migration) wherever possible. In the 1950s and 1960s, many people migrated from those rural areas, and small communities, if not being targeted for socialist modernization, were allowed to waste away. Many of the communities that were left had few options for economic renewal. Compared with developments in Western countries, many rural locales faced a relatively stagnant future as a part of CMEA cooperation. After the new capitalistic order was introduced in the early 1990s, local restructuring occurred as a response to the ongoing shift from the socialist to a market economy, which was an economic and social shock for the majority of local residents.

This paper begins by examining the different phases of state economic policy relating to the agricultural sector in Hungary over the post-war period. It discusses the process of restructuring that occurred through local adaptation to centrally planned economic policies, and the impact of these restructuring processes on peripheral regions in general, and eastern Hungary in particular. Eastern Hungary is defined as the area to the east of the rivers Tisza and Zagyva, and consists of six counties: Békés, Borsod-Abaúj-Zemplén, Hajdú-Bihar, Heves, Jász-Nagykun-Szolnok, and Szabolcs-Szatmár-Bereg (Süli-Zakar 1993).

The paper then examines the current situation in eastern Hungary in more detail, drawing on the results of a survey carried out in 1992 by one of the authors (Dr. Süli-Zakar) with the support of the Hungarian Foundation for Scientific Research (OTKA). The survey examined the situation and behaviour of people living in rural areas. In all, 2,500 questionnaires were filled out in the villages of eastern Hungary. Earlier surveys had been carried out in the 1970s and the early 1980s, and these provided a basis for assessing changes in attitudes and behaviour. All the authors have done field research in Hungary since 1990. The analysis is regional in scope, and single-resource communities, such as cooperatives, state farms, or villages, are not analysed in detail. The paper explores how people coped with restructuring, and it focuses on the intertwining of economic activities and the restructuring of agriculture. In conclusion, the role of local economic development policy and community in the post-socialist stage of development is discussed.

Changing state economic policies, 1945–1993

In order to understand the restructuring of the 1990s in eastern Hungary, the different periods of rural policy in Hungary are outlined briefly below.

Land parcelling after World War II

After 1945, radical land reform was carried out. It closed down the large private farms responsible for the majority of agricultural production. Because of the large number of claimants for land, poorly equipped "dwarf" estates emerged in large numbers (the average size was 2.8 hectares). Despite the problems arising from land redistribution, by 1948 agricultural production had approached its pre-war level, again meeting Hungary's requirements for food and even providing a surplus for export.

The foundation of cooperatives, 1949–1965

The Communist Party, or, more precisely, the Hungarian Socialist Workers' Party, came to power with the adoption of a new constitution establishing single-party government in 1949. Its objectives were to found Soviet-type agricultural cooperatives, and rapidly to develop manufacturing industry in rural areas.

Despite considerable efforts, the establishment of cooperatives did not progress as well as planned. Most of the cooperatives that did emerge could not expand their activities enough because they were unable to invest sufficiently in production – their revenues were partly transferred to the manufacturing sector. Meanwhile, the absorption of incomes from agriculture ruined the economy of the better-off stratum of peasants. The uncertainty of rural life also encouraged young people to seek work in other industries, and often to leave their villages.

In the early 1950s, agricultural production fell and constant food shortages occurred. General discontent led to the revolution of 1956. After its suppression, peasants saw their future as negative. The social and political order that followed speeded up the formation of cooperatives throughout the country between 1959 and 1962. However, the importance of the food supply in the country's political realm was also realized. Less income was taken away from agriculture and improved conditions for agricultural growth were created. These included the setting of prices, the provision of credit, and an improvement in the supply of necessary agricultural inputs. As a consequence, the country again became a net food exporter of key agricultural products in the 1960s.

In the meantime, however, the development of manufacturing industries in towns was encouraged by the policy of industrial investment. As a corollary, key infrastructure was also developed in these towns. This process occurred as a consequence of a policy that ranked towns and villages according to their economic and administrative function, and gave them financial resources for development in accordance with their rank. This administratively oriented policy guided the spatial allocation of capital and manpower. Within each county, the investments in social capital favoured selected localities. For decades, this allocation of resources defined the spatial division of labour in eastern Hungary.

County authorities paid less attention to the development of the marginal areas of their county, and allocated available funds to the development of only one or two of the county's towns and a few rural development schemes. Less developed rural regions, consisting mainly of small villages, did not receive much in the way of financial resources to promote development. As a result, the more active part of the population, together with those young people with higher expectations, migrated to urban areas. This process reached its peak between 1950 and 1965, when peasant farms were closed down and there were limited prospects for agriculture. Villagers able to commute found safer jobs in the manufacturing and service sectors. In underdeveloped areas, where poor transport facilities made commuting impossible, the only option left to villagers was migration. Restructuring through out-migration resulted in the depopulation of small villages. Only people unable to do anything to change their situation (the elderly, unskilled, etc.) remained. Schools, health care, public administration, and even large-scale farms were managed from the district centres. As a result, small towns and villages lost human and social capital.

The consolidation of the cooperatives and the restart of small producers, 1966–1979

The New Economic Mechanism (NEM) was officially announced in the fall of 1965 and put into effect on 1 January 1968. It aimed at decentralizing economic management in order to allow enterprise leaders greater scope in decision-making. This meant that, after 1968, farm enterprises had relative freedom to plan production and investment. By the end of the 1960s and the early 1970s, investment, credits, and subsidies to the agricultural sector increased considerably, and this created the opportunity for technological change in the sector. Since efficient machines and technology were mostly available in the West, Hungary's technical development was based on an adaptation of West European and American farm technology.

The method of diffusing new technology was based on an original Hungarian concept. Outstanding farms, research institutes, trading companies, and smaller farms formed economic associations or "schemes". The "scheme manager" (the leading farm) undertook to provide, for a fee, the necessary technical tools, the necessary biological inputs (seeds, breeding animals, etc.), other inputs necessary for production (fertilizer, plant-protection materials, etc.), and professional advice concerning the use of these inputs in particular forms of farming (for example, corn or wheat cultivation, pig rearing, etc.). In this way, the "scheme managers" substituted for the missing producer service sector in agriculture. More efficient production was further facilitated when, in the mid-1960s, farms ceased to follow targets set by central planning authorities. This enabled cooperatives to plan their production and development activities independently. Economic factors, such as prices, credits, and subsidies, became the main means, albeit indirect, of allocating production factors on farms. None the less, the national trusts, which dealt with the processing and distribution of agricultural products, were the sole agents for the sale of agricultural products, so they were still able to exert a significant influence on farming.

By the beginning of the 1970s, across a significant part of the country, production was being carried out using relatively modern technology. Cooperatives administered 80 per cent and state farms 14 per cent of the arable land in Hungary; the remaining 6 per cent belonged to tiny private farms and plots cultivated by non-agricultural workers. Agrarian resource communities were thus based mainly on cooperatives. In 1970, the average size of a cooperative was, in terms of agricultural land, 2,000 hectares and such a farm had a total of 450 members and employees (Keefe et al. 1987). In contrast, the average size of a state farm was 4,900 hectares of agricultural land and it employed 900 persons on average. In Hungary, there were almost 2,500 cooperatives and 180 state farms. Rationalization later decreased the number of farms.

Despite the dominance of collective farming, small-scale production was an important factor in certain sectors of the country's food production. Part-time farming and household plots accounted for more than one-third of farm output and about one-fourth of Hungary's agricultural production (Keefe et al. 1987), yet they constituted only 13 per cent of the collective farm area of agricultural land. The land that a farmer could own as personal property was restricted, as was the amount of land that cooperative members could be given as a plot to farm part time. Consequently, such land was mainly used for intensive crop production, such as vineyards, orchards, or vegetable plots, or for the production of corn as reserve fodder for household animal husbandry. The continuance of this small-scale production and of household farming was initially justified on social and economic grounds relating to the low income of agricultural workers, and because it diversified food supplies in the country.

As wages rose, however, household farming became a means of making additional money rather than a necessity. The development of small-scale animal husbandry was assisted by the distribution of fodder and the availability to small-scale producers of farm buildings that had been abandoned since the introduction of the cooperatives. Thus, this small-scale production represented the most economical way of increasing overall production. "Household integration" emerged, with large-scale farms and consumer and sales cooperatives providing the small producers with animal stock, fodder, and, in many cases, tools, and offering them advice and veterinary care for their livestock. All accounts were settled at the end of the season. The products were, in turn, sold to the processing industry through the cooperatives and state farms. For the processing industry, this meant that basic supplies of suitable quality and quantity were guaranteed under contract, without their having to maintain direct contact with thousands of small producers. The cooperatives and state farms received a fee per unit of output for their broking activity and avoided the high labour costs of labour-intensive production. The small producers could draw a regular income without requiring significant capital input.

With this strengthening of large- and small-scale farming at the beginning of the 1970s, the process whereby small villages, and even whole regions, gradually wasted away was moderated. However, in the less developed areas, where the conditions for agriculture were unfavourable, the decline could not be stopped. Eastern Hungary remained a declining transitional area during this period, and out-migration continued. Not only the ordinary labour force, but also well-trained experts, moved from the countryside. Eastern Hungary, except for some industrial and mining districts, had been characterized by an excess of labour since the end of the nineteenth century. Even the larger towns of the region had excess labour until the early 1980s. However, unemployment was not prevalent. People seeking employment could find jobs in the capital or in the western part of Hungary.

The financial crisis of socialist production, 1980–1989

Agriculture employed 1.1 million people in 1980, and many others were involved in small-scale production while keeping up their chief occupation. Agricultural employees and many industrial workers, professionals, and pensioners had a household plot. Agricultural production in the 1980s grew faster in Hungary than in Bulgaria, Poland, Romania, and the Soviet Union (EC 1991, 72), but the pace of modernization was not competitive compared with the West. For instance, labour productivity did not increase much, and agriculture employed approximately the same number of people in 1989 as in 1980 (ibid.).

However, the socialist countries had ignored the increases in oil prices in 1973, and were continuing to maintain heavy industry that was both material and energy intensive. Development could be maintained only through the input of increasing amounts of foreign capital. Given the obsolete means of production and production structure, this led to the increasing indebtedness of Hungary. This had two consequences for the agricultural sector: (a) the previously well-balanced financial contracts were once again replaced by the transfer of revenue from the agricultural sector; and (b) pressure grew to export to markets paying with convertible currency – especially with respect to agricultural products.

There was no problem selling agricultural products until the early 1980s. Although the Common Market (now the European Union) imposed stricter and stricter quotas, the Hungarian producers were able to handle the situation. In the 1980s, however, the price of agricultural products in the world market dropped significantly (in relation to Hungarian production costs), and agricultural products could be sold in foreign markets only if given increased subsidies. Regular crises of overproduction occurred. The maintenance of sales volume and increases in income required changes in the product mix supplied to the market and an improvement in the processing of agricultural products. However, the development of modern processing lagged behind, and the development of new marketable products was neglected.

The combination of the rapidly growing gap between the cost of production inputs and the price received for agricultural products, together with the increased transfers of revenues from agriculture by the state, led to a decline in the profitability of farming. Only farms with outstanding production levels and conditions could make sufficient income. To escape from this situation, cooperatives started setting up businesses by developing industrial and service activities, which had considerably higher profits. The range of their activities included almost everything from the manufacture of computers to producing champagne – the success of this adaptation depending on the skills and the connections of their farm managers. In some cases, agricultural companies were thus able to compensate for the loss in income from agricultural production. However, with the worsening of economic conditions, the progress of Hungarian agriculture became sluggish in the mid-1980s, and some 300–400 of the 1,400 large-scale farms (producing some 30 per cent of the total production) were constantly struggling with financial crises, and were only just able to avoid becoming insolvent without regular financial assistance from the state.

Many efforts were made to resolve the problems in agriculture in the 1980s. For instance, largely independent, self-financing units were established within companies, share-farming methods requiring manual work were adopted, and producers were given the right to participate in foreign trade. However, adoption of such strategies was not widespread, and legal restrictions on business and land acquisition hindered the emergence of private entrepreneurship.

Eastern Hungary, 1980–1989

The labour surplus of eastern Hungary stimulated cooperatives to establish industrial subsidiaries. From the mid-1970s, the cooperatives of eastern Hungary established as many industrial plants as possible to ensure full employment. However, this industrialization of the eastern part of the country was mainly based on obsolete technology, and was carried out by transplanting branches that had become outdated in other regions. In the long run, this resulted in considerable disadvantage (Süli-Zakar 1985). Further, the industrial basis of the eastern part of the country involved the production and primary processing of raw materials – metallurgy, heavy chemical industry, food, and light industry – not industries developing high-level techniques and technologies.

Technologically advanced factories were rare in eastern Hungary, with the result that a technological gap widened between eastern Hungary and the rest of the country. Moreover, the subsidiary branches in eastern Hungary had little contact with the production of their base enterprise. Until the mid-1980s, full employment had been "assured" in the eastern part of the country. However, this had been achieved at the cost of outdated workshops in the villages and towns and old-fashioned industrial plants and loss-producing mines in the north. In the end, population declined in most towns in eastern Hungary in 1980–1990 (Erdösi 1993).

Figure 5.1 shows the conditions of regional development in eastern Hungary in 1990. This pattern of well-being is the outcome of the industrial decline of the late 1980s, the long-term development policy as portrayed above, and natural conditions. For at least three decades, regional backwardness in Hungary has been recognized and proposals made for its mitigation. In spite of this, instances of regional disparity grew during socialism (Miklóssy 1990). Recent studies suggest that the indifference of previous regimes towards investment in advanced economic and social capital has been a cause of regional backwardness. The region's peripheral position, set during World War I, and inherited economic and social structures are other reasons.

The transition from a socialist mode of production to capitalism, 1989–1993

The transformation of the economy to a market economy started at the beginning of 1989, and affected the whole system of agriculture. When the CMEA markets collapsed, the amount of goods sold there dropped dramatically, causing crises in production. A rapid growth in sales to Western markets was taking place, but continued trade restrictions in the Western markets meant that this growth did not balance out losses elsewhere. Hungarian agriculture was cut off from a very large portion of its traditional domestic market. Between 1989 and 1991, the retail trade in raw and processed food fell by about 30 per cent, and such decreases continued in the early 1990s. The real

133

Fig. 5.1 **The spatial structure of socio-economic well-being in eastern Hungary, 1990 (Key to regions: 1 = wealthy, 2 = wealthy, but below national average, 3 = disadvantaged, 4 = backward. Source: Süli-Zakar 1993).**

loss in sales came about as a result of the declining income of the Hungarian population. Economic output dropped, and inflation rates of around 20–30 per cent became constant, weakening trade opportunities. High interest rates (30–40 per cent) caused uncertainty for the development of production, resulting in a drastic rise in unemployment.

The crisis in agriculture accelerated when the state withdrew from agricultural administration at the height of the chaos. Food-processing companies struggling with sales problems refused to take over agricultural products, dramatically cut purchase prices, and delayed payments, thus shifting their economic burden to agricultural producers. In addition, almost all of the food-processing companies that had been privatized had been bought by foreign companies. Often multinational, these companies were not always directly interested in the development of domestic agricultural production. As a consequence, large-scale producers started downsizing and, when their integration with small producers broke up as a result, small producers went bankrupt in large numbers.

At the same time as this crisis, land reform based on property held in 1947 resulted in the breaking up of farmland into little parcels of 2–4 hectares – often too small for an independent family farm. In accordance with the Compensation Acts of 1991 and 1992 and the Cooperative Act, compensation coupons were to be given for confiscated property. Cooperatives were compelled to put up for auction the amount of land that claimants and former proprietors had the right to buy with compensation coupons. Because the nominal value of these coupons proved to be far below the value of nationalized or confiscated property, land purchases were subsidized by the state, provided customers agreed to use the land bought at auction for agricultural purposes.

Cooperatives were compelled to form two land funds. One contained the land to be auctioned, the other was to satisfy demand from cooperative members and employees. Members received about 1 hectare and employees about 0.7 hectares of land if they had no claim for compensation from the compensation land fund. Members were also entitled to a share of the cooperative property to be distributed. This phase of restructuring actually led to the partial break-up and reorganization of the former, collectively managed resource communities.

As has happened in many earlier land reforms, those who acquired land in the early stages of privatization succeeded in getting more land than those who acquired land later, the gap between the nominal value of coupons and the rising price of land increasing over time. The compensation paid to the former landowners created uncertainty for cooperative members and management, who were unable to plan their future, not knowing, as of 1993, whether or not they would have enough land and property left to survive.

The survey carried out in eastern Hungary in 1992 showed that the majority of people reclaiming land and property no longer worked in agriculture and were not likely to take up farming again. Cooperative members and those demanding compensation had the right to decide to carry on farming either in a collective or privately after the compensation demands had been settled and the cooperative's assets had been distributed. The majority of the members of former cooperatives and those working in cooperatives under transition, however, intended to continue farming within cooperative boundaries – as actually happened during the following years. The reasons stated in the 1992 survey were as follows:

- farmers have grown accustomed to this method of production: the younger generation have no experience of private farming or no willingness to take risks;
- potential farmers do not have enough machinery or other means of production;
- machinery owned by cooperatives that operate on a large scale cannot be distributed among small farms – they are too large for small farms, and too few to be available for each small farm;
- small farms do not have a suitable infrastructure: storage, trade, transport, and services have been built up for big farms;
- the state is not in a position to give sufficient support and credit to new farmers;
- before the change in the political system, the cooperatives afforded a certainty of existence, as well as social security, and many people expected this social network to remain.

In fact, most farmers in the survey claimed that they were likely to choose some combination of collective and private farming. Collective farming, of course, does not exclude private land. During the surveys in 1992, there was a perception that cooperative farms might transform themselves into purchasing, selling, and servicing companies or into collective farms where mechanized field production would remain prevalent. The large-scale growing of crops might have ensured economically efficient production – this view generally being held by those surveyed who had remained cooperative members. However, although many workers did not wish to leave the cooperatives, a large number of cooperatives had gone bankrupt, forcing many people to start their own businesses under unstable economic conditions.

The interviews in the survey led to the conclusion that the paramount stimulus among local people causing structural change was the transformation of the property system. The transition was hindered in its infancy by delays in the acquisition of land, the almost complete lack of a land market, and the high proportion of owners living in urban areas, detached from the land. This last fact led to a situation where large numbers of new owners wanted to sell land but demand was low. A solution was brought about by land-leasing and the re-formation of cooperatives. This unique economic formation played a decisive role in the production of food in Hungary in the mid-1990s. One social consequence of restructuring was that the agricultural population became socially divided and was, at least during the intense years of transition, full of tension.

The transition to a market economy brought past regional devel-opment differences even more to the surface. Transition had impli-cations for the spatial organization of agricultural production. Where technical equipment had deteriorated and there was no possibility of repairing it, the formation of cooperatives was difficult. Crises in sales affected marginal farms first. Hungarian cooperatives had many eco-nomic and social commitments and were not very competitive. Employment problems did not decrease as private ownership became dominant; they just took another form. Employment in agriculture fell significantly as a consequence of the market-led competition.

Because of the recession, companies built up their operations in cities and closed down their subsidiaries in peripheral localities. An increasing number of large-scale farms went bankrupt and signif-icantly added to the number of unemployed agricultural workers. The industrial investments of the early 1990s have not contributed much to the development of less developed regions either. Industrial plants in the country towns were usually branch plants. Their managers and employees have not had much say in development-related issues. The attempt "to become independent" witnessed in peripheral regions in the 1990s was the outcome of the desire of the main companies to dispose of the burden of regional branches. The closures of branch plants, which were often created by the former regional policy aimed at establishing new manufacturing jobs, mainly took place in the towns of the Great Plain.

The results of transition

With respect to the basic trends, Hungarian agriculture was trans-formed within uniform country-wide legislation. The law stipulated that cooperatives could not own land but that they could undertake agriculture by renting the land from owners. Although the land was legally the private property of individuals, most land was in the form of shared ownership in which plots were not individually owned.

According to one estimate, 90 per cent of the land of cooperatives became farmed by re-formed and new cooperatives. The role of re-formed cooperatives is crucial. About 800 of the 1,300 cooperatives were slimmed down, but nevertheless re-formed, concentrating on agri-business; 300 were closed down; and 200 decided to choose another form of enterprise. Some 500 new cooperatives were founded during the early years of transition.

In the period of the transition to a market economy, priority was given to the rapid enactment of the laws (compensation, privatization, cooperative transformation) promoting the reorganization of property relations. The property relations and organization that dominated agriculture for decades were radically transformed in a relatively short time by the laws of compensation and privatization.

The new property structure was mostly formed and mainly completed in the autumn of 1995. The figures in the following summary are based on an OECD report (1996, 37–38):

- of the 5.6 million hectares of collective agricultural land, one-third had legally belonged to private owners during the communist period; after setting aside 1.8 million hectares for compensation purposes, the remainder was divided between farm workers, cooperative members, or their descendants;
- some 40 per cent of state farmland was set aside for compensation, while 6 per cent was distributed to employees, leaving 54 per cent (500,000 hectares) in state ownership;
- compensation vouchers and land auctions have created over 600,000 landowners; there are now 1.5 million owners of agricultural land and over 90 per cent of agricultural land is in private hands;
- each landowner acquired about 3.5 hectares on average;
- property and land formerly owned by the cooperatives was distributed among the present members, employees, pensioners, former members, and their descendants in the main;
- owners have leased their land to farms, so that up to 80 per cent of farmland is rented;
- the share of total land used by individual farms has grown rapidly, from 22 per cent in 1993 to 46 per cent by the end of May 1995.

The proportion of land privately owned was restored to that in 1950. This new land reform did not lead to considerable fragmentation of farming because of land-leasing. In 1995, farms over 100 hectares accounted for about 58 per cent of agricultural land, farms of 5–100 hectares for 20 per cent, and small farms of under 5 hectares for about 22 per cent (OECD 1996). Hungarian agriculture was (and still is) more focused on large-scale farming compared with the EU average. Nevertheless, individual farming is growing in Hungary.

After the difficult first years of transition, the economic recession came to an end in 1994, and agricultural output began to increase in 1995, but agriculture amounted to only 6.4 per cent of GDP in 1994 as compared with 15.6 per cent in 1989 (OECD 1996, 35). Exports of agricultural and food products increased rapidly in 1994 and 1995, and 43 per cent of agro-food exports went to the European Union and 33 per cent to the former CMEA counties (ibid.). It took about five years to recover from the collapse of the market and three years from the beginning of privatization to turn the agricultural sector round. Many main crop outputs, such as maize and wheat, were still below the average crop production levels of 1986–90 in 1996, and a few crops, such as of sugar-beet and sunflower seed, exceeded the output averages of 1986–1990 in 1996. Thus, recovery has taken time.

The Europe Agreement between Hungary and the European Union came into effect at the beginning of February 1994 and aimed to integrate the Hungarian economy into the European market. Hungarian products benefited from tariff reductions, and the European Union increased import quotas yearly. Hungary also concluded an agreement on duty reductions with the other members of the Central European Free Trade Association and reduced tariffs came into effect at the beginning of January 1996. Hence, the time of uncertainty and the weak market for Hungarian agro-food products was over.

Eastern Hungary: The interpretation of transition

The effects of transition on industry

The six counties of eastern Hungary have 30 per cent of the Hungarian population but accounted for 41 per cent of the registered unemployed in both 1992 and 1995 (table 5.1). Unemployment in eastern Hungary grew considerably as a result of the layoffs of the employees of cooperatives formerly engaged in subsidiary branches. A reduction in the bureaucracy in big companies meant that unemployment also grew among white-collar workers.

Measured in terms of unemployment, the economic depression in Hungary was worst in the counties of Nógrád, to the west of eastern Hungary, Szabolcs-Szatmár-Bereg, and Borsod-Abaúj-Zemplén

Table 5.1 **Counties of eastern Hungary: Population, unemployment, and economic structure**

County	Resident population, 1996 ('000)	Unemployed ('000) 1992	Unemployed ('000) 1995	Employed in agriculture, 1995 (%)	Employed in industry, 1995 (%)
Békés	403	33.9	23.3	12	35
BAZ	746	72.0	56.4	6	39
Hajdú-Bihar	550	39.2	33.5	10	30
Heves	328	24.9	18.2	8	37
JNS	421	37.9	28.4	13	36
SSB	572	61.8	44.7	7	29
Eastern Hungary	3,020	269.8	204.5	9	35
as % of country	29.6	40.7	41.2	32.2	34.7
Country	10,212	663.0	495.9	7	30

Source: *Statistical Yearbook of Hungary 1995* (1996); *Regional Statistical Yearbook of Hungary 1995* (1996).
BAZ = Borsod-Abaúj-Zemplén, JNS = Jász-Nagykun-Szolnok, SSB = Szabolcs-Szatmár-Bereg

(Sántha 1993). Nógrád and Borsod-Abaúj-Zemplén were once the pride of socialist industrialization. As large-scale industrial production based on exports to Eastern Europe and Russia decreased, the industrial plants with their outdated equipment were closed and the workers were dismissed. Between 1992 and 1995 the number of unemployed decreased by one-quarter (table 5.1), and privatization proceeded. For instance, privatization has dramatically changed the economic structure in the county of Borsod-Abaúj-Zemplén and in its largest town, Miskolc. The economy of the county has traditionally been based on heavy industries and mining, and also chemical works, engineering, and the production of textiles and furniture. Out of 3,600 companies in the county, only 50 are still state owned. In 1997, the majority of companies (about 2,600–2,700 firms) operated as limited companies. The county's search for new processing industries involves highlighting its position as a gateway to Eastern markets and emphasizing its environmental projects, such as the efforts to create nature reserves and national parks (Chamber of Commerce of North Hungary 1997).

Large towns (e.g. Debrecen, Szolnok, Nyíregyháza, and Békéscsaba) where the economic structure was more diversified did not face as severe a crisis as many resource communities in the early 1990s. The restructuring of industrial and rural areas in Hungary is comparable, albeit for different reasons, to the spatial restructuring elsewhere in Europe, where traditional industrial districts faced development problems (especially in the 1980s) and remote rural areas suffered population loss. The European experiences in regional policy have led to the conclusion that regional policy should seek not to facilitate the mobility of production factors, as suggested by traditional approaches, but to encourage the utilization of local resources and greater productivity from local resources (Cappellin 1983; 1992, 3; Garofoli 1992). Similar approaches were haphazardly adopted in the counties of eastern Hungary in the 1990s owing to a lack of appropriate alternatives.

Although there are plenty of natural resources and production capital, the number of employees engaged in eastern Hungarian industry was too high in relation to production. In local ventures, the financial capital necessary for starting independent enterprises, along with expertise and marketing skills, was missing in the more backward regions. The shrinking of the Eastern and neighbouring country markets resulted in an increased economic role for the western part of Hungary, which benefited from better infrastructure and proximity to Western markets. Domestic and foreign investments therefore mainly flowed to this region as well as to Budapest.

Because unemployment was a new phenomenon of the 1990s in Hungary, the country possessed neither the institutions nor the mechanisms to cope with it effectively. In 1993, it was thought that the unskilled and low-skilled unemployed of eastern Hungary, who constituted a high proportion of the total unemployed, would be permanently excluded from the labour market and indefinitely marginalized socially (Süli-Zakar 1993). Although unemployment is still higher in the eastern counties, unemployment has declined considerably since 1992. The worst-case unemployment scenarios have not materialized.

Individual farming in light of the survey in eastern Hungary

It was clear from the beginning of the study that agricultural activities did not offer any remarkable solution to employment problems in the resource communities under transition. Small-scale farming did none the less spread quickly during the transition. This expansion of agricultural activity helped significantly to mitigate the unfavourable socio-economic effects of the rapidly growing unemployment in the villages of eastern Hungary, but it resulted in a decline in demand for food products and hence the subsequent crises in the food production sector. The increase in small farms and plots resulted from economic pressure, and they can, therefore, be considered to be mainly "enterprises of necessity." As wages in industry decreased (or ceased altogether), the self-supporting role of farming grew. The modernization of individual farms (Fehér 1990), however, was rare, even in areas near big cities, suggesting that these village inhabitants either had not accumulated sufficient capital or had not been able to access liquid capital for purchasing modern farm machinery.

Based on the responses to the questionnaires, the phenomenon of single-household cultivation can be divided into three groups during the transition. The first two categories are:

• *household plots*, where income comes from some external occupation, but the agricultural plot provides a considerable part of the family's daily needs for foodstuffs; farming is done by family members only after work or in retirement;
• *part-time farms*, where income is derived approximately equally from an outside occupation and from the farm; these farms are basically providing foodstuffs for household use, but the amount of production for the market may still be significant.

Cooperatives and corporations carry out farming on the large scale, but individual farms too have emerged and expanded. They constitute the third category:

• *family enterprise farms*, where the primary or exclusive source of income comes from private farming; this type of activity is based on family labour and the farmer is the sole proprietor of the agricultural enterprise; land is owned or/and rented.

New individual farms have developed almost exclusively around large towns, mainly in response to unemployment rather than to the proximity of apparently stable markets. Since 1989, a great number of household plots have changed into part-time farms, and some part-time farms have turned into family enterprises. Among those running individual farms, the number of young and middle-aged people has been growing. Those running enterprises that have arisen during the years of the transition were all under 50. Women and family members played an increasing role on the farm.

The individual farms investigated in 1992 were mostly engaged in animal breeding. Arable farming or horticulture was significant east of the Tisza River (tobacco, winter apples, vegetables) and in certain agricultural regions of Borsod-Abaúj-Zemplén county (grapes, fruit, vegetables) in the north. In the survey, 91 per cent kept pigs (55 per cent for the market), poultry could be found on almost all farms, 17 per cent bred cattle (generally provided by cooperatives for this purpose); sheep and small animals were also kept as a supplementary activity. The survey revealed that the individual farms were usually technically backward – equipment consisted of outdated, discarded machines and vehicles. The environmental impacts of small farms were serious. Pigs were kept in deplorable conditions.

In general, individual farms produced ordinary products in a conventional way. The introduction of new species of plants has had unfavourable results. Several people have either lost money or completely failed with new products such as earthworms and coypu, or with growing plants such as marrows for seed. In our view, the reason for these failures is that training and development inputs were inadequate in eastern Hungary: agricultural advisory schemes did not convey enough of the necessary information to the peripheral farms.

The individual farms investigated were, as a rule, deficient in initial capital. Without exception, they had sprung up as a result of individual savings. Some farmers had used money lent by individuals or family members, but only a few had applied for bank loans. The farmers had little information on credit for enterprises or on "start-up" loans. None the less, none of the individual farms observed was insolvent. Family houses, farm buildings, machines, animals for breeding, etc. had been built or bought from individual savings. The help of friends and families had been frequently sought. There was no sign of an economic recovery and farmers were cautious about investing. Therefore, no over-indebtedness in the agricultural regions of eastern Hungary was observed during the survey. The remarkable construction of houses during the 1970s and 1980s had been achieved with minimal credit, and the majority of the loans had been repaid by early 1991. The drastic rise in food prices did not affect the inhabitants of villages to any great extent. The majority of the participants in the survey considered themselves lucky to live in villages: in their view, it was easier for them to make both ends meet than it was for town-dwellers.

The crisis in agricultural sales and the uncertainty in property relations resulted in doubtful prospects during the transition, as observed in the survey in 1992. This was confirmed by the data on trade in agricultural equipment: only a very small proportion of the machinery and materials necessary to maintain the existing level of agriculture was actually sold.

However, at that time the economic and social consequences of the transitional process were unforeseen. The bigger the individual farm, the more thought out the farmer's future expectations were. Other surveys have produced the same result (Halász 1991). However, those who had been earning their living by running agricultural enterprises for years suggested that future prosperity would depend on a number of conditions being met. They considered that prosperity would be achieved only if the acreage of the farm could be increased, if new possibilities opened up for more intensive farming, if the necessary mechanization could be carried out, if the necessary support were given, and if products could be sold at a reasonable price. Almost every part-time farm and family enterprise stressed that integrating production in line with the needs of distributors was extremely important.

Questions concerning expert advice and agricultural services were answered by many in the survey along the lines of "my grandfather knew how to run a farm, though he also learned it from his father." There was little demand for expert advice, although the larger the farm, the more urgently it was needed. Those who did want advice required it, first, on questions of marketing and farm management – which explains the sales crisis; and, secondly, on mechanization and production technology. The demand for advice on plant protection and animal health care came third, with advice on financing fourth. This ranking reflects the fact that the agricultural enterprises of the transitional years emerged with a minimum of external capital investment. It also relates to the fact that individual farms did not intend to increase their production by means of new investments during the transition.

Intertwining activities in transition: A buffer against uncertainty

The structure of small-scale cultivation reflects the legacy of the second economic phase of the socialist period. The intertwining of activities from the formal and subsistence sectors has been an important instrument whereby individual households have been able to cope with the problems of the restructuring of the 1990s.

The majority of the survey interviewees had faith in the future of individual farms, although their arguments ("agricultural products will always be needed," "you must take on some job," "at least the family will not die of hunger," etc.) are not very convincing. They think that the rural way of life has always provided reliable protection against hostile external forces. Even people who had worked in urban-located heavy industry for 15–20 years were seeking to re-establish themselves as part of a self-sufficient farming unit during the transition. Self-sufficiency was regarded as the real strategy for survival. The survey revealed serious confusion affecting rural life: there was a deterioration in social values, a moral crisis, and the end of demands for modernization. Some considered the plea not to restore the past but to build for the future to be just propaganda.

According to the research, many descendants of pre-war tenants had continued to live in their native villages. In contrast, the majority of farm labourers' descendants had left the villages permanently over recent decades. The reorganization of traditional peasant communities has resulted in some people moving back to the villages and rejoining the agrarian society. This, in turn, has led to the strengthening of family relations, because the new agricultural enterprises have been decisively based on family loans, provision of livestock, help from retired parents, etc.

The economic turmoil brought a few young people to the countryside who saw opportunities in the villages, although it is possible that they will simply leave again at the first opportunity. In the mid-1990s, there were no attractive urban regions in Hungary, so they saw themselves as agricultural "entrepreneurs." It is relatively easy to get involved in agricultural activities – especially with help from family and friends. Thus, in the age of transition this represents one way out for many in eastern Hungary. The growth of self-sufficient farming was a buffer against uncertainty in the early 1990s.

Emerging class structures

The interviews suggest that there is hardly anyone in Hungary engaged in agriculture who, speaking about recent decades, would not complain about discrimination against agriculture. Since 1945, the Hungarian peasantry has suffered from ideological and political condemnation. Many people cannot understand why the morality of the various forms of small farming was questioned during the socialist era, or why their individual diligence was treated as objectionable. At the time of the transition to a market economy, they did not understand why their work was simply considered unnecessary. Social, political, and economic uncertainty has become a dominant feeling in the eastern part of the country. This has brought about a feeling of isolation and a strong survival instinct amongst the people. Some even say that previously self-confident, resolute, and energetic locals have become listless, hesitant, and helpless peasants (Süli-Zakar 1993). In the period between the surveys, many village people have become embittered and apathetic.

The 1992 survey, and the interviews that followed, led to the conclusion that "individual farming" is not a homogeneous phenomenon. The numerous people engaged in agricultural activities cannot be considered as a monolithic mass. New social classes are arising, such as landowners, tenants, small producers, entrepreneurs, and workers. The Hungarian situation is an interesting laboratory of class structure because of the unique combination of land-leasing and cooperatives and of small producers – both of which are uncommon in Europe.

The dynamics of development in eastern Hungary

The dynamics of agrarian development can be explained by natural conditions and the legacy of the past social structures. The comparative advantage of agriculture in the counties of the Great Hungarian Plains has been in the production of grain, oil-seeds, and horticultural products. The counties of Békés, Hajdú-Bihar, Jász-Nagykun-Szolnok, and Szabolcs-Szatmár-Bereg are all located in the Great Plain, where arable land is abundant (table 5.2.). Conditions are favourable for both cultivation and meat production based on the cultivation of cereals. High productivity has been achieved through mechanization and large-scale production. As a result, the number of employees in agriculture has decreased considerably since 1990. Agriculture officially employed 0.3 million people in 1995, or 8 per cent of the labour force (*Statistical Yearbook of Hungary 1995*), the majority of whom were employed by cooperatives (58 per cent); limited companies employed a further 38 per cent of workers in agriculture (*Regional Statistical Yearbook of Hungary 1995*).

Transformations are to be expected in the system of smaller farms as well. The organization, size, and product mix of farms are dependent upon expected profits and the capital available for investment. There is no shortcut to individual farming. The conclusion to an investigation in Borsod highlights the lack of social and financial capital; in simplistic terms, there were too many potential farmers in relation to the available resources to start efficient family farming quickly:

Table 5.2 **Counties of eastern Hungary: Arable land and agricultural enterprises by legal form**

County	Arable land as % of total land area	No. of agricultural and forestry enterprises, 1995			
		Limited companies	Cooperatives	Sole proprietors	Others
Békés	77	240	143	2,352	2,938
BAZ	39	155	179	920	1,476
Hajdú-Bihar	57	266	131	1,872	2,510
Heves	43	92	77	669	924
JNS	65	186	131	1,489	1,952
SSB	49	178	222	1,442	2,102
Eastern Hungary as % of	55	1,117	883	8,744	11,902
country	40	30.7	41.7	29.2	30.2
Country	51	3,636	2,117	29,975	39,385

Source: *Statistical Yearbook of Hungary 1995* (1996).
BAZ = Borsod-Abaúj-Zemplén, JNS = Jász-Nagykun-Szolnok, SSB = Szabolcs-Szatmár-Bereg

A number of entrepreneurs who are without professional skills and do not have enough information on market conditions have rushed into the seemingly simple – but usually foredoomed – venture of animal breeding. To set up a real farm, 300,000–400,000 *forints* is too small a sum. Further, an increase in animal husbandry in an oversupplied market is likely to prove unsuccessful. (Vincze 1991)

Appropriate technology, more developed infrastructure, and good advisory organizations are indispensable in individual farming. Yet only 9 per cent of the new agricultural enterprises examined in the 1992 survey were considered to have adequate agricultural technology, skills, and premises. Development inputs and advisory organizations are needed.

Much is expected of specialized farms. Usually their operations and labour demand are adjusted to the skills available within the family. An important locational factor for such farms is easy access to consumer markets, rather than large acreages. During previous decades, a large number of agrarian specialists were trained in Hungary. A considerable number of them may still either be not fully employed or have started new companies out of necessity. The agricultural polytechnics of eastern Hungary (Debrecen, Nyíregyháza, Karcag, Szarvas, Mezőtúr), however, continue to train agrarian experts in

great numbers. These may become farmers and managers of specialized farms in the future.

The survey showed that, in the villages of eastern Hungary, there
are motivated people who are ready to adopt new types of agricultural activity and are open to information and new technologies, but
it also showed that much needs to be done in order to enhance economic and social capital in rural areas. A significant part of the agricultural potential in these villages can also be explained by the fact
that the industrialization of past decades maintained rural lifestyles.
Keeping the cottages, fostering family relations, and topping up
unsatisfactory earnings from industry by working in the "second
economy" (the informal agrarian economy) contributed to the survival of a semi-rural way of life and preserved the skills of small-scale
farming.

One central aim of agricultural policy in eastern Hungary in the
latter half of the 1990s will be to raise the incentives necessary for the
modernization of farming and to promote investment in agriculture,
which was delayed because of the transition (Illés 1993). Consequently, the second important task of agrarian policy is to support
structural changes to increase the competitiveness of farming, and to
strengthen a counselling service for farming. Agricultural unemployment increased in this part of the country in the first half of the 1990s.
Thus, the third important task of agrarian policy is to assist the agricultural population to earn a living without forcing them to leave
their place of residence, and to expand the economic base in order to
create new job opportunities in the agrarian regions.

Achieving a balance in future development

Diversification

The number of people employed in agriculture has fallen considerably since the beginning of the transition, and there is no sensible
way to increase labour-intensive, small-scale farming except during a
severe crisis. Furthermore, many new entrepreneurs in the villages
will be likely to give up their agricultural activity, which provides
them with only a hand-to-mouth existence. To relieve unemployment, it is necessary for the other sectors of the economy to develop
and grow.

Even if Hungarian products could be sold without quotas in the
EU markets in the near future, agricultural production is not

expected to grow very much, and, according to plans (Sántha 1993), at least 10 per cent of the arable land should probably cease to be utilized for agricultural production. The only solution in many of the marginal areas in eastern Hungary, as elsewhere, may be afforestation, although, in some areas, extensive animal breeding and more sustainable farming could be established. Most of these tracts are not industrialized, are less polluted than average, and have an abundance of rare species. Thus, agriculture, silviculture, wildlife, protection of the environment, tourism, and the services based on these activities could be linked and developed in these regions.

The role of local and regional authorities

An indisputable result of the transition in Hungary has been the growth of the role and independence of local and county governance. This means that the necessary resources for the operation of the local districts and the counties must be ensured. The strengthening of the administration at the intermediate level began during the transition. When the transition started there were few development projects and the lack of funding was evident. According to the post-Fordist governance model and considering the legacy of Hungarian governance, overcoming these problems requires the strengthening of actors as partners, and the development of associations between local governments and the creation of business coalitions within the same region. This development would be particularly justified if Hungary becomes a member of the European Union, because various private and public partners are assumed to exist in EU policy programmes. Otherwise, development will be constrained by the lack of partners, as Syrett (1997) envisages.

With greater responsibility for the future of their resource communities, local governments need to encourage economic development through enterprise development schemes and through the creation of infrastructure in accordance with local conditions. The allocation of funds for research and development in companies increases productivity and profitability (Husso et al. 1996). Companies need access to modern communication networks provided by up-to-date infrastructure. Various regional development strategies seek to promote factors internal to firms, such as technological, managerial, and entrepreneurial capabilities. Other strategies attempt to foster networking and creative milieux to promote the adoption of innovation in the various regional economies (Molle and Cappellin

1988; Cappellin and Nijkamp 1990; Malmberg et al. 1996). However, these strategies require research, technology, and training inputs into a region – and the funding of these inputs necessitates public–private partnerships.

The environment of these resource communities, and the countryside in general, should also be improved, so that residents consider the areas worth living in. Apart from their aesthetic appearance, local cultural values can increase the attraction of towns and villages. This can be ensured through appropriate town planning and a conscious effort to integrate environmental and economic interests.

Further, the increasing independence of regions has led to the situation of border regions seeking to restore economic contacts with regions that were intrinsically linked to eastern Hungary (Tóth 1993). This is economically important for eastern Hungary, which seeks to be a gateway to Romania and Ukraine. Supra-regional integration in the Carpathian Euro-region is evolving, which is expected to boost the resource communities of eastern Hungary in the future. On the other hand, lower wages attract companies to locate their branch plants in countries where production costs are lower than in eastern Hungary, for instance in Romania. If Hungary were to join the European Union in the early 2000s, integration into EU markets would provide new instruments for promoting development.

Conclusion

The immediate effects of the collapse of the previous socialist system can be summed up as follows:
• both serious upheaval in society and a drastic decline in the economy led to a strengthening of family ties and the growth of the informal economy (i.e. the second economy);
• the social ties and values required for self-sufficiency strengthened;
• the intertwining of economic activities in the formal and informal economic sectors provided protection against the severe consequences of economic recession;
• a return to the countryside became a solution for some in Hungary because it provided better and more secure opportunities for everyday life.

The second economy was developed during the socialist period in Hungary and it provided a flexible and valuable buffer for individuals against uncertainty during the transition.

Lively discussion on local development and local development strategies has taken place in the academic literature in recent years. Economic development policy has shifted from national and regional measures to local policy, local initiatives, partnerships, and development corporations in many developed countries. The socio-economic transition in Hungary has not been an exception, though problems have been more severe there, and the restructuring of the former socialist countries has been much more overwhelming than restructuring in the West. After the abolition of the former rigid and regulative institutions of socialism, *laissez-faire* and individualism were strongly emphasized. Simultaneously, the development of new economic structures was also begun. The rural transition of Hungary is an excellent example of the balancing of different factors in order to achieve economic and social recovery. Political choices, local-specific conditions, sectoral development paths, and individual actions are interrelated elements of development.

With respect to farming in the countryside, the recent combination of collective and individual farming and private ownership of land seems to be a solid foundation for recovery. The initial results of reformed farming, the introduction of leaseholds as a result of the privatization of land, and the reorganization of the public sector are all leading Hungarian society towards a unique community structure. Nevertheless, it is necessary to point out that the growth of the economy mainly originates from non-agricultural sectors.

The Hungarian case illustrates that the fundamental changes and development processes of capitalism are not predetermined. It also shows that the existence of community-based development practices depends largely on residents' willingness and ability to enhance social and economic development in a market economy. We can explain community development by introducing the interpretation that the resource communities are being replaced by communities with conditions that are suitable for post-Fordist production, as well as encompassing the unique local environs. Furthermore, this process is being influenced by the legacy of social structures and capital and by citizens' expectations of future development.

References

Cappellin, R. (1983), "Productivity Growth and Technological Change in a Regional Perspective," in Giornale degli Economisti (ed.), *Annali di Economia* 42, pp. 459–482.

——— (1992), "Theories of Local Endogenous Development and International

Cooperation," in M. Tykkyläinen (ed.), *Development Issues and Strategies in the New Europe*, Avebury, Aldershot, pp. 1–19.

Cappellin, R. and Nijkamp, P. (eds.) (1990), *The Spatial Context of Technological Development*, Avebury, Aldershot.

Chamber of Commerce of North Hungary (1997), "Regional Corner: Borsod-Abaúj-Zemplén County, Hungary," unpublished material.

EC (European Communities) (1991), *Central and Eastern Europe 1991*, Statistisches Bundesamt and Eurostat, Office for Official Publications of the European Communities, Luxembourg.

Erdösi, F. (1993), "Regionale Prozesse und Erscheinungen in Ungarn Ende des 20. Jahrhundert," in A. Aubert, F. Erdösi, and J. Tóth (eds.), *Regional Problems in East-Central Europe after the Political Changes*, Department of General Social Geography and Urbanistics and Centre for Regional Studies of the Hungarian Academy of Sciences, Pécs, pp. 7–40.

Fehér, A. (1990), "A vállalaton belüli vállakozások és a privatizáció a mezögazdaságban," *Gazdálkodás* 34(10), pp. 1–6.

Garofoli, G. (ed.) (1992), *Endogenous Development and Southern Europe*, Avebury, Aldershot.

Halász, P. (1991), "A mezögazdasági kistermelés szerepe a települések fejlödésében," in T. Kovács (ed.), *Válság és kiút*, MTA RKK, Pécs, pp. 39–43.

Hirschman, A. O. (1970), *Exit, Voice and Loyalty*, Harvard University Press, Cambridge, Mass.

Husso, K., Leppälahti, A., and Niininen, P. (1996), "R&D, Innovation and Firm Performance. Studies on the Panel Data of Finnish Manufacturing Firms," *Statistics Finland, Science and Technology* 1996:3.

Illés, I. (1993), *Az Alföld rövid távú területfejlesztési koncepciója*, Alföld Projekt Programiroda, Kecskemét.

Keefe, E. K., Brenneman, L. E., Giloane, W., Long, A. K., Moore, J. M., Jr., and Walpole, N. A. (1987), *Hungary. A Country Study*, United States Government, Headquarters, Department of Army, Washington.

Malmberg, A., Sölvell, Ö., and Zander, I. (1996), "Spatial Clustering, Local Accumulation of Knowledge and Firm Competitiveness," *Geografiska Annaler* 78B(2), pp. 85–97.

Miklóssy, E. (1990), "Magyarország belsö gyarmatosítása," *Tér és Társadalom* 4(2), pp. 1–13.

Molle, W. and Cappellin, R. (eds.) (1988), *Regional Impact of Community Policies in Europe*, Avebury, Aldershot.

OECD (Organization for Economic Cooperation and Development) (1996), *Agricultural Policies, Markets and Trade in Transition Economies*, OECD, Paris.

Regional Statistical Yearbook of Hungary 1995 (1996), Central Statistical Office, Budapest.

Sántha, A. (1993), "The Position and the Possibilities of the Development of Rural Areas in Hungary," typescript. Paper submitted to the editors.

Statistical Yearbook of Hungary 1995 (1996), Central Statistical Office, Budapest.

Süli-Zakar, I. (1985), "Elargissement des activités des coopératives agricoles et leur influence sur la société rurale," in *Le Changement Social dans les Campagnes*, Actes du Xième colloque franco-hongrois de géographie, Université Paul Valéry, Montpellier, pp. 217–239.

—— (1993), "A Socio-Geographical Study of New Rural Enterprises in Peripherizing Eastern Hungary," typescript. Paper submitted to the editors.

Syrett, S. (1997), "The Politics of Partnership. The Role of Social Partners in Local Economic Development in Portugal," *European Urban and Regional Studies* 4(2), pp. 99–114.

Tóth, J. (1993), "Conception of the Multidisciplinary Studies in Connection with the Carpathians-Tisza Region", in A. Aubert, F. Erdösi, and J. Tóth (eds.), *Regional Problems in East-Central Europe after the Political Changes*, Department of General Social Geography and Urbanistics and Centre for Regional Studies of the Hungarian Academy of Sciences, Pécs, pp. 110–118.

Vincze, J. (1991), "Egyes speciális pénzüyi alapok felhasználásának tapasztalatai Borsod-Abaúj-Zemplén magyében," in L. Lackó (ed.), *Válságtérségek Magyarországon*, Hungarian Academy of Sciences, Budapest, pp. 35–50.

6

Restructuring and articulation of the modes of production in Russian Karelian villages

Eira Varis

Introduction

This paper examines restructuring in rural Russia. Restructuring has been defined as a series of fundamental socio-economic changes in which the old structure of a society is replaced by a new structure that is characteristically different from the old one (Tykkyläinen 1993, 61). In a regional study of restructuring, it is essential that both historical and geographical components are considered. The concept of restructuring specifically includes qualitative changes in a community, for example the closure of old industries and the rapid emergence of new ones. In general, communities are transforming their socio-economic structures and functions in the face of external impulses and local responses (ibid.). Changes in the ownership of the means of production denote indisputably that restructuring is taking place.

The rural areas of the Karelian Republic in north-western Russia (later Karelia) have undergone a constant process of socio-economic restructuring throughout the past half-century, as a consequence of the various attempts that were made to improve the operation of the socialist system there. This socialist system has now collapsed, and a market economy is penetrating the former socialist fabric. Rural areas are again facing a new stage of transition.

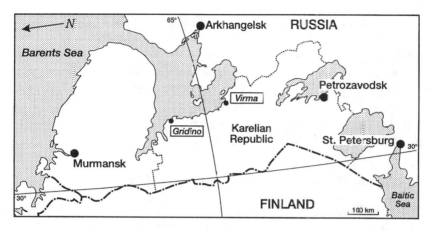

Fig. 6.1   **Virma and Gridino on the White Sea.**

This paper looks at rural development in Karelia during this extended period of socio-economic restructuring by examining development in two rural villages: Virma and Gridino on the White Sea (fig. 6.1). Originally they were resource communities in which people's livelihood was based on fishing. The data were collected through thematic interviews and systematic structured interviews (Yin 1989) carried out in the course of field studies in Virma and Gridino in 1991 and 1993. The material collected on the field trips was supplemented with statistical data and data from archives, papers, and books. Virma and Gridino represent two distinct lines of development. By comparing their development, it is possible to understand some of the different processes that have influenced the outcome of the transition, and to suggest explanations of the restructuring process of rural Karelia.

The findings of this study reaffirm the extent to which development at the local level can be determined by national decision-making, regardless of what the local inhabitants may do. However, the comparison of the two communities also highlights how, even in a centrally planned economy, the same external political decisions can have very different consequences for different communities in the same peripheral region, depending on the specific characteristics of these communities. Examination of the different patterns of restructuring that occurred in the two villages demonstrates the importance not only of factors directly relevant to productive activities, but of

155

local leadership and of local attitudes that emerge in response to the impacts of past, as well as present, processes of restructuring.

This paper also shows how the different consequences of externally initiated policies can have profound implications for the way communities restructure in response to subsequent external pressures, not only in terms of the opportunities and constraints they generate for future development, but also in the extent to which different systems of production overlap simultaneously.

The articulation of the modes of production

In the socialist system, the economy was based on centrally led planning and ideologically driven policies. The concept of the "logic of socialism" refers to this economic system and its centrally planned functioning principles, which allocate each locality a certain productive role within the spatial division of labour. The elements of the logic of socialism considered in this study are the formation of a spatial division of labour through the system of economic regions in the former Soviet Union, where production was organized according to the idea of territorial production complexes (Kolosovskiy 1961; Bandman 1985; de Souza 1989).

The logic of socialism has not been able to ensure the reproduction of the labour force, so another form of production has developed alongside it. This occurs in the form of a self-sufficient household economy, based on family relationships. In earlier times, this self-sufficiency occurred on the privately owned small farms of *kolkhoz* workers. Nowadays, it occurs as private farming and small-scale cattle rearing, which provide a source of livelihood not only in the rural areas but also in urban areas among those people who have connections with the countryside. This is linked to the idea of "the summer village," which forms one basis for food support throughout the whole of Karelia (Varis 1993; 1994).

Recently, a third form of production, a new market-based economy, has appeared as a consequence of the collapse of the former social system. This market economy, as it functions in the 1990s however, has features from the old structures superimposed on it (fig. 6.2).

The theoretical framework for this study, therefore, has been drawn from concepts underpinning articulation theories, developed mainly to understand the structure of economies in developing or

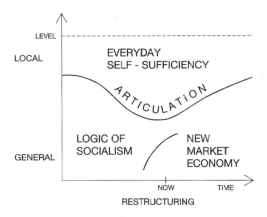

Fig. 6.2 **The articulation of the three modes of production.**

peripheral countries. These theories (Torp 1980; Amin 1976; Meilla-soux 1987) highlight the fact that two different means of production may overlap each other in the same area (Wolpe 1987). In this study, the concept of articulation has been used as a way of understanding the socio-economic restructuring that has happened in Karelia, where three forms of production have come together in the one region – one based on the "logic of socialism", one on a market-based economy, and one on everyday self-sufficiency (see fig. 6.2).

This paper examines the key factors affecting local development in each of the different periods of Soviet and associated Karelian history between 1928 and 1995. Certain external economic and social politi-cal decisions have had a decisive effect on rural restructuring and adjustment in Karelia. In analysing the restructuring process below, particular attention is paid to these decisions (Rannikko and Varis 1994, 42). The outcome of restructuring is analysed in the context of the articulation of the three different modes of production discussed above.

The restructuring of the society is examined in long periods, start-ing from the collectivization of the land at the end of the 1920s, and ending with the penetration of the new economic order in the 1990s. This chain of processes is interpreted in terms of its influence at a local level. The study demonstrates that restructuring has occurred in each period. The final section elaborates on the factors associated with the different dimensions of restructuring, from universal com-ponents to individual responses to restructuring in the communities.

The periods of restructuring in Karelia

The collectivization of agriculture

The implementation of the national economic Five Year Plans began in the Soviet Union in 1928. The collectivization of agriculture and other rural industries, including fishing, was carried out soon after.

The location of Virma and Gridino meant that fishing had traditionally been their main source of livelihood. Fishing *kolkhozy* were founded in both villages in 1930. The economy and production were organized according to collectivist principles: private property was collectivized, land ownership was transferred to the state, and almost every household joined the *kolkhoz*.

The *kolkhoz* took care not only of production but also of public services in the village. The life of the village took shape from its productive role. Life and work in the *kolkhoz* were strictly regulated, and movements were controlled by passport restrictions. The life of the 1930s was one of hard work and social control.

At the same time, the Stalinist policy of standardization was strong. Small nationalities, in particular, suffered from this policy. In Karelia, the policy was directed at Fenno-Ugric nationalities such as the Karelians and Finns, and their numbers decreased dramatically.

The impact of the war

World War II extended to Karelia, part of which was in a war zone. Villages in northern Karelia were evacuated, although after the war citizens returned to their home villages. Virma and Gridino were located outside the areas of operations, so they were not evacuated. The war, however, affected the whole of Karelia. In both villages there are memorials to villagers who died during the conflict. During the war, the *kolkhozy* were closed. Women took care of the activities necessary for day-to-day survival while the men were fighting in the war.

The war caused some significant changes in the territorial structure of Karelia. The areas taken from Finland by force were mainly incorporated in Karelia. These former Finnish territories were evacuated, and new populations, mainly Belorussians and Ukrainians, migrated to settle there.

The impact of increased forestry development

In the 1950s, forests became the region's most valuable natural resource. Forestry and forest industries were, therefore, seen as the most appropriate production sectors for Karelia, and vertically integrated forest industry complexes were built. The economic potential of forestry was also increased by production plants seized from Finland. Construction began on special forest villages (*lesopunkt*), which got new inhabitants. With this emphasis on forestry, the closure of agricultural *kolkhozy* and the reduction in fishing *kolkhozy* were seen as appropriate by central planners.

The labour from the *kolkhozy* was released to do forest work and urban industrial work. The forest industries came to represent Karelia's role in the system of production. A large proportion of the inhabitants of Virma and Gridino moved to cities and to forest work. A forestry unit was founded in a village next to Virma, and this attracted population from surrounding areas. Gridino, however, did not lose as many people, because of its working *kolkhoz* and the passport restrictions.

The commitment to the policy of big economic units

The aim of the agricultural and settlement policies was to increase productivity and efficiency. Since low productivity was associated with high costs, the rationalization of production and regional structure in rural areas was considered necessary. There were also aspirations to abolish the main differences between rural and urban areas in economic performance (Orfinski and Grisina 1994).

In the 1960s, the policy of "no prospect" villages (that is, villages with no potential for a viable future) was introduced. These villages were too small economically, and maintaining their public services was considered too expensive. In the rural villages perceived to have no future prospects, public services such as schools, libraries, medical centres, and shops were closed (Klementyev 1991, 47). In northern Russia, about two out of three villages were considered to be villages with no future (Eronen 1993).

At the same time, poor living conditions also encouraged people to move away (*Problemy Ekonomicheskogo ... * 1989). Young people, in particular, did not want to stay in villages with poor services or facilities, and the better wages of forestry work attracted them elsewhere.

The most important social and political decisions concerning Virma and Gridino proved to be those associated with the rationalization of fishing production. Fishing production was centralized in the most efficient, or in other ways advantageous, *kolkhozy*. In 1960, the *kolkhoz* of Virma was closed, together with 16 other Karelian fishing *kolkhozy*. The *kolkhoz* of Virma was a "millionaire *kolkhoz*" (which meant that it had surpassed its target for production), but its location near the Belomorsk fishing industries was a disadvantage. The catch along the White Sea coastline was limited, and competing units had to be closed. This political decision, along with the "no prospect" village policy, led to the suspension of Virma's "village soviet" status. The life of the village began to disintegrate.

In contrast, the village of Gridino was considered to be a village with future prospects. Its production unit, the fishing *kolkhoz*, was saved. Despite its isolated location, the *kolkhoz* was considered an effective centre for its district, because of its knowledge of fishing. Another important reason for its survival was that seaweed produced by the *kolkhoz* was strategically important, because it was being used as raw material in the food industry and in some manufacturing sectors. The productive role of Gridino was strong enough to keep the village alive.

The period of stagnation

The era of Brezhnev after 1964 can be divided into two phases (Iivonen and Paastela 1989). The first phase, from 1964 to the second half of 1970, was a period of relatively stable economic progress. The second phase involved the slowing down of economic growth and the centralization of power. So far as Virma and Gridino are concerned, however, it is not possible to differentiate distinct local development processes occurring in the first and the second phases of this era.

Rural conditions during this era were constantly changing in Karelia. Production was rationalized with the aim of increasing economic efficiency. By the end of the 1960s, forestry work had decreased and the need for forestry labour diminished. The consequence was rural depopulation and increased urbanization. Overall, the number of inhabitants in Karelia declined: between 1959 and 1970, external political decisions resulted in a reduction in the number of Karelian rural villages from 1,553 to 1,069. Rural depopulation became possible with the abrogation of the law on passport restrictions affecting *kolkhoz* workers, and was accelerated by poor living conditions (*Problemy Ekonomicheskogo* ... 1989).

The period of *perestroika*

In 1985, Mikhail Gorbachev was elected President of the Soviet Union and Chairman of the Communist Party. It was the beginning of the new era of *perestroika* and *glasnost*. The new political decisions aimed to consolidate the socialist foundations of Soviet society by rationalizing the national economic and political systems to counter the decline in economic growth. The first years of the period were ones of progressive development, even though some of the goals were not fulfilled. The national income increased, unemployment was insignificant, and the inflation rate was low. After 1989, however, all sectors of the national economy began to collapse, and this economic crisis led to the collapse of the Soviet Union (Iivonen 1992).

The *perestroika* policy once again meant upheavals in the rural areas of Karelia. With the rapid rationalization of the economy, rural living conditions quickly worsened. The delivery of public services was disrupted, and food supplies ran low in rural areas. There was even rationing of consumer goods. The accessibility of general services deteriorated.

This gave rise to the growth in private household gardening. The significance of old people's rural houses changed, becoming essential for the whole family's food management. The old people tend small private gardens, in which potatoes and vegetables are grown for the whole family, including its urban members. Private gardening is based on family relations, with the urban relatives helping with planting and harvesting. Cattle are also kept for the needs of the whole family. It is estimated that one-third of Karelia's food supplies come from small private gardens (Karkinen and Oksa 1994). Thus, the importance of everyday self-sufficiency increased remarkably during the *perestroika* period.

The inhabitants of Virma, having lost their *kolkhoz* and their village soviet status, felt forgotten. The period of *perestroika* did not halt the decline of the village. Decisions concerning their life were made somewhere far away. There were no deputies in the village soviet of Sumskii Posad to which Virma was joined. There were doubts about whether anyone was taking care of their affairs any more.

The reaction towards *perestroika* was different in Gridino. The *kolkhoz* got a new chairman, who began to modernize. The *kolkhoz* bought new fishing ships with refrigeration systems, which made long fishing trips to the Barents Sea possible. This meant that the significance of the fishing stations located along the coast declined. Infrastructure was also improved: the village got electricity and a new road. The influence of the *kolkhoz* was very important in every aspect of village life, whereas that of the village soviet was only marginal.

However, the modernization of the Gridino *kolkhoz* by its chairman met resistance, because people felt that the chairman was using the *kolkhoz* for his own interests. He has since left the village, even though some of the villagers supported him. The change in the social system shook the stable order of the village and caused many personal and social problems.

The collapse of the Soviet Union

After the Soviet Union collapsed, and Yeltsin became President, the transformation of the socialist system to a market economy began, together with a commitment to the democratization of the political system. The principles of private ownership of land and of the means of production were adopted, and a policy of privatization implemented. In autumn 1993, the Land Reformation Law was passed, making the private ownership of land possible, although land was not yet really tradable in the mid-1990s.

At the local level, the collapse of the previous system and its consequences have caused uncertainty about the future. The change to a market economy has resulted in upheaval and led to the self-seeking exploitation of a confused economic situation. The transformation has made everyday rural life worse. With it have come mainly negative impacts, such as the rejection of work, empty shelves in shops, and increased alcohol problems. Privatization has confused ordinary people, among whom there is no tradition of private ownership or entrepreneurship. They do not know what to do with the privatization vouchers; most of them have given their vouchers to their children or sold them to buyers from outside the village. Whereas, in Virma, attitudes to privatization were mainly negative, Gridino has more active-aged people and also more positive attitudes towards privatization.

The factors associated with restructuring

The development of Virma and Gridino demonstrates how people at the local level can react to restructuring in different ways. Restructuring has occurred in several different parts of society, but restructuring at every level has decisively affected development at the local level (Tykkyläinen 1993, 63; Tykkyläinen and Neil 1995).

Factors associated with four different dimensions have affected the evolution of the current situation in Gridino and Virma (see table 6.1):
1. broad-based policies and decision-making at the national level;
2. sector-specific factors, in this case activities associated with fishing production;
3. the locality, important in that it has determined both the productive role of each place and the possibilities for different household activities directed at everyday self-sufficiency;
4. the reaction of local individuals to external political decisions.

The general and sectoral factors, the properties of a locality, and individual reactions are not clearly separated, and many of them overlap.

General factors and decision-making

The socialist system and the process of decision-making in accordance with the logic of socialism were integral to the development processes in Virma and Gridino. The most important goal of the decision makers was efficient economic and productive development nationwide. The spatio-administrative instrument of the logic of socialism was the economic regions, in accordance with the planned spatial division of labour. The tool of the spatial organization of economic activities was the territorial production complex. Rural areas were viewed as sources of raw materials and labour, not as human environments. Attempts were made to reduce the distinction between rural and urban areas in the standard of living and economic performance.

Karelia has been the border area of a "Moscow-centric" society. It has been seen as a peripheral region, whose function was to produce forestry products. In terms of food production, Karelia has not been self-sufficient, and only its fishing industry has had any significance outside Karelia.

At the same time, the strategic location of Karelia on the borders

Table 6.1 The socialist and post-socialist restructuring in Russia and its manifestation in the rural communities of Virma and Gridino

Time	General	Sectoral	Level	
			Locality	Individual
1929	Collectivization of agri-culture Passport restriction law 1933	Collectivization of fishing	Local resources-based production Foundation of fishing *kolkhozy* Workers' commitment to *kolkhoz*	Joining *kolkhozy* Kulaks Social control and "strict" work
1939–45	War	Production shut-downs	*Kolkhozy* languish Men at war, women take care of livelihood	Stress and loss due to WWII
1950	Booming economy Forestry boosts Karelian society Policy of large economic units	Territorial division of production and specialization Rationalization of fishing	Relocation from war areas "Millionaire" *kolkhozy*	Living and welfare by working
1959	Policy of "no-prospect" villages	Centralization of production	The closeness of Belomorsk affects V. – *kolkhoz* closed, workers move to *sovkhozy* Abolition of village soviet in V. The importance of seaweed and its isolated location benefit G. Depopulation	Urban services and better wages in forestry attract young people Weakened services
1964	Period of stagnation Passport restriction abrogation	Modernization of production	Modernization aspirations in G. V. disintegrates Rural and urban differences grow	

1985	*Perestroika*	Technological development	Summer village process begins Public services weaken The importance of transport connections grows Social problems increase	Living conditions worsen and self-sufficiency grows Modernization in G. New families in G.
1991	Collapse of the Soviet Union	Reorganization of production Privatization	Road and electricity come to G. Privatization of plots Reorganization of *kolkhoz* in G. Western consumer goods available	Confusion and uncertainty Social problems, and a lack of discipline

Note: V = Virma; G = Gridino.

of Western Europe has been reflected in the evolution of the area. The areas evacuated during the war got new inhabitants from the southern Soviet Union, when Fenno-Ugric nationals were excluded, but a wide, uninhabited, border zone has been retained.

The centrally planned decision-making process extended to all areas of the state. When the Soviet Union collapsed in 1991, the creation of a new state and social order began. Nowadays, privatization is taking shape and new social structures are developing.

Sector-specific factors

Sectored production meant that every locality had its special productive role. The development of Virma and Gridino was determined by the goal of efficiency in the fishing industry. Thus, they were affected by the rationalizing of the fishing industry at the turn of the 1960s.

Because of the hierarchical, top–down system of decision-making, there was no way, at the local level, of influencing decisions. The *kolkhoz* of Virma surpassed its target, but was none the less closed. This meant the dispersal of the villagers, and the disintegration of the village as it had been. The territorialization of fishing waters also affected the amount of the catch. The most important fishing grounds are located in the Kola area, where the fishing company Sevryba also has its headquarters. There were enough fishing units there to handle the fishing along the White Sea coast, and production was centralized. On the other hand, the *kolkhoz* of Gridino was not one of the best in terms of productivity, but was none the less saved because it was an important producer of seaweed.

In the 1990s the Gridino *kolkhoz* is becoming a centre of its territory's fishing production. There are plans to combine with two other fishing *kolkhozy*. The aim is more efficient production, and the new management and technology of production are developing in association with privatization.

Local-specific features

Important local features have determined the potential for the fishing industry in Virma and Gridino: good water connections and sheltered bays.

Both villages are traditionally old "pomor" (a tribe living by the White Sea) villages, and some features of this culture have remained, despite the earlier policy of cultural standardization. These remnants of traditional culture can be seen in different fields of culture, such as religion, architecture, or craftwork traditions (Orfinski and Grisina 1994; Skvortsova 1993). The old traditions have been preserved by old women, who are transmitting them to their grandchildren.

Standardizing politics, however, have brought things like club-houses to every village. These are social centres, where official meetings also take place. In Virma, the clubhouse was no longer in use in the 1990s, but in Gridino it is used actively – there were even plans to build a new clubhouse.

Virma has good road and railway connections, whereas the road to Gridino is only a few years old. Accessibility was not, however, a saving factor for Virma. This village was located "too near" the Belomorsk fishing industry, and, therefore, competed for the same catch. The isolated location of Gridino seems to have been its source of rescue, because of its favourable position in relation to gathering important forms of seaweed.

The reaction of individuals – the human factor

The decisions of the *kolkhoz* influenced all village activities. The *kolkhoz* also worked as a part of the wider fishing organization, and this further influenced its authority. Most villagers have been members of the *kolkhoz* and, therefore, used to listen to the *kolkhoz* leaders on many practical matters. The *kolkhoz* was a very authoritative unit, and relations between the leaders and the members played a significant role in household activities aimed at everyday self-sufficiency (Jussila 1994).

During the period in which fishing production was rationalized, the management of the *kolkhoz* at Gridino were apparently very active in saving their *kolkhoz*. The *perestroika* era made it possible to modernize the enterprise. On the other hand, their "outsider" chairman had to leave the village, the resistance probably being caused by his excessive modernizing. Since he left, a village-born engineer has been leading the *kolkhoz*. He is regarded as being familiar with "village things" and knowing how to make the best of the village. The future of the village is seen positively.

Gridino is a self-governing village soviet, but the local authority has had only marginal influence over village activities. It mostly deals with recruiting school teachers, running the village shop, and collecting population statistics. In the mid-1990s, the role of the village soviet was changing in line with privatization. It will soon acquire a new role organizing public services (Karkinen and Oksa 1994).

Virma lost its productive role, the *kolkhoz*, when fishing production was rationalized in 1960. At the same time, it lost its status as a village soviet and was demoted to the category of a rural village. Nowadays, the future of the village is seen in terms of its new role as a summer village and a location of private gardening.

Conclusion

In this paper, the rural restructuring process of Russian Karelia has been analysed. At the local level, this restructuring could take different directions, as happened in the case-study villages, Virma and Gridino. The development of these two communities has been affected by the interaction of both broader social processes and distinctive local factors. Economic and social decisions were made in line with the principles of a centrally planned society ("the logic of socialism"), which extended to even the most peripheral rural villages. The most important factor in each place was its productive function, that is, its role in the spatial division of labour.

At the local level, the logic of socialism was articulated with self-sufficient action in order to maintain everyday life. The articulation of the logic of socialism and self-sufficiency in everyday life varied during the different periods of restructuring. The general mode of production has as a rule been transformed by the new market economy in Russia. This means that the countryside is adapting itself to the market-led spatial division of labour. Some villages have become summer villages, which feed people through private gardening. On the other hand, those resource communities that have been able to maintain their productive position have also had to adapt to the changes in the society.

It is likely that the near future will be mostly affected by the privatization process and the transition towards a market economy. At this stage, privatization is incomplete and its consequences can only be estimated. However, structures do not change quickly, and the transition will need at least one generation.

The art of living in remote resource communities in Russia in the 1990s means living day-by-day. Achieving everyday self-sufficiency takes all people's energies. Wages and pensions are not enough to buy basic necessities, so livelihood has to be based on self-sufficiency. Rather than understanding privatization or the political changes, an ordinary rural inhabitant is more interested in the adequacy of the potato crop, or how to get hay to the cattle in order to feed the family during the next winter. Essential in the restructuring process is the continuity of transition. The form that privatization takes will be decisive in how it proceeds and whether or not it succeeds in the long term.

References

Amin, S. (1976), *Imperialism and Unequal Development*, Harvester Press, Sussex.

Bandman, M. (ed.) (1985), *Regional Development in the USSR – Modelling the Formation of Soviet Territorial-Production Complexes*, Pergamon Press, Oxford.

Eronen, J. (1993), "Venäläinen ja suomalainen periferia: Permin Komin ja Kainuun aluetaloudellista vertailua," *Review of Economies in Transition* 9/1993, pp. 19–46.

Iivonen, J. (1992), "Neuvostovallan viimeiset vuodet," *Ulkopoliitikan instituutin julkaisuja*, no. 1, Gummerus, Jyväskylä.

Iivonen, J. and Paastela, J. (1989), *Idän muuttuvat suurvallat. Kiina ja Neuvostoliitto*, Weilin and Göös, Espoo.

Jussila, O. (1994), "Mitä oli Neuvostoliitto?" *Historiallinen Aikakauskirja* 1/94, pp. 3–9.

Karkinen, K. and Oksa, J. (1994), "Ruokaa metsätyökylille, Karjalan tasavallan metsäyhtiöiden aputalouksien kehittämisprojektin raportti," *Joensuun yliopiston täydennyskoulutuskeskuksen julkaisuja, sarja B: oppimateriaalia*, no. 7, Joensuu.

Klementyev, J. I. (1991), *Karely, Karjalazet, Etnograficeskii ocerk*, Karelija, Petrozavodsk.

Kolosovskiy, N. N. (1961), "The Territorial-Production Combination (Complex) in Soviet Economic Geography," *Journal of Regional Science* 3(1), pp. 1–25.

Meillasoux, C. (1987), "Uusintamisesta tuotantoon," in P. Valtonen (ed.), *Kulttuuri ja talous, Kirjoituksia taloudellisesta antropologiasta*, Transactions of the Finnish Anthropological Society 19, pp. 128–141.

Orfinski, V. and Grisina, I. (1994), "Karjalainen Talo," *Carelia* 6/94, pp. 118–129.

Problemy Ekonomicheskogo i Social'nogo Razvitija Karelii (1989), Akademii nauk SSSR, Karel'skii filial, Otdel ekonomiki, Nauka, Leningrad.

Rannikko, P. and Varis, E. (1994), "Rural Development in Russian Karelia and Eastern Finland," in H. Eskelinen, J. Oksa, and D. Austin (eds.), *Russian Karelia in Search of a New Role*, Karelian Institute, University of Joensuu, Joensuu, pp. 41–56.

Skvortsova, G. (1993), "Peilissä Pomoria eli visiitti Vienalandiaan," *Carelia* 12/93, pp. 110–124.

Souza, P. de (1989), "Territorial Production Complexes in the Soviet Union – With a Special Focus on Siberia," University of Gothenburg, Departments of Geography, Series B, no. 80, Gothenburg, Sweden.

Torp, J. E. (1980), "Kehitysmaiden taloudellisen kehityksen teoriat, Johdatus liberaaliin ja marxilaiseen kehitysteoriaan," in Kehitys ja kehityksen teoriat, *Helsingin yliopisto, Kehitysmaainstituutti, Interkontin julkaisuja*, no. 18, Helsinki, pp. 1–53.

Tykkyläinen, M. (1993), "Rural Development, Resource Communities and the Development Theories," in P. T. Karjalainen (ed.), *Different Geographies*, Universitas Ostiensis, Joensuu, pp. 59–75.

Tykkyläinen, M. and Neil, C. (1995), "Socio-Economic Restructuring in Resource Communities: Evolving a Comparative Approach," *Community Development Journal* 30(1), pp. 31–47.

Varis, E. (1993), "Russian Karelian Villages in Transition," in H. Jussila, L. O. Persson, and U. Wiberg (eds.), *Shifts in Systems at the Top of Europe*, KTH FORA, Stockholm, pp. 113–121.

—— (1994), "The Restructuring Process of Rural Russian Karelia: A Case Study of Two Karelian Villages," United Nations University, WIDER, Working Paper 115.

Wolpe, H. (ed.) (1987), *The Articulation of Modes of Production: Essays from Economy and Society*, Routledge & Kegan Paul, London.

Yin, R. K. (1989), *Case Study Research: Design and Methods*, revised edn, Sage, Newbury Park, Calif.

7

The role of a non-governmental organization in Vietnamese rural communities in transition

Cecily Neil, Nguyen Ngoc Triu, and Nguyen Van Gia

Introduction

This chapter examines a model of assistance being given to marginal rural communities in Viet Nam during the current period of transition from a planned to a market economy. Thus, like a number of the preceding chapters, this chapter explores local economic development in agrarian communities in the context of a nation undergoing major national socio-economic transformation. The previous chapters in this volume, however, have been concerned primarily with the roles of local residents or organizations, or of public sector agencies, in restructuring. This chapter examines the role of an external non-governmental organization in the restructuring process.

In newly developing countries, external non-governmental organizations (NGOs) are playing an increasingly important role in the local economic development of resource-poor peripheral agricultural areas. There is considerable diversity in the NGOs involved with rural development around the world – in the socio-economic contexts in which they work, the nature of their relationship with the state, and their philosophies, objectives, and modes of operation (see, for example, Farrington and Lewis 1993). None the less, most have a strong commitment to local participation in planning, and, in this respect, examination of their local economic development activities complements an analysis of models of local economic development adopted by government agencies and regional authorities.

The analysis undertaken in this chapter examines the way in which an indigenous Vietnamese NGO, the National Association of Vietnamese Gardeners (VACVINA), has gradually expanded the nature of its activities in response to the changing local circumstances, which VACVINA itself has helped to bring about in some of the communities it has assisted. VACVINA was set up in 1986 to improve the nutrition of rural households by the promotion of self-supporting household gardening, "an integrated system of land-farming in which gardening, crop cultivation and tree-planting is combined with animal husbandry and aquaculture" (Nguyen Ngoc Triu 1994, 26). It is a nationwide organization, with a central national office in Hanoi and branches at all levels of Vietnamese society, from the province to the village. It now has over 150,000 member families, and branches in every province in Viet Nam. Through the gradual evolution of the type of local development activities it facilitates in rural communities, VACVINA has been able to help communities not only to develop and expand their subsistence agricultural activities but to integrate these activities into the wider economic system in order to be able to generate income from surplus produced. The problems VACVINA has experienced in the process of this evolution, however, highlight the fact that the very strengths of the local community development participation models often adopted by NGOs may, in the context of major national transition, lead to development that is self-limiting unless the NGO can do as VACVINA has done, and put in place mechanisms to link these communities into the newly transformed national economic system.

The first section of this chapter examines briefly the national transformation process taking place in Viet Nam, and its effect on rural communities. The next section then looks at VACVINA and its philosophies and techniques for fostering local development. The third section describes the way in which the developmental activities of VACVINA have evolved in response to the changing circumstances that VACVINA itself has helped to bring about in some of the communities in which it has worked. This is followed by a discussion of several important differences between the type of local participative planning frequently fostered by external government agencies and that encouraged by most NGOs, and the way in which these differences can be strengths in helping local residents cope with

172

the immediate crises of restructuring, but also sources of potential longer-term limitations to economic development.

The concluding section of this chapter highlights the way in which NGOs can meet some of the conditions that may be prerequisites for such development to succeed, while still adopting an approach that is supportive of local residents.

Socio-economic transformation in Viet Nam

[Between 1975 and 1990] the model of economic development followed [especially in northern Viet Nam] was that of large cooperatives possessing from 300 to 500 hectares of agriculture land. The means of production belonged to a collective ownership and the farmers were subject to the management of a managerial board.... The cooperatives were under the control of the state administration in terms of production orientation, volume of trade, and prices. The area assigned by the cooperatives for household production was limited to fifteen percent of the total acreage of agricultural land. The households planted crops in their assigned plots for additional food and income.... [The cooperatives] made active contributions to the Green Revolution, irrigation, and social services ... and the building of rural infrastructure. However, the range of income distribution was heavily egalitarian ... [and] did not encourage cooperative members to work diligently. Moreover, at the macro level, the state granted the coops only limited autonomy in business management. The cooperative had to sell most of its produce to the state at fixed prices in exchange for technical materials, also at fixed prices. Under this mechanism, business in conformity with market demand did not exist. (Vu Tuan Anh 1992, 86–87)

During this period, sectors in the economy

were organised along vertical lines with production units having little idea about the ultimate use of their product, [or] even who the customers were ... [E]xpansion of markets beyond the immediate locality was a decision for higher authorities, there being no means for the production unit to gauge demand and a ceiling on output could easily be reached at a relatively small scale of production. (Beresford and McFarlane 1995, 54)

With the emphasis on rice production and the spread of cooperatives, particularly in the north of Viet Nam, traditional farming households in many areas lost not only a lot of their farm management skills but also their knowledge of traditional horticultural techniques.

By late 1979, however, many cooperatives and production teams had begun to disintegrate (Chu Van Lam 1993, 153). In early 1988, a disastrous pre-harvest period left 9.3 million people underfed and domestic animals in jeopardy. Natural calamities were the primary cause of the disaster, but the situation was aggravated by a number of facets of the management of the agricultural sector (Chu Van Lam 1993, 157). By late 1988, Resolution 10 of the Political Bureau (Renovation in Agricultural Economic Management) had been introduced, assigning land to the household for long-term use. The resolution recognized the long-term existence and equality of the state, collective, private, and individual economies. Cooperatives and production teams became voluntary, self-governing economic organizations of the farmers, and were permitted to determine their own form, scale, orientation, and mode of production (Chu Van Lam 1993, 158–159). The household became

free to make purchases and sales of its produce on the market after paying the taxes to the state and submitting the contribution to help set up the production assistance and the welfare funds of the cooperative. The cooperative [now] has the function of providing agricultural services such as irrigation, veterinary treatment, the application of chemical fertilizer and insecticide. It collects taxes, purchases farm produce for the state, and readjusts land among households after each cycle of land allotment to farmers. The cooperative carries out trade with farmers at negotiated prices. (Vu Tuan Anh 1992, 87)

This liberalization of the economy began in rural areas, but the policy of "*doi moi*" was rapidly adopted nationwide. The cooperatives are still, in 1997, undergoing evolution, to some extent influenced by the government's passing of a new cooperative law in 1996.

According to Mya Than and Vokes (1993, 240), the key elements of *doi moi* are:

- a decentralization of state economic management and a granting of autonomy to state-owned enterprises (SOEs) in making decisions relating to production, distribution, and financing;
- a replacement of *administrative* measures and controls by economic ones, and, in particular, the use of market-oriented monetary policies to control inflation;
- the adoption of an outward-oriented policy in external economic relations; key elements of this policy were the adoption of realistic exchange rates and an extremely liberal foreign investment law in 1988;
- the adoption of agricultural policies that allow for long-term usufruct rights and greater freedom in the marketing of products;
- a reliance on or acceptance of the private sector as the engine of economic growth.

Thus, the reform programme, *doi moi*, deregulated the economy, dismantled collectives, and encouraged new private business. The growth of GDP and foreign trade has been rapid in the 1990s. Viet Nam adjusted to the collapse of the CMEA and the loss of socialist aid without a decline in GDP. Although administrative control is extensive and the state has control over many enterprises, reform has been seen as bold in an East Asian setting (World Bank 1996).

There have, however, been important social corollaries to the economic reform, one of which is the polarization of rich and poor in urban areas (Nguyen Tri Dung 1994, 95; Trinh Duy Luan n.d., 6). Further, the present process of economic development appears to be widening the gap between urban and rural areas (Cleary 1994, 62). In some rural areas, there "are still poor households without enough farming implements to produce subsistence food or enough money to buy food whenever it is needed.... On a general basis. food consumed by rural households other than staples and grains, is far from adequate" (Nguyen Ngoc Triu 1994, 24). At the same time, however, the improved standard of living in Viet Nam, coupled with the national implementation of a partial "user-pays" policy with respect to education and health, has meant that producing a surplus for sale must be an important long-term goal for most farmers.

The wealth apparent in the cities has attracted rural labour, especially seasonal labour, although until recently this has been counteracted both by tight controls on population movement and by the relatively low income differentials between town and country (Economist Intelligence Unit 1993). None the less, especially in the north of Viet Nam, the spatial pattern of villages and their social composition have remained relatively stable. There is an emerging trend towards inequality within the rural sector, but the drastic differentiation of the class structure that is occurring in urban areas appears unlikely to occur in the rural areas (Cleary 1994, 62; Ngo Vinh Long 1993, 194ff.; Do Thai Dong 1991, 95).

The majority of people, 68 per cent in 1994, live in rural areas (World Bank 1996). Most communities are resource based, but they are not yet highly specialized in producing for the market as many resource communities do in the developed countries. Villages in rural areas can currently be classified into three broad categories (To Duy Hop 1995, 284): agricultural communes/villages; non-agricultural communes/villages; and mixed communes/villages – an age-old pattern that existed during the period when the country was trying to collectivize farming and restrict the growth of market forces. What has changed is that, with the weakening or total dismantling of collectives within communes, job flexibility has increased tremendously: in the days of central planning and collectivization, when a person was registered as a farmer with an agricultural collective he was not permitted to engage in other trades; today, an individual can switch professions freely, or undertake several different types of economic activities simultaneously (To Duy Hop 1995, 284). Thus, if a farming household can produce surplus products, there are no constraints on processing and trading this surplus. Other forms of mixed economic activity, such as selling seasonal labour or establishing small businesses providing transport or mechanical services, making bamboo products, or milling rice, may now also be undertaken by farmers.

For all the change that has occurred, however, it is important to note that the movement towards a market economy has not been synonymous with the adoption of a market ideology in Viet Nam. The current model is one characterized, *inter alia*, by a market economy under the management of a socialist state (To Duy Hop 1995, 281). According to Boothroyd (1992, 197),

behind the rapid and sometimes confusing changes in Vietnam there seems to be a remarkable degree of agreement within the country, and without, on the broad direction the country should take ... the agreed-on direction is ... toward the creation of a viable welfare state.... Indeed, in broad outline the welfare state seems to be an agreed-on accomplishment. It is the dominant, if not consensual, opinion that the ideological framework is in place for ongoing experimentation in developing an optimal relationship between the state and the private sector.

Further, Viet Nam is still a very traditional rural country, and its GDP per capita was approximately only one-tenth of those of Poland and Russia in the mid-1990s (World Bank 1996). In regions in which "there has been a strong and uninterrupted tradition of household gardening, it has been estimated that the income equivalent yielded by these activities may account for as much as sixty or even seventy per cent of the total inome for a rural family" (Hodder 1994, 20).

VACVINA: The organization and its philosophies and techniques for diffusing knowledge of VAC techniques

As indicated above, VACVINA was established to improve the nutrition of rural households by helping to restore the traditional system of household food production, or, to be more accurate, a system of horticulture based on tradition but incorporating updated techniques and crop varieties wherever appropriate. It advocates the adoption of an ecological system of horticulture, in which gardening, fish-rearing, and animal husbandry are integrated to achieve sustainable agricultural development (see Tú Giay and Duong Hong Dat 1988; Nguyen Ngoc Triu 1994). The particular products cultivated and the techniques employed are matched to the physical and social demands of the local environment.

Relationship with government

The move to restore traditional horticulture to Vietnamese farms began as a government initiative, and many of the most senior volunteers leading VACVINA have held top government posts in the course of their careers. VACVINA itself, however, receives no financial support from the state, its main sources of finance being:
– membership fees,
– profits from technical services,
– financial assistance from international agencies, and
– projects funded by Vietnamese government departments as part of implementing policies such as setting up employment for unemployed people and reforestation of bare hills.
None the less, there has never been any antagonism between VACVINA and the government of Viet Nam, such as that experienced between some NGOs and the state in various other Asian countries – indeed, the government of Viet Nam acknowledges that the work of VACVINA assists the realization of official state policies relating to health, environmental protection and rehabilitation, and the alleviation of poverty. Strong links have consequently been forged with many government departments at both the local and national level. Extensive and effective links have also been established with state-funded mass organizations in the communities in which VACVINA is active. This local network is one of VACVINA's major strengths, enabling it to mobilize additional resources to facilitate its local activities.

Membership of VACVINA

The establishment of a VACVINA branch in a commune usually comes about as the result of a local initiative. Membership of VACVINA is theoretically open to any eligible farming household that wishes to join, although the scarcity of resources available to VACVINA for the provision of training and agricultural extension work has made it necessary to restrict membership numbers in many communities. To be eligible to join, families must have land suitable for VAC horticulture and sufficient labour to be able to undertake successful VAC horticulture. Some branches give priority to farmers who have spent some time living elsewhere, since these farmers are often the most successful when it comes to VAC horticulture, either because of the broader knowledge they have acquired elsewhere or because of their accumulated capital, and are therefore seen as potentially providing good role models within the community. Other branches give priority to invalids or poor families, including families supported by a woman and families with many children.

Philosophies and techniques

VACVINA's activities at the village level are based on three key principles: the willingness of village members to volunteer their services; self-help; and the mutual exchange of information. An essential criterion for membership is the willingness of the family to volunteer and to be prepared to link its own activities with those of the community through the exchange of experiences.

The first activity of a new local VACVINA association is usually to help a small number of local farmers who already have a good knowledge of farming techniques, and some resources of their own, to develop VAC plots that can serve as models for the rest of the community. Help received by the local VACVINA branch from the VACVINA Central Office at this stage may include extensive training in horticultural techniques, agricultural extension work, and the provision of technical services such as the supply of seedlings and animal stock. Local VACVINA branches may set up demonstration farms and nurseries to supply farmers with seedlings and stock, and offer technical support services. The success of the households that first adopt VAC farming techniques usually results in the further growth of VACVINA membership among those in the community who have some personal resources that they can use to establish a VAC plot and who wish to adopt the techniques advocated.

A wide variety of activities is adopted to help with the diffusion of VAC horticultural techniques. Activities include:

- running both large- and small-scale free commune-level training courses on VAC techniques, provincial-level training courses for local trainers and extension workers, and seminars/workshops on specific topics;
- organizing meetings of members with common interests to exchange experiences;
- distributing documents and establishing demonstration centres;
- undertaking farming extension work;
- organizing study tours, including the opportunity for farmers to observe and exchange experiences with families that have done well as a result of VAC horticulture – people who have been successful VAC farmers are selected, and others are invited to their home, where some issue, such as techniques in the selection of small piglets, is discussed in detail.

Thus, the farmers themselves are an integral part of the diffusion process. As indicated above, when farmers become VACVINA members they accept responsibility for helping transfer knowledge about VAC techniques. Most of the work of VACVINA at the local level is undertaken by volunteers: usually there are only two or three salaried people in provincial-level VACVINA branches, while at the community level virtually all the work is voluntary.

The evolution of VACVINA's programme of activities

Diffusion of knowledge of VAC horticultural techniques

The early activities of VACVINA concentrated on the diffusion of VAC horticulture as a means of improving household nutrition and food security in rural areas. Different provinces and districts have different approaches, and varying degrees of success, in encouraging farmers to adopt VAC horticulture – success in this respect has required the ability to mobilize resources to provide training courses and study tours on VAC techniques, to carry out sufficient extension work, and to supply technical services to members. Evaluations carried out in a number of communities in 1990 showed that households adopting VAC horticulture had, indeed, significantly increased food production: production of fish and meat had more than doubled, production of vegetables had increased by 2.75 times, and fruit production by 5.6 times (Nguyen Ngoc Triu 1994, 26). Nutritional intake had been substantially improved, although often this achievement had required VAC development to be accompanied by nutrition education.

The need for capital loans

In most communes in which VACVINA is active, VAC gardening techniques have been readily adopted by farmers when they have access to some capital resources. In the early 1990s, such resources were, however, not available to many farmers. In some cases, farmers could borrow directly from the bank, but problems associated with providing collateral meant that, without external assistance, they were more likely to have to borrow from private money lenders at an interest rate as high as 10 per cent per month. International aid projects assisted in funding the adoption of VAC techniques in a number of communities with severe food security problems, but such aid was limited. Thus, for VAC horticulture to expand in rural communities, some means of helping farmers acquire capital was necessary.

In a number of provinces, therefore, VACVINA has assumed an important role in helping those farmers without capital to obtain credit. Strategies for achieving this in some cases were developed as part of the local subsistence economy. Thus, VACVINA has helped organize small-scale credit schemes using financial assistance from domestic and international organizations, or community-based loan funds from which farmers can borrow. In these schemes, loans, made in either money or kind (for example, a piglet), are provided from membership contributions or from the voluntary contributions of farmers. In other areas, local VACVINA branches have enabled farmers to borrow from banks that are part of the broader market economy. In some provinces, farmers have been helped to borrow directly from the bank, but with VACVINA acting as an intermediary, using its prestige to secure the loan. In these cases, farmers approach VACVINA with a business plan and loan application, VACVINA processes all applications, and then VACVINA representatives approach the bank to negotiate the loan and sign the contracts. Alternatively, in other provinces, VACVINA may borrow money directly from a bank or other financial institution, again using its prestige as collateral, and then use the money borrowed to provide small-scale credit to farmers. In such cases, VACVINA is responsible for the loan and charges farmers a slightly higher rate of interest to cover administrative charges.

Local processing and marketing

By 1992, VACVINA's success in achieving its initial goals had high-lighted a new problem in its local economic development model. Some income generation is essential for the sustainability and expansion of VAC horticulture in a commune, as well as to cover expanding household costs with the introduction of user-payment for social services. Consequently, many villages have now come to specialize in producing a surplus of a particular product as part of their horticultural system. Specialized activities range from the breeding of tortoises for the export market, to the growing of ornamental plants to meet the expanding local urban market in Hanoi and Ho Chi Minh City. However, the principles through which the implementation of local economic development strategies has occurred – the sharing of information, the development of a model farm, etc. – have encouraged everyone in the village to undertake the same activity, with little attention being paid to external demand.

This has presented a new problem. Many crops, especially fruit, have harvests of only 15–20 days. In those districts in which significant progress has already been made with certain forms of horticulture, the result is often a glut of fruit or vegetables in season, with low market prices for any surplus produced. (This problem has been exacerbated by the collapse of the Soviet Union, which had provided the main market for Vietnamese exports, especially for rural products processed in local state-run factories, some of which have now been forced to close.) The lack of processing facilities and the difficulties associated with the distribution and marketing of local produce create fluctuating prices that limit the scope for the continued profitable growth of similar forms of VAC horticulture within a given community.

Thus, the principles upon which the implementation of local economic development strategies has been based may generate barriers to continued local economic development. The way VACVINA has operated is incompatible with an individualistic approach to marketing in the current economic climate. There is an inherent contradiction between the logical outcomes of the traditional principles of mutual self-help and sharing that underpin VACVINA's projects and the behaviour required for entrepreneurial success in the broader context of free competition, which is an integral part of the new market economy in Viet Nam. The more successful VACVINA becomes in a region, the greater the marketing problems are likely to

181

become. Unless resolved, this dilemma could ultimately undermine some of the credibility that VAC horticulture has so far achieved.

This is not to imply that marketing concepts are new to Vietnamese rural society. As To Duy Hop (1995, 291–292) points out,

agricultural diversification and market orientation have been a constant throughout the economic history of the country.... But this practice of acquiring wealth through a market economy was ill-regarded in recent history when the state practised central planning and subsidized production during 1954–85 in the north and 1975–85 in the south. Hence, the market economy did not become widespread in rural areas, and self-sufficiency became the norm as villages and rural communities were closed to external economic forces....

Furthermore, in the old days or even during the recent period of subsidized and centrally planned economy, markets took shape spontaneously, sometimes in the form of "underground" or "black" markets, but that being the case, they were mostly rather rudimentary and irregular. The market economy of Vietnam's rural sector today exists in the context of an open-door policy. It is a modernized market and this level of modernization depends on the level and scope of relationships with the developed world outside.

Thus, if VACVINA is to continue to expand, in addition to continuing to provide the services it currently offers, local VACVINA branches need assistance in developing marketing, distribution, and small-scale food-processing strategies that are consistent with both the goals and philosophy of the organization and the resultant processes through which change is implemented. Although its primary goal remains the diffusion of VAC techniques to improve household food security, the VACVINA Central Office has recognized these changing requirements and started to respond: several projects are now being undertaken that involve training in household food processing and that have a major marketing component. However, although local communities can be provided with an understanding of the new market economy that will permit them to be actively involved in making decisions concerning how to respond to the market, it is unlikely that members of these communities will, for some considerable time, themselves develop external links with economic institutions that might enable them to dispense with the support of the VACVINA Central Office in this respect. In order to ensure that local branches obtain the assistance they need in these areas, the VACVINA Central Office is also endeavouring to develop a pool of professional expertise that incorporates not only their current extensive knowledge of agricultural techniques but additional knowledge relating to the development of marketing and distribution strategies – ideas that can be disseminated to local branches in the same way that knowledge of VAC techniques is currently being disseminated.

For local economic development initiated by VACVINA to evolve from agricultural development that improves household nutrition to wider income-generating activities, VACVINA may have to continue to provide a bridge between the two socio-economic systems that coexist. It can do this only through the provision of an infrastructure that can broker the relationship between producers at the grass-roots level and organizations firmly embedded in the market economy.

Implications of the NGO local economic development model

Recently, the effectiveness of NGOs in facilitating income-generating activities among the poorest people in rural areas has been debated, as has their ability to influence government organizations in Asian and African countries (Farrington and Lewis 1993). None the less, as some of the following chapters in this volume highlight, development projects that involve local community participation are likely to have a better chance of succeeding than those imposed from above, and most non-governmental organizations are firmly committed to the philosophy that people in rural communities have the right to participate in planning and implementing economic development strategies. Moreover, NGOs working in resource-poor peripheral rural communities tend to facilitate the development of economic activities such as improved agricultural techniques, the household processing of surplus produce, or other innovative income activities that can be carried out on-farm. Coupled with training, which is an integral part of most NGO projects, this ensures that there is no mismatch between the labour requirements generated by a local developmental project and the local labour market. Such activities, therefore, involve the labour of, and are of direct benefit to, existing local residents, rather than encouraging an influx of new residents. This is particularly important in situations in which there is no safety net available for rural poor displaced by local restructuring.

However, participation can take a number of forms (see, for example, Biggs 1989). An important distinction is whether this participation seeks to foster the participation in development of local community leaders and potential entrepreneurs who show a capacity for individual innovation, or whether it seeks to foster the participation of all members of the community, particularly the poorest members with the fewest resources, building on concepts of self-help and mutual aid.

The examination above of the evolution of the range of activities that VACVINA facilitates in local rural communities highlights the changing prerequisites for sustained local economic development that may confront an NGO fostering this kind of community participation, especially an NGO trying to facilitate sustainable local economic development in times of national socio-economic transformation, if (a) the implementation process leads to a uniform community response, rather than activities that encourage the emergence of individual, externally focused entrepreneurs; and (b) local economic development is implemented on the basis of community values that lead to local systems of production that, unlike the system of everyday self-sufficiency that has developed in Karelia (see chap. 6), depend in part on participation in the new economic system, but cannot operate independently in the wider transitional socio-economic system. Difficulties are particularly likely to arise in situations in which transition is occurring in a communal type of socio-economic system in an agricultural area that lacks members with existing external commitments and established external links. Unless carefully planned, in such situations successful agricultural innovation may contain the seeds of its own containment.

This is a potential problem facing any organization attempting to facilitate community-led, non-subsistence, local economic development. However, it is one that particularly confronts NGOs that seek to ensure the participation of all members of the community in adopting innovations, and not just to encourage the growth of a relatively small number of potentially successful entrepreneurs. It suggests that NGOs facilitating local economic development that necessitates hitherto autarkic or semi-autarkic rural communities' participation in a marketing economy for the first time, either because of their prior exclusion from the wider national economy or because of transformation of the national economy, need to be multi-issue NGOs. Such NGOs may need not only to offer advocacy but to have an infrastructure that can both help the local community understand and respond to the demands of the external system and provide the necessary links to external agencies and systems on an ongoing basis. This suggests that the agencies likely to be most successful in facilitating local economic development in this type of context are large national NGOs working in a number of different areas, which can support the necessary infrastructure and be in a position to meet changing community needs for support over a considerable period of time.

Conclusion

This paper examines the role played by VACVINA, an indigenous organization, in local economic development during the current national socio-economic restructuring in Viet Nam. It illustrates the important role that NGOs can play working with local residents to foster the use of innovative technologies and facilitate the growth of innovative income-generating activities.

However, this paper also demonstrates an issue that has arisen in a number of the earlier chapters and is often less well addressed by NGOs. In the absence of local people with pre-existing links and commitments beyond the local community, communities undergoing restructuring are likely to require ongoing assistance to enable them to understand and to develop external links to the wider socio-economic system – something that is necessary for development to be sustained. Some NGOs have placed considerable importance on advocacy on behalf of peripheral rural communities. However, there may be a need for much broader assistance with lobbying (see, for example, Hernes and Selvik 1979), accessing capital, or marketing. Such needs may be particularly strong during socio-economic transition. At such times, changes are occurring in the external economic system within the context of which a developing community may have to operate. However, the community may have few ties that could provide it with an understanding of the changes occurring, or that could be used to mobilize external support. As this case-study illustrates, the nature of the economic change resulting from those community values that enable participatory, self-help types of development to thrive may, in fact, be antithetical to a community's successful direct participation in a new economic system. In these circumstances, the type of external support and assistance that has facilitated local economic development in other countries – the provision of "facilitators" to act as "brokers" between would-be entrepreneurs at the grass roots and the professional and formal services available to assist such entrepreneurs (see, for example, Moon and Willoughby 1988) – may not be enough. Rather, what may be required is an external agency that can mediate on an ongoing basis between the community as a whole and economic institutions in the wider economic system.

This case-study revealed that non-governmental organizations can, in certain circumstances, play an important role in promoting local development. However, the applicability of any NGO programme depends, *inter alia*, on the socio-economic circumstances of the country and the production sector in which the programme is being implemented and on local-specific factors, such as the degree of match between the way production is organized locally and the requirements of the sector of which the proposed local economic development will become a part. In some countries, NGOs can be an important force in influencing the direction taken by local economic development. They can protect the interests of local residents or the local environment against non-sustaining development by external bodies. In other countries, such as Australia, NGOs can play a significant role in bringing people together to exchange ideas, lobby governments, and produce an improved infrastructure that facilitates the implementation of innovative ideas generated within the community. In less economically developed countries, NGOs must play a much more all-pervasive role, suggesting innovations, offering training, and possibly helping local people link into the wider economic system for the first time. NGOs are not a panacea, but they can be very useful in certain development stages of the country.

Acknowledgement

Some of the information for this chapter was collected when two of the authors visited VACVINA branches in eight provinces in Viet Nam as part of a joint VACVINA/CARE International in Vietnam Project undertaken in 1992 (Neil et al. 1994).

References

Beresford, M. and McFarlane, B. (1995), "Regional Inequality and Regionalism in Vietnam and China," *Journal of Contemporary Asia* 25(1), pp. 50–71.

Biggs, S. D. (1989), *Resource-Poor Farmer Participation in Research: A Synthesis of Experiences from Nine National Agricultural Research Systems*, On-Farm Client-Oriented Research Comparative Study Paper No. 3, The Hague International Service for National Research, The Hague.

Boothroyd, P. (1992), "Ideological Change in Thailand and Vietnam: Implications for Canadian Development Assistance," in A. Pongsapich, M. C. Howard, and J. Amyot (eds.), *Regional Development and Change in Southeast Asia in the 1990s*, Chulalongkorn University Social Research Institute, Bangkok, pp. 193–210.

Chu Van Lam (1993), "Doi Moi in Vietnamese Agriculture," in W. S. Turley and M. Selden (eds.), *Reinventing Vietnamese Socialism: Doi Moi in Comparative Perspective*, Westview Press, Boulder, Colo., pp. 151–164.

Cleary, P. (1994), "Vietnam Sirens Warn of a Growing Poverty Gap," *Australian Financial Review*, 24 August, p. 62.

Do Thai Dong (1991), "Modifications of the Traditional Family in the South of Vietnam," in R. Liljeström and Tuong Lai (eds.), *Sociological Studies on the Vietnamese Family*, Social Sciences Publishing House, Hanoi.

Economist Intelligence Unit (1993), *Indochina: Vietnam, Laos and Cambodia. EIU Country Report*, EIU, London.

Farrington, J. and Lewis, D. J. (1993), *Non-Government Organizations and the State in Asia*, Routledge, London and New York.

Hernes, G. and Selvik, A. (1979), "Local Corporatism," in G. F. Summers and A. Selvik (eds.), *Nonmetropolitan Industrial Growth and Community Change*, Lexington Books, Toronto, pp. 145–157.

Hodder, Allison (1994), "Household Horticulture for Improved Family Nutrition and Food Security: Issues for Development Strategies," Proceedings of International Conference on Rural Household Food Security, Hanoi, 16–19 November 1994, Association of Vietnamese Gardeners (VACVINA), National Institute of Nutrition, UNICEF, and FAO, pp. 20–23.

Moon, J. and Willoughby, K. (1988), *An Evaluation of Local Enterprise Initiatives: The Case of Esperance*, Australian Government Publishing Services, Canberra.

Mya Than and Vokes, R. W. A. (1993), "Vietnam and ASEAN: Near-Term Prospects for Economic Co-operation," in Mya Than and J. L. H. Tan (eds.), *Vietnam's Dilemmas and Options*, ASEAN Economic Research Unit, Institute of Southeast Asian Studies, Singapore.

Neil, C. C., Dinh Tuan Viet, and Nguyen Van Gia (1994), *Report on Institutional Strengthening for VACVINA Central*, CARE International in Vietnam, Hanoi.

Ngo Vinh Long (1993), "Reform and Rural Development: Impact on Class, Sectoral and Regional Inequalities," in W. S. Turley and M. Selden (eds.), *Reinventing Vietnamese Socialism: Doi Moi in Comparative Perspective*, Westview Press, Boulder, Colo.

Nguyen Ngoc Triu (1994), "Toward Integral Household Food Security in Vietnam," Proceedings of International Conference on Rural Household Food Security, Hanoi, 16–19 November 1994, Association of Vietnamese Gardeners (VACVINA), National Institute of Nutrition, UNICEF, and FAO, pp. 24–28.

Nguyen Tri Dung (1994), "Vietnam: Second in a Five-Part Series Urbanisation and Polarisation, a "Doi Moi" Side Effect?" *Vietnam Investment Review*, 20 June, pp. 95–96.

To Duy Hop (1995), "Characteristics of Changing Social Structure in Rural Vietnam in Doi Moi," *Sojourn* 10(2), pp. 280–300.

Trinh Duy Luan (n.d.), "Social Impact of Renovation in Vietnamese Cities," typescript, Institute of Social Sciences, Hanoi.

187

Tú Giay and Duong Hong Dat (1988), "The Ecosystem VAC as a Means to Solve the Food Problem in Vietnam," in Tú Giay, J. M. Dricot, J. Vuylsteke, and Ha Huy Khoi (eds.), *Applied Nutrition. Proceedings of the International Conference on Applied Nutrition, Hanoi, 25–29 April*, National Institute of Nutrition S.R. Vietnam and UNICEF, Hanoi, pp. 66–80.

Vu Tuan Anh (1992), "Approaches to Sustainable Rural Development in Vietnam," in A. Pongsapich, M. C. Howard, and J. Amyot (eds.), *Regional Development and Change in Southeast Asia in the 1990s*, Chulalongkorn University Social Research Institute, Bangkok, pp. 85–88.

World Bank (1996), *From Plan to Market. World Development Report 1996*, World Bank, Washington D.C.

8

The effect of transition on a village in south central Bulgaria: The case of a lead-zinc plant

Alfred Levinson, Cecily Neil, and Markku Tykkyläinen

Introduction

This paper deals with socio-economic restructuring in Bulgaria in the early 1990s. The restructuring is interpreted through the development of a small resource community, Kuklen, where a metallurgical plant is facing the impulses of a market economy. The paper reveals the huge productivity gap between the old and modern technologies with which the plant had to cope during the transition to a market economy. Furthermore, this case-study shows how the shrinking of the traditional market and the realization of an urgent need for environmental investments affected the transition in Kuklen. The paper reveals the structural shift in demand, i.e. the growth of new demand during the new neo-capitalistic era of the 1990s, and it deals with the structural shift associated with the setting up of new economic activities in Kuklen and its surroundings. The latter structural shift is improving the viability of both the community and nearby agricultural activities.

Kuklen, the community examined here, was originally an agricultural community. The village proper is located 16 km south-southeast of Plovdiv (the second-largest city in Bulgaria). It was built on the side of a mountain in the Rodopi mountain range overlooking the

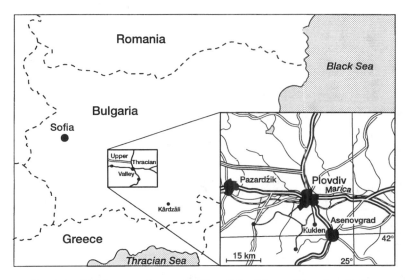

Fig. 8.1 **Kuklen, on the south side of the Upper Thracian Valley.**

Upper Thracian Valley – the best-formed alluvial valley in Bulgaria (fig. 8.1). The valley is about 100 km long and 40 km wide, and is bounded by mountains with an average height of 1,000 metres. Most of the village houses are surrounded by vegetable plots, though there are also larger fields where corn, grapes, and cherries are grown. Unlike some other agricultural communities, however, Kuklen is showing signs of potential future economic growth.

The current situation of the village is, in the first instance, attributable to the existence of KCM, one of Bulgaria's two lead-zinc manufacturing plants, in the valley on the outskirts of the village. The plant in Kuklen and its impact on the community are the subject of this study. This paper shows how the economic processes of transition placed the factory in a position to respond effectively to pressures demanding a reduction in the plant's negative impacts on the surrounding environment. Also, it appears that the local farms will be able to respond positively to new pressures arising indirectly from the political transformation of the nation.

The paper begins with a description of the transition to a market economy in Bulgaria. We then briefly describe Kuklen and the history of of the lead-zinc plant, and discuss its impact on the village and the surrounding communities. We examine the environmental and health effects of the plant, especially pollution of the food chain. The

Table 8.1   **The transition in Bulgaria: Eonomic indicators**

	1990	1991	1992	1993	1994
Real growth rate of GDP (%)	−9.1	−11.7	−7.3	−2.4	+1.4
Real growth rate of agricultural production (%)	−6.0	−0.3	−12.0	−18.3	+2.5
Manufacturing index (1980 = 100)	116	90	76	74	78

Source: WIIW (1995); *Statistical Yearbook of Finland 1995.*

changes in foreign and domestic demand as a result of the transition are discussed, as is the overall effect on Kuklen of Bulgaria's gradual integration into European Union standards and markets. The potential development of new agricultural-based industries, in response to environmental pressure and the opening up of new markets, is appraised. The final section of the paper examines the extent to which local adaptation, both at the plant and in agriculture, can be attributed to local or external initiatives, and the extent to which success in this local initiative needs to be facilitated by external support.

Bulgaria under transition in the early 1990s

Bulgaria has faced similar economic turmoil to that experienced by the other small East European countries. Production in the manufacturing sector reached a peak in 1988 (the index of production in manufacturing being 141, compared with 100 in 1980). After that, total output fell dramatically, but growth in production resumed in 1994 (see table 8.1). The economic reforms have progressed with difficulty, and the country faced an economic crisis in mid-1990 (Pautola 1997).

Under socialism, agriculture was organized primarily into state cooperatives. Since the country's transformation to a market economy, there has been a two-step process for restoring agricultural land to its former owners: (1) in 1991, the right to use (not rent or sell) land for agriculture was given to those former owners or their descendants presenting claims to the land; and (2) later on, after the land had been surveyed and ownership established, the title to the land was to be given to the former owners – only then would they have the right to rent or sell the land. Movable assets went to the employees of the farms that were split up, so former owners received only the land and had to finance the acquisition of farming equipment

191

independently. This procedure for privatizing agricultural land had a destructive effect on Bulgarian agriculture (Levinson 1993). In many cases, particularly where land was divided among descendants, the plots that were reclaimed were as small as 100 m^2 and could not be farmed efficiently. However, until surveyed, these plots could not be sold or leased. Total farm production diminished in 1992, both in monetary terms and in quantity. The result was a return to subsistence farming in many areas.

As was the case in all centrally planned economies, prior to the transition to a market economy production and management decisions in manufacturing and the base metals sector in Bulgaria were made by the central government. Local managers had little autonomy, although the necessary contacts between the various manufacturing plants were often made directly by the local managers. With the transition to a market economy came the end of central planning. The state-owned enterprises were deconcentrated and de-monopolized as a first step towards privatization. The managers of the plants were allowed and expected to find markets for their products. This meant that they had to compete not only against other plants in the country but also with foreign companies, even for markets in the former CMEA countries. Local managers had a great incentive to find new markets; if they did not, the plant could be closed. This happened in many cases. Some of the managers were able to find either new products or new markets for existing products to keep their plants open. Other managers were less innovative – the plant was closed and they and their employees were out of work. Managers had close ties with the ministry that oversaw their operation, and naturally did what they could to help other managers. A foreign investment commission was established by the government to find partners or buyers for state-owned enterprises and to find markets for their products.[1]

Kuklen and the lead-zinc plant

In 1934, Kuklen had a population of 4,300 (see table 8.2). During the war, the population increased by 10 per cent. However, as a result of post-war industrialization, which culminated in large-scale migration to the cities, Kuklen's population decreased by 17 per cent to 3,911 by 1956.

The lead-zinc works in Kuklen was designed jointly by the Moscow Ghiprotsvetment organization and some other Soviet and Bulgarian institutes. Construction of the zinc plant began in 1959. It went into

Table 8.2 **Population in Kuklen, 1934–1992**

	1934	1946	1956	1965	1975	1985	1992
Population	4,300	4,720	3,911	5,367	6,328	5,362	5,682

Source: Nationalen Statisticheski Institut (1993, 137).

operation at the end of 1961, producing zinc, cadmium, and sulphuric acid. In 1963, with the completion of the lead smelting plant, lead production started. In 1965, two years after the plant became fully operational in both zinc and lead production, the population had increased by 37 per cent over the 1956 level, to 5,367. The population continued to grow until 1985, when it reached its peak of 6,362. As production languished at KCM, people began migrating to the urban areas, following the migration patterns of the rest of Bulgaria. Between 1985 and 1992, Kuklen lost 11 per cent of its population. However, since 1990, with the beginning of the transition, the population in Kuklen has been relatively stable, owing to the decrease in jobs in urban areas, the continued operation of KCM, and the possible increase in subsistence farming that has occurred with the return of some of the state agricultural lands to their former owners. At the end of 1992, Kuklen had 5,682 people. About 45 per cent of the adults have at least a secondary education, with 5.5 per cent having a post-secondary education.

The KCM lead-zinc works in Kuklen is one of two lead-zinc plants in Bulgaria. The other, OCK, is in Kurdjali, also in the Rodopi mountains. Kurdjali is located 104 km south-east of Plovdiv. The Rodopi mountains are the source of some of the lead and zinc ore used in the plants, although the mines are unprofitable and may be closed; most of the lead and zinc is imported. The KCM lead-zinc works produces primary lead, primary zinc, sulphuric acid, and cadmium. As commercial by-products of the manufacture of lead and zinc, cobalt-cement, copper-cement, and zinc sulphates are also produced. The works contains a zinc electrolysis plant, an acid plant, a Waelz plant, and a conventional lead smelting plant. The Waelz plant and the acid plant are integrated into the zinc production process. The acid plant processes the sulphur dioxide roasting gases from the zinc plant, and the Waelz plant processes the slag from the roasting and leaching processes in the zinc plant. As in most centrally planned economies, production decisions were made in the capital, and there was an excessive number of employees. At the time of writing this paper, the lead smelter (though not the rest of the works) had been closed owing to the loss of the CMEA markets and the high costs required to bring it up to common European pollution control standards, though it was expected that it would soon be reopened as a result of the increase in the domestic demand for lead. Furthermore, the smelter appears to have been competitive: the zinc was exported, the zinc ores were largely imported, and it was not losing money.

In 1991, KCM produced 39,500 tonnes of primary lead, 31,750 tonnes of primary zinc, 45,900 tonnes of sulphuric acid, and 177 tonnes of cadmium. This is nearly 50 per cent lower than production levels in 1989, owing to environmental constraints and the collapse of its CMEA markets.

In February 1992, 2,500 people were employed in the plant. Compared with lead and zinc plants in Western Europe, the output of the KCM works was five to ten times lower, but the number of employees was two to three times higher. This was typical of factories in Eastern Europe and the CIS in the early phase of transition. There appeared to be a high level of redundancy at the plant. However, since wages in Bulgaria were only a fraction of those in Western Europe, labour costs were probably not higher. Only about a third of the plant's employees was from Kuklen. Another third commuted from Plovdiv, and the remainder came from Asenovgrad, a few kilometres from Kuklen. With populations of 340,000 and 68,000, respectively, the employment impact of KCM on Plovdiv and Asenovgrad is small. However, the number of local employees at the works represents about one-quarter of Kuklen's working age (18–60) population, and a much higher proportion of the labour force. As a result, the plant has a significant impact on employment in Kuklen.

The construction of the lead-zinc works in Kuklen was largely responsible for the 37 per cent increase in population between 1956 and 1965, and for the continued increase in population until 1985. This increase occurred during a period when there was a large migration of the rural population to the urban areas of the country. Of course, the fact that Kuklen is only 16 km from Plovdiv also meant that people from Kuklen could commute to jobs in Plovdiv.

Environmental and health impacts of the plant

Until recently, large amounts of pollutants were emitted into the environment from the KCM works. A study undertaken by Haskoning (1992) compared the emissions from the zinc plant with the emissions of a larger zinc plant in the Netherlands. The Budelco zinc plant in the Netherlands produced seven times as much zinc in 1991 as KCM, yet dust emissions by KCM were more than two and a half times higher, zinc emissions were more than double, cadmium was more than nine times higher, and sulphuric acid was over three times higher. Emissions from the KCM lead plant were also compared with the emissions of a conventional lead plant in Western Europe that produced twice as much lead. Again, air emissions were several times higher than from the West European plant. Further, waste water containing pollutants from KCM was discharged into the sewer system. These discharges too were several times higher than those from plants in Western Europe, although, since 1990, the waste generated from clinker separation has been recycled, resulting in some reduction in water pollution. Some of the slag from the fume furnace was sold to the cement industry. The remainder, together with the slag from the Waelz kiln, was dumped in a landfill on a military air base a few kilometres north of the plant.

The emissions of lead and cadmium from the lead-zinc works have had a definite impact on the local environment. Lead levels in the blood of the local population were at the limit of the acceptable level (as set by the World Health Organization) of 400 micrograms (μg) per litre, and the levels for children were considerably higher than the 150 μg/litre considered acceptable by the United States. Lead levels in the blood of workers at the plant were in some cases nearly double the limit set by the WHO. Further, the soil near the plant contained lead levels as high as 2,000 mg/kg. Since crops are grown in the vicinity of the plant, the lead has naturally accumulated in some of the crops. There are houses with vegetable gardens within 2 km of the KCM works. It is assumed that lead also accumulates in the soil fauna, affecting the whole food chain near the plant. Lead levels as high as 188 mg/kg have been found in some locally grown food. These high levels of lead in the soil around the zinc-lead works in Kuklen are not unusually high for a lead smelter. However, in contrast to the situation at Kuklen, the land surrounding plants such as the Budelco plant in Holland is not inhabited or used for agricultural purposes.

Cadmium is the other major pollutant produced by the KCM works. Here, the cadmium intake by humans is primarily through the food chain. A quantitative hazard assessment estimated that, near the lead-zinc plant, a child, on average, will consume as much as 33 μg of cadmium a day (Haskoning 1992, 31–34). Since the WHO's recommended acceptable daily intake is 57 μg per day, the intake of cadmium by a child in the vicinity of the plant, on average, will not exceed the average daily intake recommended by the WHO. However, if the lead plant is operated without being upgraded, cadmium discharges to the water are expected to exceed European Union limits, and it is expected that cadmium will accumulate in soil fauna (primarily earthworms) and crops. High cadmium levels will have a negative effect on microbiological soil processes, and will distort the growth of the root systems of some plants (Sengalevich 1993a).

Because Kuklen is located on the side of a mountain and the KCM works is in the valley on the outskirts of the village, only those living in the valley near the works are subjected to its high levels of air pollution. The plume of air emissions is carried in a north-easterly direction, usually bypassing Plovdiv. The smaller villages of Krumovo and Yagodovo, which are a few kilometres from Kuklen, lie in the path of that plume (Sengalevich 1993b). The population of these two villages has the highest exposure level to the air pollutants from KCM. Unfortunately, no health or environmental impact data are available for Krumovo or Yagodovo.

There is evidence that the groundwater in the vicinity of KCM is contaminated with heavy metals. However, it is reported that this water is not used for drinking but only for irrigation.

Kuklen provides an example of the environmental problems in a former socialist resource community. There were no possibilities for local control over industrial development, and the local environment deteriorated as a result of industrial activity using a poor technology.

Changing trade partners

Towards global markets

Of the countries of Eastern Europe, Bulgaria was the most dependent on exports to the CMEA countries. With the collapse of the CMEA, demand for lead and zinc decreased. This accounts for much of the decrease in the output of the KCM works in the late 1980s. To compound this problem, domestic demand for lead and zinc declined in 1991 and 1992 owing to a depressed economy – lead demand decreased by one-third and zinc demand by 40 per cent. During this period, the government reoriented its export markets. Both lead and zinc exports increased in late 1992. In 1993, zinc exports continued to increase, but lead exports began to decline as a result of the increase in domestic demand for lead.

Before the transition, trade among the CMEA countries was settled in transferable roubles. Under this regime, there was little competition and it was not necessary to produce quality products. With the demise of the CMEA and with the eventual admission of Bulgaria into the European Union, Bulgaria must now engage in trade using convertible currencies. Because Bulgarian products now face competition on the world markets, their quality must be improved. Bulgarian enterprises need to find new markets for their products, cease production of items for which there is no market in the West, and identify new products that can be manufactured and sold in the West. These requirements apply to the KCM plant in Kuklen as well. However, the Bulgarian base metal sector has been able to find Western markets for its zinc. This is the first step to production in Kuklen being gradually assimilated into the processes of globalization – hence into the general processes of capitalism.

Expanding the domestic market for lead

One reason for the growth in domestic lead consumption is directly connected to transition. The increase in the number of automobiles in operation has led to an increase in demand for automobile batteries manufactured in Bulgaria, and thus in demand for lead. Domestic demand for lead is expected to continue to increase.

At the time of writing, the government was planning to reopen the lead plant in Kuklen to meet this increased demand. The lead industry is one of the few industries to show an increase in domestic demand, considering that during this period (1990–1993) GDP decreased in real terms by 20 per cent and final domestic demand decreased by 25 per cent.

Growing environmental pressure and the development of non-food crops

Environmentalists played a greater role in bringing about Bulgaria's transition than in any other of the former Communist countries. The president, Zhelyu Zhelev, was a founder of Ecoglasnost, the non-governmental environmental organization, and the Greens were represented in first anti-communist government, and are represented in the current government of the mid-1990s, which is administered by the former Communists. It was the local Greens and their colleagues at the Agricultural University in Plovdiv who performed the initial studies on the environmental impact of KCM in Kuklen and alerted the new government. It was they too who conducted studies to find alternative crops for villagers to raise.

Like the other countries of Eastern Europe seeking membership in the European Union, Bulgaria will, in the future, have to meet the environmental standards of the European Union. In the more immediate present, it is the pressure from Bulgarian environmental organizations that is forcing the government to ensure that the polluted land and water are cleaned up and that pollution control equipment is installed in manufacturing plants to meet European Union standards. In 1992, at the request of Ecoglasnost, the government of the Netherlands commissioned the Dutch consulting company Haskoning to conduct an environmental impact study of the lead-zinc works in Kuklen.[2] As discussed above, the report showed that almost all emissions to the air were above European Union standards. Dust, lead, cadmium, and sulphur dioxide emissions were more than 10 times above European Union limits.

Based on the preliminary analysis of the environmental impact of the plant, to bring the plant up to European Union standards will require, at the minimum, an upgrading of the lead and zinc plants to reduce emissions. As an alternative, the consultants suggested a major restructuring of the lead plant and an upgrading of the zinc plant. The restructuring of the lead plant could mean the installation of a new smelter using state-of-the-art technology, or the elimination of primary lead production altogether by the installation of a secondary lead facility, which would rely on recycled lead as the resource for the plant.

By 1992, both of the lead-zinc works, KCM and OCK, had had their dust collectors overhauled. The companies invested 209 million *leva* of their own money and are planning to spend another 230 million *leva* to reduce the environmental impact of their operations further. Because domestic resources are insufficient for lead and zinc production and, in 1992, the government decided to phase out the money-losing ore mining facilities, both companies have been seeking new forms of cooperation with foreign partners (*168 Hours BBN*, 20–26 September 1993, 11). As was noted above, the government was planning to reopen the lead plant at Kuklen to meet increased

198

domestic demand for lead. Although no mention has been made of privatizing the KCM plant, the Privatization Agency was planning to put the works up for privatization with the expectation that the eventual investor would modernize the works (*168 Hours BBN*, 15–21 November 1993, 16).

There is a plan to rehabilitate the region surrounding the works to meet the European Union's environmental requirements. According to the plan, KCM will pay 70 per cent of the costs of the clean-up, and the government will pay the remaining 30 per cent and supply the environmental expertise.

The government is committed to halting the production of food crops in the vicinity of KCM. Agricultural experts from the Agricultural University at Plovdiv are exploring non-food crops that might be grown there. Among the alternatives being considered are raising roses for use in rose oil production, and growing mulberry bushes and raising silkworms for use in a local silk manufacturing industry. Their studies have shown that zinc and heavy metal pollution does not affect the growth of these plants or the silkworms.

Bulgaria has been renowned throughout the world for its high-quality rose oil, which is used in cosmetics. In fact, Bulgaria used to be the dominant supplier of that market. However, as a result of the manner in which agricultural land was privatized, rose cultivation has declined sharply and rose oil production has decreased. The establishment of a rose oil industry in Kuklen would help reverse that trend. Bulgarians are also acquainted with silk manufacture – prior to World War II, Bulgaria was an important producer of silk. The Japanese have offered to finance the establishment of a silk industry in Kuklen.

The transition has led to a stabilization of the population in Kuklen, largely as a result of the continued operation of the KCM works at a time when factories in the cities are closing or curtailing production – either laying off employees or making workers redundant. The fact that the KCM works has stabilized its level of production and may even be growing is looked upon favourably by the people of Kuklen. If non-food crops replace the food crops grown in the vicinity of KCM, and rose oil and silk industries are developed in Kuklen, then there should be a net increase in jobs in Kuklen. This development might well prevent a return to the past pattern of rural migration to the cities (which notably occurred during the past decade).

Local development and the transfer of expertise

Cooperation between farmers and agricultural scientists is unusual in Bulgaria. In general, there has been little transfer of knowledge from research laboratories to the farmer. The United States, in cooperation with the government of Bulgaria, has sent agricultural extension experts to assist Bulgaria in establishing an agricultural cooperative extension service, similar to the one that has been in existence in the United States for over 100 years, to transfer developments from the university agricultural laboratories to the farm.

Apart from the pressure on the managers of KCM to find new markets for zinc and lead, little initiative has come from Kuklen itself. Most of the initiative to clean up KCM and even consider alternative crops has come from the Greens and from the scientists at the Agricultural University at Plovdiv.

Conclusion

The penetration of a market economy to the East has led to a technological revolution and structural adjustments in the whole production sector. As the case of Kuklen shows, each company, plant, and factory has to develop its own ideas for profitable production, and, thus, the adjustment to a market economy is specific to each case.

Bulgaria's transition to a market economy has had a major impact on Kuklen, in some ways in an unexpected manner. Whereas most state enterprises languished, KCM was able to stabilize its production and level of employment by adjusting to the new market conditions.

Kuklen is also an example of the environmental effects of the change in ideology and in policy-related factors, such as the regulative regime. The abandonment of the country's isolation from the market economies of the West and the institution of democracy have necessitated a reduction in the level of pollution produced by the lead-zinc works and the clean-up of the surrounding environment. Although market rationality does not of course solve all problems, in this case its introduction is clearly improving the health of the community in the long run and more generally is leading to an improvement in the ecosystem in and around Kuklen.

The sectoral shift to more profitable production is an investment in know-how. The case-study illustrates that the support of outside expertise for local initiatives is an important factor promoting development. New products, modernization of the processing of raw materials, and changes in the ownership of production capital are leading to a restructuring of the countryside. Depending on the available resources and the abilities of each locality to adjust to the conditions of a market economy, transition is creating either growing or declining communities. In order for the individuals in these communities to obtain maximum benefit from the transition and the new market economy, the transfer of knowledge, training, and the encouragement of development initiatives look like being some of the most important means of enhancing production in the late 1990s.

Notes

1. A negative effect of this has been the establishment of "shadow" companies by local managers. The goods produced by a state-owned enterprise are sold to the shadow company at a loss. The shadow company, in turn, sells the goods at a profit. The local managers get the profit, which is not reported to the government. Thus, no taxes are paid on it. The state-owned enterprise records a loss and may get subsidies from the government to keep operating and keep its workers in employment. This does not appear to be the case for the two state-owned lead-zinc enterprises, whose profits provided much of the financing (70 per cent) for their upgrading.
2. Their report, *Survey on Environmental Aspects of the Lead and Zinc Industry in Plovdiv (Bulgaria),* was issued in September 1992.

References

Haskoning (1992), *Survey on Environmental Aspects of the Lead and Zinc Industry in Plovdiv (Bulgaria)*, Ministry of Housing, Physical Planning and Environment, The Netherlands.

Levinson, A. (1993), "The Impact of Privatization on Settlement Patterns in Southwestern Bulgaria," presented at the Summer Institute, University of Joensuu, Joensuu, Finland, June.

Nationalen Statisticheski Institut (1993), *Broi na Naselenieto po Oblasti, Obstini i Naseleni Nesta*, Nationalen Statisticheski Institut, Sofia.

Pautola, N. (1997), "Towards European Union Eastern Enlargement – Progress and Problems in Pre-Accession," *Review of Economies in Transition* 6, pp. 5–21.

Sengalevich, G. (1993a), "Zamursyavane na Pockvete s Tedsiki Metali v Raiona na KCM (AD) – Plovdiv," *Journal Zemedelie* 1(2), pp. 24–25.

——— (1993b), "Promishdeno Zamurdenite Zemi Ne sa Otpisani za Proizvodstvo na Selskostopanska Prodyktsiya," *Journal Ractitelna Zashtita* 1(1), pp. 11–13.

Statistical Yearbook of Finland 1995 (1995), Statistics Finland, Finland.

WIIW (Wiener Institut für Internationale Wirtschaftsvergleiche) (1995), *Countries in Transition 1995*, WIIW Handbook of Statistics, Vienna.

Part IV
The life cycles of resource communities

9

Mill closure – options for a restart: A case-study of local response in a Finnish mill community

Jarmo Kortelainen

Global versus local factors

While industrial societies were growing, the most important factor in the development of a locality was its locational advantages with respect to the production systems of manufacturing industries. Firms sought the most profitable locations for their industrial plants, and the communities around them grew and flourished for decades.

Since the beginning of the 1960s, however, industrial societies and their spatial structures have been in transition; the deindustrialization process in Western industrial countries has reduced jobs, both in manufacturing and in resource sectors. The growth of the markets of many traditional industrial products has slowed and international competition has intensified. Numerous flourishing manufacturing and resource communities have lost their status in the production system because they are now less attractive locations from the point of view of enterprises. Firms in the traditional industrial sectors have cut costs by rationalizing production and investing in new technology, and by shifting production from the old industrial regions to other parts of the country or abroad. Therefore, the number of jobs in "smokestack" industries has been declining, and the growth of the labour force and economic activities has been shifting to metropolitan regions producing services and to production complexes utilizing new technology. Many industrial and resource communities have become deteriorating "problem" regions, characterized by unemployment and out-migration. New, suitable economic activities are sought in these communities.

In Finland, forest industries dominated industrialization, and, consequently, the spatial structure of the forest sector was the basis of the settlement system in large parts of the country. The expansion of the forest industry dispersed workers into the backwoods to cut and transport timber, and also placed industrial workers in mill towns and industrial agglomerations to process it. Localities within the forest sector formed an expanding part of the settlement system in the first half of the twentieth century. In recent decades, by contrast, most of them have faced increasing problems. First, from the 1960s, small rural villages began to decline as a consequence of falling demand for labour in forestry due to nationalization. Secondly, since the late 1970s, mill towns dominated by forest industries have experienced a decrease in jobs and, therefore, also faced problems (see Oksa and Rannikko 1988; Kortelainen and Rannikko 1993).

This paper analyses the development of a declining Finnish resource community, Vuohijärvi, which had originally grown up around a plywood mill (Rannikko 1990). The theoretical starting point of the study is the proposition that the spatial and social changes of localities are tightly linked with the national and international restructuring of production (Massey 1984; Kortelainen and Rannikko 1993). In the case of Vuohijärvi, the restructuring of the plywood industry is the most important event, which is studied by combining the development of the sector with product lifecycle theory. Each product and sector has a particular life cycle that consists of different stages. In the different stages, changes in world markets and available technologies alter the competitive conditions of the sectors and enterprises. As a consequence, the economic attractiveness of different locations changes, and profitability in traditional manufacturing localities may weaken in comparison with new production in lower-cost regions (see Rothwell 1982). In this case-study, the growth and decline of Vuohijärvi is analysed by examining how the spatial attractiveness of its location has changed within the spatial division of the labour of the plywood industry during the different development stages of the sector.

The development of a locality cannot, however, be explained only by external forces. Studies on restructuring have more and more shifted towards focusing on local conditions and local actors in order to explain local differences in the restructuring processes. In the 1990s, numerous locality studies have emphasized the role of local activity in response to the negative consequences of restructuring processes (see, for example, Bagguley et al. 1990; Jonas 1992). In explaining the motives of local actors, local dependence has often been the key concept. It refers, quite simply, to all those social and economic factors that attach actors to a certain locality. Built environment investments and the knowledge of locally tied workers make a firm dependent on a locality. Local states are dependent on local tax bases and, furthermore, they, like firms, have concerns deriving from the immobility of their built environment facilities. People have personal "traditional" and "modern" local dependencies through their social interaction and relationships within the local context. Traditional local dependencies arise from such social relations as, for example, family, ethnicity, or neighbourhood, which add to the predictability of life, encourage confidence in the future, and are a source of self-identification. The growth of the welfare state has led to a decline in the importance of traditional local dependencies. However, the importance of the local context in social interaction has remained, because work and consumption are more or less locally bound. In addition to home ownership, these factors represent the modern form of local dependence (Cox and Mair 1988, 308–313).

In this study, local responses are studied by examining the role and significance of local actors during the threat of mill closure in Vuohijärvi in the mid-1980s. In conclusion, after the empirical examination, the factors that affect local economic development are discussed, and some possible measures that might slow down the downswing in declining industrial localities or other resource communities are proposed.

The life cycle of plywood production

The locality in question, Vuohijärvi, is a small one-mill community in the municipality of Valkeala in south-eastern Finland (see fig. 9.1). Its development has mainly been determined by changes in international plywood markets and the national plywood industry. The first Finnish plywood mills were built in the 1910s. At that time, Finland was an attractive country for plywood production, because a lot of birch, which is excellent raw material for plywood, was available. Most of the birch resources were in central and eastern Finland, and almost

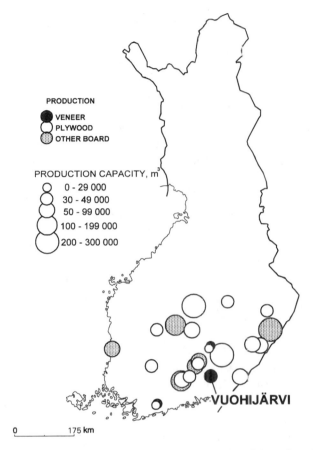

PRODUCTION

● VENEER
○ PLYWOOD
◉ OTHER BOARD

PRODUCTION CAPACITY, m³
○ 0 - 29 000
◎ 30 - 49 000
◯ 50 - 99 000
◯ 100 - 199 000
◯ 200 - 300 000

VUOHIJÄRVI

0 ____ 175 km

Fig. 9.1 **Location of the Vuohijärvi mill and the veneer, plywood, and board mills in Finland in 1994 (Source: Metsäteollisuus ry 1995).**

all plywood mills were located there. The industry was highly dependent on exports; the growth of the sector was based on increasing demand in industrialized European countries, especially England. Until the 1960s, the markets for plywood continued to grow, and Finland became the leading plywood exporter. Almost half of the exported plywood in the world was produced in Finland in the early 1950s (Väänänen 1983, 571).

The Vuohijärvi mill was established by a small company called Kalso Oy. The mill was not among the pioneers of the plywood industry, since it was not founded until 1934. The Vuohijärvi community was situated at the junction of a waterway and a railroad, at

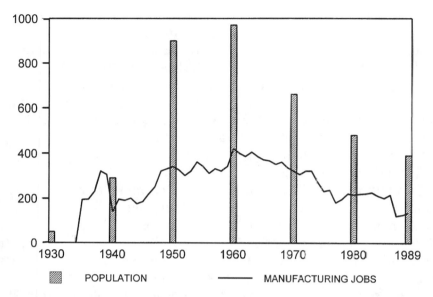

Fig. 9.2 **Manufacturing jobs and total population at Vuohijärvi since 1930 (Source: Kortelainen 1991).**

the edge of the birch forest region of eastern Finland. Given the prevailing transport technology at that time, it was a most favourable location. Timber could be floated to the mill and plywood could be transported by train to seaports. As people migrated from surrounding regions for the jobs available at the mill, the settlement began to grow in a previously almost uninhabited place. The population of the locality rose rapidly from a couple of dozen to approximately 1,000 (see fig. 9.2).

The mill and the locality grew with the expanding global plywood markets until the 1960s. At that time, the plywood industry began to reach the stage of maturity and the growth in demand began to slow down. Simultaneously, competition intensified as cheap plywood produced in lower-cost countries, together with substitute products, was introduced into the markets. As a result, the Finnish plywood producers lost part of their share in the international plywood markets. In order to avoid the decline of the sector, investments in research and development were made and new technology was introduced (van Duijn 1984, 21). Production machinery was modernized in several mills, and new plywood products were introduced in order to acquire new markets. At the same time, however, serious country-specific problems emerged. The Finnish plywood industry had increased its capacity in excess of its birch resources, and now faced difficulties in getting enough raw material. These international and national developments caused restructuring pressures in many plywood mills, especially during the oil crisis of the early 1970s. As a way of solving the over-capacity problem, the association of Finnish plywood producers drew up a plan. Production costs were to be cut through further rationalizations and investments in new technology, and total production was to be diminished by shutting down old-fashioned and small mills.

In addition to the fact that the Vuohijärvi mill was old, small, and non-integrated, there were several other factors that particularly weakened its position. When the founder of the original company, Kalso Oy, died in the early 1960s, the mill's position in the spatial division of labour began to change. The head office was moved from Vuohijärvi to one of the company's other mills in the city of Mikkeli, and, consequently, the managers did not live in Vuohijärvi as they had done earlier. The Vuohijärvi mill began to operate as part of a company called the Grahn Corporation. Also, locational advantages with respect to transportation almost completely lost their importance during the 1960s and 1970s, as transport technology improved and trucks replaced both railroads and waterways in the transportation of raw material and final products.

There were also some local social factors that weakened production conditions. The plywood industry of that time was labour intensive, and a prominent feature of the local labour market in Vuohijärvi had been the disproportionate number of unskilled workers; thus, the income level was low and the housing conditions poor. These inferior living conditions and the disproportionate number of older and retired people caused problems later on in recruiting permanent workers. They also forced many young people to move away.

The old mill building and the outdated machinery would have needed extensive investment in order to continue profitable plywood production in the 1970s and early 1980s. However, all the above-mentioned factors decreased the willingness of the managers of the parent corporation to put money into the Vuohijärvi mill. They found it more profitable to allocate investment to other plants, and, as a consequence, the production and workforce of the Vuohijärvi mill diminished. At the same time, they began to expand the Grahn Corporation by incorporating new enterprises. The relative importance

Table 9.1   **Vuohijärvi mill's share of the labour force and of the net sales of the parent corporation, 1978, 1981, and 1985**

	Share of the labour force (%)	Share of net sales (%)
1978	24	28
1981	15	14
1985	8	6

Source: Kortelainen (1991, 93).

and economic attractiveness of Vuohijärvi declined markedly from the parent corporation's point of view (see table 9.1).

There were serious plans to close the mill, because it had become unsuitable for modern plywood production. These plans were, however, changed and the company began to seek a new product that would be more appropriate for the local circumstances in the late 1970s. Veneer was selected as the main line of production because it had several advantages compared with plywood. First, veneer production had some parquet producers in Sweden and Germany as permanent main customers. Secondly, it was easier to get raw material, because veneer was produced from fir rather than birch. Thirdly, the production better fitted the local conditions: the old mill building was well suited to veneer manufacturing and a smaller labour force was needed.

The production of veneer was launched in 1979 and it increased rapidly, so that, in the mid-1980s, only 20 per cent of production at the mill was plywood. The mill, therefore, became profitable, and new investments were carried out in 1984 in order to modernize veneer production. Furniture manufacturing was chosen as the secondary line of production, and some of the former plywood workers who were not needed in veneer production were able to find new jobs there. None the less, more than 30 per cent of the manufacturing jobs disappeared in Vuohijärvi during the 1970s (see fig. 9.2).

Bankruptcy and restart

In spring 1986, Vuohijärvi faced a serious crisis when the parent corporation, Grahn, went bankrupt. This rapidly expanded forest corporation had collapsed and was dissolved within a couple of months. All employees were discharged and it seemed that the mill would be closed for good. Although the bankruptcy caused uncertainty and scepticism among the villagers, behind the scenes numerous local and outside actors were seeking solutions for the future of the mill. The local managers of the mill, the authorities of the municipality of Valkeala, and the provincial authorities were the most active. The development of the mill and the measures taken after the bankruptcy are presented in detail below.

The first task, in order to save the mill, was to maintain production. Therefore, it was necessary to convince the customers (the parquet producers) that production would not cease and orders would be filled. It was also necessary to reassure the liquidators and the financing banks that the continuation of production would be profitable. Since the supply of the raw material could be arranged, most of the former workers were called back to work and production restarted one month after their discharge. The mill stopped only during the summer holiday season, as had always happened every year.

In autumn 1986, the state government granted Vuohijärvi the status of a "Special Support Area" and, as a consequence, the highest level of regional policy benefits and grants could be allocated to it. Two companies were established to continue the production of the old Vuohijärvi mill. Four local managers and supervisors of the plywood mill and a provincial development company, Eficap, established Kalso-Teollisuus to restart veneer production. The furniture production of the Grahn Corporation was taken over by Lepofinn, and the furniture department in Vuohijärvi became a branch plant. Kalso-Teollisuus was an independent firm and its head office was located in Vuohijärvi. However, despite the fact that the mill did not close, approximately 40 per cent of the manufacturing jobs in Vuohijärvi were lost as a result of the bankruptcy.[1]

Several factors made it possible to carry on production almost without a break after the bankruptcy. With regard to furniture production, the main reason was simply the fact that furniture production had been the most flourishing and profitable part of the Grahn Corporation. The restart of veneer production was a more complex matter and thus requires a more detailed examination. Finnish plywood producers and their national association were the central actors enabling the continuance of the mill, although they were not committed to any concrete measures for the benefit of the Vuohijärvi mill. Indeed, it was the fact that certain measures were not carried out that turned out to be the crucial factor in the survival of Vuohijärvi. In order to understand the role of the large forest companies in this matter, the Vuohijärvi case must be compared with the fate of another of the Grahn Corporation's plywood mills in the city of Mikkeli. After its bankruptcy, similar measures, also involving public authorities, were undertaken in the hope of restarting the Mikkeli mill. However, although a great deal of money had been invested in the Mikkeli mill just before the bankruptcy, it never went back into production. The mill was offered to forest companies, but none of them wanted to buy it and carry on producing plywood there. The plans for a restart were a failure because the mill was a non-diversified plywood mill and competition was intense in the plywood sector in both the export and the raw material markets. Given these conditions, large companies producing plywood realized they had a chance to reduce the capacity of the plywood industry. They therefore bought up the machinery of the Mikkeli mill and removed it to prevent a planned restart.

The soundest part of Vuohijärvi was the veneer production started in the late 1970s. Kalso-Teollisuus had permanent customers, and, most importantly, a product that was not in competition with any of the large forest companies. Since the 1970s, the local management of the corporation had striven to shift the production line from highly competitive plywood to veneer, which was more suitable for local conditions. The company had invested in new production and the mill was profitable enough, although the parent corporation was not. Since the new firm was not continuing plywood production, major plywood producers had no reason to prevent production by the mill. Vuohijärvi mill did not compete in mature plywood markets and it used fir instead of scarce birch as a raw material. Essentially, the fact that the interests of large forest companies and the new firm were not contradictory offered it a niche for veneer production. If the production of Kalso-Teollisuus had interfered with the large plywood producers, they would have forced the new company, which was still in its planning phase, to close, as happened at Mikkeli. An indicator of this was that the big plywood press was dismantled and taken away from the Vuohijärvi mill. This ensured the end of plywood production, but did not harm veneer production.

Another central factor in rescuing the Vuohijärvi mill was the fact that the locality was chosen as a sort of pilot case for regional policies. When the symptoms of deindustrialization began to occur and jobs decreased in Finnish industrial localities, the old regional policy measures turned out to be insufficient. The province of Kymi, in which Vuohijärvi is located, is very dependent on forest industries.

Therefore, it was a region where the restructuring of industry hit hard and new ideas for regional policy were needed. The Ministry of Trade and Industry had appointed a "Vuohijärvi Committee" in 1985 to discuss new means of helping the development of Vuohijärvi and other industrial localities in the province. The aim of the committee was to develop measures, building on the Vuohijärvi experience, that could be applied in other localities suffering from deindustrialization. The committee, having already completed its work, was called together again immediately after the bankruptcy.

The Vuohijärvi Committee linked several influential state and municipal authorities personally with developing the locality. Several of the actors who influenced the regional policy measures had already been actively involved in the Vuohijärvi question before the bankruptcy, and, consequently, they did not think of Vuohijärvi as just one locality among many. For example, the Ministry of Trade and Industry had not previously supported bankrupt firms or closed mills in restarting production. In the case of Vuohijärvi, the principle was changed and a precedent was set. The rules of the regional policy were changed and, since then, benefits have been given on condition that the bankrupt firm or closed mill was both profitable and essential for the surrounding locality.

Actors at the provincial level were the most active of the non-local actors. Eficap, the development company of the province of Kymi, had been established as a joint venture between the state, the municipalities, and firms to relieve the effects of deindustrialization and encourage small-enterprise activities. In the Vuohijärvi case, its task was, first, to examine and report on how to deal with the situation after the bankruptcy, and then, secondly, to take part in restarting production at the mill as a minority shareholder in Kalso-Teollisuus. Later Eficap bought the majority of the shares.

The role of the government authorities was to create favourable conditions for business in Vuohijärvi. The regional representatives of the Ministry of Trade and Industry and the provincial planners maintained active contacts with the central governmental bodies in Helsinki. They played a major role with respect to arranging start-up grants, development grants, and investment loans for the new company. However, one of the key actors was the Minister of Trade and Industry himself, who had, a couple of years before, bought a vacation home a few kilometres from Vuohijärvi. Therefore, not only could he observe the development of Vuohijärvi very closely, but he had some dependence on the locality.

214

The role of local actors

Industrial localities have traditionally been regarded as places without power. It has been emphasized that their development has been solely determined by market forces, and decisions concerning local economies have been made in far-away cities by the top managers of parent enterprises (Bradbury 1984). In the 1980s, however, the experiences of the deindustrialization process and the restructuring of manufacturing began to change this perception. Numerous studies concerning local response emerged (for example, Cox and Mair 1988; Cooke 1989). According to these, locally dependent actors were not passive witnesses of restructuring but were beginning to fight back. These studies revealed community responses emerging in different forms in which local employees, local administration, and local businesses worked together in various combinations. A common theme in these studies is the importance of collective action. Action is seen to be carried out by workers' unions, local development coalitions, or other local organizations (see Fitzgerald 1991; Herod 1991; Ironside 1994). This brings us to a discussion of whether or not power existed at the local level in the case of Vuohijärvi – that is, power with significant effects on local development.

No separate local organization emerged to try and prevent the consequences of restructuring. However, a local response did occur, and it was channelled through the actions of municipal authorities and local official staff of the mill. The municipal authorities were mainly motivated by the fact that the local state is fiscally dependent on the local tax base, and restructuring can reduce taxes and, therefore, cause fiscal crises for municipalities (Cox and Mair 1988, 311). The closure of the Vuohijärvi mill would have cut manufacturing jobs by half and doubled the unemployment rate of Valkeala municipality. It would have slashed the local tax base, and created social and economic problems that would have generated extra costs for municipal institutions. Therefore, the municipal authorities were actively involved in the Vuohijärvi problem. After the bankruptcy, the municipality financed research into how to continue production at the mill, and it even became a major owner of the mill buildings. A couple of years later, the municipality sold its share of the mill buildings to Kalso-Teollisuus.

Some of the mill's local white-collar employees and management were the most active local residents during the restart process. Their role is very interesting, because their motives differed from those of the municipal authorities. The local managers' activities were not based on professional duties or institutional local dependence, but stemmed primarily from their personal, subjective, local dependence. In order to understand the motives for local activity in Vuohijärvi, local development must be examined in terms of a longer period.

When the mill faced serious problems as a result of the buyer's market and its future was at stake in the 1970s, it was the local managers who played a key role in seeking new solutions in order to continue production at the mill. They began to look for new products to manufacture, and they were also responsible for the large investments made in 1984 for the purpose of intensifying veneer production. After the bankruptcy of the Grahn Corporation, the local managers took over the new enterprise as major shareholders and took considerable economic risks. They thus combined the roles of capitalist investor and local citizen in their actions. On the one hand, their motives were economic, because the enterprise provided them with the opportunity to take part in a flourishing business. On the other hand, they had grown up in Vuohijärvi and had chosen the locality as their place of residence. They had local social networks and emotional ties, and, in addition, local economic interests, skills tied to the local mill, and social status that would have been impossible to create elsewhere. They had, in other words, very strong traditional and modern local dependencies (Cox and Mair 1988). During the bankruptcy process, their own interests and the future of the whole locality were at stake. According to the managers, concern about Vuohijärvi's prospects was one of the main reasons for taking personal risks and establishing the new enterprise.

The local managers of large corporations have usually been regarded not as local actors but rather as executors of decisions made by the corporation management (Koch and Gartell 1992, 210). In contrast, the present study demonstrates that their influence has been underestimated. The local managers of Vuohijärvi were quite able to draw up their own plans for the mill and persuade the management of the corporation to accept them. These local managers had their personal local dependencies, and they did not behave as passive messengers of corporation élites but exercised their own distinct power.

Social consequences

Although the mill was restarted in 1986, approximately 80 former plywood workers lost their jobs. In other words, over 30 per cent of

216

the total jobs in Vuohijärvi disappeared during the bankruptcy and restart process. Thus, one would ordinarily expect a severe unemployment problem and several other social problems to have emerged. However, the unemployment rate in Vuohijärvi was only 8 per cent in 1989. The rate increased immediately after the bankruptcy, but after a year it was at the same level as before the bankruptcy. Though the unemployment rate was higher than the national average in the late 1980s, it was relatively low in comparison with the number of industrial jobs lost. The factors that prevented the formation of a serious unemployment problem will now be discussed.

One of the most popular means of dealing with job decrease is to create substitute jobs in a community. Traditionally, this has been done by locating new activities in depressed resource communities. Recently, more emphasis has been put on encouraging unemployed workers to establish small enterprises and in this way to create their jobs themselves. Neither of these factors was the cause of the relatively low unemployment rate in Vuohijärvi. There were some preliminary investigations into the possibilities of establishing a distillery near Vuohijärvi in order to replace the lost jobs. The distillery would have created 100 to 150 new jobs, but it never happened. Furthermore, none of the former plywood workers established firms of their own. Plywood workers' skills and the remoteness of the community did not provide the best preconditions for becoming an entrepreneur, and the local working culture, based on monotonous industrial work, did not create the most favourable background for entrepreneurship.

Because the locality did not offer any new employment opportunities, many of the former plywood workers had to move away. During the three years after the bankruptcy, half of the discharged workers migrated from Vuohijärvi to localities where jobs were available. For those who were living in rented company or municipal houses and had otherwise weak ties in the community, it was fairly easy to move.

Out-migration has been the most common way of dealing with job loss in small and undiversified localities (Bradbury 1984). This has partly been the case in Vuohijärvi throughout its existence, since decline in plywood production has usually been followed by selective out-migration. However, in spite of some migration after the bankruptcy, half of the discharged workers were still living in Vuohijärvi in 1989.

Retirement seems to have been the second important factor in preventing the rise of an unemployment problem (see table 9.2). The

Table 9.2   **Economic activity of the people discharged after the bankruptcy and still living in Vuohijärvi, 1989**

	Number	Percentage
Retired	25	68
In work	6	16
Unemployed	4	11
Student	1	3
Activity unknown	1	3
Total	37	100

Source: Kortelainen (1991, 110).

official retirement age in Finland is 65 years, but, in certain circumstances, the pension system permits early retirement for people over 55.[2] Older age categories dominated the age structure of the Vuohijärvi mill in the 1980s, so the bankruptcy gave many of the former workers the opportunity to retire early. The early retirement system has been effectively exploited in Finland during the deindustrialization process, and, thus, the local social consequences of mill closures or job decreases have been less severe than would have been the case without this system (see, for example, Tykkyläinen 1992, 242). Older workers are the most threatened by long-term unemployment, because they are the least likely to move or to get new jobs.

Out-migration and early retirement reduced the social problems that would have emerged if long-term unemployment had been greater. But this does not mean that there were no social problems in Vuohijärvi. Problems in the housing market were especially visible. The overrepresentation of unskilled workers, low wages, and a long period of decline were responsible for the lack of improvement in Vuohijärvi's housing conditions in comparison with national development in the 1960s and 1970s (see Rannikko 1990).

In the 1980s, however, the situation began to change as the municipality became the decisive actor in the housing market. At the turn of the decade, one-third of all housing in Vuohijärvi was owned by the municipality (Rannikko 1990, 224). Not only did the municipality build rental houses but, with the bankruptcy, all company-owned housing shifted to municipal ownership. Afterwards, substandard company houses were demolished and new rental houses were built on the site. A very important reason for building new rental houses was to help recruitment for the mill by providing up-to-date dwellings, since, earlier, the company had had difficulty getting permanent workers because of the inferior housing conditions. In other words, the municipal authorities took housing policy measures to support the operation of the Vuohijärvi mill.

Most of the single-family homes were renovated during the 1980s, supported by various public renovation loans and allowances. The conversion of more and more single-family homes to holiday homes owned by city residents is a special characteristic of the housing market in Vuohijärvi. A supply of single-family houses and the unpolluted lake have been the main attractions for summer residency. Vuohijärvi and its surroundings have been transformed from a single-industry community into one with a mixed economy. In addition to being a mill town, it is also, for instance, a summer resort for cottage owners from the cities of southern Finland.

Discussion: The interplay of factors

Industrial capital, the public sector, and local actors

External forces have been the main determinant of the "long waves" of Vuohijärvi's development. Its very favourable location for plywood production shaped the development of the community from the start of the mill up to the late 1970s. The community came into existence and grew because of the good conditions for profitable production. Later on, Vuohijärvi began to decline as its economic attractiveness decreased owing to overproduction, falling prices, and a shortage of birch. Developments after the late 1970s, however, cannot be understood as resulting only from market forces or outside factors.

Although locational factors played a distinctive role in determining the spatial division of labour in the plywood sector, other functions and roles developed in the locality. Many of these functions can be described by the concept of local dependence. During the period when the locality offered favourable conditions for plywood production, different actors became dependent on it in various ways. Local dependence ties actors to a locality; in other words, it prevents spatial mobility (Cox and Mair 1988). Financial capital is much more mobile than actors, which may cause conflicts between the interests of locally dependent actors and the interests of national or multinational corporations during the restructuring processes. The closure of a mill may be rational from the viewpoint of a large corporation, but it is

219

against the interests of locally dependent actors and can be devastating for a locality. This was the case in Vuohijärvi and it was the main cause of local action.

Although local actors could not stop the decline of the locality, they did have a major effect on its development. Without their activities, the mill would most likely have been closed completely. The local managers strove consciously to find a way around the institutional barriers in the plywood sector, and, through their persistence, they were able to shift production to a new, profitable sector. In this respect, external conditions not only constrained conscious choices but also offered some opportunities. Thus, it could be claimed that the external forces had the most decisive role, because they provided the general conditions for the restart. None the less, during the restart process the fate of Vuohijärvi rested on the combination of the opportunities provided by the forestry companies and banks, the economic preconditions provided by public institutions, and the conscious actions of local actors. If any one of these elements had been missing, the plans for a restart might never have been realized. Therefore, none of these three factors can be considered to be more important than the others.

Recently, a large literature concerning the endogenous development of regions has emerged. Most of it has emphasized local abilities and opportunities to mobilize and control local economic development (see, for example, Garofoli 1992). Although the recent development of Vuohijärvi has many endogenous characteristics, it would be an overstatement to refer to it as endogenous. It has been an interactive process in which both endogenous and exogenous factors have been necessary elements.

The locational choices of enterprises have traditionally been popular research subjects among economists and economic geographers. The basic assumption has been that, in a market economy, firms are looking for optimal locations for given economic activities. This was the case when the founder of the Vuohijärvi mill was seeking the best location for his plywood mill and chose the most profitable of many other possible ones. Later, during the restructuring process in the locality, this situation was reversed. When the existing production lost its locational advantages, suitable new production was sought for the local mill. In other words, the entrepreneur was searching for the optimal activity for a given location. This switch can also be explained by the local dependence of actors. A firm can be highly dependent on a locality, for example because of its investments in built environment or because of its dependence on locally tied workers (Jonas 1992). Furthermore, especially in the case of small firms, it is common for the entrepreneur to be personally attached to a locality before he or she begins running a business. For these actors, locational choices are not necessarily the most relevant issues. Rather, the most relevant issue is the problem of selecting the proper economic activity for the particular conditions that their locality provides.

The role of social capital

In recent studies, much emphasis has been placed on local social resources as sources of effective local responses against plant closures. Existing social networks and local organizations provide a certain basis for local activity. Several concepts have been used to describe these resources; community cohesion and community consciousness have been the most common (see, for example, Fitzgerald 1991; Koch and Gartell 1992). Here, local social resources are seen in a broader context, and, consequently, the concept of social capital is applied (see Bourdieu 1986, 248–249). Social capital implies social networks and mutual social connections that enable an actor or group to enlarge its power. The volume of social capital depends on the extent of the network connections and on the power (economic, political, etc.) of those to whom the actor is linked.

In this paper, social capital has been presented in a spatial context, and in a local setting it has two dimensions. First, it implies power that depends on the density and cohesion of the locality's internal social network. Secondly, it includes connections with outside actors. Studies concerning local responses have been inadequate in this respect, because they have paid very little attention to cooperation between local and outside actors. Social networks are never purely local, and external contacts and interests do exist. As the Vuohijärvi experience demonstrates, external actors and their prestige can have significant effects on the development of a locality. The Vuohijärvi Committee linked several influential actors with Vuohijärvi, and the Minister of Trade and Industry was personally tied to the locality. These contacts enlarged the social capital of local actors and were valuable when regional policy measures and various sources of funding were planned.

One of the main practical lessons of this study is that old and old-fashioned can be valuable too. In other words, although flexible production and new technology are the bywords of today, there exist countless niches for old Fordist production. If the measures and investments of public institutions or private firms are directed only to new growth sectors, there is a risk that potentially profitable Fordist factories will be needlessly closed. The possibilities for continuing production should be examined carefully and the restart of a plant should be supported if it turns out that it will be profitable. In many cases, this is far cheaper than attracting and establishing new firms in order to replace lost jobs.

But, instead of concentrating only on production, there may be other ways of preventing or slowing down the effects of a local downswing. One of them is housing. The service class is becoming the hegemonic group in Western societies (on the concept, see e.g. Urry 1988, 40–41). The emerging culture of the service class idealizes, for example, countryside, traditional landscapes, and old built environments, a phenomenon that is visible in, for example, their residential preferences (Thrift 1989). Old mill communities are often very rich in tradition, with old buildings and parklands, and, thus, they can be very attractive places for newcomers planning on moving from the city to a smaller settlement. This development will benefit primarily communities that are located near larger centres, making commuting possible. It does not help remote depressed resource communities. Nor does it necessarily help the original inhabitants of the community, who may be faced with a change of their community from a traditional working-class to a middle-class community.

Endogenous versus exogenous forces

It is fairly fruitless to argue about whether endogenous or exogenous forces are generally the dominant factors in regional development. In some localities, exogenous forces have a dominant position; in other cases, regional development has more endogenous characteristics. The importance of internal or endogenous factors does, however, seem to be increasing. The restructuring of industrial society has increased competition between localities for economic activities and public assistance (Cox and Mair 1988, 307; Jonas 1992, 350–351; Neil and Tykkyläinen 1992, 20). Simultaneously, the balancing role of the welfare state seems to be decreasing at the national level. In Finland, and other Nordic countries, until the early 1990s the welfare state compensated for unbalanced regional development. It provided equal services, and therefore created similar service jobs, in different localities. Furthermore, the state used regional policy measures to help poorer areas. Now, various austerity programmes are cutting public services, and, instead of active regional policies, governments are putting more emphasis on private activity in order to ensure local business and regional development (Amin and Malmberg 1992, 412–413; Kortelainen and Rannikko 1993). Localities will be more and more on their own in the competition for new jobs, economic activities, and state expenditure.

Public services and income transfers are of the utmost importance for Vuohijärvi and other declining resource communities in Finland. Pensions are almost as significant as the salaries of mill workers in the local economy of Vuohijärvi, and, without public housing, the condition of dwellings would be much worse and the mill would have enormous difficulties in recruiting workers. Furthermore, public measures eased the consequences of the bankruptcy: early retirement opportunities decreased unemployment rates, and, without regional policy measures, restarting the mill would have been impossible. The support of the strong welfare state has been the main reason for the relatively weak negative social effects of deindustrialization in Finnish industrial localities. If welfare expenditure is ever dramatically cut, future mill closures and decreases in manufacturing jobs may cause much more serious and far-reaching social problems than have occurred so far in Finnish mill communities.

Notes

1. Kalso-Teollisuus was still producing veneer in 1996, but furniture production was stopped in Vuohijärvi when Lepofinn went bankrupt in 1991. The number of employees increased to 120 in 1995.
2. Retirement is allowed at the age of 55 if a person's working capacity has decreased or the work has become too hard. Furthermore, if unemployment has lasted over 200 days, a pension can be granted to a person over 60.

References

Amin, A. and Malmberg, A. (1992), "Competing Structural and Institutional Influences on Geography of Production in Europe," *Environment and Planning* A 24, pp. 401–416.

Bagguley, P., Mark-Lawson, J., Shapiro, D., Urry, J., Walby, S., and Warde, A. (1990), *Restructuring: Place, Class and Gender*, Sage, Worcester.

Bourdieu, P. (1986), "The Forms of Capital," in J. Richardson (ed.), *Handbook of Theory and Research for the Sociology of Education*, Greenwood Press, Westport, Conn., pp. 241–258.

Bradbury, J. H. (1984), "Declining Single-Industry Communities in Quebec-Labrador, 1979–1983," *Journal of Canadian Studies* 19, pp. 125–139.

Cooke, P. (ed.) (1989), *Localities. The Changing Face of Urban Britain*, Unwin, London and Worcester.

Cox, K. R. and Mair, A. (1988), "Locality and Community in the Politics of Local Economic Development," *Annals of the Association of American Geographers* 78, pp. 307–325.

Duijn, J. J. van (1984), "Fluctuations in Innovations over Time," in C. Freeman (ed.), *Long Waves in the World Economy*, Pinter, London, pp. 19–30.

Fitzgerald, J. (1991), "Class as Community: The New Dynamics of Social Change," *Environment and Planning D: Society and Space* 9, pp. 117–128.

Garofoli, G. (1992), "Endogenous Development and Southern Europe: An Introduction," in G. Garofoli (ed.), *Endogenous Development in Southern Europe*, Avebury, Aldershot, pp. 1–13.

Herod, A. (1991), "Local Political Practice in Response to Manufacturing Plant Closure: How Geography Complicates Class Analysis," *Antipode* 23, pp. 385–402.

Ironside, R. G. (1994), "Concept of Dependency: The Canadian Resource Dependent Community," in Ulf Wiberg (ed.), *Marginal Areas in Developed Countries*, CERUM, Umeå, pp. 83–89.

Jonas, A. (1992), "Corporate Takeover and Politics of Community: The Case of Norton Company in Worcester," *Economic Geography* 68, pp. 348–372.

Koch, A. and Gartell, J. (1992), "'Keep Jobs in Kootenays': Coping with Closure in British Columbia," in C. Neil, M. Tykkyläinen, and J. Bradbury (eds.), *Coping with Closure. An International Comparison of Mine Town Experiences*, Routledge, London, pp. 208–224.

Kortelainen, J. (1991), "Vanerin varassa. Tutkimus Vuohijärven tehdasyhdyskunnan elinkaaresta," *Joensuum yliopisto, Karjalan tutkimuslaitoksen julkaisuja* 99, Joensuu.

Kortelainen, J. and Rannikko, P. (1993), "Restructuring of Small Rural Centres in Finland," paper for the European Summer Institute in Regional Science, June 1993, Joensuu, Finland.

Massey, D. (1984), *Spatial Division of Labour*, Macmillan, London.

Metsäteollisuus ry (1995), *Avain Suomen metsäteollisuuteen*, Talousviestintä Oy, Espoo.

Neil, C. and Tykkyläinen, M. (1992), "Introduction," in C. Neil, M. Tykkyläinen, and J. Bradbury (eds.), *Coping with Closure. An International Comparison of Mine Town Experiences*, Routledge, London, pp. 1–23.

Oksa, J. and Rannikko, P. (1988), "The Social Consequences of the Differentiation of Agriculture and Forestry. A Case Study of Two Villages in Finnish Forest Periphery," *Acta Sociologica* 31, pp. 217–229.

Rannikko, P. (1990), "Locality Studies and the Housing Market," *Scandinavian Housing and Planning Research* 7, pp. 223–226.

Rothwell, R. (1982), "The Role of Technology in Industrial Change: Implications for Regional Policy," *Regional Studies* 16, pp. 361–369.

Thrift, N. (1989), "Images of Social Change," in C. Hamnett, L. McDowell, and P. Sarre (eds.), *Restructuring Britain. The Changing Social Structure*, Sage Publications, London, pp. 12–42.

Tykkyläinen, M. (1992), "Solutions to Mine Closure in Outokumpu," in C. Neil, M. Tykkyläinen, and J. Bradbury (eds.), *Coping with Closure. An International Comparison of Mine Town Experiences*, Routledge, London, pp. 225–246.

Urry, John (1988), "Cultural Change and Contemporary Holiday Making," *Theory, Culture and Society* 5, pp. 35–55.

Väänänen, A. (1983), "Suomen vaneriteollisuuden kehitys," *Paperi ja Puu* 10.

10

Toward translocal communities: A mine in Western Australia

Markku Tykkyläinen

Introduction

This case-study deals with the restructuring of settlement policy in Western Australia. A large, sparsely populated state, Western Australia represents new thinking in community development and local economic policy, and, more fundamentally, it demonstrates the inevitable pressures that necessitate changes in policy and planning as a result of technological progress, economics, and the choices of individuals.

The last half of the twentieth century has been characterized by the concentration of the population of Western Australia in one metropolitan area. Other agglomerations, often based on mining, have remained small. In the late 1970s, Australia's "construction stage" engaged in many resource-processing activities, especially mining. Eventually, however, the creation of new mining towns in remote locations ended, marking a considerable change in regional policy and fundamentally affecting local economic policy. In this new approach, the construction of mining townships in remote areas has been replaced by long-distance commuting with accommodation provided at the working site. This commuting-based settlement type was discussed by Newton and Robinson (1987) as an already functioning option among new, more flexible, settlement types, which was developed in order to avoid the problems experienced in single-industry communities (ibid.).

Rural communities are usually stereotyped as "typical" mining communities, "typical" service centres, or "typical" agricultural villages. They are under pressure to restructure in a way that embraces new, more efficient housing and settlement practices. It should be noted, however, that commuting-based settlements do not replace traditional rural communities, scattered settlements, villages, or towns on a large scale, but they are a solution to the problems of organizing housing and everyday life in extremely remote places.

It is important to recognize that within this commuting-based practice the traditional one-to-one relationship between a community and the respective local area such as a town or village disappears. The implementation of this advanced community type modifies a society's spatial structure, in that the individual is tied closely to two sites, a place of work and a domicile, and the traditional environment of a single living space disappears. The geographical space for an employee is no longer uni-nodal, confined to a single locality, but consists of time–space contacts across the ordinary spatial fields of activity. A community as a social unit for an employee is translocal.

Basic concepts and aims

The concept of commuter mining, in which employees spend a fixed number of days working on-site followed by a given period at home, has been introduced in the sparsely populated areas of Canada and Australia in the past few decades, and it has expanded rapidly since the early 1980s. These are not unique cases, for long-distance commuting and its applications have been in use, for instance in Russia, for a long time, and commuting by bus associated with on-site accommodation is frequently used in the region of Antofagasta in northern Chile. Mines such as Zaldivar and La Escondida were operating in this way in 1995. For clarity, the term "long-distance commuting" is considered to include employees who commute by air.

This research explores long-distance commuting in the mining industry in Western Australia, and aims at laying the foundations for possible ways of developing very remote regions or "sparselands" (Holmes 1981). It evaluates the suitability of this community development practice from the viewpoints of employees, companies, and the authorities, and it analyses it in the context of broader socio-economic transformation of values and behaviour in high-income economies and communities. This paper examines the technological, socio-economic, and behavioural reasons for the emergence of long-distance commuting, from the points of view of both the employees and the companies. Then, with the aim of contributing to a theory of development targeted in the introductory chapter of this book, the paper looks for an answer to the question of what the role of local economic development might be when remote areas are exploited.

Forrestania in the outback

The data for this paper are derived from a sample survey conducted at the Forrestania Nickel Mines in 1993, analysed in detail in other papers (Tykkyläinen 1994; 1996a). The mining complex is located in semi-arid mallee forest, 10–15 km from a sparsely populated agricultural area, and 380 km east of Perth (fig. 10.1). Forrestania Nickel Mines is a part of the globally operating Outokumpu Group, which employs 14,000 people in mines, smelters, and subsidiaries in several countries. The head office of the conglomerate is in the Greater Helsinki area, Finland, but the mine is run locally on-site and from offices in Perth.

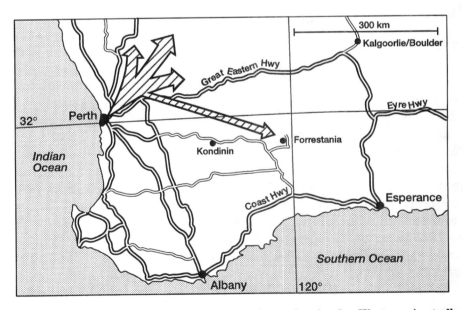

Fig. 10.1 **The directions of long-distance commuting in the Western Australia mining sector.**

228

The Forrestania Nickel Mines, consisting of underground mines and open pits, excavate 700,000 tonnes of ore and produce 7,600 tonnes of nickel in concentrate per year (1995). Nickel ore is processed at a highly automated mill in the middle of the mining area, and the concentrate is then transported to the nearest port, Esperance. When a sample survey for this case-study was conducted in April 1993, the mining complex was starting production, and a large majority of the employees were constructing mine galleries and finishing various installations. The 193 employees of the mines in April 1993 commuted chiefly from Perth and worked mainly in rotation cycles of five days on and two days off or two weeks on and one week off. The employees of the mining company and some of the contractors commuted by air and lived in a well-equipped accommodation complex, which had been completed at the end of 1992, providing board and lodging for 128 employees. The rest were lodged in two contractors' camps.

The standard of lodging in the complex can best be compared with that of a modern motel. The complex consisted of two–four-room units with private shower and toilet. Other facilities included a restaurant, laundry facilities, swimming pool, gym, cable television and video broadcasting, a bar, and a tennis court. The two small contractors' camps consisted of temporary workmen's cabins and recreational facilities such as a television room and a gym.

About 70 per cent of the employees had homes in the metropolitan area of Perth, and they made one to four return flights per month between home and the mining site. The metropolitan area of Perth is large ($5,400 km^2$), and has more than 1 million inhabitants. Mining employees typically live in single houses in a suburban environment. The mining complex is located in the shire of Kondinin, but the local authority is not very interested in developing new infrastructure near Forrestania, because the mining region is located on the fringe of the shire, 150 km from the municipal centre, and the shire has little in the way of funds for the development of its outback. Hence, the employees of Forrestania and the local authority have few common interests.

Employees sometimes go shopping and in search of recreation in the tiny, nearby towns (Tykkyläinen 1993, 68–70), and the company makes good use of local suppliers and mining-related contractors. The local supply of goods and services is, however, limited, and a mine of 200 employees cannot create sufficient demand for many new services to be profitable.

Reasons for the emergence of long-distance commuting

Technology and the spatial expansion of business

Many reasons for the disappearance of traditional mining and company towns can be traced to technological development. Furthermore, resource-processing activities are expanding into new places. Although this case-study deals with the mining sector, similar developments have been experienced in other resource sectors such as forestry, oil, and gas. This model does not fit in agriculture, although large-scale company farming may change the time–space behaviour of individuals.

First, improved communications have promoted global operations. Improvements have been considerable – for example, it took only 25–30 years to pass from manual long-distance telephone calls to the era of cellular phones, faxes, and the Internet. The effects of the abolition of trade barriers and the end of the Cold War have also been significant (Humphreys 1995). A modern resource-processing company consists of a network of primary production sites, mills, plants, and research and development facilities in different parts of the world. The working community of the whole company is, thus, multilocal, linked together by efficient communications. Modern technology has greatly facilitated the global networking of business activities.

Secondly, the availability of more efficient transport, and especially of a wide range of fuel-efficient aircraft, has improved the feasibility and economy of commuting, while increased productivity has reduced the number of employees needed on-site, and thus the number to be transported to each production site has decreased. Automation has made it possible to reduce the direct human labour input on-site, but has increased the number of visits by maintenance experts. The employees are highly specialized in most processing stages, and, therefore, they are recruited from the diversified and extensive labour market.

Thirdly, contracting is increasing, and only a specific nucleus of employees work at the site regularly. Contracting allows companies to take on experts for a short period. This is true in the pulp mills as well as in mining. For instance, 43 per cent of the employees in mines operating on a long-distance commuting basis in Western Australia in 1991 were employed by contractors (Houghton 1993, 289), and two-thirds of those working at Forrestania in its start-up phase in 1993 were similarly on contractors' payrolls.

Fourthly, economic growth has been strong in newly industrialized countries in Asia and in some countries of South America. This growth is expected to continue, and, in association with this process, the mineral sector is likely to see the withdrawal of government involvement and its deregulation (Humphreys 1995). An economic upswing is also expected to take place soon in the outlying parts of Russia, where old equipment will eventually have to be replaced by new installations. Thus, more resource-processing activities will be operating in harsh environments and very remote places in the future, which will, in turn, require new commuting and housing practices.

Finally, technological changes have reduced the perceived importance of settling sparsely populated regions for defence purposes.

Socio-economic benefits

The rise of commuting and temporary accommodation is connected with the fact that public services are provided at already existing localities such as metropolitan areas, towns, and municipalities, and local authorities, and companies to a smaller degree, wish to avoid the costs of both building new infrastructures and providing new services. Small communities possess certain limitations in the adequate provision of public services, which are expensive to start up and maintain compared with commuting alternatives.

Investment in temporary accommodation complexes does not represent a substantial part of the investments in a mining project as a whole. In the case of an advanced nickel mine with an on-site mill, the value of the accommodation investment is only a small proportion of the total investment (3 per cent in the case of Forrestania). The entire arrangements for commuting, board, and lodging accounted for an additional cost of 28 per cent over and above the actual labour costs in Forrestania in April 1993, and again in 1994. An employee's working hours of up to 2,500–2,600 hours per year compensate for these extra costs.

Although the expenses of long-distance commuting add an additional one-quarter to one-third to a company's labour costs, the company saves money because it does not need to invest in a company town. Higher costs are compensated by the longer working hours of a compressed working schedule. The company also benefits from a lower turnover of labour and less problematic labour relations.

The Forrestania case proved that long-distance commuting is the advantageous way of organizing housing, commuting, and work in the outback. Low investment costs, the competitive prices of flights, and flexibility in the use of labour, along with the relatively small number of employees, are all factors that make long-distance commuting more profitable than establishing a separate mining town.

Long-distance commuting could be regulated by introducing taxes or development guidelines, but changes in government policies have meant that this has not been done in Western Australia during the past 10 years. The shift away from mine town policies is a result of politico-ideological changes and declining revenues in the public sector. Furthermore, regional development policies in Australia have been characterized by discontinuity and a lack of integration between policies evolved by different governments at the same level and by different levels of government at the same time (Taylor and Garlick 1989, 79). There have been many concerns associated with isolated mine town development. Many of these concerns in northern Western Australia can be understood in light of the state's policies in the 1960s and the primacy given to development over other social objectives and interests (Harman 1981). Assistance to private enterprises to encourage them to develop the north included favourable tax provisions, little or no restriction on the source of development capital and low royalties, and acceding to the wishes of the companies regarding the siting of new towns. By the end of the 1970s, however, external factors were forcing pragmatic changes with respect to the application of this development ideology. Returns of the mining sector were beginning to decline, and, by the mid-1970s, the government of Western Australia was feeling increasingly obliged to contribute more to the costs of infrastructure, which had usually been supplied by the mining company.

Despite all efforts, by the 1980s, federal and state regional policies in Australia had failed to diversify the economic base of country areas significantly. The declining economy, together with scepticism about the potential for success with regional policies in Australia, led to a new focus on macroeconomic reform (Taylor and Garlick 1989). By the end of the 1980s, many local economies had demonstrated that they were unable to generate the new jobs required to meet demand. Deindustrialization and national economic restructuring in a climate of lower economic growth led to most of the growth in business and consumer services occurring in the cities (Planning Research Centre 1989). The problems of resource communities, in particular, were exacerbated by the deregulation of the late 1980s and the rapid internationalization of the economy (Taylor and Garlick 1989, 83). By the early 1990s, the attention of governments was focused on the nation's high levels of unemployment. Theoretically, importance was still attached to regional issues but, as both state and federal governments were fighting public service debt (as in other Western countries), there was less scope for significant intervention to correct the regional "imbalance" in economic activity (Murphy and Roman 1988, 268).

In the contrast to the development of remote resource communities, increased long-distance commuting has been considered economical and acceptable by the authorities. Although the tax advantages of commuters have been criticized and worries have been presented about the low employment of locals in the outback (Department of State Development 1992), the major concern has been that economic development as a whole not be jeopardized by government restrictions. Most of all, the authorities have saved money, because they have not needed to invest in outback infrastructures. The experiences of the new townships established in the north-western parts of Western Australia have not encouraged such investments, and those towns have not operated as the growth centres of regions as was originally envisaged.

Finally, the fly-in/fly-out option potentially reduces the problems associated with the boom and bust conditions of mining that affect mining companies and communities alike. In boom times, isolated mining towns in Western Australia experienced a constant struggle with labour turnover and the recruitment of sufficient employees, and industrial relations problems were rife. As mines became less viable and downsizing took place, the reverse problems occurred. Gradually, over the life of the mine, a process of self-selection had occurred among the employees, and many of those who remained were people who had sought to make the isolated mining community their permanent home. For these people, the loss of their jobs meant total upheaval in all aspects of their lives, including the loss of their homes and disruption to their supportive networks of friends. These serious problems at the beginning and end of the life of a mine are substantially reduced by the commuting option – assuming, of course, that commuting employees are not all recruited from a single, small community that is dependent on the salaries earned at the mine.

233

Choice by the employees: Behavioural aspects

Long-distance commuting becomes a viable option if employees and their families are satisfied with it and with the rotational schedule of work and leisure-time. If they do not feel that this work situation is suitable on a permanent basis, the company should seek to develop mutually acceptable alternative arrangements.

A company applying long-distance commuting expects to create commitment to the mining site where it operates. One aim of the architecture and design of an accommodation complex is to avoid the notion that the complex is temporary in nature, so on-site accommodation premises in commuter mining are usually well planned.

According to the 1993 survey, most of the employees living in the mining company's accommodation complex in Forrestania were highly satisfied with it. Overall, they would have liked more leisure activities and improvements to that part of their everyday lives. When the question "Why might you plan to leave the mine?" was posed, no one referred to the premises or to life in the complex and camps as valid reasons. Hence the condition of the accommodation and the social life at mines such as Forrestania are not crucial factors determining whether employees stay or leave.

It is a very common finding that employees express general satisfaction with long-distance commuting and do not appear to have any long-term difficulties in adjusting to work schedules that involve lengthy periods in remote mines (Houghton 1993, 286; Gillies et al. 1991). These favourable attitudes are thought to exist for several main reasons. First, companies provide higher pay to attract employees to commuter mining. Secondly, the compressed work schedules associated with commuter mining provide employees with lengthy periods of leisure in which to pursue recreational activities and to spend more time with their families than do many employees working an eight-hour day, five day weeks (Houghton 1993, 286). Thirdly, it is possible to improve spouses' career prospects and children's education if they stay in the metropolitan area.

When the employees were asked to state their reasons for having decided to come and work in Forrestania, savings and pay ranked high on the list (Tykkyläinen 1994, 98). A question was also posed regarding the goals that the employee hoped to achieve at Forrestania. On average, one-third of the employees who had a definite goal felt that it was economic in nature, often a matter of saving for a specific purpose (for details, see Tykkyläinen 1996a, 233). The higher the socio-economic status of the employee, the less important the economic motives.

Although economic factors such as higher pay served to explain the attractiveness of work in commuter mining, they should not be exaggerated, and many employees also assigned great weight to factors such as the gaining of more experience, the improvement of skills, and the seeking of promotion. Once crucial economic goals have been achieved, other goals seem to increase in importance.

Though many commuting employees had rest periods of several days, the total time spent outside the home was much longer than with an ordinary work schedule. Furthermore, those employed in the administration of the Forrestania Mines worked on weekdays and spent their weekends at home. Thus, it is access to leisure activities and family life outside the mining site that the employees themselves consider so important. The employees at Forrestania agreed emphatically with the statement that they much prefer working on a rotational basis than living and working in a mining town. The choice must be seen in context, of course, in that many of them have only two options: to work periodically in the outback or to live there permanently.

The positive image of fly-in/fly-out operations is conducive to an acceptance of the practice. The employees in Forrestania agreed with statements that working on a rotational basis and living in accommodation complexes are a modern way of organizing work at a mine. On the other hand, one might say that the mining company and the subcontractors had succeeded in hiring the "right" people, because selection was based partly on candidates' willingness to accept and adapt to these ways of working.

As regards disadvantages, compressed work schedules, robotization, and long-distance commuting involve a greater intensification of work, and they may lead to greater stress than before. These new working and commuting arrangements can be seen as a post-Fordist production paradigm, which also covers "traditional" industrial sectors (see, for example, Hudson 1995).

The employees in Forrestania did not generally disagree with the statement that the rotational work schedule causes problems for family life. On the other hand, they reluctantly agreed that any such problems could be overcome without serious difficulties or drawbacks. Thus, although the effects on family life are mainly detrimental, they can to some extent be overcome. Most of the employees in Forrestania were married and 37 per cent of them had children.

Hence, the compatibility of working schedules with family life is crucial for the future of commuter mining. The employees in Forrestania found the fly-in/fly-out operation to their liking. Gillies et al. (1991) had similar findings in an individual employee survey on personal attitudes at 17 Australian mines.

The impact on domestic life of long-distance commuting, as compared with living in an isolated mining community, is also consistent with the increasing gender awareness and the associated changes in the role of wives that have been taking place in Australian society. For example, a lack of employment opportunities was a major problem for some women in the mining towns of the 1970s (Neil and Jones 1988). This problem is significantly reduced if the family remains based in a major city. Another gender issue was reflected in the comments of miners in Kidston, a commuter mine in Queensland. The men there talked of the effect that commuting had on the decision-making processes in the family: many men who had previously been in fairly traditional families found that their wives were assuming an increasingly important role in decision-making owing to the absence of their husbands. A number of men felt this had required significant adjustment on their part – some ultimately finding it a rewarding change, others accepting it only reluctantly.

Once basic needs such as shelter and food are achieved, the satisfaction of higher-level needs becomes crucial in everyday life and in the selection of a permanent place of residence (see Hoggart and Buller 1987, 18–27). The opinions of the employees of Forrestania on this aspect were obtained by asking them to assess the strength of the factors that had influenced their decision to continue living in their current homes.

The results show that the employees have a very strong attachment to the metropolitan environment. Those living in Perth do not wish to abandon their metropolitan lifestyle, as expressed in the statement "I like the lifestyle in my home town/region," which represented the most important reason for their continuing to live there. The miners enjoy city life and its abundant supply of commodities and recreational facilities, and statements mentioning "a pleasant place to live," "climate," and "the quality of the surrounding natural environment" were also ranked very high. For those with children, it was not a spouse but children who influenced the ranking – the attribute "a fine place to bring up children" was the most important tie to their present domiciles. It has often been shown that people prefer the environment in which they are currently living, but it was something of a surprise that such factors as lifestyle and the prevailing environment were ranked above economic and employment factors – commitment to work, finances, low housing costs, spouse's work – to such a marked extent.

Apart from the lifestyle factor, emotional and social ties, which cannot easily be replaced or compensated for by extra pay, are also very important reasons for staying put. As experiences in mining towns show, a company house – even when better than a house in a suburb – does not guarantee employee satisfaction (Gribbin and Brealey 1981; Newton 1985; Brealey and Newton 1978). One's lifestyle, social relations, and home atmosphere are not transferable to other localities.

The employees have adapted to the multilocal lifestyle, and do not feel it is unnatural. Rather, they consider it a very advanced lifestyle, and accept the new forms of spatial arrangements. Current perceptions of the significance of traditional notions of "local" and "regional" in administration and planning therefore require some rethinking.

The changing role of local economic policy

From local spin-offs to network spin-offs

Long-distance commuting could be criticized because the employment and income effects of new investment do not benefit a local community – instead, they "fly over." Employees are not recruited from the vicinity of a resource site, they and their families do not spend their incomes on goods and services provided by local businesses, and, above all, the company does not create an environment, as was the case with former industrial towns, in which the basic industry provides a catalyst for the development of producer services and other industries.

This chain of reasoning is very logical in the context of the traditional model of central places and their spheres of influence, and it fits in with Keynesian thinking about the multiplicative effects of a large resource-processing production unit. This way of thinking was valid a couple of decades ago, when, for instance, the Outokumpu Group operated within the state borders of Finland, with operations consisting of mining communities and smelters in a few industrial towns. However, economic systems no longer work within these frameworks. Nowadays, the company group consists of globally

operating units that concentrate on business and avoid the responsibilities of a "company town." This new strategy gained adherents in
the Outokumpu Group in the 1980s, when mine closures increased
the mobility of employees. In 1986, the corporation started an internal labour adjustment project with the aim of creating a flexible pool
of labour available to all the units of the corporation (Tykkyläinen
1992, 242). The model of an industrial community in which employees spend their whole career in a single locality was gradually
replaced by a network and project way of thinking.

Thus, economic transactions between the factories of transnational
companies are based on point-to-point contacts between many dispersed locations, increasing the network character of the spatial
structure and intimately linking the growth and decline of communities with each locality's specialization in a global context. Technologically advanced resource-processing units require very specialized
producer services and labour, which must be recruited nationwide or
even on a global scale. This has been a problem even in mining towns
where new investment has been carried out.

During the start-up phase of Forrestania in 1992–1993, local labour
markets were not able to satisfy the demand for a highly skilled
labour force, even though it had been expected that the local labour
supply would be sufficient. However, some subcontractors were
found and some employees were hired from the surrounding area.
Furthermore, the company used local suppliers of goods, services,
and contract work when it was considered possible and economical.
The remaining necessities had to be satisfied from external sources,
irrespective of whether employees or suppliers were located in the
mining town, in outlying tracts, in a metropolitan area, or abroad.

In reality, both advanced resource businesses and automated and
specialized high-volume production are no longer able to operate by
creating local spin-offs, as used to be the case many decades ago.
Local spin-offs have been replaced by network spin-offs, creating
economic impacts on the partners with which the production units
cooperate globally.

Fragmented spatial structure

As employees choose to live periodically on-site and spend their free
time in a different environment, the spatial organization of an entire
urban–rural system changes considerably. For a planner, grasping
how these changes influence the potential of local economic policy is

important. The crucial premiss is that spatial planning should respond and adapt itself to changes in human behaviour.

The experiences gained from Forrestania show that the workforce is geographically fragmented, as Houghton (1993, 283) put it in his analysis of the spatial consequences of long-distance commuting. Long-distance commuting leads to a fragmented spatial structure consisting of various resource communities, often temporary and randomly distributed, connected with pick-up points for employees commuting over the intervening distances (Tykkyläinen 1996a).

Long-distance commuting is generating a new conceptual model of central places and their interaction, which consists of randomly distributed resource sites, a few metropolitan areas, and interaction that may vary considerably depending on the nature of housing and production in each particular place. The commuting pattern may also be a mixture of commuting by bus, car, and aircraft. A coherent community to which employees and their families belong does not exist. There is no common locality or a home town. Employees and their families are citizens of a mix of communities in metropolitan areas, villages, towns, or the countryside, according to the location of their homes. Contracting creates temporary interactions between pick-up points and resource sites. Without a knowledge of the nature of production, technology, and housing in each case, the degree of spatial interaction would seem to vary inexplicably within the whole area.

Urbanization has been a global process, and metropolitan areas have become very attractive, with their multifarious and dynamic identity and cultural composition (Knox 1995). Commuter-based activities are reinforcing the trend, which had already begun with suburbanization, towards a fragmented, polycentric, and much more complex regional structure, which helps industrial capital to escape from agglomerated working-class environments (see, for example, Soja 1989, 179–180). New social and spatial configurations become intertwined.

Where a single-industry town is replaced by commuting and by on-site accommodation, one result is social diversification as individuals become parts of several communities. Compact communities are replaced by multifarious community structures forming parts of the complex social structure of a metropolitan environment and of a work organization (Tykkyläinen 1996b). An advanced resource company recruits very sophisticated and qualified labour, usually from a "creative" metropolitan home environment.

When employees first move to the setting of long-distance commuting, de-territorialization takes place, and then a new identity of
place develops – in other words, re-territorialization gradually follows
(Knox 1995, 246–247). Employees belong to the on-site working
community and they are also part of the business community of the
company, which may be multicultural and highly international.
Alongside this, their leisure-time activities take place in the diversified social environments of a metropolitan area. The Forrestania case
showed that employees' commitments to metropolitan social networks are strong. However, the employees emphatically disagreed
with the statement "Many employees of Forrestania and their families come together also in free time," so it appears that they do not
build up a compact company-based community within the metropolitan area. On the other hand, they proved to be an efficient working
community during their stay on-site.

Commitments are thus translocal rather than strongly local and
parochial (Tykkyläinen 1996b, 231). While commuting workers live
in at least two places (their workplace and their home region), many
managers, experts, and contract workers have a much wider spatial
range and they shuttle between several localities. This suggests an
even stronger reinterpretation of spatial commitments than that
argued by Urry (1990, 189). Localities comprise a highly diverse set
of social groupings and, if most of the people of a locality travel
around the country as they are promoted upwards in their company,
their likely interest in or commitment to that locality will be very
limited. The advanced commuting practices accompanying a spatially
flexible human resource policy will deepen the fragmentation of the
spatial setting even more and create new types of spatial commitments, comprehension, and identities. The crystallization of norms,
behaviour, and way of life that takes place depends on the new
setting.

Development milieux, pockets, and networks

The fragmentation spoken of here can be seen in the broader context
of regional development in general. One notion that emerges from
this investigation is the discrete and selective nature of modernization
in a geographical space. Many advanced production units are complex collections of technologically advanced systems that are dependent on being maintained and continuously developed.

[Production] systems ... are not just fixed flows of goods and services – conducted by firms that are little more than stereotype converters of standard inputs into standard outputs – but rather dynamic arrangements based on knowledge creation.... Changes in the international economy have gradually shifted the basis of a firm's competitive edge from static price competition towards dynamic improvements and are favouring firms which are able to create knowledge a little faster than their competitors [to make a profit]. (Maskell and Malmberg 1995, 3)

A crucial issue is whether these new kinds of production system tend to cluster in geographical space and whether the post-modern world economy will be identified as a mosaic of independent regional production systems. Arguments exist for and against such thinking.

In resource sectors, the diffusion of new technological applications and advanced businesses follows a pointwise pattern rather than being a smooth process advancing from the source of innovation to the periphery. It is easy to agree with Porter's (1994) argument about the formation of spatial organization, in which the most decisive attributes of a locality include:

the presence of a continually improving pool of skilled labour, applied technology, tailored infrastructure, experienced "sources" of capital and other factor inputs that are *specialized* to a particular business; a core of sophisticated and demanding customers for the products, whose needs anticipate these elsewhere; a critical mass of local suppliers of those specialized components, machinery, and services that significantly influence product or process improvement in the business, and the presence of other locally based competitors to motivate progress. (Porter 1994, 37)

These attributes interact in a mutually reinforcing, cumulative process. However, at least two factors can convert this idea from supporting the "cluster model" in a particular locality or region to supporting a network model for entire sectors. First, what is true in the spatial behaviour of the clothing industry, for instance, is not necessarily true in the mining or in the wood-processing sector, because the ideal models, as profit-generating configurations of capital and labour, vary considerably from one sector to another. Secondly, improving technology and the possibilities for increased mobility of people, knowledge, and capital reduce the costs of maintaining the type of network organizations that may exist within the transnational companies, in comparison with the costs of maintaining a single-locale-centric model. Hence, a cluster can be composed of business units within a network, if it is the most profitable way to conduct business. A crucial reason for this is the geographically uneven distribution of natural resources and subsequent opportunities to exploit them.

Resource-oriented industries tend to develop a network strategy of business, once single localities or national markets have become too small to be operational. This strategy may find suitable locales for production in isolated areas, as in the case of mining. Further, resource-based, high-volume industry is sensitive to the availability of suitable and distinctive infrastructure. The infrastructure that may be suitable for aircraft assembling or the manufacture of cellular phones, for instance, is not suitable for a basic metal industry or paper-making. This uniqueness of places and localities, together with the specific demands of locational attributes, creates the heterogeneity of spatial development. Therefore, it is not only primary production, but also resource processing, that may have a very specific locational pattern.

From the perspective of resource sectors, economic growth and development tend to take place in favourable pockets, locales, and localities that can attract investments worldwide (Tykkyläinen 1995; Bond and Tykkyläinen 1996) and that are integrated more and more with global business, often possessing single-industry production. This metaphor seems valid for recent industrial developments in many countries in the sectors supplying raw materials, bulk products, and energy. What remains most obscure is related to human issues: although employees often welcome new ways of organizing work, as in this case, what their reaction might be when their mobility and that of their families frequently brings them up against cultural borders (such as language) remains to be seen. What kind of local planning and policy will be needed then?

Changing premises for local economic policy

Discussions of local milieux, untraded interdependencies, and embeddedness have usually emphasized localities and regions as the basic units of successful development policy (Storper 1995). A "local milieu," defined by Malmberg et al. (1996, 91), is an environment in which collective learning about conducting business occurs through intense interaction between a broad set of actors, such as companies, subcontractors/suppliers, other allied business partners, and customers. Depending mainly on industry-related factors, a milieu can be a place or a region, but it can also be a network of many business units with a common business culture, similar goals, and shared experiences about how to do business and enhance competitiveness.

The milieu is both a result of, and a precondition for, learning – an asset that is constantly being produced and reproduced – rather than a passive entity. It is an environment where physical capital and human capital are pulled together over time, which translates into sustainable competitiveness among incumbent firms. Malmberg et al. (1996, 94) argue that diversified transnational companies have thus created something of a "multi home-base" structure, involving several distinct bases for innovation, which are often called "centres of excellence." This could represent an effort to acquire strength for certain businesses from suitable milieux of global scale by gaining direct access to advanced suppliers and customers, specialized labour and technology pools, and close competition with leading rivals. At least in the case of the Outokumpu Group, parts of the corporation are efficient at transferring development capabilities internationally and they share responsibilities within specific product areas between home and foreign units.

The production process needs to be organized in ways that meet capital's requirements for profitable production, and companies assiduously seek to guarantee that this is the case. In the search for new, viable configurations of capital and labour, new ways of organizing housing, transport, commuting, and other infrastructure are leading towards new socio-spatial arrangements. The strategies of networking and increased out-sourcing and subcontracting have further served to reorganize regional structures and to alter the premisses of local development policy. The authorities are more or less adaptors in this situation. The concept of plan ideology, as defined in the introductory chapter of this book, has been proven to be a failure, and it is difficult to show that a strong and traditional involvement of the authorities in business would lead to better, sustainable solutions.

The role of small businesses and community development programmes in economic development has been the subject of lively discussion (see, for example, Wilson 1995). As we have seen within advanced capitalism, high-volume resource businesses such as mining or the wood-processing sectors do not have the kind of general production paradigms that could flourish under the development programmes of small and often "low-tech" production. The Forrestania case demonstrates the complex structure of a resource project and its ties to high technology and the global economy. In order to be successful, local economic policy should often accept sophisticated solutions. Development is increasingly a search for a profitable combination of "big" and "small," "local" and "global" ways of contributing to a business project. These combinations may also require novel settlement practices in order to function.

Conclusions

Spatial diversification increases as the short-term mobility of the population increases. Advanced commuting arrangements are expanding in marginal areas and will become increasingly feasible in many countries for economic, technical, and behavioural reasons. This research contributes by adding the lifestyle factor to the explanation of the popularity of commuter mining, and it elaborates on the effects of new commuting practices on the spatio-social starting points of local economic policy in resource peripheries.

The prevalence of a lifestyle factor as an important part of everyday life emphasizes individuality. It should be stressed that the social environment of local economic policy became more individually oriented once the phase of the traditional industrial society (that is, the fourth wave; Freeman and Perez 1988) passed in the most developed societies in the 1980s. As a corollary to this, policy measures should be based on the needs of those who will be influenced by the process and those who will directly participate in it. The principle of subsidiarity should be included in governance in the sense that economic policies implemented within development projects should ensure the welfare of the individuals involved in this business. This group is often clearly identifiable in a green-field project (such as a new mine or factory). In the case of Forrestania, it is employees and their families, because they are the most strongly involved in local development. From the human point of view, without people and their behaviour, there is no "local" *per se*, and therefore local administrative practices need to be commensurate with the new phase of society.

Local administrative practices should be adapted to the new settlement patterns and not *vice versa*, if that is what the people involved wish. The strict territorial nature of administration should be replaced by translocal practices, which should be more compatible with the time–space behaviour of individuals and should serve their needs. The provision of public services should be tailored to the new spatial behaviour. Spatiality should not be considered just as bounded, non-overlapping territories in governance (cf. Taylor's 1996 critique of state-centric thinking). This adjustment is an enormous challenge to administration and planning. So far, the expansion of commuter-based industrial activities is considered viable from the viewpoints of the authorities because the benefits outweigh the costs. The role of the authorities is to ensure the overall efficiency of spatial systems, which may be steered by taxation.

A rural locality, as a production site or a home, is by no means a dead concept. It is at least as important as before. However, as this case-study shows, the idea of "a rural locality" is becoming more complex than before and it is bound to numerous spatial relations. Rural places are necessary in economic development and have the potential for social life. At the local level, it is better to search for opportunities and then adjust rather than simply to resist the "inevitable development" of capitalism. Coping with restructuring involves taking a chance, and in this process of development the content of "local" should be constituted according to the needs of individuals and emerging opportunities.

Acknowledgements

This case-study was funded by the Academy of Finland, the University of Joensuu, and UNU/WIDER under the Special Finnish Project Fund supported by the Finnish Ministry of Foreign Affairs.

References

Bond, D. and Tykkyläinen, M. (1996), "Northwestern Russia: A Case Study in 'Pocket' Development," *European Business Review* 96(5), pp. 55–61.

Brealey, T. B and Newton, P. W. (1978), *Living in Remote Communities in Tropical Australia: The Hedland Study*, CSIRO Division of Building Research, Melbourne.

Department of State Development (1992), "Long Distance Commuting and Regional Communities, a Discussion," paper prepared by Department of State Development, Western Australia.

Freeman, C. and Perez, C. (1988), "Structural Crises of Adjustment, Business Cycles and Investment Behaviour," in G. Dosi, C. Freeman, R. Nelson, G. Silverberg, and L. Soete (eds.) (1988), *Technical Change and Economic Theory*, Pinter, London, pp. 38–66.

Gillies, A. D. S., Just, G. D., and Hsin Wei Wu (1991), "The Success of Fly-In Fly-Out Australian Mining Operations," Proceedings of the Australian Institute of Mining and Metallurgy, Cairns, 21–25 April.

Gribbin, C. C. and Brealey, T. B. (1981), "Decision Making in New Mining Towns," *Architecture Australia* 69(6), pp. 51–57.

Harman, E. (1981), "Ideology, Development and Liberal Hegemony in Western Australia, 1960–1980," paper presented to State, Capital and Labour Conference, Murdoch University, Perth, 1981.

Hoggart, K. and Buller, H. (1987), *Rural Development. A Geographical Perspective,* Croom Helm, London.

Holmes, J. H. (1981), "Lands of Distant Promise," in R. E. Lonsdale and J. H. Holmes (eds.), *Settlement Systems in Sparsely Populated Regions*, Pergamon, New York, pp. 1–13.

Houghton, D. S. (1993), "Long-Distance Commuting: A New Approach to Mining in Australia," *Geographical Journal* 159, pp. 281–290.

Hudson, R. (1995), "Regional Futures: Industrial Restructuring, New Production Concepts and Spatial Development, Strategies in the New Europe," paper presented at the Regional Studies Association European Conference on "Regional Futures," 6–9 May, Gothenburg. Revised version, mimeo.

Humphreys, D. (1995), "Whatever Happened to Security of Supply? Minerals Policy in the Post-Cold War World," *Resources Policy* 21, pp. 91–97.

Knox, P. L. (1995), "World Cities and the Organization of Global Space," in R. J. Johnston, P. J. Taylor, and M. J. Watts (eds.), *Geographies of Global Change*, Blackwell, Oxford, pp. 232–247.

Malmberg, A., Sölvell, Ö., and Zander, I. (1996), "Spatial Clustering, Local Accumulation of Knowledge and Firm Competitiveness," *Geografiska Annaler* 78 B (2), pp. 85–97.

Maskell, P. and Malmberg, A. (1995), "Localised Learning and Industrial Competitiveness," paper presented at the Regional Studies Association European Conference on "Regional Futures," 6–9 May, Gothenburg.

Murphy, P. A. and Roman, D. (1988), "Regional Development Policy in New South Wales: Contemporary Needs and Options," *Australian Quarterly*, Winter, pp. 262–275.

Neil, C. C. and Jones, J. A. (1988), "Mental Health in Resource Boom Towns," *Australian and New Zealand Journal of Sociology* 24, pp. 437–458.

Newton, P. W. (1985), "Planning New Towns for Harsh Arid Environments: An Evaluation of Shay Gap and Newman Townships, Australia," *Ekistics* 52(311), pp. 180–188.

Newton, P. and Robinson, I. (1987), "Settlement Options: Avoiding Local Government with Fly-In/Fly-Out," in P. Parker (ed.), *Developments in Local Government, 5. Resource Development and Local Government: Policies for Growth, Decline and Diversity*, Australian Government Publishing Service, Canberra, pp. 72–81.

Planning Research Centre (1989), *Rural Settlements Project Volume 1. Overview and Summary*, Planning Research Centre, Faculty of Architecture, University of Sydney, Sydney.

Porter, M. E. (1994), "The Role of Location in Competition," *Journal of the Economics of Business* 1, pp. 35–39.

Soja, E. S. (1989), *Postmodern Geographies. The Reassertion of Space in Critical Social Theory*, Verso, London.

Storper, M. (1995), "The Resurgence of Regional Economies, Ten Years Later: The Region as a Nexus of Untraded Interdependencies," *European Urban and Regional Studies* 2(3), pp. 191–221.

Taylor, M. and Garlick, S. (1989), "Commonwealth Government Involvement in Regional Development in the 1980s: A Local Approach," in B. Higgins and K. Zagorski (eds.), *Readings in Regional Experiences, Policies and Prospects*, Publication No. 10, Australian Regional Development Series, Australian Government Publishing Service, Canberra.

Taylor, P. J. (1996), "Embedded Statism and the Social Sciences: Opening up New Spaces," *Environment and Planning A* 28(11), pp. 1917–1928.

Tykkyläinen, M. (1992), "Solutions to Mine Closure in Outokumpu," in C. Neil, M. Tykkyläinen, and J. Bradbury (eds.), *Coping with Closure. An International Comparison of Mine Town Experiences*, Routledge, London, pp. 225–246.

——— (1993), "Rural Development, Resource Communities and the Development Theories," in P. T. Karjalainen (ed.), *Different Geographies*, Institutum Geographicum, Universitas Ostiensis, Joensuu, pp. 59–75.

——— (1994), *Kaupunkilaismainarit Forrestaniassa,* Joensuu University Press, Joensuu.

——— (1995), "'Stunde Null' and the Pocket Theory of Development in the Socio-economic Transition in Russia," in M. Tykkyläinen (ed.), *Russian Karelia – An Opportunity for the West*, Occasional Papers 29, Human Geography and Planning, University of Joensuu, pp. 9–21.

——— (1996a), "Commuting with On-Site Accommodation in the Mining Industry and Its Effects on Spatial Structures," *Fennia* 174(2), pp. 223–243.

——— (1996b), "Increasing Long-Distance Commuting and Its Effects on Spatial Structures," in M. E. Furlani de Civit, C. Pedone, and N. D. Soria (eds.), *Development Issues in Marginal Regions II: Policies and Strategies*, Universidad Nacional de Cuyo, Mendoza, pp. 223–234.

Urry, J. (1990), "Conclusions: Places and Policies," in M. Harloe, C. G. Pickvance, and J. Urry (eds.), *Place, Policy and Politics. Do Localities Matter?* Unwin Hyman, London, pp. 187–204.

Wilson, P. (1995), "Embracing Locality in Local Economic Development," *Urban Studies* 32(4–5), pp. 645–658.

Part V
Sectoral shift and diversification
– The example of tourism

11

Mining to tourism: Economic restructuring in Kellogg, Idaho, USA

Harley Johansen

Small towns under restructuring

America's small towns have suffered a severe decline in economic activities during the past several decades (Johansen and Fuguitt 1984; 1990), and, since about 1980, rural population decline has also been widespread (Johansen 1993a). Most American resource communities have been economically and socially integrated, with agriculture as the most important industry, although, in all areas based on primary industries, economic restructuring has occurred. In 1990, rural incorporated places accounted for over 13,000 (66 per cent) of the more than 19,000 incorporated places in the country, yet they contain only about 6 per cent of the total United States' population. Why, then, are we interested in this small segment of the US settlement system?

First, the rural places are important as independent local government units with the normal responsibilities of basic services and infrastructure. Secondly, they are residential and social communities with established commercial functions for local and area residents. Finally, it is the large number of these relatively small places that makes them important and justifies our concern about economic and social viability. The small towns of America have lost both population and business activities at a high rate during the past 15 years, and these losses represent a challenge for community planners to retain viability in the changing economy.

Kellogg, a small town that grew along with the mining and smelting industry in northern Idaho, provides an example of the local challenges resulting from economic restructuring. Its economy was abruptly altered by the closure of its main industry in 1982. This paper will describe the economic changes in Kellogg resulting from the decline in the mineral industry and the community's attempt to redevelop the economy around tourism and other industries. This case-study represents a pattern typical of mining towns and other single-industry towns in the western United States today.

Shift in the economic base in Kellogg

Kellogg is the largest of several mining towns in the Coeur d'Alene mining district of northern Idaho, in the north-western United States (see fig. 11.1). Until 1982, it was the site of the largest mine and smelter complex in the region, and a thriving industrial community. Despite the significant activities of mining and smelting, the population of Kellogg was no more than 3,417 in 1980. Many employees commuted from the surrounding area, and hence the basic industrial activities had a wider spatial sphere of influence. When the smelter and mine closed in 1982, the impact on Kellogg was severe, causing the unemployment of over 2,000 people who had worked at the Bunker Hill Mining and Smelter Co. Other mines in the district also closed during the 1980s, resulting in a regional pattern of declining employment and economic depression.

Economic decline led to out-migration and resultant structural changes in the population of Kellogg and the neighbouring communities. Following the mine and smelter closure, the people of Kellogg began to explore alternative sources of employment. Beginning with a team of consultants from the University of Idaho in 1982, the people of Kellogg sought assistance from outside the area to help them cope with the challenges of sudden economic decline and the social and economic costs of large-scale unemployment. During the period of adjustment since the closure of Bunker Hill, the people of Kellogg have explored many possible alternative industries and have embarked on a large-scale recreational development as the centrepiece of their effort to move from mining and smelting to a more diverse economic base.

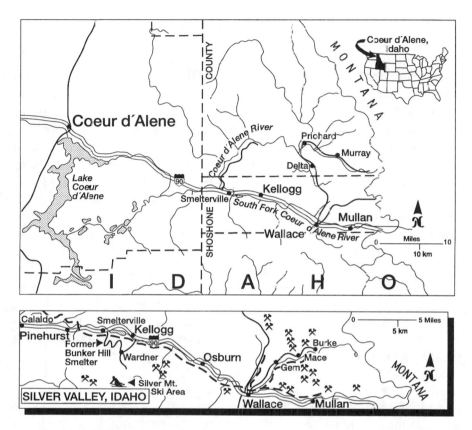

Fig. 11.1   **Kellogg, in the Coeur d'Alene mining district of northern Idaho.**

This shift in economic base has not been without challenges. Kellogg has some major environmental scars from the years of mineral industry operations. Once-forested hills around Kellogg are still bare owing to a major fire early in the twentieth century and subsequent years of smelter fumes that prevented tree growth. Large piles of mine waste materials, called tailings, remain along the highway entrance to the Kellogg area, and the empty lead smelter and zinc plant buildings stand as a reminder of past activity. The area has been declared seriously polluted and, as a result, qualifies as a "superfund" site by the United States Environmental Protection Agency. It is undergoing a major environmental clean-up to remove lead and other contaminants harmful to local residents. Tourist developments now focus on the mountains above the Coeur d'Alene valley and coexist with the remnants of Kellogg's industrial past.

253

"Silver Valley" and the road to smelter closure in Kellogg

Silver, lead, and zinc ores were discovered by Noah Kellogg on the site of present-day Kellogg in 1885, which led to the development of a large mine and smelter industry. The smelter and zinc plant were designed to serve the Bunker Hill mine at Kellogg, as well as other mines in the district extending east to the ridge above Wallace and the Montana border (see fig. 11.1). Early mining developments led to the development of a railroad through the valley corridor and, later, to a federal highway, which became part of the interstate highway system. The mining district became the centre of settlement in Shoshone County, and Wallace, the seat of Shoshone County government, is the only other significant town in the valley. Wallace has also suffered economic stress with the decline of mining in its vicinity, and has similarly made efforts to create alternative employment sources.

The Bunker Hill Company at Kellogg was a leading producer of lead and zinc, initially from locally produced concentrates and, later, also from concentrates imported from other mines, from the northwest, and from abroad. The Coeur d'Alene district became a leading producer of silver, and was the major United States source during most of the twentieth century. The term "Silver Valley" is commonly used to describe the district extending from Pinehurst to Mullan, including several smaller mining communities such as Smelterville and Osburn. Each community developed around a local mine or industry, and automobile access later made commuting between these communities possible. The region has functioned as an integrated economic area, based on mining and metal processing, but social ties to local schools and towns within the region have been strong.

Kellogg grew as a town along with the Bunker Hill and Sullivan Mining and Concentrating Co. It became incorporated in 1913 but retained elements of a "company town" until recently. A consultant's report to the company in 1955 recommended that the company should separate itself from the operations of the city and assume the position of an industrial employer, rather than a "patron," in its relations with Kellogg (McKinsey & Co. 1955). At that time, the company owned the local hostel, 235 housing units, retail stores, and the water and electric utilities, and was also the main source of funding for many local programmes and projects, such as public recreation facilities, the cemetery association, and even the local welfare account. Housing was considered inadequate for the labour force, and air pollution was recognized as a serious problem.

A study of residents' attitudes towards Kellogg in 1972 revealed a major concern about environmental pollution (Ellis 1932; Ellsworth 1972). Despite general satisfaction with Kellogg as a place to live and work, residents objected strongly to air and water pollution. Smokestack emission controls later reduced air pollution, and tailings ponds helped reduce water pollution from mine wastes. Other concerns expressed were inadequacies in housing, wages, and recreation opportunities for young people. At the time of the smelter closure in 1982, Kellogg was still dependent on the company for many community services and as the major employer. Closure forced the ultimate solution to the problem of dependency. No longer could Kellogg go to Bunker Hill for help when city funds were inadequate.

The 1970s and early 1980s were times of reorganization in the American mining and mineral-processing industry. Several mineral companies were acquired by large energy companies. Anaconda, a large mining and smelting company in Butte, Montana, was acquired by Atlantic Richfield Co. (ARCO), and Bunker Hill was purchased by Gulf Resources and Chemical Corp. Both of these events preceded smelter closure in the early 1980s (Johansen 1987). Closure of the ASARCO smelter at Tacoma, Washington, in the mid-1980s, further reduced mineral concentrate marketing options for nearly all mining companies in the north-west region. When the Bunker Hill Company closed in 1982, it was the largest smelting and refining complex in the region and the second-largest employer in Idaho. Closure of the plant, therefore, had a large impact both on local employment and on the smelting and refining industry.

After their heydays, the Silver Valley communities are faced with a need to cooperate and plan for integrated development that will help resolve the economic plight of the whole region. Although declining in number during the past decade, mining jobs have fluctuated along with silver and other metal prices. The industry may continue to be a viable part of the local economy for many years, but. as with other mechanized primary industries, it will likely employ fewer people than in years past.

Effects of the closures

The abrupt decline of mining and smelting resulted in the loss of over 2,000 high-wage jobs and had a profound effect on the city of Kellogg. The most obvious effects were a population decline from out-migration, unemployment, declining incomes, declining housing values, and the loss of local revenue. The major impact of the mine and smelter closures in Kellogg is evident in records of the demographic and employment information for the County of Shoshone.

Economic restructuring

The city of Kellogg is the largest place in the county, and the Bunker Hill Company was the largest employer in the county. Furthermore, as other mines in the county have also reduced employment since the Bunker Hill closure, the problem of restructuring has become widespread throughout Shoshone County. The economic and employment impacts hit the localities possessing fewer than 20,000 inhabitants altogether before the closure (see fig. 11.2a). Hence, although the impacts were severe for individuals, they did not embrace a large number of people, as has been the case in the many old industrial, densely populated districts in Europe and the United States.

Unemployment was relatively stable at about 5 per cent of the labour force during the 1970s (see fig. 11.2b). Closure of Bunker Hill in 1982, however, caused this to grow to over 30 per cent. The average rate remained high during the 1980s, but fluctuated along with mining employment in the county.

This was a very different outcome compared with the employment impacts of the mine closures in Northern Europe in the 1980s. In Finland, for instance, some of the redundant employees of several closures were relocated by the mining company's adjustment policy, and the regional policy cancelled out the rest of the negative employment effects for a few years (Talman and Tykkyläinen 1992). The difference reflects divergent politico-economic environments between the United States and the Nordic countries in the 1980s. Anyhow, this Nordic model of control over restructuring no longer worked well during the deep economic depression of the 1990s, as shown in the case of Kolari in chapter 12 in this book.

The Bunker Hill mine (not smelter), for example, reopened briefly under new management during the mid-1980s. Other fluctuations later in the decade represent mine closures and openings among the other mining companies in the district. Each event had a greater impact on the unemployment rate in later years because the total labour force had declined in size.

Another indicator of the economic impact is the annual wages paid in the county by sector (see fig. 11.2c). Total wages were increasing up to 1982, when the downward trend in mining and smelting began.

256

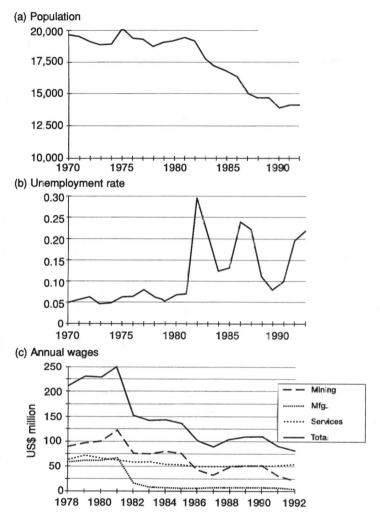

Fig. 11.2 **Population, unemployment rate, and annual wages in Shoshone County (Sources: Idaho Departments of Commerce and Employment, Annual Statistics for Counties, Statehouse, Boise, Idaho).**

Mining remained the main source of income until 1986, when relatively stable services became the leading sector. Mining rebounded briefly between 1988 and 1990, but has since declined again. After nearly 100 years of mining industry dominance, Shoshone County has apparently now become dependent on the service sector as its major employer.

A separate, but related, indicator of economic decline is the

257

reduction in real estate property values over the 1978–1993 period. The total value was over US$1 billion in 1979 (valued in constant 1992 dollars), but it dropped below US$400 million in the latter half of the 1980s. The market value of real property followed a trend very similar to that for wages and population, resulting in much lower assessed values in the early 1990s. The lower valuation of property affects the revenue of local governments and, therefore, the ability to maintain services. Shoshone County is eager to avoid a continued downward spiral of property and revenue decline.

Demographic trends

Shoshone County lost some of its population during the 20 years from 1970 to 1990, but the rate of decline increased from 2.5 per cent between 1970 and 1980 to 27.5 per cent between 1980 and 1990. The total population also dropped, from 19,718 to 13,931, during the two decades, a decline of nearly 30 per cent (see fig. 11.2a). Shoshone County ranked seventh in the United States on the 1980 to 1990 decline of 27 per cent. Interestingly, several of the other high-loss counties in the United States were also based on mining industries. The most severe decline occurred after the Bunker Hill closure in 1982, and continued until 1990. Between 1980 and 1990, Kellogg's population declined 24 per cent from 3,417 to 2,591, and Wallace dropped 42 per cent from 1,736 to 1,010. Most of this change was due to high rates of out-migration, especially of young adults (see fig. 11.3).

Net migration estimates were derived for Shoshone County during 1970 and 1990 (see fig. 11.3). The measure of net migration is the balance of total population change after accounting for the natural increase or decrease. Except for a spurt of growth during 1975 (see fig. 11.3), net migration was strongly negative during most years, and reached extreme values in 1983 and 1987. The total net migration during the 1980s of 5,872 was almost equal to the total population decline of 5,787. The mid-1970s growth is difficult to explain, but it does correspond to a time when rural areas were growing throughout the United States and, of relevance to this area, it coincides with a step upward in silver prices (Rudzitis 1987).

Births exceeded deaths by a substantial margin during the 1970s in Shoshone County, though these rates converged in the early 1980s (see fig. 11.3). The sharp drop in births after 1981 may reflect the out-migration of younger adults and the postponement of marriage and

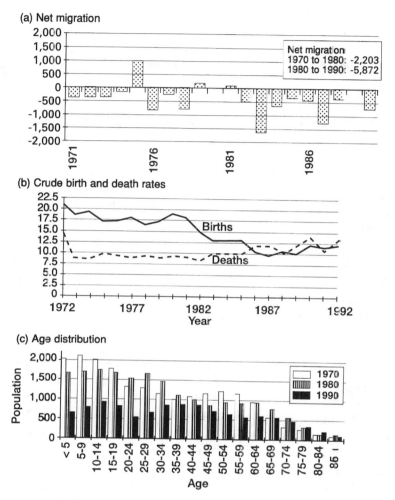

Fig. 11.3 **Net migration, birth and death rates, and age distribution of the population in Shoshone County (Source: US Bureau of the Census, *Census of Population*, Washington, D.C.).**

family following the economic recession. At those times during both decades when the natural increase was high, it was offset by high rates of net out-migration.

Continued net out-migration has affected the age distribution of Shoshone County's population (see fig. 11.3). The number of people in the 0–14 age groups declined sharply between 1970 and 1990, whereas the numbers in the oldest age groups increased slightly. The current population is more uniform by age, and it has fewer people in

259

working and school-age groups. The proportions of the population in the 45–64 age groups were also quite large, indicating the change in the workforce associated with the loss of mining and smelting jobs.

Planning for change

In the United States, there is no national policy for economic development that addresses rural communities or the impacts of industrial transition (National Commission on Agriculture and Rural Development Policy 1990). Aside from agriculture, industry-specific programmes for community or area development have not been part of federal government policy (Galston 1992), although state governments have been involved in some county- and community-based projects for economic growth. Idaho has a Department of Commerce programme to assist communities with development efforts, in which support is provided in the form of consulting services for community organization, goal-setting, strategy formation, and the funding for qualifying projects. Planning at the community level has been unequal in small towns, and most plans emphasized physical rather than development planning in the period prior to the mid-1970s.

After 1980, small towns increased their planning efforts for economic development at the local community level. Early local development efforts emphasized industry recruiting, but later changed to focus on entrepreneurial growth and the retention of existing firms (Johansen and Fuguitt 1984). Problems in rural areas resulting from restructuring in all primary industries led to concern for job retention and creation throughout rural America. Kellogg is typical of communities faced with the closure of a single large employer, but many other rural towns have faced more gradual declines in employment and local market support as a result of changes in agriculture.

Kellogg wrote its first comprehensive plan in 1957. The plan emphasized land-use and infrastructure needs in a growing community, but also recognized both the opportunities for further economic growth through an expansion of the mining and smelting industries, and the other possibilities from tourism and manufacturing industries. At that time, the problem was not a declining employment base, but one of managing expected growth. During the period 1948–1955, average monthly employment at Bunker Hill Company grew from 1,791 to 2,226 – an increase of 24 per cent (Kellogg 1957).

More specific economic development planning began in 1982 with the announced closure of Bunker Hill Company. Kellogg received funds from the Idaho Private Industry Council to support an economic development plan prepared by a consulting team of specialists from the University of Idaho aimed at alternatives to mining and smelting (Merk and DiNoto 1982). The 1982 plan emphasized an assessment of Kellogg's resources and the need for diversification in the local economy. It suggested that, in a marketing effort, Kellogg target the recruitment of manufacturing industries, and it stressed the importance of working in a combined effort with other communities in the northern Idaho region. Tourism, based on the ski area above Kellogg, was suggested for further market analysis. The plan also stressed the need for an office of economic development with a director in Kellogg to lead the effort to diversify the local economy.

As in most American communities, planning for Kellogg's development became the responsibility of an informal, non-governmental organization (NGO). People from the local community formed a committee and began pursuing the recommendations of the consultants. The committee consisted of bankers, clergy, retail merchants, private citizens, and some members of local government agencies. These people worked as a policy and planning unit for Kellogg, and also participated in a larger NGO representing the larger region of north Idaho. Later on, the communities in the mining district formed an economic development NGO with more specific responsibilities for Kellogg and other communities in the valley.

In 1984, the Silver Valley Economic Development Corporation was formed, with a goal of diversifying the economy to include tourism and manufacturing industries. The City of Kellogg began looking seriously at the potential for development of the ski area already established on the mountain above the town. Bunker Hill Company had operated a small-scale ski area for several years. One of the advantages for ski tourism was the good highway access to northwestern cities via Interstate 90. The distance to Spokane, the nearest large city, seemed competitive when compared with other ski resorts. The mountain was also challenging, but offered potential for expansion to include a wide variety of ski runs. The major disadvantage to the ski tourism strategy was the difficult access route from Kellogg and the highway to the ski area. Recognizing this, the people of Kellogg began a campaign to acquire funding to build a gondola lift that would lift skiers directly from the town to the ski area.

At the time of application to the federal government for the funding of a gondola project, the Idaho Governor's Office provided assistance to Kellogg (the Idaho Department of Commerce had not been formed yet), but the primary effort and responsibility lay with the local government and citizens of Kellogg. The mobilization of local resources based on local initiatives became the key content of the development policy at the end of the 1980s, but the promotion of the growth of the manufacturing sector was carried out in parallel.

Tourism

Dedication to the goal of local community development
Tourism has been a popular strategy for development throughout rural America, as well as in other countries (Frederick 1992; Fuguitt and Johansen 1990; Johansen 1993b). Most of these efforts combine natural or cultural amenities with marketing and promotional activities. Funding to support tourism often includes public sources. During the late 1980s, Kellogg residents decided to pursue funding from the national government for construction of the gondola lift and renovation of the old Silverhorn ski area above the town. A gondola was seen as a solution to the problem of difficult access, and a tourist attraction in itself, conveniently located at an entrance to Kellogg from the interstate highway. The old ski area was limited in scale and ability, so the expansion plan included the creation of new ski runs, additional lifts, and a new day-lodge on the mountain to serve both skiers (in winter) and summer tourists.

Kellogg's effort to raise funding for the ski area development is an example of extreme dedication to the goal of local community development among its citizens. According to local officials, city council members and other unpaid volunteers met every morning at 7:00 for two years to work on fund-raising. They called every federal and state office that could possibly provide help to them. After two years of effort, and with the help of Idaho's legislative delegation in the US Congress, a special funding item for the Kellogg ski area project was added to the appropriations bill for the US Forest Service. The bill appropriated US$6.1 million for the project with the condition that matching funds be raised from other sources. Kellogg immediately went to work getting commitments from private sources. They began with a tax levy on themselves of US$2 million to be raised over 20 years. This unusual city tax levy tested the Idaho constitution and was later challenged, but it was upheld in court. The tax levy, amounting to about US$50 per year on an average family home, was put to the voters in 1988. The referendum passed by an unprecedented 87.5 per cent. This strong commitment by the people of Kellogg provided evidence of local support and led to investments by Von Roll Inc., gondola builders in Switzerland, by Washington Water Power Company, the local electrical utility, and by the State of Idaho to provide the matching capital in the project. The result was a public–private partnership that became the largest new ski area development in the United States during the 1980s.

With a lease agreement from Bunker Limited, owners of the former Bunker Hill Co.'s land holdings, the City of Kellogg moved into the construction phase in the summer of 1989. The gondola opened in June 1990 and began serving tourists immediately. The expanded ski area and day-lodge opened in November for Kellogg's first ski season.

The gondola and ski area project became associated with a theme for marketing Kellogg's tourist planning efforts. Modelled after Leavenworth, a town in central Washington, Kellogg adopted a Bavarian (Alpine) theme as the focus for new exterior construction and signs (Egan 1989). Subsequent plans have focused on the tourist industry and the services and shops normally associated with skiing tourists. Integrating the former business district with the gondola to attract visitors to shops and restaurants in Kellogg is a goal for future development.

In 1994, Kellogg received funding from various state and federal sources to improve the streets and pavements and the landscaping in the centre of the business district. This allowed new lighting, new parking areas, tree planting, and a small park and pedestrian access to link the business district with the gondola base lodge. The aim of this project was to make the business district more attractive and more accessible to visitors who come to use the ski area and gondola.

The results of the tourism planning efforts
The expanded ski area opened in November 1990 under the management of the City of Kellogg and operated by a hospitality company in nearby Coeur d'Alene, which offered special ski packages in conjunction with its hotel. The number of visitors exceeded expectations during the first summer. The gondola proved to be attractive for travellers to get above the valley and see the mountain. It also attracted mountain hikers and bikers and visitors to scheduled concerts during the summer season. As expected, though, skiers have made up the majority of visitors every season since it opened (see table 11.1).

Attendance is subject to economic and weather conditions. The

Table 11.1　**Silver Mountain visitors, 1990–1994**

	1990	1990/91	1991/92	1992/93	1993/94[a]
Winter		68,010	91,061	90,794	98,000
Summer	71,611	91,083	73,170	65,857	68,000
Total	71,611	159,093	164,231	156,651	166,000

Source: Silver Mountain Management 1994.
a. Estimated.

four-year record shows an average annual attendance of 161,494, based on the four years of complete winter/summer data. The volume of visitors to Silver Mountain is comparable to that in the other major ski areas in the region.

The immediate goal of Kellogg's tourism programme is to increase the time spent in the business community by visitors to the ski area. The large influx of visitors is seen as a market for lodging, restaurants, gift and sporting goods shops, and other functions that can be developed in the village. A new motel opened in 1993 and condominium units were added in 1994. In an attempt to attract customers to shops, local merchants have adopted the Alpine theme for building exteriors.

Promotion of the manufacturing sector

The Silver Valley Economic Development Corporation succeeded in recruiting 12 new industrial firms to the area, creating 170 jobs. In early 1994, several firms were waiting to locate in the valley as soon as land became available. The shortage of available land led to the formation of a for-profit corporation to build an industrial park east of Kellogg at Osburn. This will create rentable space in a modern industrial building, along with other options, on a 4 acre site. The development strategy of "Silver Valley" has thus not been one-sided and directed only to tourism.

The challenge of environmental conditions and housing markets

Along with economic problems, Kellogg has inherited a legacy of serious environmental problems resulting from nearly 100 years of mining and smelting industry. Air pollution was a common complaint

264

during smelter operations (Ellsworth 1972), but airborne dust has also contaminated the local soils. High lead levels were discovered in the blood samples of children from Kellogg during the 1970s, and the federal government has declared the smelter vicinity a "superfund" site, worthy of funding for immediate clean-up. Other problems resulting from smelter operations include the denuded slopes on the mountain sides above Kellogg, and the large tailings piles lining the entrance to the town from the highway.

Kellogg has faced a difficult challenge to overcome these visual blights and to make the community attractive to tourists. The early returns seem to indicate a successful effort on the part of the city and the people of the community.

Immigrants and tourists see a community undergoing change, though with some remaining difficulties. The removal of lead-contaminated soil is under way, and tree planting has helped reveg-etate the hillsides, but considerable scars remain in the form of the tailings piles and vacant industrial buildings. Kellogg may change its image to that of an Alpine village, but it is likely that, underneath the facade, the old industrial base of mining and smelting will be visible for some time (Egan 1989).

In spite of these environmental issues, economic recovery started in the housing markets in the early 1990s. The coincidence of high unemployment and the opening of the gondola and ski area in 1990 had a stabilizing effect and led to a modest revival of the local real estate market in Kellogg. Houses were priced low because of the local depressed economy, and tourists from outside the area saw this as an attractive opportunity to invest in recreational property. Houses of former miners and smelter employees were bought for weekend ski lodging and summer recreation retreats by people from Spokane, Seattle, and elsewhere in the north-west. The strengthened real estate market also caused an upswing in the construction of homes: building permits in Kellogg and Shoshone County increased from 158 in 1992 to 216 in 1993.

Conclusion

Evidence of economic restructuring can be seen in Kellogg, Idaho, following a shift from mining and metallurgical processing to tourism and more diverse activities. The mining industry in northern Idaho has been faced with low metal prices during much of the period since the late 1970s, and 100 years of mining have resulted in greater depths and, therefore, greater costs of production. The closure of Kellogg's smelter and mine, an event that shocked not only the local community but the whole region, occurred during a general reorganization of the industry in North America (Johansen 1987). The decline in the base metals industry can be linked to the changes in other industries and to a general shift away from materials in the US economy (Galston 1992). The industry has also shifted to lower-cost production areas in Asia, Latin America, and Africa. Tykkyläinen (1993) described several factors causing economic restructuring in resource-dependent communities. Although several theoretical perspectives may apply here, the Coeur d'Alene mining district, and Kellogg itself, seem to have been affected by the forces of technology and innovation and by global capitalism. It is a situation that has been repeated in numerous mining communities throughout the western United States. Furthermore, the importance of local activity for promoting development proved to be significant, but it works only if those responsible for planning have something to offer that can lead to business ideas that are productive and profitable, at least in the long run.

Restructuring has affected the demographic composition of Shoshone County's population. The out-migration of families with young children is evident from the change in age distribution during the past two decades. The labour force population is smaller as a result of this demographic shift, as is the total population. The natural increase has declined substantially and, in some years, was negative, indicating a sharp reduction in births and a slightly increased rate of death, which might result from a higher proportion of elderly people in the population.

Communities in the Coeur d'Alene mining district have gone through 100 years of mining and related industries. That length of continued production and occupancy is uncommon in mining areas of the world. This district will continue to experience economic restructuring if the mining industry follows its current path towards a reduction in labour and the closure of mines in the area. Future developments will depend on a combination of metal market conditions, ore reserves, and mining costs, and increasingly on the success of the communities in attracting and developing new economic activities to replace the lost jobs in mining and the base metal sector.

The profound restructuring of the local economy in Kellogg has been an ongoing process since the early 1980s. Had the mining company not closed, it is unlikely that Kellogg would have undertaken the efforts to restructure its local economy. Economic conditions

266

prior to the closure were quite good – wages were higher in 1981 (US$11 per hour for entry-level jobs) than they have been ever since, and unemployment was low. The commitment to diversify the economy came from an effort to replace jobs lost in mining and smelting. It was driven by a strong desire among the majority of local residents to salvage the Kellogg community and allow the citizens and merchants to remain in the valley. The attitudes of the local residents at the time of the closure revealed a preference for living in the valley and a willingness to support efforts to replace lost jobs. This widespread community support helped Kellogg launch a new direction and gave community leaders the courage to take bold steps in development strategies. Kellogg will continue to seek diversity in its local economy by encouraging the development of industries that can benefit from the location and resources of the community. The development of diversity will depend on continued advantages for manufacturing and service industries, including tourism.

References

Egan, T. (1989), "... In Effort to Be a Resort," *New York Times*, 13 July.

Ellis, M. M. (1932), *Pollution of the Coeur d'Alene River and Adjacent Waters by Mine Waste*, US Bureau of Fisheries, Washington, D.C.

Ellsworth, L. E. (1972), *Community Perception in the Coeur d'Alene Mining District*, Idaho Bureau of Mines and Geology, Pamphlet 152, Moscow, Idaho.

Frederick, M. (1992), "Tourism as a Rural Economic Development Tool: An Exploration of the Literature," US Department of Agriculture, ERS Bibliographies and Lit. Ag. No. 122, Washington, D.C.

Fuguitt, G. V. and Johansen, H. (1990), "Development Planning in American Villages during the 1980s," paper presented at the Commission on Changing Rural Systems, IGU, Ljubljana, Yugoslavia, July 1990.

Galston, W. (1992), "Rural America in the 1990s: Trends and Policy Choices," *Policy Studies Journal* 20, pp. 202–211.

Johansen, H. (1987), "Recent Trends in Marketing and Shipment of Mineral Concentrates in the Western United States," in H. Johansen, O. P. Matthews, and G. Rudzitis (eds.), *Mineral Resource Development*, Westview Press, Boulder, Colo., pp. 192–203.

——— (1993a), "Local Development Strategies and Local Resources in Finland's Rural Communes," paper presented at the European Regional Science Association 33rd European Congress, Moscow, Russia.

——— (1993b), "The Small Town in Urbanized Society," in D. L. Brown, D. Field, and J. J. Zuiches (eds.), *The Demography of Rural Life*, Northeast Regional Centre for Rural Development, University Park, Pa., pp. 58–83.

Johansen, H. and Fuguitt, G. V. (1984), *The Changing Rural Village in America: Demographic and Economic Trends since 1950*, Ballinger, Cambridge, Mass.

267

—— (1990), "Infrastructure, Development Efforts, and Other Factors in Small Town Business Growth," in F. W. Dykeman (ed.), *Entrepreneurial and Sustainable Rural Communities*, Mt. Allison University Press, Sackville, N.B., pp. 177–192.

Kellogg (1957), *The General Plan*, Kellogg, Idaho.

McKinsey & Co. (1955), "A Proposed Community Relations and Housing Program: Bunker Hill and Sullivan Mining and Concentrating Co.," unpublished report.

Merk, L. H. and DiNoto, M. J. (1982), *A Marketing and Economic Development Plan for the Silver Valley*, Centre for Business Development and Research, University of Idaho, Moscow, Idaho.

National Commission on Agriculture and Rural Development Policy (1990), *Future Directions in Rural Development Policy*, US Department of Agriculture, Washington, D.C.

Rudzitis, G. (1987), "Silver Prices and Market Speculation," in H. Johansen, O. P. Matthews, and G. Rudzitis (eds.), *Mineral Resource Development. Geopolitics, Economics and Policy*, Westview Press, Boulder, Colo., pp. 203–235.

Silver Mountain Management (1994), unpublished data obtained via telephone interview.

Talman, P. and Tykkyläinen, M. (1992), "Finland: Restructuring Policy in the 1980s," in C. Neil, M. Tykkyläinen, and J. Bradbury (eds.), *Coping with Closure. An International Comparison of Mine Town Experiences*, Routledge, London, pp. 313–326.

Tykkyläinen, M. (1993), "Restructuring in Resource Communities and Regional Development Theories," paper presented at the European Regional Science Association 33rd European Congress, Moscow, Russia.

12

Extracting local resources: The tourism route to development in Kolari, Lapland, Finland

Heikki Jussila and Jari Järviluoma

Introduction

Declining employment in agriculture and forestry, out-migration from rural regions, an ageing population, and a reduction in private services have weakened the development of the peripheral regions in Northern Europe during the past few decades. In many resource communities in northern and eastern Finland, local conditions have gradually worsened to the extent that some villages are facing total out-migration and "death" unless something extraordinary enables these regions to create new alternative paths for local economic development.

Regional development policies have had the task of reducing this decline by creating new jobs for those forced to leave their jobs in the primary sector – usually agriculture and forestry (see Robinson 1990, 22–24). In practice, regional policy instruments have been geared towards the industrialization of rural regions in Finland and in most other OECD countries. The goal of early regional policies in Finland was regionally balanced, and regionally equal, industrial development. The regional policy instruments through which this was to be achieved were the development of infrastructure and the provision of subsidies to start enterprises in the remote rural municipalities of northern and eastern Finland. Various grants were financed by the state (Tykkyläinen 1992, 231), and the provision of public services was financed generously.

This equality goal of regional policy has been kept as one of the basic objectives in current approaches to regional development. Industrialization, or, more precisely, the goal of creating industrial jobs extensively, has not paid off very well in the rural peripheries of Finland since the late 1960s (Tykkyläinen 1988), for three reasons. First, the loss of jobs in agriculture and forestry was so rapid and intense that policy measures were not sufficient to mitigate the problem to any great extent (ibid., 381). Secondly, the skills and labour practices of local people were not always in line with the endeavours of those responsible for local development (i.e. the municipal industrial secretaries and politicians responsible for economic development).[1] Thirdly, the primary goal of the authorities and financial institutions was the development of processing industries and manufacturing. For most peripheral regions, this left very little room for manoeuvre. The financial incentives available were geared towards capital investments, not people, who are really the main "resource" in any service industry. This meant that tourism, for example, got publicity and money was given for new resorts, but the training of the labour force was not given due priority. It was as if people were looked upon as "a necessary evil," not as a way of creating economic prosperity.

This was evident in the first regional policy laws emphasizing that Finland should be turned into a modern industrial society (*Law on Regional Development 1967*). In light of this policy, both the state and municipalities worked towards a new regional and local structure, both in a business sense and in a social sense. This meant that regional policy was a tool to create new and, in peripheral locales, previously unseen economic structures. The investments in local infrastructure and the rapid development of the public service sector have changed the content of regional policy, but the primary target is still the diversification of the local economic structure. In practice, the emphasis on the development of infrastructure turned out to be a policy for developing regional municipal service systems. This is most evident in the policy outcomes of the 1970s and 1980s, when the public sector increased its magnitude and scope by incorporating many new tasks within the social service sector, and thus also gave employment to people made redundant in the traditional peripheral industries. With hindsight, the older type of regional policy did not achieve the goal of diversification but rather created another "singular" economic mode – a public service economy.

Tourism and local and regional development policies

The original emphasis on the role of industrial development was not altogether in vain, although industrialization today means a more versatile spectrum of operations than before. The role of different service-based industries has grown and given impetus to the current calls for a "post-industrial" or "knowledge-based" society (Paasivirta 1991). For remote rural and peripheral areas, however, development based on information technologies is not that easy, and even the centres of these regions must work hard to overcome the various obstacles created by distance (see Andersen et al. 1993). Those policies that seek to create development based on the newer resource of "knowledge" often fail to see that the only real resource in a periphery is the local environment and it is, therefore, important to look at opportunities for local development based on the evolution of the concept of, and an appreciation of the utilization of, the peripheral environment (Jussila 1992).

In Finland, as in other industrialized countries, the revision of the national regional policy (Ministry of the Interior 1991) made tourism one of the preferred methods of diversifying local economies in peripheral rural regions (Archer 1978; Duffield 1977; Pearce 1980; Williams and Shaw 1988). Tourism has some characteristics that make it particularly suitable as a development tool for peripheral areas. Tourism differs from other spatially oriented economic sectors, which today favour concentration rather than dispersion. Naturally, though, the deconcentrated nature of tourism does not include all forms of tourism. In Finland, for example, Helsinki, as a densely populated locality, received more overnight tourists in 1992 than the whole administrative province of Lapland (Statistics Finland 1993).

From a local development perspective, tourism as an industry is also beneficial because of its high labour intensiveness: in favourable conditions, tourism can give a big boost to the local labour market. Further, tourism traditionally provides jobs for women and the young, who, in peripheral regions, tend to be in the worst position in the local labour market. However, tourism has a drawback – it tends to keep the level of local skills low. This is not to say that tourism as a source of livelihood is less important than the currently popular "high technology." The important point is that regional development

271

policies should also at least try to enhance the abilities of local people.

Other drawbacks attached to tourism are leakage from the local economy, local inflation, and seasonal unemployment. As a spatial form of development, tourism inevitably increases the utilization of local physical natural resources as pressure from large numbers of tourists visiting the region increases.[2] The impacts on nature are concrete, but the non-material sociocultural impacts of tourism are at least equally important (Mathieson and Wall 1982). In spite of the above criticism, tourism is a widely preferred alternative in local economic schemes owing to its income and employment effects. Furthermore, some cultural effects can be considered positive.

This chapter looks into the problem of peripheral local development from a micro-perspective. The municipality of Kolari is used as an example of community restructuring. The chapter analyses the changes in the economy and the job structure that occurred over previous decades. In addition, the question of the local attitude towards tourism and its repercussions is analysed. The aim of this article is to estimate, in general policy terms, the feasibility of tourism as a tool for local development in Kolari. Finally, the question is raised of what alternative development paths might have been available to the municipality of Kolari after the closing down of mining activities. The analysis of Kolari is an attempt on our part to understand how local development works. It is also an attempt to illustrate the difficulties of local decision makers when they try to envisage the future of their local community.

The case-study: Kolari

The rural municipality of Kolari, located approximately 100 km north of the Arctic Circle in western Lapland, has 4,700 inhabitants. In spite of its remote location and harsh environment, Kolari is a representative example of regional policy in peripheral Finland from the late 1960s. The same regional policy instruments, investment grants, and labour subsidies and loans have been available as elsewhere in Finland. Development policy in Kolari was also planned on the basis of experience elsewhere. Similar problems existed in a number of mining communities in Finland and other Nordic countries in the 1980s, and many development projects were carried out in these resource communities (Neil et al. 1992).

With respect to tourism development, the hilly landscape of the

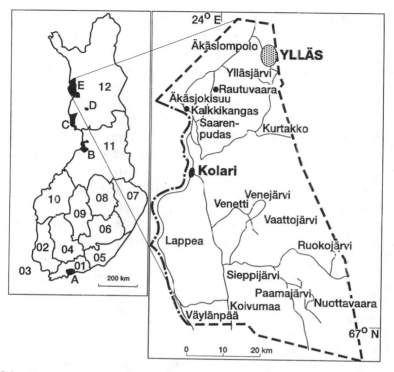

Fig. 12.1 **Kolari and the tourist region of Ylläs in Kolari municipality (Key: 12 = the administrative province of Lapland; A = Helsinki, B = Oulu, C = Kemi-Tornio, D = Rovaniemi city, E = the municipality of Kolari).**

north-eastern corner of Kolari is the most important resource (see fig. 12.1). The skiing resort of Ylläs (the major mountain in the area) offers excellent natural conditions for cross-country skiing, and, in the Finnish environment, good potential for downhill skiing. Within a 60 km radius of the Ylläs region, there are also three other major ski resorts – Levi, Olos, and Pallas. Together, these four resorts form one of the largest and most popular winter and spring holiday destination areas in Finland. In the low season, tourism in Kolari, as well as in other places in Lapland, is based on through-traffic, because many tourists head towards the most northerly point in continental Europe, the Nordkapp. In autumn, the autumn colours have been used as an additional attraction to extend the tourist season.

After World War II, the economic structure of Kolari changed dramatically. First and foremost, the importance of traditional rural occupations in agriculture and forestry diminished. The local scene

273

changed particularly during the period of the "great move" in the late 1960s and early 1970s, when people migrated in search of employment in Sweden and in the main centres of southern Finland. The number of dairy farms, for example, more than halved around this time. In 1992, the number of active dairy farms was 51, which was about 80 per cent of all active farms in Kolari.[3] Given that the number of dairy farms was almost 600 in 1965, the restructuring of Lapp agriculture has been dramatic. Kolari is located in the marginal area of agriculture owing to its cold climate, and hence the farms were very sensitive to changes in agricultural policy.

A second major change was more specific to Kolari. This change can be traced to the 1970s and 1980s, when Kolari was one of the most industrialized rural municipalities in Lapland. At that time, two large Finnish companies – Rautaruukki Ltd., owned at that time by the state, and the privately owned Partek Ltd. – had operational units in Kolari. Rautaruukki had an iron mine in Rautuvaara, 15 km southwest of Ylläs, and Partek had an open quarry and a cement factory, Kalkkikangas, in the municipality (fig. 12.1). Manufacturing employment (including mining) doubled in the early 1970s. These two industrial units employed over a fifth of the total labour force of Kolari; in the peak year of 1975, this exceeded 400 people. The industrial labour force declined rapidly in Kolari after this peak, and the mining operations and the cement factory in Kolari were shut down completely during the last years of the 1980s.

The closing down of the Rautaruukki mine and the Partek cement factory revealed that, although these industrial activities had increased the general well-being of the municipality and its inhabitants, not all their effects had been positive so far as long-term local development was concerned (Salkoaho 1993). The firms did not add much to the local industrial base. In fact, it could be argued that the big firms had hampered the development of local indigenous small businesses, because independent development was not achieved while the big firms were in operation.

A third, decisive change in Kolari, as everywhere else in rural Finland, was the growth of the public sector. The number of people engaged in public sector activities almost doubled during the 1970s and 1980s, increasing from 500 to almost 800 in two decades. The growth in Kolari occurred in the municipal sector, whereas the number of state jobs decreased slightly. In 1970, the municipality of Kolari employed some 172 employees; in 1990, the corresponding figure was 506 – an increase of 194 per cent. This growth in public sector jobs was also a way of diminishing the impact of mine closure. At that time there were no pressures to improve productivity in the public sector. However, as the economic situation in Finnish municipalities deteriorated in the 1990s many of the public service jobs disappeared. Thus, this local economic development model based on an increase in the jobs in the public sector did not prove sustainable.

Reaction to mine closure: Tourism development

In resource societies, "a closure" is a very difficult process, because it influences not only those directly employed but the whole area and its future. Most of the public and private services in a resource region depend on the income that the utilization of a resource, such as iron ore, generates. A closure also influences the small and medium-sized enterprises of the region because they, too, quite often depend on the "big" industry close by – this was the case in Kolari. The closure of Rautuvaara mine and the cement factory of Partek led to a collapse in the industrial base of Kolari. There may be plans to deal with the problems of the mine community and the miners' loss of jobs after such a closure, but these plans are effective only if those responsible for the planned closure have something to offer, either education or an alternative path for economic development. This is important because, when the whole basis for existence has gone, it is natural to question whether or not one has a future. In the case of Kolari, despite the problems, there was something available – the natural environment and its tourist potential.[4]

Following the announcements of the closure of Rautaruukki's iron mine and Partek's cement factory, the authorities – both state and municipal – started to look at the "old new" resource (the environment) for new forms of economic activities. At that time, the Finnish economy was booming and all kinds of services seemed to offer opportunities. For Lapland and for Kolari, tourism-based development was one of the most promising ways to alleviate the problems from the economic nose-dive (Matkailun edistämiskeskus 1988). In 1987, the provincial government of Lapland appointed a committee to coordinate all the different regional policy actions that were geared towards alleviating the economic crisis caused by the loss of industrial jobs in Kolari (Lapin lääninhallitus 1990). In the following year, a special Ylläs committee was formed by the State Board of Tourism to enhance local development. The basis for the work of this committee was the realization of the tourist potential of Kolari, given that tour-

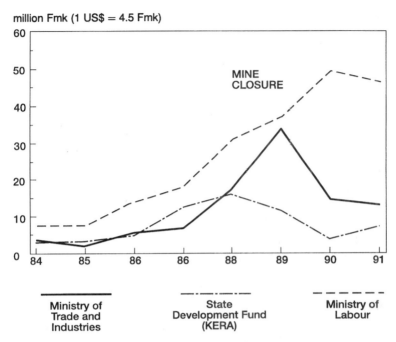

million Fmk (1 US$ = 4.5 Fmk)

MINE
CLOSURE

| | Ministry of Trade and Industries | State Development Fund (KERA) | Ministry of Labour |

Fig. 12.2 **Public aid allocated to Kolari by the State Development Fund, the Ministry of Trade and Industries, and the Ministry of Labour (Lapland District), 1984–1991 (Sources: statistics of the State Development Fund, the Ministry of Trade and Industries, and the Ministry of Labour, Lapland District).**

ism already played an important role in the Äkäslompolo area. These two committees were the beginning of a large effort to change the difficult economic conditions in Kolari during the latter part of the 1980s. For instance, in 1989, the State Development Fund (Kera Oy), the Ministry of Trade and Industries, and the Ministry of Labour (District Organization of Lapland) gave financial aid, loans, and grants to Kolari totalling some Fmk 84 million (see fig. 12.2). This represented approximately Fmk 18,000 (about $US4,500) per capita in Kolari. The main target for this assistance was tourism, which was seen as having the best possibility of success.

The support paid off relatively fast. New firms started to locate in Kolari. Between 1986 and 1990, the employment figures for restaurants and hotels in Kolari more than doubled – from 100 to almost 250. At the end of the 1980s, the immediate and indirect employment effect of tourism in Kolari was about 460 full-time jobs (Naalisvaara and Rantakokko 1991). Construction in the Ylläs region was continuous, and the number of construction jobs had gone up by five times within a few years. By the end of the 1980s, the number had reached 100. There was actually a period when there was a shortage of carpenters in Kolari.

Despite the dismissals from the mine and the cement factory in Kolari, the percentage of people employed improved in Kolari much faster than the average in Lapland at the end of the 1980s. In 1986, the unemployment rate in Kolari was 23 per cent, but, by the end of the 1980s, it had dropped to under 10 per cent – although this was only a temporary decline. Besides tourism and construction, the decline in unemployment was due to active measures of direct employment support and employment education. The migration of many of those who lost their jobs in the closure of the mine and cement factory also reduced the unemployment rate of Kolari municipality (Lapin lääninhallitus 1990). According to Alajärvi et al. (1990), every third employee to be given notice had moved away from Kolari within six months of the mine closure.

Construction of the Ylläs ski resort took place rapidly. Between 1985 and 1990, the Ylläs region was one of the fastest-growing tourist regions in Lapland. According to the approved construction licences, over 5,000 new tourist beds were built during that period. At the beginning of the 1990s, the total bed-capacity of the Kolari region had risen to some 10,000 beds, making the Ylläs region the largest single resort in the whole of Lapland (Niittyranta 1991). Most of the accommodation was in the form of private holiday or time-share apartments that did not receive public support to any major degree. During the late 1980s, public support for tourism in Kolari was needed because there were three new hotels and projects to enlarge the three existing hotels or motels in the Ylläs region. By the mid-1990s, taking into account the oldest hotel in Äkäshotelli, the Ylläs region had seven major hotels. The hotel build-up was also an incentive for other tourist service projects, such as restaurants, entertainment companies, shops, etc. In 1992/93, the region had 33 different routes for down-hill skiing and 18 lifts. Those interested in cross-country skiing could make use of the 280 km of cross-country tracks. At the beginning of the 1990s, the Ylläs region had some 100 firms, all deriving most of their business from tourism.

This rapid development of tourism in Kolari meant that, between 1987 and 1991, the number of registered overnight stays in hotels and motels more than doubled. The growth in tourism in Kolari was at that time much faster than in the province of Lapland as a whole (see

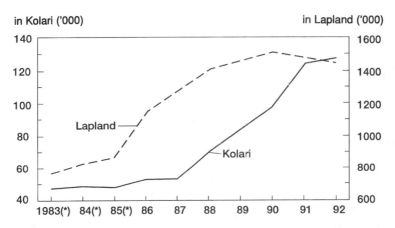

Fig. 12.3   **Registered hotel nights in Kolari and in Lapland, 1983–1992 (Note:** * =
excluding overnight stays at campsites. Source: Statistics Finland 1993).

fig. 12.3). The seasonal peak for tourists in Kolari is in the spring,
because both winter skiing holidays and the Easter holidays attract
tourists to Kolari. In 1992, the eight hotels operating in Kolari[5] had
close to half (46 per cent) of their customers in February, March, or
April. Kolari depends on domestic tourism, which accounts for about
90 per cent of all registered hotel nights. This shows that tourism in
Finnish Lapland is much more Finnish than international. During the
economic boom years of 1988–1990, it was customary for a growing
proportion of disposable income to be spent on leisure-time activities
by Finnish people. Although the relative strength of the Finnish mark
(Fmk) in the late 1980s and early 1990s made it possible to take a
holiday abroad, Finns still wanted to have their skiing holidays at
home. Developments during the late 1980s were aimed more towards
international tourism, but, because Finland is an expensive country,
this strategy did not have the success that had been forecast.[6]

The development of Kolari at the end of the 1980s was based on
very optimistic expectations about the future of tourism in Lapland.
This comes out very clearly from the general master plan for the
future development of the Ylläs region (see Suunnittelukeskus Oy
1990), prepared in 1989/90. This plan assumed that the Ylläs region
would increase its hotel bed-capacity to over 30,000 by the end of the
1990s. According to the plan, the Ylläs region would house a very
large tourist resort. The facilities would include 70–80 down-hill
routes and 36 ski lifts. The Äkäslompolo and Ylläsjärvi villages

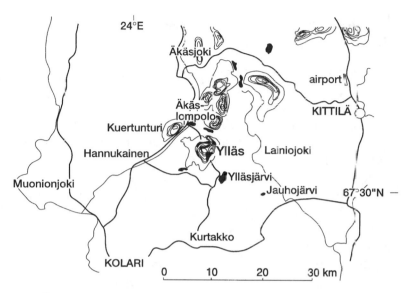

Fig. 12.4 **Äkäslompolo and Ylläsjärvi villages in the Ylläs tourist region (Source: Suunnittelukeskus Oy 1990).**

located on either side of the mountain (see fig. 12.4) were to be the main locations for the new hotels and motels. In addition, the land-use plan proposed that a tunnel should be built under the Yllästunturi to connect the villages. The plan also suggested that this tunnel would house facilities for tourism such as restaurants, shops, and a gym, and it would also be possible to get to the top of the Yllästunturi by elevator (Lapin tiepiiri and Suunnittelukeskus Oy 1990). The idea of constructing the tunnel was foiled by the long-lasting economic depression of the 1990s.

This master plan was, and is, a "good" example of the optimism that existed in Finland at the end of the 1980s. It was only about a year later that the recession hit Finland. At first it seemed that the recession would be like those in the middle of the 1970s and the 1980s, but it soon became clear that the current recession is much deeper and more structural that was originally believed. The unemployment rate in Kolari, which had fallen below 10 per cent during the late 1980s, rose again, and more than a quarter of the total labour force in Kolari was suddenly unemployed in the early 1990s. The slide into recession in Finland was extremely rapid and the recession was the deepest of all the OECD countries. Although, at the end of

279

the 1980s, Finland had got used to a standard of living that briefly surpassed even Sweden's, it faced economic problems that were much tougher than those of other West European countries.

The economic recession hit real estate businesses in Finland, and, consequently, also the construction of tourist resorts, especially hard. The most severe problem was, however, the huge and rapid growth in unemployment. In Kolari, the unemployment rate doubled during the early years of the 1990s, although in many other regions the rate increased even faster.[7]

The recession in Finland was fundamental in its character. The problems in the Finnish banking sector had grave consequences for local and regional development. The decision of the Finnish government to bail out the banking system increased government expenditure, and thus diminished the possibility of tackling the problems of unemployment and the reduction in domestic consumption, which, in turn, increased the problems of tourist regions like Kolari. The question of domestic consumption became an important issue in the debate on what measures should be taken and how the economic crisis should be tackled.

The economic recession of the 1990s hit the hotel and tourism business in Kolari hard, as it did Lapland as a whole. In particular, at the beginning of 1990s, interest rates went up and at the same time the value of the Finnish mark fell.[8] This was a serious blow to the domestic tourism industry, which had taken on currency-based loans at the time when the Finnish mark was at its "peak" value. This also halted most of the plans for new construction in the Ylläs region, and rapidly increased unemployment among construction workers. The hammer moved from the hand of a construction worker to the hand of a judge in court as the bankruptcy trials of hotels started in Lapland and in Kolari. Most of the seven hotels in the Ylläs region went bankrupt, although all of them were still operating in the mid-1990s, albeit in the hands of trustees appointed by the court.

It was not just the hotel business that ran into trouble. Private holiday homes also faced problems because their prices started to fall. These problems were especially difficult for those who had bought real estate as an investment at the end of the 1980s. At that time, the highest prices for housing in the vicinity of the main skiing areas were around Fmk 15,000 per m^2, and in 1993 those same cabins and houses had a price tag of only Fmk 6,000 per m^2. Despite this drop of some Fmk 8,000 in two years, business was slow, and this meant that the later investors, and banks with them, were hit very hard indeed (Sahiluoma 1993).

The economic problems of Kolari were, however, no more severe than those faced by other tourist resorts in Lapland. In addition to the inevitable bankruptcies, the fact that Finland became a relatively cheap tourist country proved to be a factor saving the tourist operators in Kolari. It is, however, important to see that the infrastructure development that took place in Kolari was an investment for a much longer period than just one decade. The mistakes of the 1980s may have halted the development in tourism, but they could not divert the municipality from the path it had chosen to take.

Local residents' attitudes towards tourism and its expansion in Kolari

The use of tourism as a way of achieving regional economic prosperity and growth has effects that traditional industrial programmes do not have. The service nature of tourism has important implications for local residents. It is thus necessary to look at the whole of the development picture, and this usually means dealing with the questions of in whose interests, by whom, and on whose terms.

From the perspective of the local population, most of the construction and hotel development was carried out by developers from southern Finland. The economic development was also carried out with the help of regional policy funds, and that kind of development did cause some problems within the region. The local population was, according to Järviluoma (1993), rather overwhelmed by the pace of economic development and, moreover, they felt that all the development projects came from "above" and that they themselves had no say about how and by what methods the development of the Ylläs region, for instance, would take place. It can be argued that this very rapid, externally based development of the region did little to increase the "average" citizen's commitment to tourism as a way of developing the area.

None the less, the attitude towards tourism among the local population was fairly positive, at least at the beginning of the 1990s. This is clearly apparent among the 200 inhabitants of Kolari who were interviewed in autumn 1990 at the "dawn" of the deep economic recession (Järviluoma 1993). The aim of the study was to estimate how the local population had taken the rapid development process of the late 1980s. According to the study, more than 90 per cent of those interviewed had a positive attitude and feeling towards tourism. This did not, however, mean that people wanted to have more tourists in their region. The majority of the respondents actually felt that the number of tourists in 1990 should be the maximum number of tourists visiting Kolari annually. This contradiction between a positive attitude and a wish to keep the numbers constant might be explained by the fact that people felt that more tourists would disrupt the "natural" peace of the region. The importance of silence could be seen in the answers of many respondents. People were also worried that the unwanted effects of tourism, such as crowding, would change their own living environment if the numbers and volume of tourists should increase. It is thus possible to argue that the social carrying capacity (Mathieson and Wall 1982, 21–22; O'Reilly 1986) of the region would be exceeded.

This rather ambivalent attitude towards tourism is understandable when looking at the unemployment figures of the municipality. The fact that tourism, and the related construction business, rectified the unemployment situation by lowering the high unemployment figures is reason enough for having a positive attitude towards a "new" source of livelihood in a region. The fact that people are more environmentally conscious and concerned is also clearly apparent, for many of the respondents felt that the most problematic issue related to tourism is the environment. The environment was the very reason tourists came in the first place, but, if there were too many tourists, the environment would suffer and, thus, so would business.

Besides the environmental issues, there was the problem of local resource allocation. The main tourist region in Kolari is located in the north-eastern corner of the municipality, and some people, especially those living rather far away (up to 100 km from the region being developed), felt that not all of their requests were met. This criticism was not against tourism as such but, rather, it reflected the desire spatially to expand the positive impact of tourism. People wanted more evenly targeted development. Development based on urbanized infrastructure investments met opposition within the municipality. The question of the use of municipal resources came into the open quite clearly in the pages of the local newspaper, which printed many open letters criticizing the way that the municipality of Kolari was handling the Ylläs region development (Järviluoma 1993).

Local development that changes local economies is never easy, and it is always bound to encounter opposition, as was the case in Kolari.

People did see that jobs were being created, but they also realized that not all of them were for the local people. Tourism as a service industry requires its labour force to have some qualifications, and this was something that the local population perhaps did not take into account.

The role of decision-making is another source of the unease felt by the local population. People did not consider that they had enough opportunities to take part in the actual process of decision-making. The fact that many of the big projects were run from outside the region strengthened this criticism.

The above are economic, environmental, and political concerns, but there is also a cultural and social dimension that needs to be discussed, namely the question of work and the work ethic within this peripheral municipality with respect to tourism as a source of livelihood. People in the region had been working in different types of jobs for a long time and their world incorporated various values. Work for them had a specific meaning. Work was seen as something concrete – farming, mining, production in a factory, taking care of the sick in a hospital; serving someone in a hotel was not the same thing. It was a job, but not work. Middle-aged and older people in particular felt this way. This cultural inheritance still influences the way tourists are served and how service work is valued in the peripheral communities.

At the same time, there is a process of change going on. People are looking at their local resources in a different way, and this is influencing their attitudes. It is the changing face of resource utilization that might, and indeed will, change attitudes. In a peripheral resource-bound area, resources have traditionally been seen as there to be used and "exploited." Now, when growing environmental awareness poses more serious threats to the older ways of using the local natural resources, new modes of resource utilization are developing, although the old attitudes and cultural traditions may still generate local opposition.

Was there a choice?

The economic difficulties that tourism experienced in Kolari are similar to those being experienced in the rest of Lapland, and, indeed, the whole of Finland. The devaluation of the Finnish mark in the early 1990s increased the number of foreign tourists, and, as the cost of going abroad also rose for Finns, domestic demand was expected to recover. The problem was that, at the same time, prices for hotel rooms and other services were falling, and this pushed many of the entrepreneurs in Kolari to the brink of, or into, bankruptcy. Fierce competition drove prices down and worsened the economic health of the tourism industry. In this sense, tourism in Kolari is suffering the after-effects of "boom and bust" development, a development that is typical of resource exploitation.

Looking at the situation from the perspective of resource development, one could, however, argue that the boom-like development of tourism in Kolari has not all been in vain. The development and building of high-quality cottages, etc., are an asset for the region. The economic forecast for the future may, as a result, be much brighter than the economic situation of the mid-1990s would lead one to believe. In order to improve the competitiveness of business, one key factor is marketing. The construction of an image and the right mix of local services are essential if one is looking for prosperity in the tourism of Kolari.

The question remains whether or not tourism was, or is, a suitable solution for rural peripheral municipalities such as Kolari. This is not an easy question to answer, and, to some extent, it is almost impossible to do so. The reason is that, since the tourism facilities were built, the community itself has changed its thinking patterns – from a mining and rural community towards a more open service community. It is yet to be seen how far this process has gone, but it is certain that there is no turning back.

The fact that Kolari has experienced problems in developing a tourism industry and was still, in the mid-1990s, suffering from the bust after the boom years of the late 1980s, and consequently also from very high unemployment, is not, in our judgement, a good reason for declaring that it was wrong to choose tourism as a way out of the structural development problem. The causes of the economic problems are to only a minor extent related to the local area. Looking at the development path, the choice was, in a way, the next natural step on the path of resource development in Kolari.

It is, however, relevant to ask whether or not there were any other possibilities and paths for local economic development in Kolari in the mid-1980s, and what these solutions might have been. In the case of Kolari, it is possible to imagine three alternative courses.

One option was for the municipality and all other authorities to do nothing. This could be called "the zero option." The probable outcome of this choice would have been massive out-migration and, in today's circumstances, an even higher unemployment rate.

Secondly, there was the option of using the investment money that was put into tourism to develop other sectors of the local economy, such as small-scale wood-processing, metal works, food-processing, "ecological farming products," or, indeed, the development of distant work. However, Kolari municipality did not possess any significant advantages in those fields, whereas there was some foundation for the choice of tourism.

Thirdly, there was the option of using tourism more diversely than has been the case so far. A diversified approach to tourism development would have included farm holidays and reindeer farm holidays, as well as fishing, hunting, and hiking. The likely outcome would have been that Ylläs, as a tourist resort, would have been a bit smaller than today, but the effect of tourism development in outlying areas would have been larger. This is, perhaps, the route that development will take naturally.

These three options for local development each reflect different approaches to resource development. The first approach is to surrender to the pressures of economic restructuring. The second approach is to invest in other industries such as small-scale manufacturing and services that would gradually become large enough to provide employment within the whole municipality. The third approach is to make broader use of local people and the local environment in order to widen the benefits and economic scope of tourism, so that it becomes the main source of livelihood for the whole of the community, not just a small subregion.

A strategy that utilized local resources more broadly than the one-resort approach would have a dispersed social and developmental effect, which can be characterized as follows:

- economic development control would be more in the hands of local entrepreneurs;
- capital by-passing (out-flow) would be smaller, because the integration of tourism would be more firmly based;
- the degree of dependency on a small segment of tourists, and on one season, would be smaller, because the basis for attracting visitors would be wider;
- a more even economic development pattern within the municipality would lead to more harmonious economic development, and to a broader acceptance of tourism as the method of local development;

- a larger and deeper commitment to and interest in tourism would be present among the local population;
- there would possibly be a more stable employment situation in the municipality of Kolari;
- there would be fewer environmental problems in the Ylläs region.

It is, however, possible to say that tourism, as a reaction to mine closure, was not very successful from the standpoint of the miners. It is evident from the labour statistics within Kolari that miners did not go to the jobs created in tourism and the related services. Miners are proud experts in their field and feel that only mining (that is, "concrete" work) can be looked upon as "proper" work. It is, however, difficult to determine to what extent traditional attitudes towards work have been a hindrance to tourism development. The local population is in an important position when development is based on a service industry, which means that the developers need to take into account the reaction of the local population.

Conclusions: The nature of the tourist economy

It is very difficult to estimate the effect of tourism in relation to the total local economy. In Kolari, tourism has been a good solution for certain resource communities that otherwise would probably have lost most of their population. However, the figures concerning economic benefits vary considerably according to the basis chosen. The municipal authorities do not know what the financial impact of tourism is in Kolari. This became apparent in the interviews with those responsible for economic development in Kolari, though the local economic adviser agreed that tourism plays an important and decisive role in income formation and the maintenance of services. If one analyses the number of people with jobs within service industries, tourism actually became the major source of employment in Kolari in the 1990s. This does not mean that all people are engaged in tourism activities – a number of people in other services also depend on the well-being of the tourism industry.

Measured against the above criterion, tourism has been central for Kolari in the creation of new economic activity. The growth in job opportunities has been substantial, although the mining community that was closed during the 1980s did not directly benefit from the establishment of the tourist resorts. This is quite common in other regions as well (see, for example, Neil et al. 1992). The general development and increase in jobs in services did not alleviate the unemployment problem created by mine closure, because the miners did not possess the skills needed in the service sector. A common problem in peripheral regional development is that the skills of local people do not meet the needs of the newly established industries. In the case of tourism, there was, and is, substantial recruitment of people living outside the region. This in itself is not a bad thing, because it can bring in new ideas and skills to the region. It does, however, diminish the employment effects, which, in most cases, are the prime goal of a particular economic development effort.

Looked at in a broader and longer perspective, tourism development in Kolari, and in Lapland as a whole, has many positive aspects. The construction of all the facilities during the 1980s created a high-quality capacity for serving tourists. This is an important asset, because Finland has become a much more affordable country for foreigners to visit. When foreign demand for Lapland and Kolari increases, it will be possible for the Kolari and Ylläs regions to capitalize on this demand. Many places in Lapland can be characterized as wilderness, and this is an important potential for tourism development. Joint marketing and joint reservation systems are also under development and will, in the future, increase the service potential. The move towards specialized tourist products and packages will undoubtedly have a positive effect on tourism in Kolari and Lapland.

It seems clear that tourism will become a major industry for utilizing or extracting a local resource in many peripheral places. This will lead to economic development in suitable locales. Developers, planners, and politicians alike should have the wisdom to pursue development based on sustainable future growth, since the natural environment is the resource on which they must rely in the future. The Kolari case demonstrates that the development of tourism is dependent not only on the natural landscape, but on external impulses, social capital, and cooperation within the business. The development of an attractive environment related to tourism is a gradual process, and the sector is sensitive to business cycles.

Notes

1. One must emphasize that economic development during the 1970s and early 1980s almost exclusively meant job creation within manufacturing industries. Services were not looked upon as being in the mainstream of local economic development, with the exception of tourism, which was already emerging in the 1970s.
2. The typical environmental impacts arise from waste disposal, construction, and sheer over-utilization of the physical environment.

3. The diminishing number of farms has, however, not influenced production, because the amount of milk delivered to dairies has stayed almost constant.
4. The ski resorts in Äkäslompolo and in Ylläsjärvi already existed. It was, however, the closing of the mine that made local decision makers really active on tourist issues. The economic boom in the real estate business in Finland at the time did, of course, help in this, although it soon proved to be just another economic bubble. At the time, developing the Ylläs region was the way out of mine closure, and it did give hope to the community as a whole.
5. Only one of the hotels is located outside the Ylläs ski resort area, and that hotel is in the centre of the Kolari region.
6. It is interesting to note that, during the recession and the floating of the Finnish mark, the number of foreigners staying overnight in Lapland increased, but, at the same time, the number of Finns taking their holidays in Lapland decreased.
7. The highest growth in unemployment in Finland occurred in the most prosperous regions around the city of Helsinki. In 1990/91, the unemployment rate in Helsinki was almost non-existent (2.5 per cent), but in 1993 it was around 15 per cent of the total active labour force.
8. In September 1991, the Bank of Finland devalued the Finnish mark for the first time, and, a year later, in autumn 1992, the Finnish mark was taken off its unilateral link to EMS and put on a floating rate, which meant an immediate devaluation of close to 20 per cent.

References

Alajärvi, A., Suikkanen, A., Viinamäki, L., and Ainonen, M. (1990), "Kaivos-yhdyskunnan purkautuminen: Tutkimus Kolarin Rautuvaaran kaivoksen sulkemi-sesta ja yhdyskunnan uudelleen rakenteistumisesta," *Lapin korkeakoulun yhteis-kuntatieteellisiä julkaisuja B, Tutkimusraportteja ja selvityksiä* 10.

Andersen, J. O., Arbo, P., Jussila, H., Nilsson, J.-E., and Sandersen, H. (1993), "Høgskolene i Nord-Skandinavia – Drivkrafter for Regional Næringsutvikling?" *NordREFO*, Copenhagen.

Archer, B. (1978), "Domestic Tourism as a Development Factor," *Annals of Tourism Research* 15, pp. 126–141.

Duffield, B. (1977), *Tourism: A Tool for Regional Development. Leisure Studies Association Conference, Edinburgh, 1977*, Tourism & Recreation Research Unit, University of Edinburgh, Department of Geography.

Järviluoma, J. (1993), "Attitude of the Local Population towards Tourism and its Repercussions in the District of Kolari," University of Oulu, Research Institute of Northern Finland, Research Reports No. 110 (in Finnish with English abstract).

Jussila, H. (1992), "The Role of Centres in Fringe Area Development," in M. Tykkyläinen (ed.), *Development Issues and Strategies in the New Europe: Local, Regional and Interregional Perspectives*, Avebury, Aldershot, pp. 145–162.

Lapin lääninhallitus (1990), "Kolari-työryhmän loppuraportti," *Lapin lääninhalli-tuksen julkaisusarja* 10, Rovaniemi.

Lapin tiepiiri and Suunnittelukeskus Oy (1990), "Yllästunneli: Tekninen, ympäris-töllinen ja taloudellinen selvitys," mimeo.

Law on Regional Development 1967, Finnish State Statutes Collection, Helsinki.

Mathieson, A. and Wall, G. (1982), *Tourism: Economic, Physical and Social Impacts*, Longman Scientific & Technical, London.

Matkailun edistämiskeskus (1988), *Ylläs-työryhmän raportti*, MEK, Helsinki.

Ministry of the Interior (1991), *Evaluation of Finnish Regional Policy*, Ministry of the Interior, Municipality and Regional Development Department, Helsinki.

Naalisvaara, L. and Rantakokko, M. (1991), "Kolarin matkailuselvitys vuonna 1990," *Nordia Tiedonantoja* B:2.

Neil, C., Tykkyläinen, M., and Bradbury, J. (eds.) (1992), *Coping with Closure. An International Comparison of Mine Town Experiences*, Routledge, London.

Niittyranta, T. (1991), "Ylläksen matkailun kehitysvaiheita," *Torniorlaakson Vuosikirja*, pp. 107–108.

O'Reilly, A. M. (1986), "Tourism Carrying Capacity: Concept and Issues," *Tourism Management* 7, pp. 254–258.

Paasivirta, A. (1991), "Suomen alueellinen uusiutumisstrategia: Aluepoliittinen selvitysmies Anssi Paasivirran ehdotus aluepolitiikan uudistamiseksi," *Sisäasiainministeriö, kunta- ja aluekehitysosaston julkaisuja 18*, Helsinki.

Pearce, D. (1980), "Tourism and Regional Development: A Genetic Approach," *Annals of Tourism Research* 7(1), pp. 69–82.

Robinson, G. M. (1990), *Conflict and Change in the Countryside: Rural Society, Economy and Planning in the Developed World*, Belhaven Press, London and New York.

Sahiluoma, V. (1993), "Pankit omistavat Ylläksen: Nauti pankkituesta Lapin lomallasi," *Kauppalehti*, 18 February, Helsinki.

Salkoaho, U. (1993), "Oi ihminen tule tunturirinnoilleni ..." Paikallistutkimus Ylläksen alueen matkailukuvasta ja väestön suhtautumisesta matkailun kehittämiseen: Julkaisematon pro gradu-tutkielma, Tampereen yliopisto, Sosiaalipolitiikan laitos, mimeo.

Statistics Finland (1993), *Accommodation and Hotel Statistics,* Helsinki.

Suunnittelukeskus Oy (1990), *Ylläksen alueen osayleiskaava: Kaavaselostus*, Suunnittelukeskus, Rovaniemi.

Tykkyläinen, M. (1988), "The Periphery Syndrome – A Reinterpretation of Regional Development Theory in a Resource Periphery," *Fennia* 166(2), pp. 295–411.

———— (1992), "Solutions to Mine Closure in Outokumpu," in C. Neil, M. Tykkyläinen, and J. Bradbury (eds.) (1992), *Coping with Closure. An International Comparison of Mine Town Experiences*, Routledge, London, pp. 225–246.

Williams, A. M. and Shaw, G. (eds.) (1988), *Tourism and Economic Development: Western European Experiences*, Belhaven Press, London.

13

The development of community-based rural tourism in Ireland

Micheál Ó Cinnéide and John Burke

Introduction: Towards community initiatives

The general economic decline of rural areas in the advanced economies of Europe and elsewhere is well documented (e.g. Commission of the European Communities 1991). Clearly, the relative disadvantage of rural areas compared with urban areas has not been overcome, despite well-funded sectoral policies such as the Common Agricultural Policy of the European Union.

Many factors precipitate these problems. Above all, technological advances and capital intensification have so increased the productivity of labour in the primary sector that vastly increased output is achieved by less and less labour (Troughton 1992). This increased labour productivity has led to greatly reduced numbers engaged in agriculture and other primary activities. Furthermore, technological change has facilitated specialization in production and increasing economies of scale, which, when combined with external economies, have tended to lead to an intensified concentration of economic activity in urban centres, largely at the expense of rural areas, which lack the natural advantages of agglomeration and economies of scale. More recently, an increasing emphasis has been placed on the role of the market in the allocative process. This is bringing increasing pressure to bear on rural areas, in many of which population thresholds are insufficient to ensure the economic provision of many services, thus leading to their curtailment and eventual withdrawal. The greater internationalization of markets is buttressing this process at the local level.

The net result of these and other related processes is that most rural areas in Europe are characterized by a spiral of decline. The diversification of the rural economy through the creation of new economic opportunities in non-traditional sectors is vital to the future of rural society. Local communities, regional development agencies, national governments, and supranational institutions such as the European Union are placing increased emphasis on means by which successful structural transitions of local rural economies can be effected. National and supranational policies generally focus on enhancing the competitiveness of rural areas by attempting, for example, to reduce the isolation of rural places through improvements in communication systems. Local and regional bodies are actively exploring new approaches, such as integrated rural development, and new forms of economic activity, such as rural tourism. New administrative arrangements with an emphasis on partnership between public, private, and community actors are being tested and implemented.

The main purpose of this chapter is to illustrate how some communities in Ireland are responding to the international forces of change that are affecting rural areas, by pursuing a programme of rural tourism development. The chapter does not analyse development in single communities in detail, but it focuses on representing a model of cooperation needed when small entrepreneurs attempt to prosper in small resource communities based on tourism.

The declining role of agriculture has exacted a heavy toll on the rural population in this traditional agricultural economy (Ó Cinnéide 1992a). Top–down sectoral policies have been largely ineffective in stemming out-migration and arresting rural decline. The net result is an ageing, imbalanced rural population imbued with apathy and a sense of powerlessness in the face of the crisis confronting rural society. However, in this study, we report on how some local communities have organized locally, and combined nationally, to effect a programme of rural community tourism development that is injecting new life into the local areas concerned. In particular, we report on the recent establishment of a national cooperative for the promotion of rural community tourism in Ireland, and assess it as a model vehicle that could be usefully adopted in other places seeking to promote tourism amongst rural communities.

The growth of tourism in Ireland

The economic and social importance of tourism to the Republic of Ireland is evidenced by the fact that, in 1991, it provided employment for 87,000, contributed 7 per cent of the gross national product, and generated a net surplus of over IR£500 million in the balance of payments (Tourism Task Force 1992). Tourism accounts for 1 in 14 jobs in the economy as a whole, and 1 in 8 in the services sector. Its potential to create jobs is shown by the fact that employment in the industry increased by over 31,000 between 1986 and 1991. In the same period, total employment in the economy increased by just 44,000.

An important feature of tourism in Ireland is that it is a widely dispersed economic activity that makes a significant contribution to local and regional development (Ó Cinnéide and Walsh 1990–91). On the international scene, in sharp contrast to the picture of decline and marginalization in agriculture, tourism trends are generally very buoyant (Lane 1993). The World Tourism Organization reported a 56 per cent increase in international visitor arrivals over the decade 1980–1990. This represents a cumulative growth rate of just over 4 per cent per annum. Considering the significant contribution that tourism is already making to the Irish economy, and the potential for further major expansion afforded by global trends, it is not surprising that Ireland is targeting the industry for major expansion.

Tourism development – its strengths and weaknesses in Ireland

Bord Fáilte, the Irish tourist board, was established in 1955 to develop and promote tourism in the Republic of Ireland. It is a body corporate, established under statute, and financed by annual government grants. Permanent staff in 1990 numbered 224, most of whom were based in Ireland, but with representatives in Britain, the United States, Germany, France, Holland, Belgium, Italy, Scandinavia, and other countries (Ó Cinnéide and Walsh 1990–91). Bord Fáilte co-ordinated the activities of six Regional Tourism Organizations (RTOs) established in 1964 as companies limited by guarantee to service the needs of individual regions. The RTOs represent an attempt to decentralize tourism promotion and development functions. Their main functions relate to (a) overseas marketing and promotion; (b) operating a network of visitor information and reservation centres; (c) encouraging environmental awareness and monitoring physical planning standards; and (d) promoting the development of tourism products. The RTOs receive a subvention from Bord Fáilte, but they have to raise most of their funding requirements through their own activities.

The particular strengths of Ireland as a tourism destination include: (a) a tradition of friendliness and hospitality, which gives the country an advantage over other Northern European destinations, especially in short-haul markets such as France, Benelux, Italy, Germany, and Britain; (b) a clean, unpolluted natural environment that offers an ideal setting for a wide range of outdoor leisure activities in uniquely beautiful surroundings; and (c) the fact that it is the ancestral home of up to 70 million people worldwide, giving Ireland comparative advantages in countries such as the United States and Australia with strong ethnic Irish traditions. To these can be added generic strengths that are common to many, if not most, of the competitor set of destinations viewed by the consumer as alternatives to Ireland. These strengths include beautiful scenery, interesting history and culture, lack of mass tourism, availability of good angling, golfing, and equestrian sporting facilities, conviviality and informality (including a relaxed pace of life), and an English-speaking, receptive, host population (Bord Fáilte 1992).

Weaknesses associated with the Irish tourism product may be classified into perceptual, structural, and quasi-generic. Perceptual weaknesses that emerge recurrently in research into potential overseas customers who have not visited Ireland include an image of Ireland as having a bland, boring countryside, with poor-quality accommodation and food, and dull shopping facilities (Bord Fáilte 1992). Structural weaknesses relate to difficult and expensive access, lack of high-profile tourism attractions, the country being expensive for car touring holidays, a lack of knowledge about Ireland overseas, and inadequate marketing of the country as a tourism destination. The quasi-generic weaknesses present the most intractable obstacles. Foremost among these is the perception of Ireland as a country beset by civil disturbances. Bad, unpleasant, generally rainy weather is another major quasi-generic weakness.

Rural tourism

Recognition of the contribution that rural tourism could make to supplementing farm incomes and providing new economic opportunities for rural communities evolved only slowly in Ireland. The initial stimulus came from a shortage of suitable tourism accommodation in the mid-1960s, leading to its provision, in limited supply, in Irish farmhouses (Gannon 1992). Yet, by 1987, only 491 farmers offered tourist accommodation and, by 1992, there were still only 650 registered farm providers. In addition, there were in excess of 1,000 registered country homes that had had no direct links to agriculture providing tourist accommodation (Ó Cinnéide 1992b).

The coordinated provision of a diversified range of rural tourism products, and the professional marketing of these, has been attempted only during the past few years. Despite its slow and inauspicious start, a strong emphasis is now being placed on rural tourism development in Ireland. This is due, in large measure, to market signals that indicate a swing away from traditional tourism resorts and, more particularly, from sun destinations. Holidays are also becoming more fragmented, leading to a demand for a greater diversity of holiday types, including sporting activities such as horse riding and golfing, countryside activities such as walking and cycling, and simple relaxation. The overall growth in the tourism industry and the swing toward "soft" or "green" tourism, especially among the most discerning market sectors, present rural areas with an unprecedented opportunity to capture a significant portion of this new and expanding economic activity.

The current emphasis on tourism in rural areas also relates to the somewhat belated recognition that rural communities could not survive on agriculture alone. With the publication by the Commission of the European Communities (1988) of the seminal document entitled "The Future of Rural Society," the limitations of the Common Agricultural Policy were officially accepted, and the search for measures that would contribute to the restructuring of the rural economy was initiated in earnest. The promotion of rural tourism was specifically mentioned as having promising potential for the future of rural society. It would help to alleviate the problems arising from the European Commission's decision to reform the Common Agricultural Policy in a way that would reduce agricultural output and so reduce farm incomes. In order to give impetus to this strategic thinking, policy measures that favoured the stimulation of new economic

activities in rural areas, including tourism, were evolved and implemented to compensate, at least in part, for the constraints on agriculture, upon which most rural communities were heavily dependent.

The recent emphasis on rural tourism development in Ireland
took place against the background of an ambitious national plan
(the Operational Programme for Tourism 1989–1993) to double the
number of inbound tourists to the country within five years. Both the
Operational Programme for Tourism and a parallel operational programme for rural development included measures to enable rural
areas to capture a share of the overall targeted growth in tourism.
Between 1986 and 1992, the number of visitors to Ireland rose substantially, from 2.4 million to almost 3.7 million (*Statistical Yearbook
1992*, 956; *Statistical Yearbook 1994*, 898). This was an exceptional
performance by international standards. However, owing to a combination of factors such as the Gulf War and the global economic
recession, the doubling of the number of visitors during the course of
the plan was not achieved.

Failure to attain the very ambitious targets set in the Operational
Programme did not deter the Irish government. The subsequent
plan (Bord Fáilte 1992) focused on increasing tourism revenue by
an average of 8.3 per cent per annum over the period 1993–1997,
thus creating an additional 23,000 jobs in the economy. In this subsequent plan there is a new emphasis on the development of tourism
that is socially, economically, and environmentally sustainable. In
that context, there is special recognition of the potential contribution of rural tourism areas, and 25 such localities within the country were targeted for development as "centres of excellence for
environmentally-friendly holidays, steeped in the living traditions of
Ireland" (Bord Fáilte 1992).

The Rural Community Tourism Cooperative Society

The new emphasis on sustainable tourism in rural Ireland is evident
today in the embodiment of strategies and approaches devised by 13
local community tourism groups, which form interdependent limbs of
a national body, namely the Rural Community Tourism Cooperative
Society (Ireland) Ltd., generally known as "Irish Country Holidays."
The progress of these groups shows how expertise, skills, and information can be maximized in the development and marketing of rural
tourism.

In an effort to stimulate the diversification of the rural economy, an agri-tourism pilot project was established in 1988 by a national co-ordinating committee, formed by two of the main farming organizations, namely the Irish Farmers Association and Macra na Feirme, together with Teagasc (the Farm Advisory Service) and Bord Fáilte. These groups had already developed marketable community-based rural tourism holiday packages based on accommodation and a choice of leisure activities. The objectives of the national coordinating committee grew out of a belief that considerable potential for economic development lay in community-based agri-tourism. These objectives included (a) setting up rural community tourism groups; (b) developing the agri-tourism product; (c) developing, maintaining, and monitoring standards; and (d) identifying training requirements and ensuring that necessary training was provided for group members (Keane and Quinn 1990). The committee selected four local rural communities for their agri-tourism pilot project.

Test marketing of packaged community-based rural tourism holidays took place during the 1989 tourist season. The marketing, which was targeted on the German market, was carried out in conjunction with C.I.E. Tours International, a holiday company specializing in coach tours. Marketing costs were met by the community groups and members of the national coordinating committee. An analysis of the results suggested that, if viability and sustainability were to be achieved, nationally and at the local level, action would need to take place in relation to the following four issues: (a) the formation of a national legal structure; (b) a planned and professional approach to marketing community-based rural tourism packaged holidays on behalf of member groups; (c) a development strategy to include national coordination and networking; and (d) an extension of the pilot project to include more community tourism groups as members of the national organization.

A legal structure

An important milestone in the history of this model vehicle for the organizing and marketing of community-based rural tourism was the formation of a legal structure in 1990. The organization was registered as the Rural Community Tourism Cooperative Society (Ireland) Ltd. The shareholders consisted of four community rural tourism groups, the Irish Farmers Association, and Macra na Feirme. Teagasc and Bord Fáilte became advisers to the board of this newly formed voluntary organization. Monthly meetings provided members with a forum for cooperative planning and organization. Plans centred on the objectives of the cooperative as stated in its articles of association, that is, to coordinate and assist in the marketing of rural tourism generally, and to represent the interests of the members of the Society and assist them in their work of developing all local resources for the benefit of their local communities.

Marketing

The biggest challenge that faced the national cooperative was successfully to market community-based rural tourism package holidays. Performance and success in the marketing field would depend on access to markets. Human and financial resources, combined with expertise, were considered to be essential tools in the process of achieving success. Agricultural cooperatives, insurance companies, and financial institutions were successfully targeted as funding sources to support the marketing exercise.

In contrast with the previous approach to marketing through C.I.E. Tours International, it was accepted that marketing would have to be undertaken through direct involvement in the market place. C.I.E. Tours International was not prepared, as a commercial tour operator, to take on the costs of market development for a new product for Ireland, because these costs might not be recouped by the company (Keane and Quinn 1990). Following discussions with Teagasc and Bord Fáilte (during 1991), financial support was committed by the latter organization to the national cooperative to fund the employment of a marketing executive for a period of two years. This appointment was a major advance for the cooperative.

In evolving a marketing strategy, group representatives at the national cooperative level shared their expertise and agreed on a marketing plan. Taking advantage of opportunities provided through Bord Fáilte tour operator contacts and promotional workshops was an obvious route. Targeting specific tour operators with an interest in rural tourism proved a very successful strategy. Through the invaluable experience of the newly appointed marketing executive, who had been previously involved in the travel trade, many new markets were developed. Package holidays with a wide variety of choice and price were compiled in an effort to attract special-interest groups and also with a focus on particular niche markets.

High priority was given by the national cooperative to maximizing exposure in tour operators' holiday guides and brochures. This objective was very successfully achieved. The branded cooperative product, Irish Country Holidays, is currently illustrated in 18 high-quality tour operators' guides throughout Europe. Packaging, pricing, and marketing in the field of tourism had to allow for a time-lag of approximately one year before results began to transpire. Tour operator prices were negotiated and travel brochures were printed almost one year ahead of client uptake. By the end of 1993, however, the number of bed nights booked through the central sales office had increased by 3,108 (1,064 per cent over the 1992 total of 292 bed nights).

National coordination

National coordinating and marketing by the cooperative provide the local groups with an important support mechanism. The main advantages lie in the central approach to marketing. Through the central sales office of the National Rural Tourism Cooperative, additional bookings are directed toward local groups. Clients can select and book a holiday spread over any 3 of the 13 participating areas by making just one telephone call to the central sales office. In this way, the tourist is given variety and choice. A very important outcome from a local economic developmental point of view is the potential for a fair distribution of business. Weaker local groups, located in more remote areas, are supported by the better-established groups, which enjoy comparative advantages such as location and ease of access. The common problem of internal competition between product providers is minimized owing to the approach of the national cooperative.

The extension of the national cooperative

Market research and an awareness of an increasing customer base indicated a great need for an increased volume and variety of product. This led to the gradual expansion of the national organization. Current membership consists of 13 community rural tourism groups, widely dispersed throughout Ireland (see fig. 13.1). The advisory panel was also expanded to include the participation of the Irish Cooperative Organization Society Ltd. (the parent organization governing all cooperative societies in Ireland). The extension of the national cooperative has been greatly facilitated by the work of Teagasc's socio-economic advisers at local community levels. An

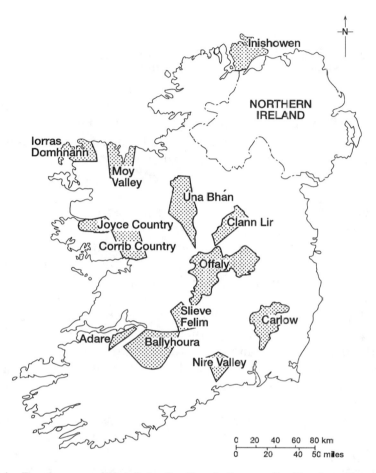

Fig. 13.1 **Rural areas affiliated to the Rural Community Tourism Cooperative Society.**

increasing awareness of the economic development potential of community-based rural tourism has also generated a lot of interest among local community groups.

Úna Bhán – a local organization

Úna Bhán is one of the 13 local groups that comprise the Rural Community Tourism Cooperative. The group is located in the north midlands of Ireland (see fig. 13.1). Bordered by the River Shannon to the east, the Úna Bhán region encompasses all of County Roscommon and the adjoining parts of the counties of Leitrim and Sligo. The

299

origin, structure, functions, and performance of the Úna Bhán group illustrate how community-based rural tourism may be organized at the local level to contribute to the economic diversification of rural economies.

During the summer of 1988, farm guest-house owners in the Úna Bhán area were invited by Teagasc to meet, with a view to setting up an agri-tourism group. The thinking behind the targeting of accommodation providers was to build on the knowledge and expertise of established operators who were already committed to tourism. It was a brain-storming session mainly focused on highlighting individual and group needs. A second objective was to evaluate the group's suitability to participate in the aforementioned national agri-tourism pilot project.

Marketing emerged as the outstanding common need of the product providers. An individual provider with five twin-bedded rooms, operating over a six-month season, had a capacity of 1,700 bed nights over that period. Maximum occupancy during a season could turn over in excess of IR£17,000 on bed and breakfast sales alone, excluding additional revenue from meals and other services. However, the national occupancy rate over the three-month peak season in 1988/89 was only 35 per cent, and the occupancy rate in Úna Bhán country was even lower, hence the need to engage in a concerted marketing drive.

By January 1989, an agri-tourism group was formed and officers had been appointed. The decision by the members to contribute IR£100 per person to a central marketing fund was an expression of their confidence in the potential of the cooperative approach. The investment was also regarded as a means of attracting matching support from funding agencies and sponsors. The short- and medium-term objectives of the Úna Bhán group were: (a) to carry out a resource audit of the Úna Bhán area; (b) to market community-based activity holidays; (c) to establish a group structure with an area office and support staff; (d) to participate in leadership and group training; and (e) to promote innovative product development.

As part of the resource audit, an inventory of the Bord Fáilte approved-accommodation bed-bank available within the group was prepared. A second focus of study was existing activities that tourists could undertake within the area. Information was also compiled on local services such as transport, car hire, bicycle hire, fishing boats, tour guides, banks, and theatres. Lists of parks, cycling and walking routes, historic houses, stately homes, castles and abbeys, fishing stands on lakes, etc., were compiled. Local amenities and natural beauty spots, along with archaeological sites, were also documented with a view to emphasizing the uniqueness of the area as a rural tourism holiday destination. The resource audit drew attention to the strengths and weaknesses of the area and provided important information in relation to potential areas for further product development. Identifying product gaps led to an increased awareness of the potential of tourism for local economic development in a rural resource community. However, the most relevant short-term outcome was the identification of saleable rural tourism products that needed to be packaged and marketed.

With the main focus on marketing, the next task for the group was to encourage non-accommodation product providers to join Úna Bhán. The group was extended to include owners of open farms and historic houses, specialists in local history and heritage, skilled craft workers, restaurateurs, guides, and many others. Most of the new members had no previous experience in tourism but displayed great enthusiasm and willingness to cooperate. Knowledge of the markets by some of the more experienced farm guest-house owners and an awareness of customer needs provided the group with a good launching pad for their marketing strategy. Through the guidance of the local Teagasc adviser, the group also explored a number of potential new markets. Packaged activity holidays were costed and prepared for marketing, based on the approach of pooling local resources to provide the customer with variety, choice, and value for money. With financial assistance from Bord Fáilte, a brochure illustrating accommodation and activity holidays was produced in four languages. It offered stress-free holidays in a clean and healthy environment. A well-presented photographic album was also prepared as a means of illustrating the quality, variety, and attractiveness of the various products. Two members of the group were assigned responsibilities relating to spearheading the marketing drive. Events such as workshops organized by Bord Fáilte, trade fairs, clan rallies, and in-store promotions were targeted as cost-effective means of reaching a wide market. Contacts were made with tour operators and consumers in an effort to attract new business. The experience gained in the marketplace indicated a need for follow-up contacts to be made in order to finalize bookings and guarantee sales, and these too were vigorously pursued.

In order to provide an efficient local booking service and implement its plans, the Úna Bhán group decided to structure itself for-

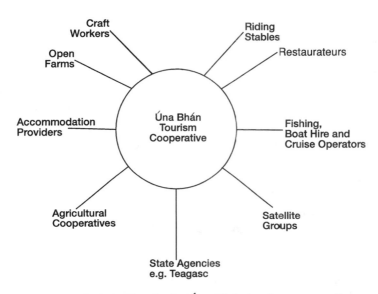

Fig. 13.2 **Stakeholders in the Úna Bhán tourism cooperative.**

mally as a cooperative society. This was formed in 1990, and it provided the local group with a legal structure that ensured limited liability. A board of management composed of seven members is appointed annually. It meets on a weekly basis. Monthly general meetings are held for the purpose of involving the wider group in decision-making and planning. A subcommittee system operates to ensure a fair distribution of tasks and responsibilities.

Local agricultural cooperatives, farming organizations, and state agencies are members of, and advisers to, the Úna Bhán tourism cooperative. Figure 13.2 illustrates the main actors involved. The headquarters of the Úna Bhán cooperative is based in a unique tourism centre that it has developed in the grounds of King House, Boyle, Co. Roscommon.

The idea of developing a unique tourism centre, which would interpret the rural tourism product of the Úna Bhán countryside, was supported by FÁS (the national training and employment authority), the county council, and other statutory bodies. Through the FÁS Community Enterprise Programme, members of Úna Bhán developed a plan for their centre. The main element of the plan is a centre for administration, communication, and reservations. Another aim was to establish, on a commercial basis, a sales outlet for locally produced crafts, as well as a coffee shop to service an estimated 35,000 visitors per annum to King House. FÁS agreed to provide Úna Bhán with a commercial aid grant to employ a manager for the tourism centre. One condition attached to the FÁS grant aid was that the project should become economically viable and self-financing within three years. Local job creation was another condition. The appointment of the manager in 1992 represented an injection of new dynamism into the group and the tourism centre has already become the heart of the Úna Bhán cooperative.

The management committee believes that the successful development of the tourism centre will act as a catalyst for local economic development. This assumption is based on the high level of success achieved to date. Since the formation of the cooperative, shareholder numbers have increased by 30 per cent, a number of satellite groups have joined the cooperative, and many of the product providers have gained financially through increased sales. The local marketing strategy, linked to the Irish Country Holidays' central sales office, is generating substantially increased tourist business through the direct targeting of potential customers. However, the economic viability of the Úna Bhán cooperative is still a source of major concern. An important revenue-earning activity will be the servicing of visitors to King House. Through a successful retail outlet at this centre, combined with a 10 per cent commission charged on all bookings made through the cooperative, the Úna Bhán group hopes to generate sufficient revenue to ensure the continued employment of the manager and staff after the cessation of state support schemes for the venture.

The successful establishment of a project such as the Úna Bhán tourism cooperative required strong and well-balanced leadership combined with group training. The Úna Bhán group understood from an early stage that the process of transforming a voluntary organization into a commercially viable venture would require sacrifice, commitment, and careful planning. The FÁS community enterprise training modules undertaken by a core group of the Úna Bhán shareholders helped focus the minds of the participants on the challenges involved. The preparation of a plan for the development of the tourism centre was one of the main outcomes of the training process. Training in relation to the general developmental needs of the Úna Bhán cooperative was not easily arranged. This was due mainly to the uniqueness of the new approach of organizing and engaging the wider community in the process of developing rural tourism. Furthermore, the Irish Country Holidays product is a special type of holiday package that needs a very specific after-sales service. Training of product providers in relation to understanding the concept of an "Irish Country Holiday" was particularly important. Tourists who buy an Irish Country Holiday expect to experience living within a rural community. They want to feel part of, and participate in, the living traditions of rural Ireland. To become involved in life on the land and have real contact with nature is a life-time dream for some. A stress-free, clean, and healthy environment with silent open spaces and woodlands full of enchanting birdsong is a typical holiday expectation of the discerning rural tourism client. To meet these expectations, the Úna Bhán tourism cooperative organized training inputs at both an individual product provider level and a group level.

The need for innovative product development on an ongoing basis has been created by the increasing diversification and enhancement of the rural tourism product by competing groups throughout Europe. In Ireland and elsewhere in the European Union, European Commission initiatives, such as the LEADER Programme, have provided an invaluable financial support for the development of viable rural tourism products. The Úna Bhán cooperative has developed a very high profile locally, nationally, and internationally in relation to the standard and quality of its product, and its endeavours in this field led to the winning, in 1991, of a major prize in the Tourism Group Awards. The cooperative continues to encourage the development of high-quality rural tourism products with special emphasis on the uniqueness of the area and maximum use of the comparative natural advantages of this unique region.

The feasibility of community-based tourism

Rural tourism is not a panacea for the economic crises confronting so many rural communities, even in the most developed countries in the world. Despite impressive growth in tourism generally, and a swing toward "soft" or "green" tourism, for which rural areas are particularly well placed, this industry is not, in itself, capable of stemming the long-term decline that characterizes rural economy and society. However, the experiences of the national Community Rural Tourism Cooperative and the affiliated local Úna Bhán cooperative demonstrate that many rural communities can revive their fortunes through tourism, provided they adopt a professional approach in promoting their areas as tourism destinations, and provided they are given the necessary encouragement and support by development agencies and the various tiers of government that impinge on their activities. The efforts of these cooperatives have enabled many marginal farmers to increase their total incomes by diversifying into agri-tourism products, and several new off-farm job opportunities have been created locally in craftshops, restaurants, etc.

Because so many rural communities are targeting tourism as a means of diversifying their local economies, rural tourism is becoming a highly competitive industry. In order to succeed, the rural tourism product must have sufficient attraction to generate significant tourism flows on a recurring basis. Otherwise, the initiative will prove to be unsustainable. The Irish experience to date suggests that the product must offer quality, uniqueness, and authenticity, at a competitive price. The product range must be developed with the needs of the customer in mind and not from the suppliers' perspectives. These products must be carefully packaged and professionally marketed. The coordinated development and marketing of tourism products requires the cooperation of the product providers themselves and effective local and national partnerships between a range of private, public, and statutory stakeholders. This is not easily realized in practice.

Conclusion: A model?

The above model is a network solution assisting small resource communities to survive with the help of tourism. Based on its considerable progress over a short period of time, the *modus operandi* of the Community Rural Tourism Cooperative and local affiliated groups such as the Úna Bhán is recommended as a model approach to the promotion of community-controlled rural tourism.

The Irish experiences show that this kind of operation must be planned carefully and operate on a long-term basis and the business sector must be explicit participants in implementation. Furthermore, this model works when other factors (markets, price competition, legislation, etc.) create a niche for business operations. Thus, there are several necessary conditions for success.

References

Bord Fáilte (1992), *Tourism Marketing Plan 1993–97: Delivering Sustainable Growth*, Bord Fáilte Éireann, Dublin.

Commission of the European Communities (1988), "The Future of Rural Society," *Bulletin of the European Communities Supplement* 4/88, Luxembourg.

―――― (1991), *The Regions in the 1990s: Fourth Periodic Report on the Social and Economic Situation and Development of the Regions of the Community*, Luxembourg.

Gannon, M. (1992), *An Analysis of the Effectiveness of the Agri-tourism Grant Scheme*, Submission to Bord Fáilte Éireann, Dublin.

Keane, J. and Quinn, J. (1990), *Rural Development and Rural Tourism*, Research Report No. 5, Centre for Development Studies, University College Galway.

Lane, B. (1993), "What Is Rural Tourism?", paper presented at the Second International School of Rural Development, University College Galway, Ireland.

Ó Cinnéide, M. (1992a), "Restructuring of Rural Areas in Ireland," in P. Huigen, L. Paul, and K. Volkers (eds.), *The Changing Function and Position of Rural Areas in Europe*, Netherlands Geographical Studies, Utrecht, pp. 87–93.

―――― (1992b), "Some Spatial Dimensions of Tourism in Ireland," in M. Ó Cinnéide and S. Grimes (eds.), *Planning and Development of Marginal Areas*, Centre for Development Studies, University College Galway, pp. 37–57.

Ó Cinnéide, M. and Walsh, J. A. (1990–91), "Tourism and Regional Development in Ireland," *Geographical Viewpoint* 19, pp. 47–68.

Statistical Yearbook 1992, United Nations, New York.

Statistical Yearbook 1994, United Nations, New York.

Tourism Task Force (1992), *Report of the Tourism Task Force to the Minister for Tourism, Transport and Communication*, Government Publications, Dublin.

Troughton, M. (1992), "The Restructuring of Agriculture: The Canadian Example," in I. R. Bowler, C. R. Bryant, and M. D. Nellis (eds.), *Contemporary Rural Systems*, CAB International, London, pp. 29–42.

Part VI
A multicausal approach and theory of development

14

Factors in local economic development

Cecily Neil and Markku Tykkyläinen

Contextual explanation, structuration, and human agency

This research project started by asking how the restructuring of the 1990s, and the associated local economic developments in resource communities, could be explained, and what forms of local adjustment were available in this context in the early 1990s. As stated in the introduction, the project sought to develop a solid theoretical framework for understanding socio-economic restructuring in resource communities in both old and nascent capitalist systems (chap. 1). An analysis of existing theories showed that the collection of development theories is amorphous. The explanations of spatial economic development have mostly been one-sided, emphasizing only some aspects of development. This has been the case throughout the history of geography, development studies, regional science, and related topics. New explanations have been presented as pivotal new theories without clearly recognizing their narrowness in explaining the complex real world (Tykkyläinen and Neil 1995), and, when one explanation has proven to be weak, a new, easy-to-follow approach has been declared to be epoch-making.

Theoretical discourse and practical everyday policy have shifted from one paradigm to another. For instance, in industrialized countries since the 1970s, the paradigms in regional economic studies have shifted from Keynesian policy to supply-side doctrines, from a growth centre strategy to the promotion of small industries, from the attraction of footloose industry to endogenous development. For a considerable period of time, explanatory models of rural development were formed from the theoretical framework of universal regional theories, and the theoretical elaboration of rural economic development was narrow (Hoggart and Buller 1987). In the theoretical discussions of the 1980s, researchers in geography began gradually to elaborate upon the complex time–space settings where human activity produces socio-spatial structures (cf. Pred 1984; Thrift 1983) – the environment in which we live. The significance of the context of human activity, and of human agency itself, became central in theory and in the interpretations of research results.

Since the late 1980s, a wave of agency-centric conceptualization and theory-building has been in progress, one that deals with the information-based mode of production, post-modern socio-economic relations, local innovative milieux, and the network society (on the latter concepts, see Castells 1989; 1996; Harvey 1989; Malmberg et al. 1996). The changing world reflected in these concepts is of great interest for both economic and rural geography. Rural geography, in the latter part of the 1990s, has focused on the current sustainability of rural systems, rural cultures, marginalization, and processes such as globalization and deregulation (e.g. Bowler et al. 1995; Cloke and Little 1997; Jussila et al. 1998).

As mentioned above, attempts have been made to overcome the problems of inadequate explanations of local economic development arising from narrowly delimited methodological and theoretical approaches, by presenting broader approaches that take into account the links between social theory and the geographical diversity of social practices. For instance, Hoggart and Buller (1987) explore the interpretation of rural development and discuss how universal conditions could produce dissimilar local manifestations and how socio-economic systems interact causally with universal forces explored in social theory. Numerous locality studies from the late 1980s onwards revealed that development paths are complex and diverse. This led to the conclusion that simple models and very general explanations of local economic development must be avoided (e.g. Cooke 1989; Harloe et al. 1990; Murdoch and Marsden 1994). This conclusion has been complemented by studies based on regulation theory (e.g. Degiovanna 1996; Jones 1997), which have also highlighted the importance of historically specific and place-specific development paths. Hence, the answer to the question "What sort of local economic policy should be carried out?" is not simplistic in nature. Urry (1990, 187), for instance, on the basis of experiences in the United Kingdom, concluded that "in each case it has been shown that the emergence, implementation and effectiveness of local policies depend upon the complex of economic, social and political conditions found within and beyond a given locality."

The chapters in this part of the book explore the pattern of multi-causality that is inherent in explaining development in resource communities. While the same general principles of capitalism are applied in many different contexts and settings, the specific nature of the complex set of economic, social, and political conditions may be quite different in the different kinds of market and transitional economies in which development has taken place in the 1990s. These differences may be exacerbated in peripheral localities. This and the following chapters aim at providing a structured view of the development processes taking place in resource communities in different institutional contexts.

Pressures on resource communities to restructure

As indicated in the preceding chapters, the factors in local economic development consist of attributes, processes, and actions on an empirical level. The introductory chapter of this book highlighted a few fundamental processes, of a general, sectoral, and political nature, that have redefined the external environment confronting resource communities in the 1990s. These include broad changes in national socio-economic philosophies and institutions, industrial sector rises and declines, the globalization of economies, the reorganization of international trade, the introduction of automation and improved technologies, and the "crisis" in public sectors.

The empirical analysis of the case-studies has enabled us to move from a discussion of the broad global processes to an examination of the impact of processes emerging from national policy responses to these broad global trends. Both these global and national processes have redefined the external environment confronting resource communities in the 1980s and 1990s and have generated direct pressures on resource communities to restructure (see fig. 14.1). These pressures are very concrete and mostly based on policy changes at the national level.

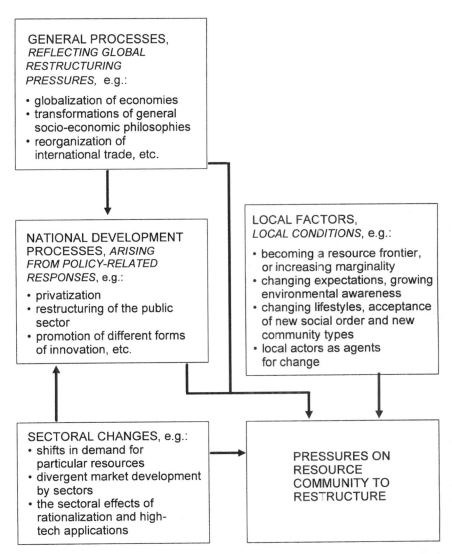

Fig. 14.1   **The pressures on resource communities to restructure in the 1990s.**

Figure 14.1 summarizes the occurrences that we considered during the progress of this research project to be the important mobilizers of restructuring in the early 1990s. Such trends, political choices, and decisions represent observed processes and are the empirical origins of the original four factors discussed in chapter 1 and further on in this chapter. The framework in figure 14.1 is only a starting point for both the further elaboration and the introduction of new conceptualizations derived from the case-studies.

These pressures to restructure have led to great socio-economic adjustments in many localities and communities in the 1990s. General, sectoral, and national development processes are leading to new patterns of competition between nations and localities. Each locality also experiences internal pressures for change. These pressures, and people's reactions to them, enshrine causal powers, which are elements of understanding the nature of the 1990s' local-level restructuring. As local responses, the role of individuals as agents for change, long-term commitment, and lobbying, careful planning and innovativeness, partnerships, business coalitions, and the role of external assistance and funding are crucial at the community level.

The general conclusions derived from the case-studies may be of use in responding appropriately in both varying countries and throughout the continuing restructuring process. However, it is necessary to keep in mind that the case-studies' applicability to other situations is restricted by the scope of the project. Because the case-studies cover only three types of society (transitional neo-capitalist economies, advanced market economies, and welfare states), the explanation and interpretation of the development processes are limited to communities in those institutional contexts.

We came to a conclusion that the processes presented in figure 14.1 can be reduced to five key actions. Based on the analysis of the case-studies, the key actions that have influenced resource community development in societies experiencing major socio-economic transition in the 1990s are:

1. privatization processes (first and foremost in transitional countries);
2. the restructuring of the public sector in accordance with market ideology and the deregulation of the economic environment;
3. the promotion of innovation and technological improvements;
4. changing local policies – towards new patterns of competition between localities;
5. sectoral shifts within and between the production sectors.

The case-studies make evident that the concept of a multicausal approach provides a setting in which the key actions of the 1990s can be elaborated upon. The task is not easy because restructuring contains numerous interdependencies and overlapping processes. The key actions are investigated in detail in chapter 15.

Table 14.1   **The sets of factors influencing local development**

The original concepts	The renamed concepts
General processes	General factors
Sector-specific processes	Sectoral factors
Policy-related factors	Political factors
Local-specific features	Local factors
	The human factor

Revising the conceptual framework and terminology

The preliminary process of conceptualization undertaken for this project led to the conclusion that, in order to understand local restructuring in any given context, it is necessary to take into account the interplay between a combination of factors that significantly influence local development (Tykkyläinen and Neil 1995). These factors each represent a bundle, or some may refer to it as a cluster, of attributes, processes, and actions that influence development. In an earlier paper, these factors were referred to as "general processes," "sector-specific processes," "policy-related factors," and "local-specific features" (Tykkyläinen and Neil 1995, 42).

The authors of the case-studies do not often refer to the original concepts presented in the preliminary work, although many processes and actions may fall within the scope of those concepts. In table 14.1, the factors are listed in their original form on the left and are given in a simpler form on the right. The renaming of the key concepts used in the initial conceptualization has been carried out in order to ensure that these concepts better reflect the concepts used in the case-studies. In addition, the role of individual actors and various social networks proved to be significant in the results described in many of the case-studies, and hence could not be ignored. Accordingly, the concept of the "human factor" (a term proposed by Smailes in chap. 3) was added to the initial list of explanatory factors.

To clarify further the terminology used in the following discussion, the term "general factors" is used to refer to the global processes of capitalism discussed in many of the case-studies, while the term "political factors" refers to supra-local decision-making. However, it should be noted that the terminology in the case-studies is sometimes less precise; in chapter 6 "general level" is used to refer to political factors.

As examples of overlapping, privatization is a political factor, but the market mechanism consists of the general processes associated with capitalism, representing a general factor. The restructuring of the public sector in market economies is a political factor related to the prevailing circumstances in each country, but the resulting private economy is increasingly guided by the general processes of capitalism. Sectoral shifts are related to the renewal of production sectors and shifts in demand, and the issue of local policy clearly demonstrates the differences both in the performance of localities and in the measures instituted to improve local competitiveness. The significance of innovations and technology in economic development is obvious in capitalism, but, as we have seen in the agricultural sector of transitional economies for instance, many sectoral, local, and political issues are interwoven with this modernization.

Changes in any or all of these factors may place resource communities under pressure to restructure. By examining the interplay of the four causal sets of factors combined with the human factor, it is possible to understand the course that restructuring takes in a given resource community. A corollary of this observation is that each phase of restructuring is structurally connected to its earlier phases. Each phase generates locally specific characteristics and structures that, in turn, generate constraints and opportunities for a new phase of restructuring. Thus, when considering the sustainability of a proposed new activity in a local economic development strategy, it is important that consideration is given not only to the sustainability of the particular new advocated economic activity, but also to the potential impact such an activity may have on the future flexibility of a community to restructure further. One must be careful not to lock a community into a course of action that may become fruitless in the face of future global changes.

The relative significance of the factors in the case-studies

It was not possible formally to test all of the ideas within the confines of the presented case-studies. Nevertheless, it became clear that local development consists of phenomena that could ultimately be explained only by understanding the causal processes and attributes that are described by the above sets of factors and the interplay between them. These factors provide an explanatory framework within which to study the pressures of restructuring that face a com-

Table 14.2　**The impacts of the factors according to the case-studies**

Case-study	Factors				
	General	Political	Sectoral	Local	Human
Härjedalen	+	+ + +	+ +	+ +	+
Cleve	+ + +	+ + +	+ +	+	+
Lower Silesia	+ +	+ + +	+	+	+ +
Supraśl	+ +	+ +	+	+ + +	+
Zabłudów	+ +	+ + +	+	+ +	+
Eastern Hungary	+ +	+ + +	+ + +	+	+ +
Virma	+ +	+ + +	+ +	+ +	+
Gridino	+ +	+ + +	+ +	+ + +	+ + +
Kuklen	+ + +	+ +	+ + +	+ +	+
Rural Viet Nam	+ +	+ + +	+	+ +	+
Vuohijärvi	+	+	+ +	+ + +	+ + +
Forrestania	+	+ +	+ +	+	+ + +
Kellogg	.	+ +	+	+ +	+ + +
Kolari	.	+	+ + +	+ +	+ +
Irish communities	.	+	+ +	+ + +	+ + +

+ + + Very significant, + + Significant, + Less significant, . Not considered

munity and the opportunities and constraints that channel social (and individual) action. Thus, the initial basic conceptualization of the research question from which the collection of case-studies evolved, combined with the role of human agency, seems to work as a valid theoretical construct.

The impacts of the different factors on the outcomes described in the case-studies are outlined in table 14.2. The relative significance of the different factors is the subjective assessment of the authors, but, that notwithstanding, reflects the multicausality of the development process and its outcomes. Table 14.2 is an a priori summary of the results in the sense that the findings of the case-studies are discussed after it. It is also an ordering framework for the results of the case-studies.

The most crucial conclusion arising from this collection of papers is that there is no single, simple, and universal explanation of local development, nor is there a single uniform policy or scheme that can offer a universal panacea for the problems of local economic development. This is not, of course, to assert that it is not possible to define some general underlying principles that affect the success of local economic development schemes. It became clear from these case-studies that any such scheme should consist of well-argued, social-capital-enhancing, participative measures, which take into account the processes that – be they any combination of "global," "political," or "local" – generate a pattern of constraints and opportunities for local economic development in any given resource community. The case-studies revealed various (often unique) combinations of such actions that have shaped local socio-economic development in resource communities.

References

Bowler, I., Bryant, R., and Marois, C. (eds.) (1995), *The Sustainability of Rural Systems*, Département de Géographie, Université de Montréal.

Castells, M. (1989), *The Informational City*, Blackwell, Oxford.

────── (1996), *The Rise of the Network Society*, Blackwell, Oxford.

Cloke, P. and Little, J. (eds.) (1997), *Contested Countryside Cultures*, Routledge, London.

Cooke, P. (ed.) (1989), *Localities. The Changing Face of Urban Britain*, Unwin Hyman, London.

Degiovanna, S. (1996), "Industrial Districts and Regional Economic Development: A Regulation Approach," *Regional Studies* 30(4), pp. 373–386.

Harloe, M., Pickvance, C. G., Urry, J. (eds.) (1990), *Place, Policy and Politics. Do Localities Matter?* Unwin Hyman, London.

Harvey, D. (1989), *The Condition of Postmodernity*, Blackwell, Oxford.

Hoggart, K. and Buller, H. (1987), *Rural Development. A Geographical Perspective*, Croom Helm, London.

Jones, M. R. (1997), "Spatial Selectivity of the State? The Regulationist Enigma and Local Struggles over Economic Governance," *Environment and Planning A* 29, pp. 831–864.

Jussila, H., Leimgruber, W., Majoral, R. (eds.) (1998), *Perceptions of Marginality: Theoretical Issues and Regional Perceptions of Marginality in Geographical Space*, Ashgate, Aldershot.

Malmberg, A., Sölvell, Ö., and Zander, I. (1996), "Spatial Clustering, Local Accumulation of Knowledge and Firm Competitiveness," *Geografiska Annaler* 78 B (2), pp. 85–97.

Murdoch, J. and Marsden, T. (1994), *Reconstituting Rurality*, UCL Press, London.

Pred, A. (1984), "Place as Historically Contingent Process: Structuration and the Time-Geography of Becoming Places," *Annals of the Association of American Geographers* 74(2), pp. 279–297.

Thrift, N. J. (1983), "On the Determination of Social Action in Space and Time," *Environment and Planning D: Society and Space* 1, pp. 23–57.

Tykkyläinen, M. and Neil, C. (1995), "Socio-Economic Restructuring in Resource Communities: Evolving a Comparative Approach," *Community Development Journal* 30(1), pp. 31–47.

Urry, J. (1990), "Conclusions: Places and Policies," in M. Harloe, C. G. Pickvance, and J. Urry (eds.), *Place, Policy and Politics. Do Localities Matter?* Unwin Hyman, London, pp. 187–205.

15

Comparing the key actions of the 1990s' rural restructuring

Markku Tykkyläinen

Introduction

Keeping the idea of the multicausal approach in mind, this chapter elaborates on the implications of the observed key actions of local economic development in the 1990s. The chapter compares the main processes and policy responses of the 1990s' local economic restructuring in the case-study communities. The processes and actions are: (1) privatization, (2) the adjustment of the public sector, (3) innovation and technological advance, (4) local economic policy, and (5) the sectoral shift in the economy.

This chapter serves as an independent summary and comparison of the empirical material of the case-studies. Furthermore, this chapter provides a necessary elaboration of the case-study material from which the multicausal theory of local economic development is constructed in the final chapter of this book. The general conclusions derived are limited to communities in their particular institutional contexts, and it is necessary to keep in mind the vast diversity of local economic processes found in the case-studies when making generalizations.

Privatization and local economic development

Geographically uneven processes

Privatization has been the most fundamental political occurrence in the development of resource communities in the former socialist bloc in the 1990s. The case-studies reveal the difficult economic conditions at the beginning of the socio-economic transition. The Bulgarian and Russian examples clearly show the poor state of affairs under socialism, and the Polish paper gives an example of a society's inability to enhance productivity in agriculture through structural reforms during the socialist period.

The modes of socialist production were not efficient enough to compete with the market economies and this was a primary reason for the transition of the 1990s. However, in a more local context, the socialist governance did not meet the expectations and the needs of the locals. The everyday quality of life in the villages and towns of the Soviet Union and the other socialist countries was poor compared with the lifestyles in advanced capitalist countries. Furthermore, this gap between the blocs continued to grow. There was economic and social discontent with the ways that the socialist societies operated and, once the transition began, people were eager to dismantle all the old socialist production systems, irrespective of their technical performance. This zeal is illustrated, for example, by the fact that previously capital-intensive agricultural production units were downsized in Bulgaria, Poland, and Hungary, on the basis solely of new political principles rather than of efficiency.

The socio-economic goals set at the beginning of the economic transition were not well defined in these countries, usually consisting of images of a new market economy derived from the wealthy OECD countries (which were far from what could realistically be achieved in the Eastern bloc). It was virtually impossible to predict the outcomes of transition, and development was very path dependent (on this concept, see Storper 1995, 204–207). In rural areas, the process of transition was actually a leap into the unknown rather than a well-planned transformation to a predetermined market economy. Consequently, individuals in resource communities were forced to face the unfamiliar consequences of collapsing economies and the experiments of the emerging market economies.

The former modes of production were widely rejected in the small

East European countries, and privatization and new ways of organizing social institutions were introduced. After the abolition of
the rigid and regulative institutions of socialism, *laissez-faire* strategies and individualism were quickly adopted, as is illustrated in
particular by the Hungarian and Polish examples of local economic
reforms.

The transition from the socialist mode of production to the market
economy partially broke down both the traditional working communities of cooperatives and the administrative structures. However,
the diffusion of the new market economy has yet to reach peripheral
areas such as the hinterlands of Russia. The situation in Russia is
the result of a different sociocultural environment: the legacy of the
old Russian social order and the longer period of socialism are still
deeply embedded in the Russian economy.

Trial and error

Laissez-faire was the dominant social doctrine during the first years
after the collapse of both the communist regimes and the entire
CMEA trade in East-Central Europe. The liquidation of the former
socialist division of labour had the most pronounced effects in
resource communities, as the Bulgarian case-study shows. The large
resource-based factories had to find new markets and the agriculture
and rural industry sectors were restructured, resulting in a great
pressure to diversify. This reorientation led to new community structures and social institutions.

Transition has been multifarious, and the consolidation of the neo-
capitalist fabric of society and its spatial forms has taken place by trial
and error in each locality. Although the profit-maximizing logic of
capitalism has been the driving force in transitional economies, the
change in resource communities has progressed sporadically. No
widely accepted plans of transition and no solid theoretical models
have been used, and the solutions have been very individualistic in
nature.

Social and economic institutions have looked to the West for their
operational model, but those parts of institutions proving to be competitive have, so far, been maintained in many places. Hungarian
development, for instance, reflects this pragmatic trend: adaptation,
new combinations of capital, and mergers have been characteristic of
the local economic solutions.

The impacts of turmoil and recovery

The immediate reactions following the collapse of the previous production system in resource communities can be summarized as follows:

- great turmoil in society and a drastic decline in the economy threatened people's livelihoods; this led to the strengthening of family ties and of social structures that assist individuals in realizing their basic needs;
- the creation of self-help and household growing plots was the solution for many in the neo-capitalist countries of the former Eastern bloc, because they provided almost the only opportunities for everyday survival.

Neo-capitalist European countries faced turmoil in the agricultural sector in the first half of the 1990s, and only the considerable productive capacity of agriculture in each country (a legacy from the spatial division of labour in the CMEA) saved the East-Central European countries from food production shortages. With respect to the means of production in the countryside, the result of the Hungarian transition was a mixture of jointly managed property (enterprises and cooperatives) and family farming. The extensive privatization of land introduced leaseholds, and the manufacturing sector of former cooperatives was privatized. This combination of factors led Hungarian society towards an experimental community structure from the European standpoint. In Poland, family farming, which was already dominant during the socialist era, displaced collective farming, and the rationalization of private farming radically altered life in the countryside. Russia is an obvious exception in the privatization process: large-scale corporate farming is still dominant on state land.

The neo-capitalist countries have numerous factories in the rural communities of the outlying areas. These include metallurgical and food-processing plants as well as machine works and wood-processing plants in the forested areas. The large resource-processing factories faced the need for modernization due to outdated production technologies. The reorganization of business activity was no easy task, because the companies themselves had to find new markets for their often outdated products while simultaneously modernizing their production technology, as the Kuklen case shows. The Russian situation was even more difficult because of the widespread insolvency crises (Hirvensalo 1995). Overall, there have been varying forms of transi-

321

tion between countries and localities but, basically, new and reformed companies and economic units everywhere are attempting to be more flexible and to adapt themselves to the globalized division of labour and to post-Fordist production conditions.

The new role of local communities

All the neo-capitalist case-studies show that the justification of community-based development practices depends on the successful enhancement of social and economic development. Also, the Vietnamese case illustrates how individual and community-based development begins from the realization of the demand of "locally produced" commodities. I conclude that the following are important characteristics of community development in transitional economies:

- the abandonment of the top–down policy of socialism: this has led to a rise in the need to establish local authorities, agencies, and coalitions in order to promote economic and infrastructural development;
- the establishment of information dissemination mechanisms: local, non-trained entrepreneurs need business advice in order to start up production, and associations or local community-based institutions should strive to meet this demand – however, the existence of advisory organizations does not necessarily guarantee success if the general economic environment does not complement opportunities for operating profitably (as the numerous problems of small farms in Russia in the mid-1990s indicate);
- an urgent search for economic activities: these are hoped to generate new jobs and income and employ people from local labour markets;
- the reorganization of the management of production from a top–down to a decentralized market-led system; and
- innovativeness: economic development is increasingly based on innovations, local initiatives, and the competitiveness of a locality, which all call for market-oriented local development policy.

The case-study of north-east Poland demonstrates the nature of local governance transformation: centrally led organizations were gradually displaced by local governance. In Russia, however, companies continue to be seen as powerful institutions and are expected to fulfil social responsibilities. Local communities in Russia had been dependent not only on incomes from a factory, but also on factory-supplied services, such as housing, water, and heating. Since transition, there has been little progress in replacing these discontinued services in countries such as Russia.

The diversity of solutions and the revival of community-based activities

The privatization process was not just a rational course of action, but also an emotional one. There was little interest in cooperative and community-based action in the early years of the transition, and many citizens voted for privatization no matter what the price or the ramifications. The private ownership of the means of production was considered superior, being seen as valuable in itself and expected to bring wealth – if not immediately, at least in the future. This process was still continuing in the mid-1990s and is leading to the considerable redistribution of the means of production among citizens, and to numerous economic, social, and class-forming outcomes. One outcome, for example, is the incorporation of small farms into larger family farms, a process that looks to be inevitable in Poland. Another outcome is that the early privatization led both to the deconcentration of industrial decision-making from the central authorities and to considerable worker-ownership in Russia (Kalmi 1995). The movement of capital from workers into the hands of investment trusts and investors was clear by the mid-1990s, leading back to concentrated organizational structures. The Hungarian rural transition gave rise to an extensive land-lease system. Thus the new-born capitalism in the former Eastern bloc is taking fundamentally diverse forms, at least from the viewpoint of the relatively homogeneous European Union.

The unpopularity of community-based local development in the early stages was particularly apparent in Eastern Europe, where people wished to restore the lost glory of pre-war capitalism, and cooperatives and production collectives were dismantled. In these circumstances, proposals for community initiation schemes were interpreted as a return to the "old" socio-economic practices and were usually rejected. However, ownership, management, and production needed to be structurally adjusted in order to establish a market economy. It was time to build private economic layers into the economy (on the term "layers of investment," see e.g. Massey 1984). Despite this turmoil, only a few industrial communities have collapsed completely; however, they are (or will be) undergoing a restructuring process (see e.g. Tykkyläinen 1995b).

In the quest for up-to-date economic activities in the transitional countries, new infrastructure, new policies, and local environmental controls are established and community-based development activities gradually emerge. Although local governance was not very far advanced in the transitional economies in the mid-1990s, organizations to provide local infrastructure and development policy were under development. However, rather than a uniform method of rural development, sporadic and country-specific, or even locality-specific, development principles have been applied. It is essential to note that infrastructural differences were (and are still) vast between localities. The results of policy factors such as privatization influenced how and at what rate social institutions and production were (re)organized in geographical space. And, because of the complex transformation processes, many of the development targets are likely to be realized only over the long run. Certainly, the expectations and conditions of EU enlargement will boost this regionalization of power in East-Central Europe and Russia in the near future.

The shift to market ideology and the adjustment of the public sector

The geographical implications of ideological change

As discussed in chapter 1, the changes in the overall policy of Western governments have been interpreted as a movement towards market ideology. The corresponding phenomenon in the neo-capitalist countries suggests that this policy reorientation was based on subjective arguments as well. The radical shifts of opinion in the Eastern bloc in the late 1980s and in the 1990s indicate that the policy chosen was, in general, the result of ideological arguments, simple reactions against the old regime, and subjective evaluations. Changes in policy may well rise from very subjective arguments and be influenced by observed poor development. The transition in the neo-capitalist countries also shows that responses may differ, and that, therefore, there is no one way of achieving this transformation of economic policy. Although all crises have to be sorted out, the way in which it is done will vary.

In advanced capitalist countries, a wide range of individual decisions have been made on the basis that they represent further stages in adapting to a market ideology. One example of this is the deregulation of the banking sector and the subsequent upswing–downswing cycle in rural resource communities, as the Finnish and South Australian case-studies show. The South Australian case describes the double-edged effects on agriculture of the use of deregulation to encourage restructuring. On the other side of the globe, the deregulation of the Finnish banking system in the early 1990s created similar economic turmoil. These kinds of deregulation schemes were implemented in one OECD country after another, and many of them had a profound influence on marginal regions. Deregulation measures have been considered one of the antidotes to the stagnation of economic growth, especially in Europe and Oceania, because some NICs, the United Kingdom, and the United States have been successfully operating in a less regulated economic climate.

Deregulation is part of a wider process of reorganizing local and national governance. Goodwin and Painter (1996) link the restructuring of local governance to the decline of the Fordist mode of regulation and the demise of Fordist strategies of governance. A geographical corollary of the new, market-led strategy is that new institutions and agencies of governance allow different local and regional service provision strategies to be developed in different places, according to the social and economic structure of each community.

The rationalization of the public sector has meant shrinking public funding for the provision of services in rural areas, as the case-studies indicate. Development strategies have focused more and more on searching for new economic activities and establishing "flexible" labour economies in resource communities. The two Australian case-studies and the Swedish case exemplify this restructuring toward a market ideology in wealthy Western countries. The South Australian case highlights the effects of the withdrawal of the public sector from providing assistance with problems in the agricultural sector, and the Swedish case analyses the effects of cutting public services and imposing a market ideology on rural areas. The result of the Australian restructuring has been the depopulation of the small South Australian communities or, in the "best"-case scenario, the diversification of the rural economy toward producing new, more profitable products. Better social benefits in Sweden mean that the rural population will not be forced to move to the same extent as in Australia. The social consequences of these market-led policies could have been more dramatic than they were in Australia and Sweden, as has been revealed in other studies (e.g. Conradson and Pawson 1997).

Toward post-Fordist governance

The post-Fordist development of local governance has led to partnerships between different actors and administrative levels, such as various business coalitions of private, quasi-public, public, and voluntary actors. These partnership and cooperative approaches are initially emerging from the practices of non-welfare states, as the examples from the United States and Ireland portray. These practices are also discussed in the cases of north-east Poland and Sweden. Market-led and partnership practices have, in fact, diffused to the post-welfare states and neo-capitalist countries in the 1990s. It seems that new ideological underpinnings are a consequence of the breakdown of the possibility (and willingness) of pursuing traditional planning and governance strategies. In the advanced market economies, the reasons for partnerships have officially been a search for efficiency in the provision of services and the combination of funding from different interest groups. In East-Central Europe, one crucial reason for the emergence of various partnerships and of volunteer organizations has been the lack of funding from the central government (Kovách 1997). The cases from Sweden and South Australia indicate that shrinking public funding is a challenge in the advanced market economies as well.

The case-study in Western Australia depicts the shift in regional policy from a "new town" policy to an acceptance of metropolitan development. This shift was originally a result of the change in the government's settlement and employment policy priorities. The abandonment of the new town policy also reflects wider cultural changes in society. New metropolitan-oriented lifestyles are replacing the old lifestyles of frontier towns. Because of this cultural change, it becomes evident that the question of how to organize society should not be addressed by the "plan rationality/market ideology" dimension, as presented in chapter 1. The answer is increasingly found in the elaboration of the role of the public sector within the post-industrial consumption pattern, post-modern values and lifestyles, and individuals' extended spatial behaviour. The crucial question is how to satisfy the needs of people in a society in which values have changed from territorial and industrial to individualistic and post-industrial. The Western Australian case represents the post-modern organization of individual socio-spatial relations, which is based on time–space compression, production systems grounded in discursive knowledge, global networks, and detraditionalized ad hoc communities (see Lash and Urry 1994, 38, 60–61, 311). In these post-modern social circumstances, the role of the public sector is understood to be to provide only a few services. The case-study also shows that the role of the public sector can dramatically change when the organization of work becomes post-Fordist and lifestyles move to a post-modern setting.

The questioning of the welfare model and geographical marginality

The significance of the public sector in Western welfare countries reached its peak in the late 1980s when economic crises hit. The restructuring toward market-led socio-economic regulation actually occurred first in New Zealand in the 1980s, much earlier than in any other OECD countries (e.g. Le Heron et al. 1992; Pawson et al. 1992).

The maintaining of the welfare state is especially important for marginal areas, where the public sector grew to be a larger employer than the traditional sectors (agriculture, manufacturing, and private services). It usually accounted for more than one-third to one-half of employees in communities in outlying areas, which allowed for economic stability and relatively high incomes. Also, it was the service sector, rather than the manufacturing sector, that replaced many of the jobs lost in primary production after World War II in countries such as Finland and Sweden. Thus, the effects of shrinking the public sector were profound in these countries in the 1990s.

The move to a market ideology was a surprise to many people in the Nordic countries. No signs of the changes in policy were visible before the economic depression of the 1990s, although there had been some public debate surrounding certain political doctrines, such as those implemented in New Zealand and the United Kingdom. But this sort of policy was not expected to reach welfare states such as Sweden and Finland.

As the Swedish case-study shows, public sector employment played a significant part in increasing educational levels and job opportunities for women in outlying areas. Hence, the social fabric of the peripheries was greatly shaped by the earlier expansion of public sector employment, and the current shrinking of that sector is expected to have a similar influence in education and gender-related issues in rural areas. Shrinking public spending decreases the provision of services subsidized by the public sector, and it also decreases government resource expenditures per capita. The Swedish case shows that peripheral areas are much more sensitive than the wealthy core areas (cities and metropolitan regions) to cutbacks in public expenditure.

One result of the cutback in public service provision is an increase in productivity. However, unemployment simultaneously increases, which, in turn, calls for public expenditure and new measures in employment policy. The role of the private sector is often small in marginal areas and, therefore, public sector cost-cutting does not lead to a corresponding rapid shift of employment to private industrial activities or to the growth of small enterprises that could employ the redundant public sector labour. Unemployed labour is paid to do nothing, while, on the other hand, there is much work that will not be done owing to the shrinking budgets in the public subsectors. Because voluntary organizations, small enterprises, and "new co-operatives" operate with lower costs, they usually emerge to replace the relatively cost-inefficient services previously provided by the public sector (Lorendahl 1996). The Swedish case-study as well as the persistent unemployment in Finland attest to the fact that shifts of labour from the public sector to the private sector do not take place rapidly in the Nordic countries. The slowness of this shift is principally an issue of appropriately training a new generation for new situations.

Furthermore, the welfare state used to provide a range of regional policy instruments to mitigate the imbalances of economic performance between different geographical areas. However, these policy instruments proved to be inadequate during the deep depression of the early 1990s. As the case from Lapland shows, they were not able to solve the crisis. Sweden coped somewhat better than Finland in terms of unemployment rates. Overall, peripheries are often on the margins of profitability and, hence, very sensitive to changes in political and general factors.

Changing perceptions and the public sector

An example of a new, enterprise-driven spatial policy in a market economy is presented in the Western Australian case, where the construction of new, permanent towns in remote areas has been abandoned in favour of an enterprise-led strategy based on long-distance commuting. Such a development could be induced by introducing legislation or taxes, of course, but this has not occurred in

Western Australia. Commuting and on-site accommodation are a growing trend in marginal areas and have proved to be feasible for economic, technical, and behavioural reasons, although they appear to be radical when compared with the "balanced" regional policy concepts discussed in regional policy literature.

This Australian case does not necessarily reflect a shift towards policies driven by market ideology, but it does represent a new perspective on the entire doctrine of spatial policy. Regional and local ties and identities are not so binding as before, as multiculturization and improved communications help people accept new forms of settlement and non-traditional lifestyles. The globalization of business culture has been a vital force, deregionalizing and denationalizing the values and the behaviour of the business world. Rather than indicating a shift to a market ideology, this new model of a resource community reflects the changing "social" values of individuals, technological progress, and the profit-seeking nature of companies. Notions of traditional regional structures have lost their significance in the minds of employees, and new privately initiated transnational development schemes are being accepted. In addition to this economic aspect, individuals find the new solutions to housing and settlement appealing.

It is a matter of debate whether regionally based development approaches, emphasizing the local and regional authorities' monopoly provision of services and infrastructure, will be replaced by an enterprise-led arrangement, which, of course, would emphasize individuals as the predominant actors. If a "region" loses its status as the basic unit for the spatial allocation of economic and social resources in advanced economies, traditional regional policy will cease to exist, and will instead be superseded by projects, partnerships, and schemes based on various ad hoc spatial dimensions. This is why it is argued that the allocation of public funding should be based on the network character of communities rather than a traditional territorially based resource distribution mechanism. The traditional idea of a national state as a mosaic of landscapes reflects the traditional concept of agrarian villages and industrial communities of the past, whereas the Western Australian case is illustrative of the network structure of the globalized society. The "network" trend in rural economy and life anticipated by many researchers (e.g. Mormont 1990; Cloke and Goodwin 1993) is linked to the development of the information society, new labour codes, and new layers of investment.

The Western Australian case shows that people have multifarious spatial commitments and that the significance of a particular space originates from the quest to satisfy needs related to food, transport, housing, culture, and lifestyle. Spatially broadening everyday activities determine people's conception of space, and not vice versa. The traditional way of providing public services does not necessarily meet the demands generated by this new spatial setting. If this is the case, many public sector services and operations will no longer be justified and the modern forms of local dependence, as described by Cox and Mair (1988, 313), will weaken and will be replaced by translocal interests (Tykkyläinen 1996). This particular phase seems to be applicable, at the moment, in advanced countries. In contrast to this translocal development, however, some of the case-studies in this book show the continuing importance of traditional local ties in such activities as subsistence production for private use, for instance. Overall, it is essential to keep in mind that the outcomes of restructuring processes vary depending on a bundle of different factors in each place.

Innovation and technological improvements

Research and training, as part of overall innovation, are considered to be sources of economic development (Magrini 1997; Kangasharju and Nijkamp 1997). As a general example of this, the superiority of the post-Fordist production paradigm is based on the flexibility of technological learning and the absolute advantages it generates for its learners (Storper 1995, 206). Governments in advanced countries and the European Commission have developed large research and technological development (RTD) programmes, funding arrangements, and organizations to promote technological advance in industry. By and large, these inputs have been considered to be very productive (e.g. Husso et al. 1996). The Western Australian case exemplifies the results of numerous high-technology projects around the globe.

The case-studies indicate that the role of innovation is central in all economic systems. First, innovation is more than simply the innovation of a product or production method. An innovation is often institutional or organizational – for instance, planning, as in north-east Poland, the new mode of production in agriculture observed in Hungary and Viet Nam, community-based tourism in Ireland, and the new institutional setting of a multi-locale community in Western Australia. Secondly, because the level of local participation by investors and entrepreneurs in development varies greatly, local authorities often serve as catalysts for greater local actor participation and innovative behaviour. Thirdly, according to the non-centralized economic ideology of post-Fordist development, local economic development is a self-piloting and creative process aiming at the highest possible returns. Fourthly, development is increasingly based on a vast base of know-how and discursive knowledge on the global scale, making efficient communications essential. Fifthly, the Finnish example reveals a complex search for a means of producing profitably within the traditional resource-processing set-up; this search process is, at the very least, driven by organizational innovations. Finally, the Western Australian case shows that peripheral production units can be leaders in introducing technical and organizational innovations; it also indicates the importance of the global development of sophisticated production technology and its application worldwide.

There are two trends in the neo-capitalist countries that may have considerable spin-off effects in the economies of neighbouring countries:

• The transfer of technical innovations rationalizes the agricultural sector and technologically backward industries and influences labour markets. This can affect neighbouring countries by supplying excess labour to their labour markets.
• The needs to invest in the resource-processing sector are huge in transitional countries, and especially in Russia (Tykkyläinen 1995a). This will probably increase imports of investment goods and know-how from neighbouring countries.

Although it is generally believed that many peripheral communities are somewhat backward, there is no support for the idea that innovative projects cannot be implemented in peripheral areas. Intelligent mining technology and the most advanced pulp and paper production complexes, for instance, are implemented in remote regions. Furthermore, the friction of distance may serve as a challenge that results in the invention of sophisticated technology, as the Western Australian case depicts. There are, of course, differences in technology between places. However, these differences can usually be explained by economic and social factors. Within the European Union, for instance, the technological sophistication of ski lifts at ski resorts is more likely to reflect the customer profile or the expected number of customers than core–periphery relations.

Resource communities are often branded as non-innovative, but the lack of innovation cannot automatically be blamed on the locals' inability to adopt new technology. Other factors, such as obsolete technology that is still profitable, shrinking markets, or nationwide economic upheaval, may prevent the adoption of innovations. Or a region may have specialized in one type of production, and, when demand for that production is low, there is no impetus to invest in improvements. The explanation for not initiating innovative changes may simply be that there is no need for innovation. A lack of support services may also prevent innovations from taking off.

Agricultural communities, in particular, may lack social capital (in the form of residents) with interests in both the local area and the wider community. A community lacking network contacts will be less able to obtain information about appropriate technology, marketing opportunities, skills, etc. that could be used to develop successful economic enterprises. The Polish, Vietnamese, and Hungarian papers highlight the problems of agrarian communities in this respect. As a contradictory example, the Irish case provides a model for community-based development in the field of tourism.

Institutional factors, such as trade blocs and trade regulations, are barriers to the development and adoption of innovation. Moreover, innovativeness itself may have many different meanings. For example, one might consider that, in Poland, state farms would have been more efficient than small farms, where hay was cut and turned by hand and transported by horses. However, small farms were ranked high by the locals because private ownership *per se* was considered innovative and progressive in Poland in the early 1990s. Similar views were expressed in Hungary in the early stages of transition. Both these case-studies demonstrate the crucial importance of organizational innovations during the transition period. The preconditions for a successful transition are efficient and appropriate legislation and the formation of economic organizations such as enterprises, companies, and public and local authorities.

Innovation is a broad concept that intertwines general, political, sectoral, and local factors. The preconditions for innovative development are created by the entire society and its particular conditions.

Paradigm shifts in local economic policy

Various policies: Local, regional, structural, and spatial

Each country or bloc of countries has schemes, programmes, and a range of instruments to enhance the competitiveness of peripheral regions. They are part of the mode of social regulation (see Tickell and Peck 1992, 192). In discussing this enhancement of spatial competitiveness, this next part of the discussion will focus on what has happened in "regional policy" doctrines (as defined broadly and in the academic literature) in the advanced countries over the past three decades. Attempts have been made to broaden the viewpoint to resource communities in general.

Examining the experiences of advanced countries can be justified by the fact that these experiences are relevant when addressing geographically oriented policies in transitional countries. The use of the EU term "spatial policy" refers, generally, to measures taken in order to influence the spatial organization of a socio-economic system. Of course, all policy measures have spatial effects, but spatial policy is defined more precisely as encompassing "urban systems," infrastructural policy, and environmental management that will strengthen structurally weaker areas (Informal Council of Spatial Planning Ministers 1994). "Regional policies" are policies carried out by regional, provincial, or state governments, and "local policies" are those carried out by local authorities, although the term "regional policy" is often used to cover both local and regional policies in general discussion. The "regional policy" of the European Union is called "structural policy."

The design of alternative geographically oriented policies is also under discussion in developing countries, especially in those that are now industrializing and possess spatially uneven socio-economic development. To be most fruitful, this geographically oriented policy discourse should be challenged by new theoretical insights and ideas from the presented case-studies.

The case-studies discussed here show the clear divide between local policy carried out by local authorities and policies financed by supra-local authorities. Local policy, or in other words community policy, has a very "local" role in administration, because it deals with the everyday services provided to the members of a community. It is directly dependent on local financing in most cases. Other geographically oriented policies deal with more "structural" issues and local people have no direct control over those policies. Therefore, local policy lies within the domain of a bundle of local factors. It is a matter of a locality and a community. None the less, the theoretical bases of local policy, and especially of broader geographically oriented policies motivated by political factors, are derived from fairly general socio-economic philosophies.

Policy doctrines – from plan to market

The fundamentals of geographically oriented policies over the past few decades have been derived from the "plan rationality/market ideology" types of philosophies discussed in chapter 1, as well as from the idea that politically acceptable socio-economic goals should determine the content of geographically oriented policies in each country. The types of policy are divided according to which one of the four arguments (listed below) they are based upon. The fundamental principles of these four types of policy differ widely.

1. *Evenly distributed welfare.* The important attributes for production and consumption are unevenly distributed. This imbalance of competitiveness should be compensated for by development schemes, and, if they prove insufficient, appropriate subsidies should be distributed.
2. *Local endogenous opportunities.* People in rural communities have the right to participate in economic developments. Jobs and entrepreneurial activities should be tailored to local residents' skills and abilities to do business.
3. *Equal opportunities.* Less-developed regions are the result of poor physical and socio-institutional infrastructures. These bottlenecks should be removed by infrastructural investments.
4. *Free-market competition.* Geographical space offers opportunities for the development of production and wealth as such. Infrastructural investments must be carried out by market-led principles.

The "evenly distributed welfare" argument is typical of most Keynesian regional policies. The state subsidizes industrial investments and labour expenses in lagging regions and subsidies are intended to be distributed to new enterprises for the first few years, allowing the businesses to get off the ground. "Regions" are stimulated to grow by financially encouraging industrial companies to set up and expand in backward regions.

The "local endogenous opportunities" argument engenders grassroots development schemes and a wide range of small-enterprise programmes. This particular argument was partly a consequence of the poor results from the first type of policy in many developed countries in the 1980s. The predominant theme is the mobilization of idle labour accompanied by small governmental financial inputs in their home region. Some of these programmes have been very local, some national, and some created and supported by the European Union or non-governmental organizations (NGOs), for example.

The "equal opportunities" argument stresses neoclassical arguments and the recognition that localities are in open and free competition for industrial investments. The locational attributes relevant to industry are not distributed homogeneously and, hence, differences in economic performance exist between localities. The "key" belief of this argument is that structural adjustment of the socio-economic conditions of the lagging areas (that is, investments in roads, communications, education, etc.) is the appropriate way to increase their competitiveness and their transformation into potentially prosperous regions. Structural adjustment through structural policy is the prevailing doctrine behind the distribution of European Union funds to its less developed regions.

The ability of market mechanisms to allocate the factors of production optimally, and the built-in and balancing feedbacks of markets, are ideas supported by neoclassical doctrines, and they are the driving concepts behind the "free-market competition" argument. This argument posits that most socio-institutional infrastructure is built, usually on an ad hoc basis, without any regard to "balanced" regional policy. The competitiveness of a region is a matter of market forces, and the private sector itself could take on many infrastructural duties of society and still expect good returns, at least in the long term.

In addition to the above four main premisses, personal interests are often powerful bottom–up motives for local economic schemes. Such interests arise in both institutional and individual contexts. Communities are organizations that are accustomed to receiving certain tax revenues and/or state subsidies, and want to continue doing so. Their actions are usually supported by the local service sector (for example, through some form of local business coalition). Individuals too claim their rights to subsidies in order to make use of rural opportunities. National interests or small cliques of citizens acting as pressure groups can lead to an avoidance of risk-taking – the authorities take responsibility for the risks of unstable production conditions facing (usually marginal) areas.

Increasingly, NGOs concerned with specific issues, such as environmental protection, influence local policy (e.g. Dalby and Mackenzie 1997). In some countries, NGOs act by providing a range of resources, including social capital for particular projects – albeit this assistance is based on the "donor" NGO's philosophy. The non-economic motives of NGOs are, however, outside the for-profit philosophy of most private sector entities. Another benefit of local NGOs may be their effectiveness in clearing the way in the preparatory phases for official local organizations.

Elements from the reasoning of all four of the main arguments discussed above are (implicitly) involved in the interventionist policies of the restructuring process described in the case-studies of this book. For instance, the "evenly distributed welfare" argument has been the basis of life in Härjedalen in Sweden for decades, although a shift has taken place towards the type of policy emphasizing the private sector and infrastructural aspects as the prime motors of local development. The "equal opportunities" policy has also prevailed in the case of Kellogg, in the United States, and regional policy moved from the first to the third type in Kolari in Lapland. The "local endogenous opportunities" argument was presented in both the Irish and the Vietnamese papers, and outlined in the Polish paper. The papers examining Australian communities clearly illustrate the "free-market competition" type of thinking.

"Evenly distributed welfare," "local endogenous opportunities," "equal opportunities," or "free-market competition" may describe the ideological standpoints of the geographically oriented policies, but, ultimately, policy implementation is a political choice. On the other hand, these case-studies reveal that ways of thinking and courses of action arise from everyday policy-making, and, therefore, models provide only rough representations.

Dynamism and reflexivity of local development policy

There is clear evidence that market forces and various partnerships play a larger role in the geographically oriented policy decisions of the 1990s than they did in the 1980s. It is also clear that each society, as indicated in this comparative research, is eagerly searching for a more efficient spatial organization of its industrial and social capital. Therefore, shifts in policy reflect the changing ideas of what would benefit society most or, more precisely, would be most beneficial to certain interest groups. The collapse of the implementation of plan rationality in spatial management indicated internal problems in the planning doctrine. Also, slow economic growth in the welfare states challenged politicians to search for market-oriented measures in geographically oriented policies.

The changes in the organization of local governance and policy are fundamental. Various private/public coalitions, partnerships, and ad hoc organizations are increasingly becoming prime agents in local policy and, crucially, this new approach has often been found to permit greater efficiencies. Two reasons for this change are that, firstly, each developmental endeavour requires expertise that transcends the social capital of the locality in question, and, secondly, such joint organizations are able to mobilize additional resources by overcoming traditional agency and policy divides.

This doctrine of flexible organizations and partnerships in local development becomes embedded in a community if it has sufficient and suitable socio-institutional infrastructure to facilitate such developments. Syrett (1997) concluded that the poor local institutional structures in Portugal have been a hindrance to implementing advanced local policy. Similar poor local institutional structures are hampering communities in neo-capitalist countries, as the case-study of north-east Poland demonstrates. A noteworthy point, however, is that even well-embedded organizations may reach a deadlock if there are subsequently declining conditions of development. Overall, regional development success is a combination of many initial and ongoing factors.

In addition to institutional and organizational change, the spatial organization of governance is under pressure to change. Vigorous competition between regions and problems of economic growth in many areas are creating new spatial structures. Furthermore, the entire culture of work and leisure is changing, as the Western Australian case-study indicates, furthering spatial restructuring. The fragmentation of the spatial uniformity of local governance is also leading to questions of how better to conceptualize the actors operating in localities. In addition to the concepts of networking and translocality, "community power" may conceptualize the complex local use of power better (Harding 1996).

Successful local economic policy is self-organizing. It creates new instruments and institutional forms capable of responding to restructuring pressures. Therefore, it would be misleading to recommend the perpetual employment of an a priori model of local policy – unless it encompasses adequate responses to complex developmental processes containing different factors, as outlined in this book. Local policy should be an ongoing, flexible, and dynamic learning process rather than a predetermined, fixed course. Successful local policy takes into account local opportunities, is based on local commitments, promotes investments in profitable and appropriate technology, provides appropriate funding, and evolves improved organizational structures. Local policy should also be a tailor-made, locally specific, and reflexive response that enhances the competitiveness of a community.

The most important lesson from this project for planners and policy makers is that successful and effective planning should, in both theory and practice, take account of the different processes occurring in both local communities and the broader society. Some of these processes are "inevitable," some are the outcome of choice; some are predictable, others not. Policy makers should continuously seek to understand all the processes currently affecting development, to anticipate new processes that are likely to occur, and to understand what measures are needed to rectify potential developmental problems in affected communities. The very nature of a community is dynamic, and the socio-economic institutions related to a community must be capable of appropriately reacting to pressures and changes. In other words, unless the theoretical backgrounds and causes of restructuring processes are understood, there is no rational way to influence development.

Sectoral shifts

The role of the primary sector

Almost all the papers in this book deal with sectoral shifts of production from one sector to another in the economy. The shifts are most explicitly presented in the papers analysing the situation in which tourism replaces traditional rural occupations. Similar sectoral shifts can also take place within a specific industrial sector, as when companies seek to increase the degree of processing and specialization. The productivity gap between neo-capitalist and advanced market economies is huge, which engenders pressure for sectoral shift from traditional rural occupations. Therefore, the expected rationalization in agriculture will keep this topic in the forefront in the neo-capitalist countries, where millions of jobs will be lost in agriculture, as the Polish case-study exemplifies.

The sectoral shift has been important in encouraging migration from rural communities in advanced market economies over recent decades. Attempts have been made to control and relieve such migration by introducing agricultural and regional policies designed to encourage restructuring. A sectoral shift, nevertheless, is not a process *per se* but is the result of a change in consumption patterns and the rationalization of production. Therefore, the ultimate causes of sectoral shifts are changing consumer behaviours and the new opportunities to manufacture goods using relatively few human resources.

The development of profitable products for the market is an integral part of the operation of manufacturing and service enterprises, but it is not a part of traditional farming. Creating innovative products and adopting innovative production methods is a time-consuming and unevenly diffused learning process owing to the heterogeneous structures of farming (e.g. farm size, education, demographic factors). The feasibility of individualistic or cooperative models is dependent on local circumstances and the stage of development (see and compare the case-studies on Ireland, Poland, Hungary, and Viet Nam, for instance). Competition may increase efficiency in some situations, but not always, competition often being regulated by local circumstances. Individualistic, entrepreneurial marketing, in which one household competes against another, may be inconsistent with the accepted patterns of cooperative village farming, in which neighbours learn from each other (with respect to the growing of new crops, for instance). Encouraging innovation in such contexts is considered to fall within the domain of advice bureaux and consultative projects. Often these advice entities must both dispense practical techniques as well as provide a bridge between the "new" and traditional values.

The search for new products and alternative production methods in rural communities is a global phenomenon (as each case-study shows by listing new production that might be worth trying in rural areas). Finding the "right" product to meet market demand may, however, require knowledge of external markets, which the residents of a peripheral area are not in a position to tap without some centralized assistance.

The case-studies indicate that:
- both restructuring within the primary sector and diversified production are eagerly sought in neo-capitalist countries and traditional market economies – these countries often searching for absolute advantages based on native products or unique local production conditions;

- local initiatives, local organizing, and financial assistance from such bodies as cooperatives and NGOs have proved to be productive in many regions, as the cases of Ireland and Viet Nam indicate;
- development schemes have usually been considered promising, but few projects have achieved the expected long-term results.

Although failures are common with rural development schemes, they are, nevertheless, essential starting points and important stimuli for development. In general, sectoral shifts and development have to be understood as involving much more than simply the introduction of development projects. The entire gamut of societal attitudes toward development ought to change, as is recognized in the research conducted on the performance of technology and incubation centres (Wilhelm 1997).

Tourism as a panacea

The widespread emphasis on tourism in rural areas relates to the recognition that employment in manufacturing is not growing and that the expansion of the public sector has come to an end in advanced market economies (at least temporarily). The role of the main economic sectors can vary from society to society, as Lash and Urry (1994) demonstrate; hence, a non-growing manufacturing and/ or public sector is also a matter of choices, policy, and ideology. Not all countries need to follow the same development path.

Tourism is considered an important source of livelihood in neo-capitalist countries. For instance, tourism was expected to be a prime stimulant of development in north-east Poland in the early 1990s. Similar notions exist almost universally.

As referred to in the Irish case, tourism was officially brought up by the present European Union in the 1990s and it was strongly endorsed as having potential for the future of rural society. It was expected to help alleviate the problems arising from the European Commission's decision to reform the Common Agricultural Policy in a way that would reduce agricultural output and, subsequently, reduce farm incomes. To compensate for the effects of the rationalization in agriculture, upon which most resource communities were heavily dependent, and in order to give an impetus to the rural development strategy that aimed at economic diversification, policy measures favouring the stimulation of new economic activities (Bryden 1994), including tourism, were evolved and implemented.

A similar policy was adopted in northern Sweden and Finland in the 1980s. The policy simultaneously supported small-scale business activities at the grass-roots level and promoted large investments in manufacturing and tourism. A large number of winter sports resorts, complete with hotels and apartments, were constructed in the 1980s. Those investments were meant to compensate for the loss of jobs in the primary sectors. The Kolari case-study, however, indicates that the new jobs did not necessarily require the qualifications that the local residents possessed. Furthermore, many of the new jobs were located a long way from the previous ones. The mismatch of the local job market and the actual local skills base is well known in mining communities and sparsely populated vast areas; the case of Kolari demonstrates this complication. However, the significance of the spatial restructuring of a local labour market should not be exaggerated – people are often accustomed to commuting long distances, for example in metropolitan areas.

Community-based tourism in Ireland gives an example of a more optimum spatial match of changed labour demand and supply resulting from translocal development schemes. Local circumstances in more densely populated areas are much more suitable for such local community-based development than are those in mountainous areas where winter sports are dominant. Moreover, winter tourism is capital intensive and sites for winter tourism are located only within certain natural environments. Considerable basic investments are usually a prerequisite for boosting the development of small businesses related to winter sports.

The outcomes of more spatially deconcentrated tourism strategies, discussed in the Kolari case-study, suggest that the alternative approach of promoting small tourist enterprises throughout the municipality might have been more beneficial (from the standpoint of the scattered rural population) both because it would have placed development more into the hands of the locals and also because it would have dispersed development geographically. Deconcentrated development would certainly have reduced the mismatch of the local labour market and local skills base and would have been desirable as far as the locals were concerned. There were no obstacles to implementing deconcentrated development in Kolari, but the "resort alternative" was expected to bring the best returns. For the future, the alternative "dispersed model" is expected to gain increasing support, because of both the economic recovery and the increasing popularity of cross-country skiing compared with downhill skiing. Hence, it is market forces that will have the last say.

The experiences of the Irish model offer important lessons for Poland and Hungary, where settlement patterns and the attractions of nature are more similar than those in remote winter sports sites. The Irish case is a good example of networking applied successfully to small-scale business (see also Keane 1993). The Irish experience suggests that a tourist product is a package that needs to be tailored to customers' needs, and that the creation of appealing tourist products is crucial for the success of the tourism industry.

Resource communities and the secondary sector

Case-studies of small rural communities have tended to deal with the "negative" impacts of sectoral shift, that is, job losses in agriculture or in the so-called "smokestack" industries. From a recent, more theoretical standpoint, modernization or a transition to a post-modern society represents a shift from mass production to flexible manufacturing, services, and consumption.

Although the tertiary and quaternary sectors employ the majority of people in all developed countries, this fact should not diminish the importance of material production. The outputs of the secondary and primary sectors are still important sources and means of livelihood in post-industrial societies. One of the reasons for the lower visibility of the resource sector is that industrial activities have increasingly undergone metamorphosis so as to blend in with the surrounding environment through new architecture and cleaner production technologies. Moreover, resource communities are not necessarily facing closures and declining development, as is often supposed. On the contrary, many activities in the resource sector are essential and are expanding, and they are often the most sophisticated systems of current industrial culture. The Western Australian case indicates the importance of this culture.

Hence, it would be wrong to conclude that the resource sector and its employees are becoming less important in the economy and that there is a continuous shift in production towards the service sector. The shift of labour towards the service sector may be questioned if automation increases rapidly in the production of services. The service society model may also be rejected by a society, as has been the case in Germany (Lash and Urry 1994, 81–93, 180–192). It has been a target for increasing criticism – "junk" jobs, a growing underclass, civil unrest, and crimes all being a source of growing concern. In any case, a certain amount of primary and secondary production will always be necessary to satisfy both the basic needs of human beings and the infrastructure needs of the service sector. Technology and work methods are changing, but material production will continue to be essential.

None the less, the indispensability of the primary and secondary sectors does not mitigate the fact that the production technology of resource processing requires continuous modernization. The Kuklen case indicates that the transformation process is leading to the updating of low-tech mass production. Old-fashioned industrial factories in Kuklen have had to install cleaner technologies and find new markets. Thus there is a desire within the resource sector to adapt advanced technology so as to meet new standards of production.

The Vuohijärvi case is a good example of the complex path of restructuring and the reorganization of social and industrial capital within the secondary sector. The development of a profitable ensemble of capital, labour, and appropriate technology to produce marketable products has been a continuous, dynamic, and reflexive process.

There will always be a search for a more profitable spatial organization of production, sharp competition between rivals, and developments in production methods. Local communities have the human resources to cope with new challenges. These human resources should be viewed as a large network of internal and external actors who can successfully respond to the pressures of restructuring. Such a network may be local or, more often, a mix of people from varying localities. The essential thing is that a network is capable of mobilizing development, for instance by starting business activities, financing starting enterprises, coming up with profitable business ideas, or attracting external support for a community.

The secondary sector continues to struggle to cope with restructuring in many old industrial communities. To maximize the use of the local social capital and infrastructure, new manufacturing activities are usually established. This situation is referred to in the Vuohijärvi case-study and, to a lesser degree, in the Kuklen and Kellogg cases. Such struggles are common in single-industry towns (see, for example, Tykkyläinen 1992). Very often, new industries will find some useful links to traditional industrial bases, but these links do not need to be based on low technology. They can be related to telecommunications, resource processing, research and development laboratories, or machine works in the same resource community. Furthermore, useful links may simply consist of an advanced infrastructure in a suitable location, as in Kiruna (Liljenäs 1992, 262–264).

Conclusion: The geography of unique development

This chapter has shown that the local development processes of rural resource communities are inextricably bound to space and time through human action. Progress is dependent on space-bound assets, such as knowledge, institutional settings, and various natural, social, and human resources, and prosperity is a result of the systematic enhancement of these assets. The wealth of a single community is the outcome of many complex actions originating from decision-making at various levels (from individual to supranational policy). Development is (almost) always possible but never automatic.

An important lesson of this comparison is that there is a great variety of means by which to develop communities and localities. The diversity of socio-economic development is very challenging both for the communities as well as for geography and the social sciences.

The topical issues of the 1990s were privatization and the squeeze on the public sector. During the next decade, modern technology will have a great impact on many resource communities; telecommunications and technological advances will change the production landscapes of most countries. Such advancement is no longer a characteristic limited to certain segments of society, but is spreading to every structure, geographical place, and level of society. This progress will change lifestyles and culture in rural settings and it may fundamentally change the concepts of rurality, community, and locality in the future.

References

Bryden, J. (1994), "Prospects for Rural Areas in an Enlarged Europe," *Journal of Rural Studies* 10(4), pp. 387–394.

Cloke, P. and Goodwin, M. (1993), "Rural Change: Structured Coherence or Unstructured Incoherence?" *Terra* 105(3), pp. 166–174.

Conradson, D. and Pawson, E. (1997), "Reworking the Geography of the Long Boom: The Small Town Experience of Restructuring in Reefton, New Zealand," *Environment and Planning* A 29(8), pp. 1331–1520.

Cox, K. R. and Mair, A. (1988), "Locality and Community in the Politics of Local Economic Development," *Annals of the Association of American Geographers* 78(2), pp. 307–325.

Dalby, S. and Mackenzie, F. (1997), "Reconceptualising Local Community: Environment, Identity and Threat," *Area* 29(2), pp. 99–108.

Goodwin, M. and Painter, J. (1996), "Local Governance, the Crises of Fordism and the Changing Geographies of Regulation," *Transactions of the Institute of British Geographers* 21(4), pp. 635–648.

Harding, A. (1996), "Is There a 'New Community Power' and Why Should We Need One?" *International Journal of Urban and Regional Research* 20(4), pp. 637–655.

Hirvensalo, I. (1995), "Maksurästit Venäjän transitiotaloudessa," *Review of Economies in Transition* 1995/7, pp. 43–72.

Husso, K., Leppälahti, A., and Niininen, P. (1996), "R&D, Innovation and Firm Performance. Studies on the Panel Data of Finnish Manufacturing Firms," *Statistics Finland, Science and Technology* 1996:3.

Informal Council of Spatial Planning Ministers (1994), *European Spatial Planning*, Leipzig, 21–22 September 1994, Bundesministerium für Raumordnung, Bauwesen und Städtebau, Germany.

Kalmi, P. (1995), "Insider-led Privatisation in Poland, Russia and Lithuania: A Comparison," *Review of Economies in Transition* 1995/9, pp. 37–52.

Kangasharju, A. and Nijkamp, P. (1997), "Innovation Dynamics in Space: Local Actors and Local Factors," paper presented at the 37th European Congress of the Regional Science Association, 26–29 August, University of Rome "Tor Vergata," Rome, Italy.

Keane, M. (1993), "Rural Tourism – The Passport to Development," in M. Murray and J. Greer (eds.), *Rural Development in Ireland*, Avebury, Aldershot, pp. 113–124.

Kovách, I. (1997), "The Changes of the Comparison of Eastern and Western Border Regions," paper presented at the Conference of Border Regions in Transition, 14–18 June, University of Joensuu, Joensuu and Sortavala.

Lash, S. and Urry, J. (1994), *Economies of Signs and Space*, Sage, London.

Le Heron, R., Britton, S., and Pawson, E. (1992), "Introduction," in S. Britton, R. Le Heron, and E. Pawson (eds.) (1992), *Changing Places in New Zealand: A Geography of Restructuring*, New Zealand Geographical Society, Christchurch, pp. 1–16.

Liljenäs, I. (1992), "From Mine to Outer Space: The Case of Kiruna, a Town in Northern Sweden," in C. Neil, M. Tykkyläinen, and J. Bradbury (eds.), *Coping with Closure. An International Comparison of Mine Town Experiences*, Routledge, London, pp. 247–265.

Lorendahl, B. (1996), "New Cooperatives and Local Development: A Study of Six Cases in Jämtland, Sweden," *Journal of Rural Studies* 12(2), pp. 143–150.

Magrini, S. (1997), "On the Effect of European Integration on Economic Growth and Regional Disparities," paper presented at the 37th European Congress of the Regional Science Association, 26–29 August, University of Rome "Tor Vergata," Rome, Italy.

Massey, D. (1984), *Spatial Division of Labour*, Macmillan, London.

Mormont, M. (1990), "Who Is Rural? or, How to be Rural: Towards a Sociology of Rural," in T. Marsden, P. Lowe, and S. Whatmore (eds.), *Rural Restructuring*, David Fulton, London. pp. 21–44.

Pawson, E., Bevin, J., Scott, G., James, B., Booth, K., Le Heron, R., McQueen, E., Barnett, R., Stubbs, J., and Kearns, R. (1992), "The State Sector," in S. Britton, R. Le Heron, and E. Pawson (eds.) (1992), *Changing Places in New Zealand: A Geography of Restructuring*, New Zealand Geographical Society, Christchurch, pp. 163–186.

Storper, M. (1995), "The Resurgence of Regional Economies, Ten Years Later: The Region as a Nexus of Untraded Interdependencies," *European Urban and Regional Studies* 2(3), pp. 191–221.

Syrett, S. (1997), "The Politics of Partnership. The Role of Social Partners in Local Economic Development in Portugal," *European Urban and Regional Studies* 4(2), pp. 99–114.

Tickell, A. and Peck, J. A. (1992), "Accumulation, Regulation and the Geographies of Post-Fordism. Missing Links in Regulationist Research," *Progress in Human Geography* 16, pp. 190–218.

Tykkyläinen, M. (1992), "Solutions to Mine Closure in Outokumpu," in C. Neil, M. Tykkyläinen, and J. Bradbury (eds.), *Coping with Closure. An International Comparison of Mine Town Experiences*, Routledge, London, pp. 225–246.

—— (1995a), "'Stunde Null' and the Pocket Theory of Development in the Socio-economic Transition in Russia," in M. Tykkyläinen (ed.), *Russian Karelia – An Opportunity for the West*, Occasional Papers 29, Human Geography and Planning, University of Joensuu, pp. 9–21.

—— (ed.) (1995b), *Russian Karelia – An Opportunity for the West*, Occasional Papers 29, Human Geography and Planning, University of Joensuu.

—— (1996), "Increasing Long-distance Commuting and Its Effects on Spatial Structures," in M. E. Furlani de Civit, C. Pedone, and N. D. Soría (eds.), *Development Issues in Marginal Regions II: Policies and Strategies*, Universidad Nacional de Cuyo, Mendoza, pp. 223–234.

Wilhelm, B. (1997), "Technology and Incubation Centres (TICs) – A Living Legend or Current Centres of Competence," paper presented at the 37th European Congress of the Regional Science Association, 26–29 August, University of Rome "Tor Vergata," Rome, Italy.

16

A multicausal theory of local economic development

Markku Tykkyläinen

The conditions of community-based development

The aim of this research project was to find a solid theoretical framework for understanding socio-economic restructuring in resource communities in nascent capitalist economies so as to reveal a structured interpretation between generality and individual/place-bound specificity in geographical reasoning. One could say that the objective was to find causal powers and liabilities (i.e. causal mechanisms and empirical regularities) that are realized under specific local conditions. This final chapter summarizes and theorizes the results of the project by presenting a multicausal theory of local economic development. Finally, the future of local economic development in the post-Fordist rural setting will be discussed.

The societies from which the case-studies have been drawn range from peripheral communities in neo-capitalist states to very sophisticated communities in advanced market economies. To date, the scope of "local" policy models in geography and related sciences has not been very exhaustive. In order to broaden theoretical insights into local restructuring, the problems of local development have been presented in a comparative spatial and socio-economic context in this project. This has enhanced the understanding of the restructuring process in a community and the influence of various conditions and of the possibilities of local policy.

One of the results of this project is, as stated in the previous chapter, the reinforcement of the view that local policy needs to match changing socio-economic circumstances and reflect the wishes of the people in a community. There are numerous kinds of circumstances in which local economic development takes place, and, indeed, the entire socio-economic system is dynamic. Thus, no ideal, fixed model of local economic development will ever be suitable for all communities. Even if one could be found, it would soon be obsolete.

The case-studies show that local initiatives are crucial, but that these initiatives vary greatly, depending upon whether they are the outcome of a policy or an individual's drive. The power of local policy is greatly dependent on the willingness of individuals themselves to react and adapt in a collective way. Reactions may differ even in neighbouring, apparently similar localities, as Simon and Gagnon (1967) show. Each community has its internal social and political structures and agencies, which influence the outcomes of restructuring. The contents and structures of community power vary greatly in geographical space. Socio-economic circumstances, from culture to pure economic calculations, create a niche for local development policy. The domain of local policy measures must be seen as embedded in supra-local processes and policies, because small communities are increasingly dependent on the entire network of global business, national and transnational decision-making, and individual responses.

The study of resource communities reveals the artificial and contractual nature of a community – actual communities are often neglected when administrative communities (such as towns and shires) are seen as independent subjects, almost like organisms. Hence, communities are usually considered to be entities that can "grow," "flourish," and "die." Thus, when, for instance, a community "dies," this is usually considered negative. This may, however, only be a symptom of the fact that a higher quality of life is available somewhere else, and people have been eager to migrate. Welfare may be maximized by starting business somewhere else. Similarly, a community may survive in a spatial sense and yet change so much in character that it no longer functions as a community for those residents who lived there prior to the restructuring. Furthermore, the network character of a community is usually neglected. Therefore, to avoid the shortfalls of planning, the starting point for planning should be both understanding individuals and their needs and viewing the community as being the way to satisfy collective needs.

A multicausal theory of local economic development

Human response, multicausality, and spatial filtering

The processes of spatial restructuring and the responses to pressure are depicted by further developing the multicausal approach into a multicausal theory. The basic idea is that the interplay of general, political, and sectoral factors (determined by supra-local structures) puts pressure on resource communities to restructure. Based on the experiences discussed in the case-studies, it is important to recognize the crucial role of various actors in community development. People create development and, on the other hand, they create social conditions and rules within which development can take place. Most of the case-studies emphasized not traditional collective action as a response, but rather the actions of individuals, groups, enterprises, and ad hoc organizations in shaping development. In elaborating upon the model, individual responses are fundamental; individuals are both actors and recipients (represented by the arrows of two-way communication in fig. 16.1). Individuals are, as we noted in chapter 14, an additional agency in restructuring. This human factor must be interpreted in the broad sense, constituting both individual human behaviour and the behaviour of various coalitions of individuals aiming at creating development.

The local factor is, first, a bundle of complementary and locally derived processes and outcomes that act locally, such as local policy, local initiatives, locally specific projects, and grass-roots actions. This local action is often referred to as a locality effect (Duncan 1989), but, as seen in this research, the network character of social relations in a community should be increasingly taken into account in defining what "local" is in a rural setting. Secondly, the role of the local factor in the form of social capital and the environment is significant. It partially consists of the "deposit of productive knowledge" (Bellandi 1997), but such concentrations of knowledge cannot emerge exclusively in a single small locale. External linkages are all important. All manifestations of local embeddedness, institutional thickness, and local associationism, as presented by Amin and Thrift (1993; 1995),

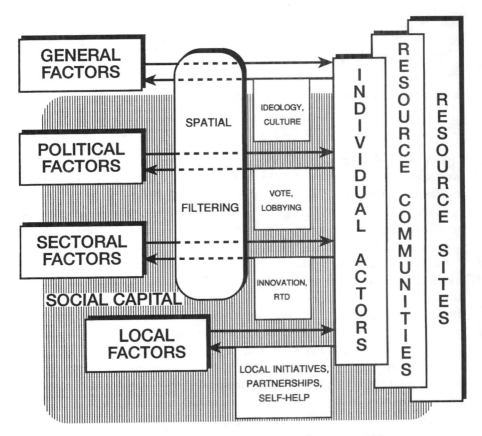

Fig. 16.1 **Spatial filtering shaping resource communities.**

vary spatially and are path dependent in rural settings (see Storper 1995). Each place holds a unique position in geographical space and each community possesses a unique socio-economic legacy.

The unique natural and social environments of a resource site and its community have an influence on the local manifestations of the general, political, and sectoral factors. Furthermore, each factor has a dynamic demand for spatial attributes and has internal mechanisms to regulate this demand. People in a community too may shape these "external" forces. The active, two-way communication between the institutions representing factors and local actors produces different spatial outcomes in each place in a process called "spatial filtering" (fig. 16.1). Finally, this synergy produces the concrete outcomes of development in a community. Hence, referring to Sayer's "structure of causal explanation" (Sayer 1992), contingent conditions are not only local but interdependent with wider spatial relations within all the bundles of factors.

The role of human agency

Development is a reflexive process, with the flows of influence occurring between structure and agency. Figure 16.1 points out that human agency, both directly and indirectly through institutions, legislates and regulates the outcomes of development. The contents of ideology, culture, voting, lobbying, innovative behaviour, RTD inputs, local initiatives, partnerships, and self-help are all finally dependent on human behaviour. Human constructs have different local manifestations, which create different conditions for development.

Individuals can realign their ideological beliefs, as in Eastern Europe in the late 1980s. Alternatively, the culture of a region can gradually alter the basic principles of the socio-economic system, leading to a change in the general conditions of economic activity. Simultaneously, there is a bundle of political factors, such as changes in national governance, that influence the development of a community. Again, people can influence the formulation of the practical measures of policy. These measures are more or less spatially planned, and not independent of the spatial context of a country. Hence, spatial filtering takes place when policy instruments are implemented.

The case-studies show that the conditions of locally derived causal effect are dependent upon the actions of local people and local circumstances. As observed, initiatives and opportunities for development, and obstacles to it, vary locally. Local entrepreneurs are sensitive to changes in the conditions of profitability and larger companies investigate attributes of geographical space continuously by searching for more profitable locations and markets. This locality effect is, nevertheless, dynamic. Spatially varying networks of human agency are increasingly central in creating conditions for sectoral transformation and acquiring benefits from it. Various forms of restructuring also induce spatial restructuring, and local actors in resource communities must have a finger on the pulse of this transformation in order to create the potential for progressive development.

The conditions of innovative behaviour and local response

As a progressive response to the pressure of competition, resource communities can compete by enhancing their social capital and by being innovative (fig. 16.1). Up-to-date social capital is usually the best guarantee for keeping a resource business in a community, and, if that strategy does not succeed, social capital can facilitate the acquisition and development of compensating businesses in the community.

The innovative potential of labour is dependent on the workers' everyday living conditions, not only in terms of education and training but in terms of the overall social and cultural milieu, which continuously produces and stimulates innovative development. This social capital, labour, and social milieu is a central productive force; it has traditionally been locally specific, but it is increasingly characterized by translocal networking. When economic systems become more open and global, many inputs (some skills, technology, etc.) are acquired externally and these outside linkages must be recognized in each local community as crucial conditions of development. The network character of RTD inputs is also perceived to be at least as important as local independent innovation centres (Koschatzky and Muller 1997; Wilhelm 1997). A successful combination of local and global know-how is a precondition for development.

Each resource site with its corresponding community provides unique potential for development. A site linked to a community has to make its locally specific opportunities available for business, and such a community – or rather the members of such a community – must be active in developing businesses. Development is the successful combination of active participation and discovered opportunities – all successful business ideas in the case-study communities were locally specific.

Local proactivity and responses to crises have varied, as the cases portray. In most cases, people have a variety of social and emotional ties to social networks and the places where they live. This dependence decreases people's willingness to change life radically in a community. Local dependence, as described by Cox and Mair (1988) for instance, consists of people's mutual commitments and togetherness, which facilitate local policy and development measures. On the other hand, this dependence is also a source of power and commitment. Three preconditions are central for a successful local response:

- *capability*: actors (entrepreneurs, business managers, economic advisers, etc.) must be capable of carrying out a development project and bringing together a unique combinations of skills for its creation;

- *commitment*: the conditions of development are created over the long term and success is the result of systematic work;
- *integration into local opportunities*: successful development is based on advantages provided by local characteristics and/or social capital, with successful enterprises being parts of growing economic networks.

These three preconditions are fulfilled in the cases of Forrestania, Irish tourism, Kellogg, Kuklen, the Vietnamese advisory organization, and Vuohijärvi.

The case-studies reveal that the actor reacting to the pressure of restructuring has not been a traditional collective community. Rather it has been individuals, re-formed groups, and ad hoc organizations who have developed responses to restructuring. Moreover, reorganization has usually crossed the borders of a single community and brought in new resources (know-how, funds, etc.).

Socio-economic crises and turmoil often change the institutional fabric of society, leading to the reorganization of the regimes of accumulation and the mode of social regulation. In such situations, organizational innovations, as observed in the case-studies, are crucial for development. Evolving business organizations and cooperation, local initiatives, and self-help processes take various forms, and they may gradually be institutionalized into the new socio-economic practices of society. The Irish case is a good example of this.

It is not realistic to expect that a traditional community, that is, a local authority or local residents, will operate as a collective and coherent organization in the restructuring phase. The consequence of the heavy pressure to restructure is usually disorder rather than increased cohesion in a community. From the policy makers' perspective, although disorder may arise, they must design policies that take into account the individuals who are searching for a means of livelihood and better lives, or who are trying to develop more profitable configurations of capital and labour. The majority of new economic activities start from these kinds of policies and entrepreneurial individuals.

This research project has portrayed how rural development is socially constructed in numerous divergent ways and how it depends on individual and collective actors but, on the other hand, how it is constrained by various processes and circumstances. The multicausal theory of local economic development is the conceptualization of spatially unique restructuring. It relates to development in the 1990s and is based on the case-studies of the project, but it may also lend itself to other circumstances.

Signs of new spatial forms of communities

A resource community is traditionally situated in a place where natural resources are located. However, the process of restructuring is reorganizing the spatial forms of communities where we live. Communities and resource sites are ceasing to coincide spatially. Although resource communities can be identified by their traditional scope, they are clearly facing a new era of multi-locale structure and changes in the mixture of social strata. One corollary is that the spatial form of a community becomes complex, necessitating an adaptability and "spatial flexibility" on behalf of the public organizations that provide services and promote development.

The case-studies also illustrate how community structures are being fundamentally changed by technological advance, information technology, and networking. It is important to recognize the rapid transformation of business and social life toward the information society. This transformation is also increasing the significance of the concept of "community," because part of everyday life takes place in these networks of social relations.

New models of future communities are penetrating societies very rapidly. Much work is done and much leisure time spent in a symbolic environment where connections are maintained by computers and advanced communications, which are no longer just a world of numbers and letters, but include a virtual world of pictures, motion, voice, and on-line interaction. People are increasingly linked to each other by digital networking, and this networking is also a necessity of everyday life among people in resource companies.

As regards resource communities, this networking needs be seen from the viewpoint of local economic development. Working in cyberspace is gaining momentum, and an increasing share of work (such as design, process control, and administration) is done in this telematics-intensive way rather than by traditional face-to-face interaction in workplaces and offices. This networking is also a basis for new resource community structures, which it is important to take into account when planning "locally."

In order to understand the current course of development, it is necessary to focus on what "local" really means within this emerging "network society," and the feasibility of the various new types of evolving communities in relation to the development of resource sites. New social formations may be likened to cyber-communities. Although the development of a cyber-community into a fundamental, socially meaningful concept has little relevance to today's rural villages in Poland and Hungary, the direction of development is clear: towards networking, multi-locale structures, work in cyberspace, ad hoc organizations, post-modern lifestyles, and new spatial identities.

References

Amin, A. and Thrift, N. (1993), "Globalization, Institutional Thickness and Local Prospects," *Revue d'Economie Régionale et Urbaine* 3, pp. 405–427.
———— (1995), "Institutional Issues for the European Regions: From Markets and Plans to Socioeconomics and Powers of Association," *Economy and Society* 24(1), pp. 41–66.
Bellandi, M. (1997), "Localised Productive Knowledge and Industrial Districts as Learning Regions," paper presented at the 37th European Congress of the Regional Science Association, 26–29 August, University of Rome "Tor Vergata," Rome, Italy.
Cox, K. R. and Mair, A. (1988), "Locality and Community in the Politics of Local Economic Development," *Annals of the Association of American Geographers* 78, pp. 307–325.
Duncan, S. (1989), "What Is Locality?" in R. Peet and N. Thrift (eds.), *New Models in Geography, Volume II*, Unwin Hyman, London, pp. 221–252.
Koschatzky, K. and Muller, E. (1997), "Firm Innovation and Region – Theoretical and Political Conclusions on Regional Innovation Networking," paper presented at the 37th European Congress of the Regional Science Association, 26–29 August, University of Rome "Tor Vergata," Rome, Italy.
Sayer, A. (1992), *Method in Social Science. A Realist Approach,* 2nd edn, Routledge, London.
Simon, W. and Gagnon, J. H. (1967), "The Decline and Fall of the Small Town," *Trans-Action, Social Science and Modern Society* 4(5), pp. 42–51.
Storper, M. (1995), "The Resurgence of Regional Economies, Ten Years Later: The Region as a Nexus of Untraded Interdependencies," *European Urban and Regional Studies* 2(3), pp. 191–221.
Wilhelm, B. (1997), "Technology and Incubation Centres (TICs) – A Living Legend or Current Centres of Competence," paper presented at the 37th European Congress of the Regional Science Association, 26–29 August, University of Rome "Tor Vergata," Rome, Italy.

Contributors

John Burke, University College Galway, Galway, Ireland

Jari Järviluoma, University of Lapland, FIN-96100 Rovaniemi, Lapland

Harley Johansen, University of Idaho, Moscow, Idaho 83843, USA

Heikki Jussila, University of Oulu, FIN-90570 Oulu, Finland

Jarmo Kortelainen, University of Joensuu, FIN-80100 Joensuu, Finland

Alfred Levinson, 219 South Orange Ave., South Orange, N.J. 07079, USA

Jan Łoboda, University of Wrocław, 90–137 Wrocław, Poland

Cecily Neil, CSIRO, Highett, Vic. 3190, Australia

Nguyen Ngoc Triu, VACVINA, Hanoi, Viet Nam

Nguyen Van Gia, Catholic Relief Service, Hanoi, Viet Nam

Micheál Ó Cinnéide, University College Galway, Galway, Ireland

Lars Olof Persson, KTH, S-100 44 Stockholm, Sweden

Zbigniew Rog, Technical University of Białystok, 15–351 Białystok, Poland

Attila Sántha, Janus Pannonius University, H-7266 Pecs, Hungary

Peter J. Smailes, University of Adelaide, Adelaide, South Australia 5001, Australia

István Süli-Zakar, L. Kossuth University, H-4010 Debrecen, Hungary

Markku Tykkyläinen, University of Joensuu, FIN-80100 Joensuu, Finland

Eira Varis, University of Joensuu, FIN-80100 Joensuu, Finland

Index